Education and Postponement of Maternity

European Studies of Population

VOLUME 15

The book series *European Studies of Population (ESPO)* aims at disseminating population and family research, with special relevance for Europe. It may analyse past, present and/or future trends, as well as their determinants and consequences.
The character of the series is multidisciplinary, including formal demographic analyses, as well as social, economic and/or historical population and family studies.
The following types of studies are of primary importance: (a) internationally relevant studies, (b) European comparative studies, (c) innovative theoretical and methodological studies, and (d) policy-relevant scientific studies. The series may include monographs, edited volumes and reference works.
The book series is published under the auspices of the *European Association for Population Studies (EAPS)*

Editorial Offices:
Gijs *Beets*
Netherlands Interdisciplinary
Demographic Institute (NIDI)
PO Box 11650
NL-2502 AR The Hague, Netherlands
Phone.: +31 70 356 5200
Fax.: +31 70 364 7187
E-mail: beets@nidi.nl

Technical Coordinator:
Jacqueline *van der Helm*

The titles published in this series are listed at the end of this volume

Education and Postponement of Maternity

Economic Analyses for Industrialized Countries

edited by

SIV GUSTAFSSON
University of Amsterdam,
The Netherlands

and

ADRIAAN KALWIJ
Utrecht University,
The Netherlands

Springer

A C.I.P. Catalogue record for this book is available from the Library of Congress.

ISBN-10 1-4020-4715-0 (HB)
ISBN-13 978-1-4020-4715-2 (HB)
ISBN-10 1-4020-4716-9 (e-book)
ISBN-13 978-1-4020-4716-9 (e-book)

Published by Kluwer Academic Publishers,
P.O. Box 17, 3300 AA Dordrecht, The Netherlands.

www.springer.com

Printed on acid-free paper

Printed in the Netherlands.

CONTENTS

PREFACE

Increasing age of women at motherhood and below replacement fertility characterize industrialized countries during the last decades. At the same time the educational attainment of young women has been increasing. The contributions to this book examine various economic aspects of education and motherhood timing for as many as ten different industrialized countries.

In October 2002 a conference with the theme *Education and Postponement of Maternity* took place at the University of Amsterdam, Department of Economics. This conference has been sponsored and organized by the Scholar Institute for Schooling, Labor Market and Economic Development (SCHOLAR), University of Amsterdam. At the conference Gijs Beets, the series editor of *European Studies of Population* at *Springer* expressed interest in the conference contributions for a book publication in this series. We have taken a selection of the conference contributions, covering a wide range of research issues, and made a coherent volume. Most of the chapters were submitted to scholarly journals in the field and benefited greatly from referee comments. Seven Chapters were accepted for publication in refereed journals including the *Journal of Population Economics*, *Demography*, *Review of Economics of the Household* and *Demographic Research*. Copyright for individual chapters remains with those journals. This book also serves as one of the outputs of the project *Rationality of Motherhood Choices* (MOCHO); a European Union sponsored project that ran from October 1, 2001, to September 30, 2004.

We are grateful to Henriëtte Maassen van den Brink, director of the research institute SCHOLAR, the researchers from this institute who acted as discussants at the conference, Danièle Meulders and other members of the MOCHO project, Gijs Beets for making this book publication possible, and to the authors of the individual chapters. Further thanks goes to the invaluable secretarial support of Robert Helmink, Sebastiene Postma and Loes Lotze.

Amsterdam, January 2006
Siv Gustafsson
Adriaan Kalwij

ABOUT THE EDITORS

Siv Gustafsson, Ph.D., Stockholm School of Economics 1976, is a professor of Economics at the University of Amsterdam. She has published several refereed articles in international edited books and journals, and she has also herself acted as an editor for books and special issues of journals. She is an associate editor of the *Review of Economics of the Household* (REHO). Her articles have appeared in *Journal of Labor Economics*, *Journal of Human Resources*, *Journal of Population Economics*, *European Journal of Population*. Her research topics have included: Male-female wage differentials; Income tax regimes and female labor supply; subsidized childcare and female labor supply; Welfare state regimes and family policies; Labor force transitions around first birth; Timing of Maternity.

Adriaan Kalwij, Ph.D., Tilburg University, 1999, is a lecturer at the Utrecht School of Economics. He is a research fellow at the Amsterdam Institute for Advanced Labour Studies, University of Amsterdam, and the Institute for the Study of Labor, Bonn, and is on the Editorial Board of the *Oxford Bulletin of Economics and Statistics*. His articles have appeared in *Journal of Population Economics*, *Labour Economics*, *Economics Letters* and *Journal of the Royal Statistical Society.* His research interests are econometrics and consumer, labour and population economics.

ABOUT THE AUTHORS

Catalina Amuedo-Dorantes Ph.D., in applied economics, Western Michigan University (1998). Worked at the Center for Human Resource Research at Ohio State University, San Diego State University and where she is currently associate professor of economics. She is a research associate at CentrA, a recently created research institute established by the Spanish government with the purpose of advancing economics research in Spain. Her areas of interest include labor economics, international migration, and international finance, and she has published on contingent work contracts, the informal work sector, immigrant saving, international remittances and immigrant health care. Her research papers have been published in such academic journals as the *American Economic Review Papers & Proceedings*, *Southern Economic Journal*, *Applied Economics, Industrial Labor Relations Review,* the *Journal of Labor Research, International Journal of Manpower, Economic Development and Cultural Change*, *World Development,* the *Review of Development Economics,* the *Journal of Development Studies, Journal of International Money and Finance*, and the *Journal of Macroeconomics.*

Massimiliano Bratti. Ph.D., University of Ancona, 2001, is an Assistant Professor of Economics at the University of Milan. He is a research fellow at the Center for Household Income Labour and Demographic Economics (CHILD, Turin) and the Work Training and Welfare (WTW, Milan), and a research affiliate at the Institute for the Study of Labor (IZA, Bonn). His articles have appeared in *Economics of Education Review, Journal of Population Economics* and *Journal of the Royal Statistical Society*. His main research interests are education economics, labour economics, household and demographic economics and applied econometrics.

Sara de la Rica, Ph.D., Universidad del País Vasco (Spain) 1991, is an associate profesor of Economics at the Universidad del País Vasco. She has published several articles in international journals. Her articles have appeared in *Journal of Human Resources, Economica, Applied Economics, Scottish Journal of Political Economy, Spanish Economic Review, Investigaciones Econónicas, and Review of Economics of the Household.* Her research interest are: Labor Economics, applied microeconometrics, labor and demography. She is a council member of European Society of Population Economics.

Amaia Iza, Ph.D., State University of New York at Stony Brook 1992, is an associate professor of Economics at the Universidad del País Vasco. She has published several articles in international journals. Her articles have appeared in *Journal of Population Economics, Journal of Public Economics, International Tax and Public Finance* and *Review of Economics of the Household.* Her research interests are: Economic Growth Theory, Demography, Public Economics.

Vladimíra Kantorová, Ph.D., Charles University in Prague, 2004, is an associate population affairs officer at the Population Division, Department of Economic and Social Affairs of the United Nations in New York. Previously, she was a doctoral candidate and postdoctoral fellow at the Max Planck Institute for Demographic Research in Rostock, Germany, where her contribution for this book was written. She has published articles in *Demographic Research* and *European Journal of Population*. Her main research interest is fertility and family dynamics with a focus on family formation in times of social, political and economic change in Eastern Europe. She is currently working on issues related to population policies.

Jean Kimmel is Associate Professor of Economics at Western Michigan University in Kalamazoo, Michigan. Kimmel earned her B.A. in Economics from the George Washington University in 1982, her M.A. in Economics at the University of Delaware in 1984, and her Ph.D. in Economics from the University of North Carolina at Chapel Hill in 1990. Prior to joining the faculty at WMU in August 2001, she was Senior Economist at the W.E. Upjohn Institute for Employment Research, where she was a researcher for 12 years. She is a labor economist whose research interests include child care, female employment and wages, employment-related health and disability issues, and multiple-job holding. New research topics include child care worker wages and retention, household time allocation, and the motherhood wage penalty. Her research papers have been published in such academic journals as the *Review of Economics and Statistics*, the *Journal of Monetary Economics*, *Labour Economics*, *Southern Economic Journal,* and *Industrial Relations*.

Hans-Peter Kohler is Associate Professor of Sociology and a research associate of the Population Studies Center at the University of Pennsylvania. Kohler earned his MA in Demography in 1994 and his Ph.D in Economics in 1997 at the University of California at Berkeley. His primary research focuses on fertility and related behaviors in developing and developed countries, and a key characteristic of his research is the attempt to integrate demographic, economic, sociological and biological approaches in empirical and theoretical models of demographic behavior. He is the author of a recent book on fertility and social interaction, has co-edited a book ok on the biodemography of human reproduction and fertility, and has widely published in leading journals including *Demography, Population Development Review and the Journal of Development Economics.*

Michaela Kreyenfeld, Ph.D., Rostock University, 2002, is a Junior Professor for the Causes and Consequences of Demographic Change at Rostock University and a research scientist at the Max Planck Institute for Demographic Research. Her articles have appeared in *European Journal of Population*, *European Societies*, *Journal of Marriage and Family*, *Population and Population Research* and *Policy Review*. Her research interests are in the field of demography, family sociology and life course research.

Ghazala Naz, Dr. Polit., University of Bergen 2002 is a postdoctoral researcher of economics at the University of Bergen. She has published in the *Journal of Population Economics*. Her research interests are family and labour economics.

Øivind Anti Nilsen, Dr. Oecon, Norwegian School of Economics and Business Administration 1998, is an associate professor of economics at the Norwegian School of Economics and Business Administration and an IZA Fellow. His research interest are applied microeconometrics and labour economics. He has published in journals such as *Oxford Bulletin of Economics and Statistics*, *Review of Economics and Statistics*, but also in sociological journals such as the *European Sociological Review*.

Cathal O'Donoghue, Ph.D., London School of Economics, 2001, is a lecturer in Economics and director of the Economics of Social Policy Research Unit (ESPRU) of the National University of Ireland, Galway. He is also a research fellow of IZA, ICER and CHILD. He has degrees in Mathematics, Statistics, Economics and Social policy from UCC, Oxford, UCD and the London School of Economics. He has worked at the Department of Applied Economics, University of Cambridge for 6 years and previously at the Economic and Social Research Institute, Dublin and as a Fast-Stream Civil Servant in the UK Government. His research is mainly in the area of social policy modelling and he has acted as an advisor to the UK Department of Work and Pensions in this area for a number of years. He has also worked as a consultant for the World Bank, European Commission, OECD, Inter-American Development Bank and UNDP. He has published in journals such as *Economica* and *Cambridge Journal of Economics*.

Eamon O'Shea received a B.A and an M.A. from University College Dublin. He received a M.Sc. from the University of York, specialising in health economics, and a Ph.D. from the University of Leicester. He is currently senior lecturer in economics at the National University of Ireland, Galway. Dr. O'Shea's research interests include health economics, the economics of ageing and the economics of the welfare state. His work has been published in journals such as the *Journal of Health Economics*, *Applied Economics*, *Social Science and Medicine*, *Age and Ageing* and the *International Journal of Geriatric Psychiatry*. He has also worked as a consultant for the European Commission and the Council of Europe in the field of ageing research. He has also published a number of reports and policy documents in the field of ageing and related studies in Ireland. His most recent report for the National Council on Ageing and Older People is titled: *Healthy Ageing in Ireland: Policy, Practice and Evaluation.* His most recent book *Policy and Practice for Dementia Care* in Ireland was published by Ed Mellen Press in June 2004.

Alexia Prskawetz is Deputy Director and Head of the research group on Population Economics at the Vienna Institute of Demography of the Austrian Academy of Sciences since 2003. She received her Ph.D., at Vienna University of Technology in 1992. Her research topics include: population ageing and economic productivity, age structured modeling in population economics, fertility and female labor force participation at the macro level, long run population and economic development, poverty dynamics and fertility, agent based computational demography and the interaction of population, economic and environmental dynamics. She has co-edited a supplement of *Population and Development Review* on Population and Environment: Methods of Analysis and a book on Agent-Based Computational Demography. Her articles have appeared in *Journal of Population Economics, Population Studies, European Journal of Population, Mathematical Population Studies*, *Economics Letters* and *Journal of Economic Growth.*

Vegard Skirbekk is Research Scholar at the International Institute for Applied Systems Analysis (IIASA) in Laxenburg, Austria since 2003. He received his Ph.D., from Rostock university in year 2005. His research interests concern aging, fertility, population forecasting, age-differences in productivity, education, religion, divorce and pensions. He has investigated ways to extend the working life, both by lowering the age of labour market entrance through educational reforms and by increasing the retirement age. His articles have appeared in *Demography,* and *Population and Development Review.*

Steinar Vagstad, Dr. Polit., University of Bergen 1994, is a professor of economics at the University of Bergen. His research interests include population and family economics, contract theory, and industrial organization. He has published articles in the *Journal of Population Economics, Journal of Public Economics* and *Scandinavian Journal of Economics*, among others.

Seble Worku is a Ph.D. student at the University of Amsterdam and Tinbergen Institute. She is currently working at Statistics South Africa. Her research interests are population and labor economics.

Chapter 1

INTRODUCTION AND CONTRIBUTIONS OF THIS VOLUME

SIV GUSTAFSSON

1. INTRODUCTION

In this chapter the main trends are presented in fertility, age of the mother at having her first child and time spent in fulltime education by young people. Fertility is declining and is now well below the replacement of the population rate in all European countries. To some extent the fertility decline is caused by postponement of maternity in the sense that without mothers of successive generations being older and older the decline would have been smaller. But why do women and men form families so late and what role does the extension of youth education play? These and related issues for ten different countries are addressed by the contributions of this book. This chapter gives an overview of the different contributions.

Young women nowadays are considerably older when they have their first child than used to be the case a few decades ago. For example, the mean age of a first time mother in the Netherlands in 1970 was 25 years. By 2000 it had increased to 29 years, making first time mothers on average four years older in 30 years. All European countries are in the process of postponement of maternity although it started at different points of time, with western and northern Europe being earliest starting from 1965-1970, southern Europe following from 1980-1985 (Bosveld, 1996) and east and central Europe developing postponement of maternity since the fall of the Soviet Union in 1990 (Kohler and Philipov, 2001). Kohler, Billari and Ortega (2002) suggest that what we witness is a 'postponement transition' which will at least not stop in Central and Eastern Europe until age at maternity is similar to that of the rest of Europe.

There are several reasons why a better understanding of postponement of maternity is useful. First, such knowledge contributes to the prediction of fertility trends. As Bongaarts and Feeney (1998) and Bongaarts (1999) have pointed out, postponement of maternity leads to falling fertility rates even if there were no decrease in the cohort completed rate. Simply, if a cohort of women has an equal number of children later in life, than the previous cohort the age-specific period total

Siv Gustafsson and Adriaan Kalwij (eds.), Education and Postponement of Maternity, 1–30.

fertility rate decreases. The reverse process, preponement of maternity, having children earlier in life, leads to increases in total fertility rates for the same reasons.

A second reason for studying postponement of maternity is that, as the aging of maternity increases, a number of women will hit the biological limit of their reproductive capacity, leading to increasing medical costs, as couples seek medical assistance in order to procreate (Te Velde and Pearson, 2002), or individual unhappiness if such assistance fails (Hewlett, 2002). There are increasing trends of ultimate childlessness particularly among high-educated women (Beets, 1998).

A third reason, is that many European governments worry about below replacement fertility and the resulting ageing of the population and attempt to design public policies, that would make it less costly for young people to form families.

The overall purpose of putting these 12 chapters together in a volume is to try and find policy implications from the studies. What kind of policies could a government try that wants to help young couples to start families? However, this book also aspires to show how difficult it is to arrive at clear policy conclusions even after the most careful statistical analyses because of the interdependency between decisions on family formation, labor force participation, investment in human capital in school and post-school and other life time plans.

2. TRENDS IN EUROPEAN FERTILITY, EDUCATION AND TIMING OF MOTHERHOOD

The most common measure of fertility is the period total fertility rate, which has the interpretation of the total number of children born to a woman over her life cycle, if the age specific fertility rates of that year were to prevail. In Table 1.1 we present total fertility rates for a number of countries over the period 1960 through 2000. The lowest fertility rates in 2000 were found in South and East and Central Europe with the Czech Republic at the bottom of the scale at 1.14.[1] In 2000, not a single country among the 16 European countries included in Table 1.1 reached the replacement level of 2.1. This is in sharp contrast to the situation in 1960 and 1970 when almost all European countries had fertility rates above the replacement level or close to it. We include figures for the US, Japan and South Africa, as a comparison to the selected European countries. Whereas in 2000 in Japan, the low fertility rate was comparable to those in the European countries, the fertility rates in the United States and South Africa were higher than the replacement rate in 2000.

2.1 Tempo and quantum effects

Postponement of maternity is one of the determinants of the decrease in total fertility rates in Europe. In an influential paper Bongaarts and Feeney (1998) explain how total fertility rates can be decomposed into the quantum effect and tempo effect. The quantum effect is the total fertility rate, that we would have observed, had there been no change in the timing of births. The tempo effect is the effect of timing changes. To decompose fertility into the quantum and tempo effects one needs birth order specific birth rates by one-year periods and single year of age of the mother. Then one can compute:

$$(adj)\ TFR_i = TFR_i/(1-r_i) \tag{1}$$

where TFR_i is the observed birth order specific total fertility rate, r_i is the increase in the mean age of the mother at having her child e.g. if the mean age at first births increases from 27.0 to 27.1, $r_i = 0.1$. and $(adj)TFR_i$ is then the tempo adjusted birth order specific total fertility rate in that year.

To get a measure of tempo and quantum effects one has to compute adjusted total fertility rates by birth order (i) and summarize them over birth orders:

$$(adj)TFR = \sum(adj)TFR_i \tag{2}$$

The difference between the observed total fertility rate (TFR) and the adjusted total fertility rate (adj) TFR is then a measure of the tempo effect.

Table 1.1. Total Fertility Rates Selected Countries, 1960-2000

	1960	1970	1980	1990	2000
Belgium	2.56	2.25	1.68	1.62	1.66
Czech Republic	2.11	1.91	2.10	1.89	1.14
Denmark	2.57	1.95	1.55	1.67	1.77
Finland	2.72	1.82	1.63	1.78	1.73
France	2.73	2.47	1.95	1.78	1.89
Germany E.[1]	2.33	2.19	1.94	1.52	1.21
Germany W.[1]	2.37	2.02	1.45	1.45	1.41
Hungary	2.02	1.98	1.92	1.87	1.32
Iceland	4.17	2.81	2.48	2.30	2.08
Ireland	3.76	3.93	3.25	2.11	1.89
Italy	2.41	2.42	1.64	1.33	1.23
Japan	2.00	2.13	1.80	1.54	1.36
The Netherlands	3.12	2.57	1.60	1.62	1.72
Norway	2.91	2.50	1.72	1.93	1.85
Portugal	3.10	2.83	2.18	1.57	1.52
South Africa**	5.92	5.44	4.56	3.51	2.42
Spain	2.86	2.90	2.20	1.36	1.24
Sweden	2.20	1.92	1.68	2.13	1.54
United Kingdom	2.72	2.43	1.90	1.83	1.65
United States		2.48	1.84	2.08	2.13

Source: OECD Health data 2001, 2002. *OECD Health data 2000.
**U.S. Bureau of Census:
http://www.cencus.gov/ipc/www/idbconf.html
[1] For West and East Germany Statistisches Bundesamt (2000): Bevölkerung und Erwerbstätigkeit. Gebiet und Bevölkerung 1999. For 2000 the data was supplied upon request (from Michaela Kreyenfeld).

A number of studies on the decomposition of total fertility rates into the quantum and tempo effect for European fertility development are now available (Kohler, Billari and Ortega, 2002; Lesthaege and Willems, 2002; Philipov and Kohler, 2001). The main result is, that postponement is responsible for some of the decrease in fertility, but that there are also substantial quantum effects. As pointed out by Kohler, Billari and Ortega (2002), it is a well-established result that there is a connection between tempo and quantum effects, so that later first births also result in smaller completed cohort fertility.

2.2 Postponement of maternity and ultimate childlessness

In Table 1.2, the mean age of the mother at first birth for selected countries is presented. In most of the countries in Table 1.2, we observe that there is a U-shaped pattern over time with the bottom in 1970 or 1975, i.e. the lowest age of the mother at giving birth to her first child occurs in all these countries around 1970 or 1975. Age of the mother at first birth, first decreases from those births that occurred in 1960 to the lowest level around 1970, and then it increases again to the highest level ever observed in the year 2000. There is no country that has had older mothers at any point of time, than what is observed in the year 2000. The pattern is that of increasing trends. Not even in those countries where the trend towards older mothers started first, like the Netherlands, is there any tendency for this trend to level off.

For example, in 1960 in the Netherlands mothers' age at their first birth averaged 25.7 years, in 1970 it had decreased to 24.8 years, in 1990 it had increased to 27.6 years and in 2000 the mean age of the mother at first birth was as high as 28.6 years. There are also clear differences between countries with the East European countries having the youngest mothers. The largest increase in mean age of the mother at first birth is observed in former East Germany, from 24.1 in 1985 to 27.6 in 2000. Interestingly, in 2000 the mean age of mothers at first birth was younger in the United States than in any of the European countries, presented in Table 1.2, whereas Japan has experienced the same recent trend of postponement of maternity as the European countries.

Is there a reason to worry about these trends? Having a child at age 29 is well within the biological limit. Looking at the mean age of the mother there could be little to worry about, but there is a distribution around the mean with particularly old mothers among high educated women and also a large share of them remaining childless (Gustafsson, Kenjoh and Wetzels 2002).

Beets (1997) presents median, first and third quartiles of age of the mother at first birth according to birth cohort of the mother. The age of the mother at first birth when 75 per cent of women have had a first birth has increased spectacularly comparing the cohort of women born in 1945 to that of women born in 1955. Among the 15 European countries analyzed by Beets (1997), the third quartile is older than age 30 for seven countries namely Ireland, the Netherlands, Sweden, Denmark, England and Wales, Finland and West Germany. For West Germany the third quartile for women born in 1955 is as high as 34 years. This means that a large share of these 25 per cent of women of this cohort will never give birth to a child, since very few first births occur after age 35 (Gustafsson, Kenjoh and Wetzels, 2002). Beets (1998) presents figures split according to the education of the mother for a number of countries and on the proportion women still childless at age 35. Beets analyzes two cohorts, namely women born 1948-1952 and women born 1953-1957 and three educational groups high, medium and low educated for a number of countries. Among high-educated Dutch women born between 1948 and 1952 as many as 43.2 per cent were still childless at age 35 and for the cohort born 1953-1957 the proportion is 37.0 per cent. Other countries that also have large numbers of childless women for the younger cohort are: Italy (33.0), Spain (35.3) and Canada (37.6).

Table 1.2. Mean Age of the Mother at First Birth, Selected Countries, 1960-2000

	1960	1970	1980	1990	1995	2000
Belgium#	24.8	24.3	24.7	26.4	26.9[c]	
Czech Republic*	22.9	22.5	22.4	22.5	23.3	24.9
Denmark	23.1	23.8	24.6	26.4	27.4	
Finland	24.7	24.4	25.6	26.5	27.2	27.4
France#	24.8	24.4	25.0	27.0	28.1	28.7[e]
Germany W*#	25.3	24.2	25.5	27.0	27.6	28.0[e]
Germany E*#	23.9	23.3	23.5	24.6	26.3	27.6[e]
Hungary	22.9	22.8	22.4	23.1	23.8	25.1
Iceland		21.3	21.9	24.0	25.0	25.5
Ireland		25.8[a]	25.5	26.6	27.3	27.8
Italy	25.7	25.0	25.0	26.9	28.0	28.7[d]
Japan**	25.4	25.6	26.4	27.0	27.5	28.0
Netherlands	25.7	24.8	25.7	27.6	28.4	28.6
Norway				25.6	26.4	26.9
Portugal			24.0	24.9	25.8	26.4
Spain			25.0	26.8	28.4	29.0[e]
Sweden	25.5	25.9	25.3	26.3	27.2	27.9
United Kingdom#				27.3	28.3	29.1
United States***		21.4	22.7	24.2	24.7	24.7[d]

* Former (countries with border changes around 1990).
The following are for different years than stated above, a=1972, b=1986, c=1993, d=1997 and e=1999.
Source: Council of Europe (2001), *Recent Demographic Developments in Europe* (hhtp://www.coe.int/t/e/social_cohesion/population/demographic_year_book/2001_Edition/default.asp#TopOfPage)
** Japan's Ministry of Health, Labor and Welfare (2000), *Vital Statistics*.
*** United States' National Center for Health Statistics (www.cdc.gov-nchs-data-stabat.tabl).
# Birth order within current marriage
Such data could not be found for South Africa

2.3 Increased age at leaving full time education

Since the mid 20th century there has been an increase in the length of education in OECD countries. Both men and women spend much more of their young adult lives in full-time education. An increased demand for skilled labor has resulted in educational expansion and this is one of the major explanations of postponement of parenthood both among women and men, although the gender effects may differ, since age differences between husband and wife have been narrowing (Bergstrom 1997). Gustafsson, Kenjoh and Wetzels (2002) estimate that mean age at finishing full-time education for women born in the 1960s compared to those born in the 1930s has increased between 1.2 to 2.8 years in a 30 year period in Britain, Germany, the Netherlands and Sweden.

In Table 1.3 and 1.4, school life expectancy for selected countries as computed by UNESCO (2002) is presented.[1] This statistic is computed as follows:

$$E(S)_t = \sum_{i=a}^{n} S_{it} \tag{1}$$

where $E(S)_t$ school life expectancy in year t is the sum of age specific enrolment ratios S_i at all levels of education for the years t that countries have delivered workable data. Countries have to report data by single year of age and by gender for both the population in school and the population of school age not in school in order to make it possible to compute this statistic.

The interpretation of the data of Table 1.4, taking the example of an Austrian male child, who was in school in a given year e.g. in 1995, is that he is expected to spend in total 14.5 years in school. This means that if school-starting age is six, he is expected to be 20.5 years old at finishing education. UNESCO cautions that comparing school life expectancy across countries does not take account of cross-country variations in the length of the school year, the quality of education and the occurrence of grade repetition in school. This measure also does not take account of variations in school starting age. Whereas the official age of starting primary school education in Sweden is at age seven, the corresponding age in the Netherlands is at age four (see Table 1.5). Most Swedish children, however, go to public subsidized childcare from age 18 months, which incorporates some pedagogic activities. From age six, there is compulsory preschool, which is not counted as school. One would think that Dutch four-year-olds do not do much more academic work, than Swedish four-year-olds do. In 1995, a Swedish young male was expected to spend 14.4 years in school making him 21.4 years old at finishing education, while a Dutch young male would spend 16.8 years in school making him 20.8 years old at finishing education. The difference in age at finishing education is therefore 0.6 years while expected number of years in school differs by 2.4 years.[3]

However, the point we want to make using Tables 1.3-1.5, is that there has been considerable expansion of education over time. All countries show increasing trends. For female children in the Netherlands, the increase is as large as 5.5 years more of being in school in 1995 in comparison to 1970, in the UK the corresponding increase is 4.9 years. Time spent in school by young women in the 1990s was thus about 5 years longer than in the 1970s both in the Netherlands and in the UK.

Table 1.3. School Life Expectancy of Women, Selected Countries

School life expectancy	1970	1980	1990	1995
Austria			14.1[d]	14.3
Belgium			14.2	16.9
Bulgaria	11.1	11.2	12.3	
Czech Republic				12.9
Denmark		13.3	14.3	15
Estonia			12.3[d]	12.9
Finland			15.6[d]	16.2
France			15[d]	15.7
Germany			14.5[d]	15.1
Greece	10.1		13.2	13.5
Hungary			11.4	13.1
Iceland	9.7			15.5
Ireland	10.8	11.6	12.8	13.9
Italy	11.5[a]			
Latvia				11.9
Malta	10.5	11.4	12.5	13.1
Netherlands	10.8	12.6	14.6	16.3
Norway		13	14.5	15.5
Portugal	8.6		14[d]	
Poland		12.1	12.4	
Romania			10.7[d]	11.6[g]
Spain	9.4	12.5		
Sweden			13.2	15.1
Switzerland		11.9	13.1	13.5
The Former Yugoslav Republic of Macedonia				11.3
United Kingdom	11.8	12.8	13.9	16.7
Japan	11.6	12.6		13.7[e]
United States		14.9[b]	15.9	16.4
South Africa			13.4[c]	14.1[f]

Source: UNESCO (2002) (http://www.uis.unesco.org/uis/en/statsO.htm)
a) 1975 b) 1985 c) 1991 d) 1992 e) 1993 f) 1994 g) 1996

Table 1.4. School Life Expectancy of Men, Selected Countries

School life expectancy	1970	1980	1990	1995
Austria			14.8[d]	14.5
Belgium			14.1	16.7
Bulgaria	11.2	11	12.3	
Czech Republic				12.8
Denmark		13.4	14	14.6
Estonia			12[d]	12.3
Finland			14.6[d]	15.1
France			14.3[d]	15.3
Germany			15.3	15.1
Greece	11.5		13.4	13.5
Hungary			11.3	12.7
Iceland	9.3			14.7
Ireland	10.9	11.3	12.4	13.5
Italy	12.8[a]			
Latvia				11.3
Malta	11	12.2	13.3	13.6
Netherlands	12.3	13.3	15.2	16.8
Norway		12.7	14	14.9
Portugal	9.2		13.2[d]	
Poland		11.8	12	
Romania			10.9[d]	11.5[g]
Spain	10.7	12.6		
Sweden			12.7	14.4
Switzerland		13.3	14.1	14.7
The Former Yugoslav Republic of Macedonia				11.2
United Kingdom	12.3	13.1	13.5	16.2
Japan	12.4	13.5		14.0[e]
United States		14.5[b]	15.1	15.5
South Africa			13.2[c]	14.1[f]

Source: UNESCO (2002)(http://www.uis.unesco.org/uis/en/statsO.htm)
a) 1975 b) 1985 c) 1991 d) 1992 e) 1993 f) 1994 g) 1996

Table 1.5. Structures of Education, Selected Countries

Official age of school education	Starting Primary	Finishing secondary	Compulsory until
Austria	6	19	15
Belgium	6	18	18
Bulgaria			
Czech Republic			
Denmark	7	18-19	16
Estonia			
Finland	7	19	16
France	6	18	16
Germany	6	18-19	18
Greece	5.5	18	15
Hungary			
Iceland	6	17	16
Ireland	4	18	15
Italy	6	19	14
Latvia			
Malta			
Netherlands	4	18	16
Norway	7	19	16
Portugal	6	18	15
Poland			
Romania			
Spain	6	18	16
Sweden	7	20	16
Switzerland			
The Former Yugoslav Republic of Macedonia			
United Kingdom	5	18-19	16
Japan			
United States			
South Africa			

Source: European Commission (1995). Structures of the Education and Initial Training Systems in the European Union.

3. CONTRIBUTIONS AND OUTLINE OF THIS VOLUME

In this section a summary of the contribution of each chapter is provided. Chapters 2 and 3 are methodological in character. Chapter 2 aims at bridging an often experienced gap between on the one hand those scholars, who have contributed to methodological advancement and criticism, the econometricians, and on the other hand those scholars who are mainly interested in particular issues around postponement of maternity the applied economists and demographers. Chapter 3 makes a contribution to the understanding of the effect of being in school on timing of maternity by showing that the school age cohort i.e. the in months age at which the individual finishes compulsory school has an independent effect on timing of maternity, although the latter event takes place about 9 years later. Chapters 4 and 5 study two catholic countries Ireland and Italy, where fertility decline has been very rapid lately. In Ireland age of maternity has always been rather high and chapter 4 focuses on decomposing the fertility decline. On the other hand in Italy postponement of maternity contributes a great deal to explaining the decrease in fertility and chapter 5 on Italy therefore focuses on the interrelation between fertility and labor force participation of young Italian women, showing for example that if the child's grandmother is available the young mother is more likely to work. In both countries higher educated women postpone maternity the most. Chapters 6, 7 and 8 focus on the two main determinants of postponement of maternity the career planning motive and the consumption smoothing motive respectively. The career planning motive, trying to time maternity when it makes the least damage to your job market career is treated in chapters 6 and 7. Chapter 6 shows that in Spain the widespread use of fixed-term job contracts make young men and women uncertain about their income and creates an incentive to wait until a permanent job is found before starting a family. Chapter 7 analyses if waiting to start a family from a career planning motive has been worthwhile for American college graduated women. Chapter 8 focuses on the consumption smoothing motive by studying saving and consumption of young Dutch couples around the time they have a childbirth. In chapters 9 and 10, the analyses focus on effects on birth timing of changes of the whole institutional structure determining costs of children in the transition economies, when the former German Democratic Republic and the former state socialist Czech part of Czechoslovakia turned into United Germany and the Czech Republic respectively. In both cases the transition period showed much later maternity timing particularly for higher educated women in comparison to the state socialist period. Many of the chapters of this volume control for husband's education, income or job characteristics e.g. chapters 5, 6, 7 and 8, but only chapters 11 and 12 focus on the additional effect of husband's education. Chapter 11 focuses on timing of couple formation and parenthood, whereas chapter 12 studies completed fertility of married couples.

In *chapter 2 Siv Gustafsson and Adriaan Kalwij* discuss methodological problems in the analysis of timing of parenthood. The motivation for this chapter is a feeling that there are two groups of social scientists studying demographic issues. One group, the econometricians focus on the model specification and estimation, and concentrate on solving different problems arising from biases. The other group, applied economists or demographers, focus less on econometric techniques and more on the institutional setting and the policy implications of their results. An ideal contribution is equally good in both respects. The purpose of the chapter is to build a bridge between econometricians and applied economists and demographers. The chapter starts with an explanation of dynamic economic theory of fertility building on work by Becker (1973), Willis (1973), Cigno (1990) and Hotz, Klerman and Willis (1997). It is shown that economic theory acknowledges that decisions to have children and when to have them depend on time and money costs of children both realized in the past, current prices and expected prices in the future. Such inclusive fertility models are very difficult and perhaps it is not an exaggeration to say that they are impossible to estimate. One of the most important problems to try and solve is the problem of causality. In order to say that a particular variable causes an outcome one needs exogenous variation in this explanatory variable. Some researchers rely on sequential models attributing causality to the timing of events so that an event that occurred earlier in time can be said to cause events later in time (e.g. Blossfeld and Timm, 2003). However, this interpretation of causality needs the assumptions that a person is not taking expectations about the future into account and, related to this, that there are no time-constant household specific unobserved effects. When analyzing timing of maternity these are troublesome assumptions because, for example, it is very likely that the reason for a young couple to decide not to have a child in time period t is influenced by the expectation that in time period $t+2$ for example, when they have finished their education and secured permanent jobs, the time and money costs of having a child will be smaller than in a more vulnerable situation for the career planning and for consumption of other goods and services in addition to fulfilling the child wish (Gustafsson 2001).

Econometric theory like demometric theory has suggested hazard models and systems of hazard models as a reasonable approach to modeling birth timing. The advantage of this approach is that hazard models acknowledge the intrinsic dynamic character of birth decisions. Developments of the hazard model approach include taking account of the interdependence of decisions by modeling jointly the decisions of timing of births of each parity and stopping behavior which can also be at parity zero i.e. some women remain childless (Heckman and Walker 1990, Bloemen and Kalwij, 2001). In spite of these econometric contributions most work in the field by applied economists and demographers proceeds by analyzing separately the different durations until life events.

The hazard models approach has been criticized for not estimating a behavioral or structural model. A structural model would estimate the parameters of utility maximization given the budget constraint for each period relevant to the decision of birth timing. One such method has been suggested by Wolpin (1984) and with more recent applications by Van der Klaauw (1996), Francesconi (2002) and Kalwij (1999). This method proceeds by backwards recursion i.e. you start by the end of the period and estimate constrained utility maximization of that period and then proceed to utility maximization of the previous period. This structural discrete time method is extremely demanding in programming skills and computer time- and only a few contributions exist applying this method. However, for the same reasons systems of hazard models as initiated by Heckman and Walker (1990) have only been estimated by a handful researchers.

An ideal empirical model should be directly related to a theoretical model, i.e. a behavioral model, and use truly exogenous variation in all past current and expected future prices to explain the decision of when to have a child. Most models estimated in this book are reduced form models, i.e. they estimate the effects of exogenous variables on the dependent variable rather than estimating the parameters of the constrained utility maximization problem as economic theory tells us to do. A researcher must always make choices, solving some problems while accepting the problems associated with others. For example in order to have information about the spouse only married couples may be analyzed as in chapters 11 and 12. this may solve an omitted variables bias but employs a select sample, which may introduce a selectivity bias. Another problem is a simultaneity bias, which results when models that should be modeled jointly are not. Bratti in chapter 5 models labor force participation and fertility jointly, but this is done by employing a linear model, whereas simultaneous estimation of nonlinear models are a so far unsolved problem. Some researchers claim that only by estimating a structural model one can say something about effects from public policies on people's behavior. However, in order to estimate a structural model one has to make assumptions about the shape of the utility function, which theory does not guide us on and one has to make simplifying assumptions like ruling out possibilities to save or borrow or assuming that a child only has positive costs the first year of its life in order for the estimates to converge. The estimated structural models reviewed in chapter 2 all ignore institutional characteristics and the contributions from the 'Types of Welfare States' literature, which instead are important in most chapters of this book. As methodological contributions in econometrics develop and new software becomes available, applied economists improve their econometric tools. The contributions to this volume have all employed best available techniques, for that policy relevant question which they have asked.

In *chapter 3 Skirbekk*, *Kohler* and *Prskawetz* study fertility behavior of Swedish women according to their birth month. This study contributes an interesting analysis about the causality from school leaving age to age of the woman at maternity. It is of course no policy interest to find that women born early in the year are younger at maternity than women born late in the year. But also from a policy point of view it is interesting to find that the younger one is at finishing compulsory school the younger one is as a first time mother although this event takes place about 9 years later. The authors use the fact that Swedish children start school in August of that calendar year in which they turned seven and remain in school at least until they graduate from the basic school (*grundskola*), which is in June during the calendar year in which they turn sixteen. For older cohorts compulsory school was shorter, since the nine year compulsory school was gradually introduced during the 1960s over different geographical areas. But school years start in August and graduation takes place in June. Only in university schooling graduation dates are spread over the year. This means that women born early in the year are older when they graduate from compulsory school than women born late in the year. Skirbekk, Kohler and

Prskawetz show convincingly that the woman's age at finishing education is more important for determining age at maternity than her own calendar age in months. The January born women are older when they graduate from school by 11 months compared to the December born women. The difference in woman's age at first birth between those born in December and the subsequent January is 4.9 months, which implies that 45% of the variation in the school leaving age is still present at the time of first birth.

Chapter 4 by O'Donoghue and O'Shea tries to explain the decline in fertility in Ireland. Ireland until recently has been a high fertility country (see Table 1.1 above). Similar to the South European countries in 1980 the Irish total fertility rate was well above the replacement rate of 2.1 children per woman. By 1990, when the fertility rates in the South European countries had already decreased to the lowest ones in Europe, Ireland still had a total fertility rate of 2.11. During the 1990s fertility decreased rapidly to levels below replacement and in 2000 the Irish total fertility rate is 1.89. O'Donoghue and O'Shea explain in their introductory part how contraceptives and family planning remained illegal in Ireland until 1973, and how restrictions such as doctor's prescriptions and sales through pharmacists remained until 1993. Interestingly, age of the woman at having her first child was always high in Ireland as was age at marriage. This fits with the low accessibility of contraceptives, which made postponing marriage age the main family planning measure, as later marriage age exposed the woman to the risk of childbearing during fewer fertile years, a Malthusian rather than a neomalthusian family planning which requires access to contraceptives. But things change in Ireland and O'Donoghue and O'Shea show that higher educated women postpone maternity in comparison to lower educated women just like in other European countries, resulting in lower fertility rates for the higher educated groups.

In their final Table 4.6 O'Donoghue and O'Shea show that the variables female wage, male earnings and male unemployment rate only account for between 43 and 14 per cent of the change in fertility between 1970 and 1994 the variables cohort and time explain the major part of the change in fertility. The important change in average schooling time in this way is incorporated in the cohort and time variables. According to Table 1.3 above expected time in school for an Irish young woman increased by 3.1 years from 1970 to 1995, while Irish postponement of first birth in the same period was only 0.4 years according to Table 4.3. But this fits with the fact that Irish first time mothers were always relatively old compared to new mothers in other countries. Different from many other countries for example Spain and Italy postponement of maternity is therefore not the main reason for decreasing fertility in Ireland.

Bratti in chapter 5 analyses female labor force participation and marital fertility in Italy. He analyzes the 1993 cross section of the Italian Survey of Household Income and Wealth data (ISHIW) by multinominal logit model with four different outcomes. A woman can be participating in the labor force (P) or not participating (NP) and she can be experiencing fertility (F) i.e. have a child or not experiencing fertility (NF) i.e. not have a child. This gives four different combinations for the year 1993.

Only married or cohabiting couples are selected, so that marital fertility is analyzed, which leaves out the possible effects from education on couple formation and marriage. Fertility is measured as the presence of a child aged more than one year and less than two years, a flow fertility variable, that is a variable measuring a recent birth to match the information on recent labor force participation. This data set does not have information about birth dates of the children in the household nor does it contain information about the women's work history. The focus of the paper is to analyze the effect of education on the four different outcomes of the multinominal logit model.

Bratti addresses the possible endogeneity of education in the fertility and labor force participation choice by two strategies. First, he introduces a wide range of controls for a woman's family background which proxy for the woman's 'taste for market work' and second he performs a Smith and Blundell's (1986) weak exogeneity test. This latter test is done by including the residual from the education equation into the 'parsimonous' multinominal logit model. He finds that there is no residual evidence of endogeneity of education with labor force participation and fertility. This means that women first decide on an educational plan and from their educational plan follows labor force participation and fertility. As discussed in chapter 2 there is a methodological discussion on whether education can be taken as a predetermined variable in the fertility decision or not. One can think of a case of reversed causality, if an unwanted early birth prevents a woman from finishing her planned educational investment, however Bratti's test shows that this case is unimportant for Italy.

The timing of fertility decision is incorporated into his model by interactions of age and education as explanatory variables for the multinominal logit outcomes. The results are in line with other research, showing that more educated women have their children later. In an interesting analysis of effects of other factors than education on the probabilities of the multinominal logit outcomes Bratti finds that increasing husband's income has a negligible effect on the woman's labor force participation and fertility. Another interesting variable is grandmother availability, which is constructed from information about province of birth, province of residence and if for either the wife or the husband of the couple the mother was alive in 1993. This grandmother availability increases the woman's labor force participation substantially. Also if the woman's mother or mother in law were working for pay the labor force participation of the woman increases. Grandmother availability might have a positive effect on fertility as a childcare resource. This is not generally found. Some of the effects on fertility seem to go the opposite way: more fertility with no grandmother availability, and more fertility if the mother in law worked but there is also more fertility if the woman's mother was a housewife. But in most cases those variables that increase labor force participation also decrease fertility indicating the sharp conflict between family formation and career planning in the Italian society at least until 1993.

In *Chapter 6 Sara de la Rica and Amaia Iza* study the effects of fixed-term jobs on the entry into marriage and maternity. Having a fixed term job rather than an indefinite contract may result in postponing parenthood until a permanent job is found. Chapter 6 therefore studies one aspect of career planning. Spain is the country that has the oldest mothers in 2000 according to Table 1.2 above, the lowest fertility rate 1.24, only after Italy at 1.23 and the Czech Republic at 1.13. As de la Rica and Iza note, postponement of maternity has taken place also within educational groups so that there is not only the compositional effect of more women studying longer but also a behavioral effect causing postponement of maternity.

One candidate factor explaining these behavioral effects are the changes that took place in the Spanish labor market leading to wide spread use of fixed-term contracts particularly among young employees. The Spanish labor market at the beginning of the 1980s was basically characterized by indefinite labor contracts with high severance payments in case of layoffs as an effect of redundancy. In 1984 a type of fixed-term contract called 'employment promotion contracts', were introduced in order to increase flexibility in the labor market and make it less costly for employers to dismiss workers for economic reasons. These contracts could be used to hire any worker up to three years, and at that moment the firm had to decide whether to dismiss that worker, without having to pay severance payments, or to contract her/him on an indefinite basis. These contracts were very attractive for employers in comparison to previous indefinite contracts and during the period 1986 to 1992 it has been estimated that almost all new contracts (98%) were of this type. Since older workers already had indefinite contracts this created a situation where particularly young workers to a large extent were the ones who had this type of fixed-term contracts. De la Rica and Iza believe that the insecure labor market situation of the young may be one reason for the fact that Spain has the oldest mothers among European Countries (Table 1.2 above).

To analyze the effects of temporary contracts on marriage and motherhood the authors use the eight available waves 1994-2001, of the Spanish data from the European Household Panel. The analysis studies the incidence of marriage among individuals both men and women who are single and not cohabiting, and the incidence of motherhood among women, who are married or cohabiting in the first wave. The panel is very short, which does not allow selecting women from different cohorts at a given age interval, say age 15-39, which is common in marriage and fertility studies. Instead individuals included are at different ages when observed and the incidence of marriage and motherhood is studied by age-educational groups. The main results are that men have a very small probability to marry, when they are not working, a finding that is in line with an earlier study by Ahn and Mira (2001) but they are also less likely to marry if they have a fixed-term contract. With respect to the decision of whether to enter into parenthood, results indicate that for all childless women, either with or without a partner, holding fixed-term contracts delay entry into motherhood in comparison to holding indefinite contracts. The discouragement effect is stronger for women with no partner, as expected. The lesson to be learned from this study is that the labor market reform that took place in Spain in 1984, i.e., the creation of the so called "employment promotion contract", not only created a segmented labor market, but also delayed men's decision concerning when to get married, and women's decision concerning when to enter motherhood. This postponement of marriage and maternity is at least partially responsible for the overall fall in fertility rates in Spain in the late 1990s.

In *Chapter 7 Catalina Amuedo-Dorantes and Jean Kimmel* make a contribution to the family wage gap discussion for the United States. This chapter is also a contribution to an evaluation of whether the career planning motive for postponing maternity has been worth while. The United States has not experienced a big decrease in fertility, and different from all European countries presented in Table 1.1, its fertility rate is at the replacement level in 2000. Also, the mean age of the woman at motherhood in the United States is by European standards low (Table 1.2), although it has increased from 21.4 in 1970 to 25.1 in 2002. However, decomposing the women by education shows that white college educated American women are postponing motherhood to a similar extent as their European sisters. For example, among women with four years of college education, as many as 56 per cent were childless at age 30 as an average for 1990-1995, while only 17 per cent were childless at age 30 among those with less than high school education.

While chapter 6 focuses on the birth timing decision, chapter 7 takes birth timing as an explanatory variable and asks if those women who postponed motherhood improved their wages by doing so. In other words, do college educated American women, who had their first child after age 30 earn more than similar women, who had their child earlier?

This chapter fits into a rather large literature about the family wage gap and the chapter starts by reviewing this literature. In the field of analysis of the wage structure a number of econometric concerns have been proposed. Amuedo-Dorantes and Kimmel address these concerns by including step by step corrections. First, because wages are observed only for working women there needs to be a correction for being included in the sample of working women. Second, a fixed effects estimation is carried out to correct for the fact that the sample is pooled across waves of a panel, which means that the same individual is observed several times. Finally, an estimation is carried out where rather than observed probability of motherhood and of delayed motherhood the predicted probabilities are used. This third step is intended to take care of possible endogeniety of motherhood and delayed motherhood. Their main findings are that college-educated mothers do not experience a wage penalty; in fact they enjoy a wage boost. This finding is robust to different specifications, however when the endogeneity corrections for motherhood and delayed motherhood are performed the estimated wage boost increases significantly to 22 per cent, a value that the authors have a hard time believing in. They focus their discussion on the results from the fixed effects sample selection corrected analysis with observed explanatory values on motherhood and birth timing rather than predicted values. Amuedo-Dorantes and Kimmel speculate that mothers, in their search for job matches with family-friendly employers, achieve job matches with employers who are also friendly to female workers and so more likely to offer female workers opportunities for career advancement and wage growth

The authors speculate that the fact that college educated women profit from delaying motherhood, happens because these women are in a position to negotiate a family friendly work environment with flexible work schedules.

In *Chapter 8, Adriaan Kalwij* analyses an issue related to the second motive for postponing maternity, namely the consumption smoothing motive. In his chapter, the financial situation of Dutch couples around the birth of children is analyzed using the Dutch socio-economic panel data set. He needs to determine the years until first birth and therefore the sample includes only couples who experienced the birth of their first child during the panel period 1987-1993.

Data on income, consumption and saving of households as well as education, age and employment status of both husband and wife are available. The empirical analysis focuses on explaining consumption growth around the time of births. The analysis takes into account the endogeneity of children in the econometric analysis, hereby acknowledging that households take consumption and fertility decisions simultaneously.

This chapter shows that households save on average more before than after having given birth to their first child. This is in line with a standard lifecycle model of consumption behavior where households make provisions for future consumption needs and with the empirical findings in Kalwij (2003) that the liquid assets of a household have a positive and significant effect on the conception probability. This suggests that the consumption smoothing motive may play a role in postponing maternity. However, households do not reduce savings enough to offset the reduction in income due to women leaving employment, and consumption is therefore observed to decrease with the arrival of children in the household. As a result consumption is shown to track income around the time of births. That is, as income decreases consumption follows the same pattern rather than there being a pattern of saving and dissaving to keep consumption at a level to smooth the marginal utility of consumption. This result suggests that young households may face tight liquidity constraints and have strong precautionary motives.

The following two chapters analyze timing of maternity in transition economies. The transition from a state socialist economy to a market economy created drastic changes in the institutional setting, which in turn changed the costs of having children. The variables of women's education in duration analyses are in the focus. Thc transition happened in East Germany when the former German Democratic Republic (GDR) was united with the Federal Republic of Germany (FRG) in 1990. *Michaela Kreyenfeld in Chapter 9* analyses the effect of these changes on maternity decisions. She describes the institutional setting in the GDR and contrasts it to that of the FRG. The expectations in the GDR were that after one year of paid maternity leave, the woman returned to full-time work, making use of the full day public childcare system. After unification the eastern states in united Germany had to adopt the institutional environment of the FRG. This meant much less focus on helping mothers to combine family life with job market demands and full-time jobs. The situation after unification meant for East German women less compensation during maternity leave, less access to jobs as unemployment increased, more uncertainty about labor market prospects, a wider wage dispersion with larger returns to education, loss of marriage and child premiums in access to housing. These changes can be expected to influence maternity decisions.

Kreyenfeld analyzes the 2002 wave of the German Socio-Economic Panel (GSOEP) comparing the West German sample to the east German sample by a piece-wise constant event history model. She splits the samples into births taking place before unification and births taking place after unification and finds that before unification there were no educational differences in the probability of entry into maternity in East Germany unlike in West Germany, where university trained women enter maternity much later. Both in East and West Germany are women very unlikely to enter into motherhood before they have finished their studies. After unification similar educational differences in maternity timing appear in East Germany as in West Germany. The transition of East Germany has not (yet) equalized patterns of maternity timing between the two parts of Germany. Comparing East and West Germany, East German women still have their children on average earlier than West German women.

In *Chapter 10 Vladimíra Kantorová* analyzes entry into maternity in the Czech Republic distinguishing between the state socialist period, analyzing births that took place 1970-1989, and the transition period, analyzing births that took place 1990-1997. The state-socialist period was characterized like in East Germany (see chapter 9) by policies that assumed that mothers were full-time workers, so there were paid maternity and parental leaves and access to subsidized childcare. Entry into early parenthood was economically stimulated also like in the GDR by housing loans for married couples under age 30 and repayments of the loan were partly cancelled, when the first child was born.

Kantorová points out that there was little information and little availability of contraceptives in the state-socialist period, a situation which also lead to early births. But these economic incentives in education and the labor market, which in market economies make postponement of maternity an economically advantageous option, were absent in the state-socialist Czech Republic, that part of Czechoslovakia which became the Czech Republic. There was little return to human capital and employment was defined as a state-guaranteed social right. In 1988 a university educated woman earned a 33 per cent higher wage than the average female wage, in 1996 the difference had increased so that a university educated woman had an earnings advantage of 61 per cent.

After 1990 the private sector of the labor market has increased and demands for higher education and job-related experience has increased. More women entered university education and would be confronted with similar opportunity costs of having children, as has been hypothesized in western market economies. In the year 2000, the Czech Republic had the lowest fertility rate, only 1.14 children per woman, of all the countries selected in Table 1.1 above. The age at entrance into motherhood was still comparatively low at age 24.9 years, however it experienced a considerable increase from age 22.5 years in 1990 (see Table 1.2 above). Kantorová presents two possible explanations: one is the increased opportunity costs of having children, which would mostly affect higher educated women, and the second one is that the transition period has been characterized by more economic hardship which would mostly affect the less educated people.

Kantorová then analyzes the Czech Family and Fertility Survey (CFFS) for 1997, which has complete retrospective fertility and educational histories for 1735 women. She uses a method where transition to first birth is estimated by women's age and by time passed since education completion. Her main conclusions are, that there is little support for the hardship hypothesis. Those who changed their fertility patterns the most were the higher educated women. These women postponed their first births not only until finishing education, but also until several years later, allowing for a period of post school investments. The less educated women postponed their first births the least in comparison to similarly educated women in the state-socialist period. Fertility dynamics in the Czech Republic therefore is becoming more like that of western countries.

The purpose of *Chapter 11 by Siv Gustafsson and Seble Worku* is to separate timing of maternity into two durations, first the timing of couple formation and second the timing of maternity given that the couple has been formed. Also in chapter 11 the educational variables in duration analyses are in the focus, but here education of each partner in 3 groups high, medium and low educated are combined to form 9 different groups. Another purpose is to compare timing of maternity between Britain and Sweden using these two separate durations. Is it the case that longer education delays the age at which a couple moves in together or does the couple live together for a longer period if high educated before they have a child?

Their results obtained by estimating Weibull hazard models show significant educational differences for both durations and for both spouses but the duration from the woman's age 13 until couple formation varies much more with education than does the duration until first birth once the couple is formed. These results are obtained holding constant some characteristics of family of origin, marriage market conditions and labor market conditions, in addition to time varying variables such as being in school, having finished school and the logarithm of current age. This result suggests that postponement of maternity by extended youth education works more by delaying couple formation than by delaying parenthood once the couple is formed. In previous work Gustafsson and coauthors have analyzed institutional differences between Sweden and Britain as regards their economic consequences for childbearing and the combination of family and work. (See Chapter 11 for references). There is no doubt that the Swedish policies of paid parental leaves and subsidized childcare which have been effective since the early 1970s are more pronatalist than the corresponding British setting. In this respect comparing Sweden and Britain is a similar comparison as the comparisons over time in the two transition economies of chapters 9 and 10.

The results show that for given educational levels of each spouse and other fixed and time-varying variables held constant in the Weibull duration analyses age at couple formation is equal in the two countries but once the couple is formed Swedish couples have their first child sooner. Swedish young people are older than British people when they achieve a given level of education but they shorten the time after finishing education until couple formation to be about the same age as the British people at this life event and then they shorten the time until having the first birth so that Swedish first parents are younger than British parents. This pattern is most pronounced if both husband and wife are high educated.

In *Chapter 12 Ghazala Naz, Øivind Anti Nilsen and Steinar Vagstad* study completed fertility in Norway. Also in chapter 12 like in chapter 11 education of both husband and wife are in the focus but the dependent variable is total number of children born to a couple rather than timing of maternity. They use the cohort of Norwegian women born in 1955, which is observed until 1995, i.e. when the woman is 40 years old. Because there is monthly information available about marital status, it is possible to create a sample of women who have been married only once and remain married to the same man throughout the observation period (stable married) Furthermore, an additional sub-sample includes women who have never been married until the age of 40.

The focus of this paper is on the effect of education of husband and wife on completed family size. There are about 20,000 stable married women from the 1955 cohort in the Norwegian Database of Generations (approximately 58 percent of the female cohort). The construction of the database restrict the authors to only study stable married women with husbands born 1950, 1955, 1960 or 1965. Among these women 57 percent have husbands who are born in the same year as themselves. The stable married sample, for whom the husband is in the sample, is representative of stable married women whose husband is not in the sample. For instance, the distribution for women over number of children, years of education as well as the means of age at first birth and mean income are indeed very similar to the stable married whether the husband is in the sample or not. Naz, Nilsen and Vagstad use one variant of a count data method (Restricted Generalized Poisson Model). The main result is the following: In analysis where the wife's education is included as an explanatory variable but husband's education is not, they find that higher educated women have more children than less educated women. Many studies seem to have shown the contrary, that higher educated women have fewer children than less educated women. These latter studies have often included all women independent of their marital status. If higher educated women are more likely to remain single, the finding that married women of higher education have more rather than fewer children may not be in contrast to these earlier results. As such it is also interesting to see that when the authors study the sub-sample of unmarried women, they find that education is negatively related to fertility. The authors argue that the significant difference in the importance of education for the completed fertility between married and unmarried women may be caused by the effect of education on childlessness.

For the stable married sample an interesting result appears when entering husband's education in addition to wife's education. Wife's education ceases to be a significant explanatory variable instead husband's education explains the number of children. Another way of explaining this result is to say that comparing two women with the same education, the one whose husband has higher education will have more children. This looks like an income effect because higher educated men earn more and therefore have the financial capacity to have more children.

Cohabitants, who in the study by Naz, Nilsen and Vagstad are recorded as single, are likely to behave like married ones. Together with increasing divorce rates, the percentage always married to the same husband (stable married) is shrinking over time. So the measured effects of education on fertility may not be valid for younger cohorts. This is also recognized by the authors who conclude their study by saying "To get a better understanding of the overall effect of increased education on the total fertility one needs to analyze family formation and fertility decisions jointly."

4. CONCLUSIONS

European women have never been so old before in history at having their first child. Education postpones maternity in the sense that the longer the education of a woman, the older she is when she becomes a mother. But is this relation the same in different countries? Is it the lack of income during student life that delays motherhood or is it competing time use? Or are future income prospects determining? Was it worth waiting to have a child until later in terms of career outcomes? Is finding a husband being delayed during student life or do higher educated couples wait longer to become parents? Do highly educated couples have fewer children than less educated couples? The chapters of this book contribute to an answer to these and related questions.

There is a vivid methodological debate on how one can identify causal effects in the area of fertility, since choices about education, marriage, labor force participation and motherhood are typically interrelated and perhaps simultaneously determined. Chapter 2 reviews and evaluates this debate and shows how the different chapters of this volume have dealt with methodological issues.

There are two approaches in the econometric literature on fertility, which both claim to model the full fertility history. The system of hazards approach initiated by Heckman and Walker (1990) on the one hand and the structural discrete time method by backward recursion suggested by Wolpin (1984). Each of these methods requires programming and extensive computations by the researcher and can not be estimated using available software. Only a handful of followers exist for either method. One review of econometrics of fertility Hotz, Klerman and Willis (1997) concludes that empirical work is much less developed than either the economic theoretical modeling or the econometric techniques. None of the chapters of this volume attempts to model the whole fertility history of a woman rather the focus is on different aspects of timing of maternity. The starting point is rather a specific empirical issue. Starting with a specific research question it rather seems as if both theory and econometrics is rather underdeveloped. Our view is that there is an interaction between the three branches of analysis: developing economic theory, developing econometric techniques and software and asking the relevant and interesting questions.

Some of the main results from the country studies of chapters 3 to 12 are summarized in Table 1.6. In Table 1.6 particularly results on the effects of education on timing of maternity are emphasized. The outline of Table 1.6 is to present results according to which country has been studied organizing the countries in alphabetical order. Table 6.1 starts with reporting some results on Britain in comparison to Sweden. It is well known that Sweden has had potentially pronatalist family policies since the early 1970s and such policies are also today compared to the British situation more favourable to becoming a parent. Yet, Swedish women of a given education are not younger mothers than British women. In chapter 11 it is shown that Swedish women are older at finishing education, older at entering a marriage or cohabitation, but once the couple is formed they are quicker to have their first child. Perhaps we have identified the pronatalist effect which in cross tabulations is not visible. Since Swedish people are older at finishing a given degree of education than British people who have the same education, the family formation process is delayed. The fact that a given educational degree takes longer in Sweden can be an effect of inefficiency in the Swedish educational system. But British couples live longer as a couple before they have their first child. The predicted age at couple formation in Sweden across all educational groups is 13 + 11.5 = 24.5 years and in Britain it is 13 + 9.5 = 22.5 years. The predicted value of women's age at having first birth only differs by 0.8 years and it is later in Britain than in Sweden. Once the couple is formed first birth comes earlier in Sweden. This result may imply that the pronatalist policies have intended effects making it more affordable for Swedish couples to start a family.

Timing of maternity in transition economies is analysed in chapters 9 and 10. Both for East Germany after unification and for the Czech Republic after the fall of the Soviet Union postponement of maternity has increased. One of the major effects is that educational differences in timing of maternity has increased in both countries during transition to market economies. This suggests that career planning has become more important in comparison to the state socialist period when child care and maternity leaves were more abundant and individual choices were less important to earnings. In the Czech Republic the relative risk ratio obtained by estimating event-history models shows that, women with university education before 1990, where even a little earlier in staring a family the relative risk ratio was in 1.12 in comparison to women with upper secondary certificate, which is similar to US high school graduation. After 1990 in the transition to a market economy the relative risk ratio for university women have decreased to 0.63 meaning that university trained women waited considerably longer than high school graduates before they had their first child (see Table 1.6).

A similar story is told about East Germany. The relative risk ratio of university educated East German women in the time of the German Democratic Republic (GDR) was 1.51 meaning that having a high education made women start a family earlier than low educated women (see Table 1.6). This situation has been reversed after unification of Germany. East German university educated women after 1990 have a relative risk ratio of 0.41 very close to the West German risk ratio of high educated versus low educated women which is 0.44. Both in East and West Germany high education postpones maternity.

Table 1.6 Effects of Education on Timing of Maternity

Country	Source	Definition of Result	Econometric Result			Main Conclusion
Britain in comparison to Sweden	Table 11.7	Predicted mean duration since woman's age 13 couples with education high (HH), medium ((MM), low (LL)		Couple formation	First birth	British couples live together childless longer. Swedish people are older when they start as a couple but have first birth sooner once the couple is formed. Both life events occur later for higher educated
			HH	12.9	16.1	
			MM	10.5	14.1	
			LL	9.7	11.6	
			Sweden	11.5	12.0	
			Britain	9.5	12.8	
Czech Republic	Table 10.3	Relative risk ratio of university education on woman's age at first birth		Coeff.	(Std.)	Increased postponement of high education women after 1990.
			1970-89	1.12	(0.20)	
			1990-97	0.63	(0.27)	
Germany	Table 9.3	Relative risk ratio of university education on woman's age at first birth		Coeff.	(z)	After 1990 university degree postpones birth as much in East as in West Germany while before in East high education women had births earlier.
			West bfr.1990	0.53	(-3.4)	
			East bfr. 1990	1.51	(0.91)	
			West aft. 1990	0.44	(-4.2)	
			East aft. 1990	0.41	(-.1.9)	
Ireland	Table 4.5 and 4.6	Mean age at motherhood	1970	28.6		Irish mothers were old relative to other countries in 1970 but have delayed first birth primarily because married couples wait longer until having a child and women's career prospects have improved.
			1980	30.0		
			1990	32.1		
		Percent of change 1970-1994 explained by				
		couple waiting longer	28.7%			
		wife's job career	41 %			
		other	30.3%			
			100%			

Table 1.6: continued

Country	Source	Definition of Result	Econometric Result			Main Conclusion
Italy	Table 5.5	Predicted probabilities from multinominal logits of labor force participation (lfp) at age 35-39 and of having a child (fert.) during age 21-39.	Education	lfp 35-39	fert. 21-39	Total fertility increases when education increases to upper secondary education but not for university. Labor force participation increases also for university.
			S = 5	34%	10.4%	
			S = 8	53%	25.5%	
			S = 13	75%	28.4%	
			S = 17	99%	13.3%	
Netherlands	Table 8.5	Income change and consumption change when children arrive in household in comparison to before they had a child. Effect on the logarithm.	Child No.	Income:	Consumption	Income decrease completely explained by less employment income by the mother. Households with children consume less and there is not enough saving before having children to smooth consumption
			1st	-0.30 (0.05)	-0.26 (0.10)	
			2nd	-0.37 (0.08)	-0.39 (0.45)	
			3rd	-0.49 (0.13)	-0.75 (0.23)	
Norway	Table 12.4	Marginal effect of education on completed fertility at women's age 40. Restricted, generalized poisson Regression.		Coeff. (t-value)	Coeff. (t-value)	When husband's education is included wife's education ceases to have an effect. Income effect dominates over substitution effect.
			Wife's edu	0.027 (3.0)	0.08 (0.9)	
			Husband's edu	not incl.	0.033 (4.3)	

Spain	Table 6.8	Probability of having a first birth all childless women. Hazard estimation		Coeff.	(z)	Women postpone first birth - if they have secondary or university education, - and if they have no work, or-a fixed term rather than an indefinite contract.
			Univ	-0.36	(2.78)	
			Second	-0.45	(3.11)	
			Fixed term	-0.36	(2.38)	
			No work	-0.62	(4.66)	
			Age	-0.09	(0.87)	
Sweden	Table 3.2	Marginal effect of birth month given birth year on mother's age at first birth OLS		coeff.	(std. d.)	Birth timing is sensitive to age in months at leaving compulsary school e.g. timing of first birth between women born December 1954 and January 1955 differs 5.59 months
			Jan=base			
			Dec	-3.09	(0.35)	
			'46=base			
			1954	14.36	(0.39)	
			1955	16.86	(0.39)	
			until 1962			
United States	Table 7.7	Wage effect of having high education and having kids late in comparison to women without children (model 5)		Coeff.	(t.value)	By having children later after age 30 the family wage gap is closed and there is no wage penalty for being a mother among college educated.
			mothers	-0.09	(14.7)	
			late moms	-0.08	(7.5)	
			childless college	-0.00	(0.0)	
			late moms college	0.01	(4.10)	

Competing time use to raising children as workers in the labor market are emphasized in chapter 4 on Ireland and in chapter 5 on Italy. The Irish study shows that the propensity of first births in 1994 in comparison to 1970 decreased mainly because female wages had increased and the proportion time women spent in the labor market had increased but also because couples waited longer after marriage. Chapter 5 finds that Italian women with higher education tend to combine work and family to a larger extent than less educated women and they also postpone motherhood more.

Some crucial results are shown in Table 1.6 In Ireland the mean age at motherhood for the sample used increased from 1970 at 28.6 to 1990 at 32.1. This is old mothers already in 1970 in comparison to other countries. This sample the 1994 Survey of Living Conditions in Ireland, reproduced in Table 1.6, shows higher age at maternity than Table 1.1 above for Ireland but also Table 1.1 confirms that Irish first time mothers have been older than in most countries all the time since 1970. Most of the increase in mother's age at first birth is due to better labor market prospects for women, 41% is ascribed to this factor and to couples waiting longer and living as childless couples than was before the case. This factor explains 28.7 per cent of the increased age at motherhood (see Table 1.6).

The predicted probabilities from multinomial logits of chapter 5 show that labor force participation increases with length of education of the wife monotonically, that is the longer her education the higher the probability that she is a labor force participant. For women with university education this probability is 99% in the age group 35-39 years. Summarizing, fertility across age groups to include all the studied age groups from age 21-39 shows that fertility does not increase monotonically. Instead the highest fertility is among women who have 13 years of education called 'upper secondary education' and university educated women have less fertility. The predicted fertility rates are quite low. The highest being 28.4% for upper secondary educated women for the entire age group of 21-39 years (see Table 1.6). These results are similar to how a total fertility rate is computed.

In chapter 8 the focus is on savings behaviour around births in the Netherlands. The main findings are that couples do save more before having a child than after, which is in line with a consumption smoothing hypothesis but they do not reduce savings enough to offset the reduction in income due to women leaving employment. Couples with children consume less, not more than when they were childless. One way of interpreting this result is that people are not behaving in an ideal rational way, saving before starting a family and then dissaving to deal with the costs of having children. The income decrease is substantial, in Table 1.6 the coefficients of income change from having children, is shown in comparison to income of the couple before having a child. This analysis is based on panel data, so that we are really comparing a given couple's situation before having a child and after. Some couples in the data have their first child during the panel period 1987-1993, others have their second or third child. The decrease in income and consumption by the arrival of first, second and third children are shown in Table 1.6. If there had been a pattern of saving and dissaving to smooth consumption over the young children period one would have observed less decrease in consumption than the income decrease. This is not what we observe.

The Norwegian completed family size is analysed in chapter 12. This chapter shows that higher educated married couples in Norway have more children than less educated couples and that this effect is primarily driven by husband's education rather than by wife's education. This is not a contradiction to other findings, that higher educated women have fewer children, than less educated women. The difference instead comes from lower probability to form a couple among highly educated women. The sample is restricted to married women. The numbers shown in Table 1.6 observe the positive and significant coefficient on number of children at age 40 from wife's education when husband's education is not included and contrasts it to the insignificant results when husband's education is included. In many studies wife's wage or wife's labor force participation has been shown to have a negative effect on number of children. This would be the case if the substitution effect of the opportunity cost of time dominates. A positive effect on the other hand would mean that the income effect dominates, so that higher income women have more children and make use of market childcare. This result for Norway indicates that the income effect dominates. Men's income or men's education are most often shown to have a positive effect on number of children and this has been interpreted as a pure income effect assuming fathers experience less of an opportunity cost of time. However, since the effect of wife's education after controlling for husband's education is essentially zero, one can draw the conclusion that substitution or opportunity cost of time effects are unimportant in Norway, whereas income effects are important.

Uncertainty about future income is emphasized in chapter 6 on Spain. Fixed-term contracts rather than permanent contracts have grown on the Spanish labor market particularly for young people. The results show that having a fixed-term, rather than an indefinite labor contract, delays entry into marriage for men, but not for women, whereas a fixed-term contract held by a woman makes her delay motherhood.

The Spanish analysis is based on a short panel, the Spanish data of the European Household Panel 1994-2001. The hazard estimates reported in Table 1.6 show that in comparison to low educated women, university and secondary educated women have a much smaller probability to become mothers and any Spanish woman who is either out of work or has a fixed term job contract is also much les likely to become a mother than if she has an indefinite job contract. Having a job contract that one knows is only for a limited period is very different than having a job contract that is indefinite that is a contract that will continue until either the worker or the employer wishes to terminate the contract. The coefficients of the hazard analysis are reproduced in Table 1.6.

Chapter 3 shows, that there is a special compulsory school cohort effect, at least in Sweden. Those who are born in January, because they are older at finishing school than those born in December, are also 4.9 months older when they have their first child. This effect remains although the latter event takes place 8 to 10 years later than completion of compulsory school. The conclusion is that age at finishing school rather than calendar age is important for timing of maternity.

In Table 1.6 the regression results underlying this conclusion are shown. The study is based on Swedish register data including 863304 women born 1946-62. In comparison to being born in January a person born in December is 11 months older at finishing compulsory school. This is because compulsory school starts in August during that calendar year, when the child is seven years old and ends with graduation in June of that calendar year during which the person will be 16. This is a natural experiment, which helps in sorting out the cause and effect problem because the fact of being 11 months older when you are a December born person is truly exogenous variation in age at finishing compulsory education. The significant results taken from Table 3.2 and reported in Table 1.6 show that timing of maternity is sensitive to age in months at leaving compulsory school. Timing of first birth between women born in December 1954 and women born in January 1955 is 5.86 months although they only differ by one calendar month in age when they finish compulsory school. This effect is significant although age at maternity occurs some 9-10 years later than age at finishing compulsory school.

Was it worthwhile career-wise to postpone maternity? This is the question asked in chapter 7 for college educated US women. The results show that women who delayed motherhood in comparison to equally educated mothers who had children earlier in life earn substantially higher wages, so it was worth waiting.

The data analysed are the national longitudinal data for young women (NLSYW). The results reproduced in Table 1.6 show that mothers in general have smaller wage than childless women in general by about 9 per cent the logarithm of the wage being –0.09. This is in line with many earlier findings about the family wage gap. Childless women who are college educated are exactly on the mean of the wage included in the study i.e. the coefficient is 0.0. However, and this is the interesting result if you are a college educated late mother defined as being 30 years or older at maternity, there is no family wage gap any more.

In summary, institutions matter because although education postpones maternity in all the countries studied, the size of the effect differs between the countries. In order for there to be an effect from education on postponement of maternity there has to be a labor market that demands skilled female labor and skills have to make a difference for the sort of career a woman can expect. Both past incomes and savings, labor market career in the past, current and expected future situation matter for both the woman and for the man, for their decisions on when to form a couple and have a child. In chapter 2 of this book, the ambitious econometric work on modeling many of these decisions jointly is presented and discussed. Most of the chapters of this book focus on one particular transition of that of having the first child and the contributions are in that respect partial. This volume gives answers to many questions around timing of maternity covering 10 different countries. As with all good research the contributions open up a new field of questions.

NOTES

[1]Tables one and two have been put together by Eiko Kenjoh, see also Kenjoh (2004).
[2]Table 1.3-1.5 has been put together by Seble Worku.
[3]There may be an efficiency gain to the Dutch system in comparison to the Swedish system. The Dutch young man is only half a year younger than the Swedish young man when he is ready for the labor market. But may be he learnt more than the Swedish young man because he spent 2.4 years longer in school.

REFERENCES

Ahn, Namkee and Mira, Pedro. "Job Bust, Baby Bust?: Evidence from Spain". *Journal of Population Economics* (vol. 14, 2001): 505-521.

Becker, G.S., 1973, A theory of marriage: Part I, *The Journal of Political Economy*, Vol. 81, No. 4, pp. 813-846.

Beets, G.C.N. "Kinderen worden later geboren: een demografische analyse." In: Beets, G.C.N., Bouwens, A. & Schippers, J.J. (eds.), *Uitgesteld ouderschap*, Amsterdam: Thesis publisher (1997): 13-31.

Beets, G.C.N. Onderwijs en de geboorte van het eerste kind in Europa, FFS gegevens, *Bevolking en Gezin*, 27(2) (1998): 99-121.

Billari, Francesco C., Philipov, Dimiter and Baizán, Pau. "Leaving Home in Europe: The Experience of Cohorts Born Around 1960". *International Journal of Population Geography* (vol. 7, 2001): 339-356.

Bloemen H. and Kalwij A. 2001, Female Labor Market Transitions and the Timing of Births: A Simultaneous Analysis of the Effects of Schooling, *Labour Economics* (8) 5, pp. 593-620.

Blossfeld H.P. and Timm A., (ed.), 2003, Who Marries Whom? Educational Systems as Marriage Markets in Modern Societies, Kluwer Academic Publishers.

Bongaarts, J. and G. Feeney. "On the Quantum and Tempo of Fertility". *Population and Development Review*, (24(2), 1998): 271-291.

Bongaarts, J. "Fertility in the Developed World: Where Will it End?" American Economic Review. Papers and Proceedings (May 1999): 256-260.

Bosveld, W. *The Ageing of Fertility in Europe: A Comparative Demographic-Analytic Study*. PDOD, Amsterdam: Thesis Publishers, 1996.

Cigno, A. *Economics of the Family*, Oxford: Clarendon Press, 1991.

Council of Europe, 2001, *Recent Demographic Developments in Europe*. (http://www.coe.int/t/e/social_cohesion/population/demographic_year_book/2001_Edition/default.asp#TopOfPage)

Francesconi M., 2002, A joint Dynamic Model of Fertility and Work of Married Women, Journal of labor Economics, Vol. 20, No. 2.

Gustafsson, S.S. "Optimal Age at Motherhood: Theoretical and Empirical Considerations on Postponement of Maternity in Europe." *Journal of Population Economics* 14 (2001): 225-247.

Gustafsson, S.S., Kenjoh, E. and Wetzels, C.M.M.P. "The Role of Education on Postponement of Maternity in Britain, Germany, The Netherlands and Sweden." In: Ruspini, Elisabetta & Dale, Angela (eds.), *The Gender Dimension of Social Change. The Contribution of Dynamic Research to the Study of Women's Life Courses*, The Policy Press, Bristol, UK (2002b): 55-79.

Gustafsson, Siv. S. and Wetzels, Cecile. Optimal Age at First Birth: Germany, Great Britain, the Netherlands and Sweden in Gustafsson Siv, S. and Meulders, Danièle E., (eds.) *Gender and the Labour Market, Econometric Evidence of Obstacles to Achieving Gender Equality*, London: MacMillan Press Ltd. (2000): 188-209.

Heckman, J.J. and J.R. Walker, 1990, The relationship between wages and income and the timing and spacing of births: evidence from Swedish longitudinal data, *Econometrica*, 58, 1411-1441.

Hewlett, Sylvia Ann, *Baby Hunger. The New Battle for Motherhood.* London: Atlantic Books, 2003.

Hoem, J.M. “The Impact of Education on Modern Family-union Initiation”. *European Journal of Population* (Vol. 2, 1986): 113-133.

Hotz, V.J., Klerman, J.A. and Willis, R.J. The Economics of Fertility in Developed Countries. In: Rozenzweig, M.R. & Stark, O. (eds.), *Handbook of Population and Family Economics*, volume 1A, Amsterdam: Elsevier, 1997.

Kalwij, Adriaan S. (1999), *Household consumption, female employment and fertility decisions: amicro-econometric analysis*, Ph.D. Dissertation, Tilburg University.

Kalwij, Adriaan S. Female Employment and Fertility Decisions: an Analysis of the Effects of Household Financial Wealth, *Applied Economics Quarterly*, Volume 49, Issue 3, (2003): 231-252.

Kenjoh, E., 2004, Balancing Work and Family Life in Japan and Four European Countries. Economic Analysis on Mother’s Employment and Timing of Maternity, No. 337, Thela Thesis.

Kohler, Hans-Peter, Billari, Francesco C. & Ortega, Jose-Antonio, *Towards a Theory of Lowest-Low Fertility*, Working Paper Max Planck Institute for Demographic Research, Rostock, Germany, 2002.

Lesthaege, R. and Willems, P. (1999), Is Low Fertility a Temporary Phenomenon in the European Union? *Population and Development Review*, 25: 211-228.

Liefbroer, A. and Corijn, M. “Who, What and When? Specifying the Impact of Educational Attainment and Labour force Participation on Family Formation.” *European Journal of Population* vol. 15 (1999): 45-75.

Philipov, Dimiter and Kohler, Hans-Peter . “Tempo Effects in the Fertility Decline in Eastern Europe: Evidence from Bulgaria, The Czech Republic, Hungary, Poland and Russia.” *European Journal of Population* vol. 17 (2001): 37-60.

Smith. R.J., Richard W. Blundell. “An Exogeneity Test in a Simultaneous Equation Model with an Application to Labor Supply.” *Econometrica*, 54 (3): 679-685.

Te Velde, E. and Pearson, P.L., 2002, The Variability of Female Reproductive Ageing, *Human Reproductive Update*, 8: 141-154.

UNESCO http://europa.eu.int/comm/education/struct/struct.html).

Van der Klaauw W., 1996, Female Labor Supply and Marital Status Decisions: A Life Cycle Model, *Review of Economic Studies*, 63:199-235.

Willis, R.J., 1973, A new approach to the economic theory of fertility behavior, Journal of political Economy, March/April, Part 2, S14-S64.

Wolpin K., 1984, An Estimable Dynamic Stochastic Model of Fertility and Child Mortality, Journal of Political Economy, 92:852-874.

Chapter 2

FERTILITY DECISIONS: ECONOMIC THEORY, EMPIRICAL ANALYSIS, AND POLICY RELEVANCE

SIV GUSTAFSSON AND ADRIAAN KALWIJ

1. INTRODUCTION

This chapter discusses methodological issues concerning empirical research on the determinants of household fertility decisions. We hope to facilitate exchange of research results between researchers, who have shaped their research methods in different environments.

Economic theory shows that past, current and expected future prices affect behaviour. The costs of a child include expenditures on larger housing, the schooling of the child and of course on goods such as clothes, food and toys and sports equipments. In addition to these child related expenditures, much emphasis in economic theory is placed on the opportunity costs of time spent with the child. For example a woman who is thinking of when to have her first child will be interested not only in the income, that she will not earn during a year of career break if she decides to have her child now but also the effects of a career break on future earnings. These considerations may as well interrelate with her education decision and saving plan. Indeed she will be interested in the full lifetime earnings consequences of her timing of maternity. Differences in opportunity costs results in differences in the timing of births. Economic theory offers less clear guidance on what the benefits are of having children and, in particular, how these benefits may differ across women or households. The benefits are considered the joy of having children, i.e. most households prefer having children to remaining childless. Once children are present, the well-being of parents is affected by their children's well-being and they will therefore invest in, for instance, the schooling of their children. Children as an insurance against financial difficulties at old age is a financial incentive for having children and investing in their education. However, in societies with well-developed old age provisions such as, for instance, public old age pensions, this is unlikely to be the dominant explanation for why a household has children.

Siv Gustafsson and Adriaan Kalwij (eds.), Education and Postponement of Maternity, 31–64.

These theoretical considerations of if or when to have children are most often the point of departure of empirical economic research on lifecycle fertility. When modelling patterns of lifecycle fertility and its determinants many assumptions have to be made to get to a statistical model that is feasible to estimate. The resulting models proposed in the literature are mainly of a reduced form, i.e. a model that approximates the costs and benefits of children and the way these affect the choice of when to have a child. For instance, using educational levels of the woman as a proxy for the opportunity costs of having children. A few empirical studies remain close to a tightly specified theoretical economic model, usually based on a constrained intertemporal utility maximization problem, and they model explicitly preferences and expectations. Such a model can be referred to as a structural model.

This chapter discusses also what one can expect from a statistical analysis with respect to economic interpretations and policy relevancy of the empirical results. This issue is related to causal inferences and the definition of an exogenous variable as against an endogenous variable. In principle only exogenous variables can explain behaviour while another endogenous variable should be treated as simultaneously determined. One solution to this problem proposed in the literature is to use predetermined variables. However, attempting to explain timing of maternity using only variables that were determined in the past may not be enough since expectations about the future play a role when making fertility decisions and may as well affect variables that are assumed to be predetermined.

Timing of maternity is an intrinsically dynamic decision. Since we are interested in the timing, a dynamic statistical model is to be preferred. The first economic theory models of fertility were static i.e. they attempted to explain complete life-cycle fertility and they considered only one period, thought of as consisting of the whole life-time period from age at marriage to the end of the fecund period or until retirement (Becker 1973, Willis 1973). Such models are linear regression models and for these models methods have been developed to control for endogeneity. However these methods cannot always be applied to nonlinear models For example instrumental variables techniques like two stage least squares are, generally speaking, available for linear models and not for non-linear models like hazard models.

Hazard models are by far the most common tools for analysing timing of events like timing of maternity. The dependent variable in such a hazard model is the duration until an event occurs. In this volume hazard models are used in chapter 6 de la Rica and Iza, chapter 9 Kreyenfeld, chapter 10 Kantorova and chapter 11 Gustafsson and Worku. If one studies the duration until first birth starting at the age of marriage the major reason for postponement of maternity may fall outside the analysis. The explanation for postponement of maternity is more likely to be the extension of youth education and women's desire to complete education and secure a job before entering into a long-term relationship with the intention to start a family. Most studies on timing of fertility therefore start the clock of the duration at age 15 of the woman. Not yet mentioned is that husbands characteristics such as education and earnings are known to be important determinants of household fertility (see, e.g., chapter 11 Gustafsson and Worku). The empirical difficulty with taking this into account in an empirical analysis is that husbands' characteristics are usually only observed for married women. Many studies therefore choose a select sample of only married women thereby introducing sample selection bias.

The outline of the chapter is as follows. Section 2 discusses and presents achieved economic theory of fertility to serve as the reference for the methodology discussions. Section 3 discusses econometric solutions to the endogeneity problem in fertility research. Section 4 discusses hazard models with extensions to cover simultaneity. Section 5 discusses a structural method namely recursive discrete choice dynamic models. Section 6 discusses institutional and policy approaches and section 7 concludes.

2. ECONOMIC THEORY OF FERTILITY

Recent reviews of the economics of fertility include Cigno (1991, ch. 7 and 8), Hotz, Klerman and Willis (1997) and Ermisch (2003, ch. 6). The origins of the economics of fertility are described by Hotz et al. (1997 p. 293) as consisting of two important contributions:

> "The first, the quality-quantity model of fertility, acknowledges that parents not only demand numbers of children but also children with certain qualities. The second contribution was to acknowledge the importance of parental time, especially mothers' time in the rearing development of children. Elements of these two model features are found in Becker (1960) and Mincer (1963) and are synthesized within the Becker (1965) household production framework by Willis (1973) with some further implications of the quality–quantity model developed in Becker and Lewis (1973)".

Much of this early literature is collected in Schultz T.W. ed. (1974) and Gary Becker's own contributions are synthesized in Becker (1981, 1st ed, 1991, 2nd ed). In the following we give our own interpretation of the status of received theory of fertility. Becker (1981) proposes that parents value both the number of children (n) and the quality of life of each child (q) in addition to their own consumption (C). This assumption produces a utility function of the form:

$$U = U(C, n, q) \tag{1}$$

By this assumption Becker is able to explain the puzzle, that children are likely to be normal goods with poor substitutes, and yet we have witnessed in Europe a hundred years of fertility decreases as income increases over time, rather than a positive correlation between income and fertility, which Malthus (1798) predicted. Becker (1960, 1981) suggests, that parents simply invest more money in each child, than have more children when their incomes increase. Following Cigno and Ermisch (1989); Cigno (1991) Ermisch (1990) we will simplify the model in order to concentrate on timing choices and write the utility function

$$U = U(C, B) \tag{2}$$

where B is a quality adjusted index of fertility and B is identically equal to n times q, which means that B is a continuous variable since it is made up by the number of children times the quality produced by investments in each child.

$$B \equiv nq \tag{3}$$

Quality in a child can be produced by parents investments of time and money in the child.

$$Q = v\,(I) \tag{4}$$

In order to study timing choices we will assume that consumption (C) and the quality adjusted fertility index (B) in (5) depend on the time period when they are realized. Therefore

$$B = \sum_t v_t\,(I_t) B_t \tag{5}$$

and

$$C = \sum_t u_t (C_t) \tag{6}$$

In Cigno (1991) v_t and u_t are summarized over a couple's married life. However, empirical research (see below) sets t = 0 at the time, when the woman is aged 15 and looks at her timing decision. We argue that a woman and a man have individual optimal timing of family formation, and that the timing of couple formation, is a step in this process, which may be a compromise between the woman's and the man's optimal couple formation age as Bergstrom and Lam (1989) suggest.

The utility function (2) with (5) and (6) substituted into (2) so that birth timing and consumption timing are chosen so as to maximize utility subject to the lifetime budget constraint (7):

$$\sum_{t=0}^{T} (C_t + I_t B_t) r^{-t} \leq A + \sum_{t=0}^{T} L_t w_t r^{-t} \tag{7}$$

where the present value of consumption and investments in children must not exceed the present value of life-time income, which consists of unearned income A, including present value of lifetime earnings of the spouse, and earned income $L_t w_t$, where L_t is labor force participation in period t and w_t is the wage in period t, the discount factor is r with (r-1) being the interest rate. The woman as well as the man each has a life-time budget constraint so that (7) above will be represented with a super index j = m, f and A^j includes the present value of the earnings of the spouse, that each individual takes as exogenous to his or her labor supply decision.

The general quality adjusted index of fertility B is also subject to physiological restrictions that allow only a maximum of:

$$B_t = n_t . \mathrm{v}_t(I_t) \tag{8}$$

to be chosen in any period, so that the realized fertility in period t is between zero and the biological maximum

$$0 \leq B_t \leq \overline{B}_t \tag{9}$$

Of course in (8) and (9) the biological maximum is dictated by the number of children n_t which can only increase by one child every year if t equals a year unless twins or multiples occur and cannot increase more when the woman reaches the age of infecundity. Investments per child I_t does not have a maximum. This formulation also acknowledges that investments in children can take place in every period t. If (9) is not binding in any period the chosen sequence of B_t, C_t, I_t will satisfy the conditions (Cigno 1991, p. 120):

$$\frac{U_t'(C_t)}{U_{t+1}'(C_{t+1})} = r \tag{10}$$

$$\frac{\mathrm{v}_t'(I_t)}{\mathrm{v}_{t+1}'(I_{t+1})} = r \tag{11}$$

$$\frac{[P_{t+1}/\mathrm{v}_{t+1}(I_{t+1})]}{[P_t/\mathrm{v}_t(I_t)]} = r \tag{12}$$

The first two conditions (10) and (11) show, that any form of expenditure must be distributed over time so that its marginal utility will decline at the rate of interest. If the marginal utility of consuming in period t, (u_t') is smaller by more than the discount rate of consuming in period t+1, (u_{t+1}'), consumption is delayed. Similarly the marginal utility of investing in a child $\mathrm{v}_t'(I_t)$ in a given period t must be larger by the discount rate than delaying such investment to the next period.
However, the interesting condition is (12) where P_t is the cost of having a child in period t. This cost (P_t) can be written:

$$P_t = I_t + w_t + \beta\omega \sum_{\tau=t+1}^{T} L_\tau r^{t-\tau} \tag{13}$$

where I_t are outlays for the child in period t, w_t is the wage foregone by making a labor force interruption to care for a child in period t and the last term is the human capital cost. This cost depends on the rate of return to human capital ω, the investment profile β, and the labor supply (L_t) of the parent after the child has been born discounted by the interest rate (1-r), where $0 \le L_t \le 1$ with $L_t = 0$ for those who are not supplying any hours of work and $L_t = 1$ for full-time workers. The human capital cost is investment in human capital foregone due to less investment in human capital after the child has been born multiplied by the return to such investment (ω). In principle L_t before a child is born might differ from L_t after the child is born. In most cases labor supply is smaller among mothers than among women, who are not parents, but there may also be differences in L_t between fathers and men, who are not parents.

The product $\omega\beta$ increases the cost P_t for every potential year of labor force participation (L_t). Usually one cannot empirically distinguish between ω and β. If one could differences in ω between parents and non-parents would be a measure of discrimination between the groups, since it would be differences in return to a given amount of human capital. Differences in β between parents and non-parents would be a measure of differences in the on the job investment profile rather than in the return to human capital.

Expression (13) is very useful. It shows that the costs of having a child P_t differ depending in which time period (t) the child is born. In order to finance the I_t or money expenditure on children, incomes of the spouse will do equally well as own income. To cover their costs couples would think about the consumption smoothing motive for covering the costs of the child. The second term of expression (13) is the current opportunity cost of time and the third term is the expected future opportunity costs of time. These two terms together make up the career planning motive in the decision for birth timing. Gustafsson 2001 expands on this idea.

Empirical estimates are in De Cooman, Ermisch and Joshi (1987), Ermisch (1988), Wetzels (1999), Gustafsson and Wetzels (2000). In a number of Studies Heather Joshi and coauthors estimate the effects of motherhood on life-time earnings e.g. Joshi (1990), Joshi, Paci and Waldfogel (1990) and Joshi and Davies (2002). The net wage at the time t is:

$$w_t = \omega k_t \tag{14}$$

where k_t is the stock of market specific human capital at time t and ω is the market rate of return (net of taxes) to that capital. Assuming that human capital (k_t) increases linearly from an initial stock k_0 over the τ time periods considered:

$$k_t = k_0 + \beta \sum_{t=0}^{t-1} L_t \tag{15}$$

In periods, when $L_t = 0$ there is no growth in what Jacob Mincer (1974) called post-schooling investments. If we want to consider the length of education, k_0 must also be split into a period of schooling investments (s) when $\beta = 1$ and all available time is spent investing in human capital, and a post-school time after finishing education (ts), and (15) will be rewritten:

$$k_t = k_0 + s + \beta \sum_{t=ts}^{t-1} L_t \tag{16}$$

It is realistic to assume that (16) is an individual life-time plan, so that the male (m) and the female (f) that form a couple and have a child differ in (16) and we may rewrite (16) with an upper index i = m, f

$$k_t^i = k_0^i + s^i + \beta^i \sum_{t=ts}^{t-1} L_t^i \tag{17}$$

Next to the literature on birth timing there is also a literature on marriage markets and the timing of marriage (Becker 1981; Grossbard-Shechtman 1984; Grossbard-Shechtman (ed.) (2003); Lam 1988; Bergstrom and Lam 1989; Bergstrom 1997; Ono (2002). Bergstrom (1997) building on earlier work by Bergstrom and Lam (1989) suggests the following model for the determination of age at marriage (a). People are supposed to have a preferred age at couple formation (a*), which in addition to consumption C gives them utility:

$$U = C - (a - a^*)^2 \tag{18}$$

where a is actual age at marriage. Suppose all males prefer a_m^* and all females prefer a_f^*. Bergstrom (1997) and Bergstrom and Lam (1989) assume that a_m^* and a_f^* are exogenously given. Bergstrom and Lam (1989) estimate their model on Swedish birth cohorts of men born from 1895 to 1942 and women born from 1898 to 1945. They assume, that the difference $a_m^* - a_f^*$ is 3 years, so that a man always wishes to be 3 years older than his wife. The actual marriage age of a male will depend on the sex ratio. Because of period fluctuations in the total fertility rates the sex ratio M_t/F_{t-3} fluctuated in Bergstrom and Lam (1989) between 0.9 and 1.25. Other marriage market studies use regional variations in sex ratios. A recent example is Ono (2002). Angrist (2002) uses variations in sex ratios by ethnicity among immigrants to the United States in the 20th century using data from three censuses. Given the fact that 50% or more married within their own ethnic group the large male dominance among immigrants produced large sex ratios among some ethnic groups.

The assumption of exogenously determined preferred age at marriage can be relaxed and instead one can argue that preferred age at marriage may not be determined by men desiring to be three years older than their wives, but by men finishing education and other training three years later than women, so that desired marriage age is a function of the human capital investment plan:

$$a_m^* = a_m^*(s^m,\ k_0^m,\ \beta^m,\ L_t^m) \quad a_f^* = a_f^*(s^f,\ k_0^f,\ \beta^f,\ L_t^f) \tag{23}$$

where in addition to youth fulltime education (s) planned labor force participation (L_t) for each year t=0...T matters, as well as the planned occupational choices, because these determine the on the job investment profile (β) and the return to human capital investment (ω).

3. METHODS TO CONTROL FOR ENDOGENITY IN FERTILITY RESEARCH

Explaining fertility is not an easy task as is clear from the outline of received theory in section 2 above. The basic static model, i.e. the model of one period comprising the whole life cycle from usually age at marriage to retirement, proposed by Gary Becker (1973) and Bob Willis (1973) explain lifetime fertility as an effect of prices and income. The prices of children include the opportunity cost of the mothers time and her market wage is a proxy for that. However, her market wage depends on her previous investments in human capital so that the number of years that she worked in the labor market determines her current market wage as is clear from the expressions (14) to (17) above. But she may have worked fewer years in the labor market if she has children so that fertility determines her market wage rather than her market wage being one of the prices that enter into the shadow price of children. Explaining fertility by wages and income means then that the estimates of the effect of the woman's wage will be subject to endogeneity bias. Explaining labor supply by the number of children is for the same reason subject to endogeneity or simultaneity bias particularly in a one period static model supposed to comprise the woman's total adult life, where labor force participation of women in general is seen as being determined by the number of children they have. (see Browning, (1992) for a discussion of this endogeneity problem.

One solution proposed to this simultaneity bias is if one has instead of a static one period model a sequential model where the timing of the events matter. One can argue that labor supply of a woman in period t is determined by the number of children she has until t-1, or that education a woman has already completed until time t-1 will determine her behaviour in period t.

Some demographers are very careful in the time sequence of different events (see e.g. Blossfeld & Timm, 2003, p. 13):

> "The causal interpretation of the transition rate requires that we take the temporal order in which the marriage process evolves very seriously. In other words, at any given age, t, the transition rate r (t) can be made dependent on conditions that happened in the past (i.e. before t), but not on what is the case at t or in the future after t."

But economic theory as explained in section 2 above also assumes that expectations about the future play a role. A woman, who decides on the optimal time of couple formation and maternity will also consider future prices, such as her expected wage two years from t, when she has finished education and got a permanent job, and the effect on this wage by having a child at t rather than at t + 2. Hotz, Klerman and Willis, 1997, p. 335:

> "Even in a perfect certainty framework, current period choices are a function of all past, current and expected future prices."

The task is very complicated and it is not surprising that Hotz, Klerman and Willlis , p. 342, conclude:

> "As is true in much of applied economics, the theory and econometric methods are much better developed than the empirical literature. The crucial challenge is to find plausibly exogenous variation in proxies for the price and income concepts appearing in the theories."

Hotz et al. (1997) distinguish between three approaches to control for the potential endogeneity of the variation in prices and income: 1) social experiments, 2) fixed effects, and 3) instrumental variables. In the following we will discuss each of these methods.

3.1 Social experiments

A social experiment would guarantee that an individual will be randomly confronted with the different prices that are caused by the social experiment so that the price variation is exogenous to the individual. In discussing the different methods Hotz et al. (1997) give what they call best practice examples. The best practice example given for the use of a social experiment is an analysis of an experiment in the United States, where poor young women dependent on social assistance who have had a first child were assigned randomly to either an enhanced services program or to the regular program for Aid for Families with Dependent Children (AFDC). The enhanced program included advice to the young women as to their further labor market training and parental training as well as increased awareness of contraceptive methods. The study (Maynard and Rangarajan 1994, cited by Hotz et al. 1997) analyzed the probability of use of any contraceptive and if the woman became pregnant again. The logistic regression models controlled for the heterogeneity of the women by age, race-ethnicity, family background, living situation, family size, reading level, educational status, contraceptive use at baselines. The observation period is only two years after the experiment was conducted. The results are disappointing. There is no reduction in subsequent fertility among those who got extra help in comparison to those who got the regular help. The women in the experimental group got advice and information at a lower cost than women in the control group. This is the exogenous variation in the price of avoiding a subsequent birth.

In reality it is quite difficult to find cases of social experiments but it is not uncommon to see research papers refer to natural experiments. For example Plug and Vijverberg (2003) refers to a natural experiment in analysing schooling and earnings outcomes between adopted children and natural siblings in order to distinguish between nature and nurture effects. Also a school reform making compulsory schooling in Britain one year longer has been referred to as a natural experiment (Harmon and Walker, 1995). In this volume, chapter 3 uses birth months of Swedish women as a natural social experiment.

3.2 Fixed effects

The idea of the fixed effect methods is that policy changes create group fixed effects. If the unobserved taste variation for a group of people is approximately constant through time for a given geographical area, then fixed effects for that region will control for omitted variables, and fixed effects regressions on grouped data would consistently estimate the exogenous effects of interest. The approach is also called differences in differences because it first was used on comparing means.

An example of a fixed effects regression given by Hotz et al. is

$$n_{st} = \alpha\pi_{st} + X_{st}\beta + \gamma_s + \gamma_t + \varepsilon_{st} \tag{24}$$

where the fertility rate (n) in one of the 51 states (s) of the United States in time period (t) is regressed on the price of interest (π), other covariates that vary both by year and by state (X_{st}), fixed effects for the state (γ_s) and years (γ_t), where ε_{st} is an idiosyncratic standard error[1].

A best practice example mentioned by Hotz et al. is a study by Blank et al. (1994) on state abortion rates in the United States from 1974 to 1988. They estimate linear regression models for the log of the abortion rate i.e. abortions per woman aged 15-44. This model includes policy variables (like Medicaid funding, parental involvement, AFDC payment levels) political climate variables, the number of abortion clinics provided in the state, demographic variables and economic conditions. The estimated effects are sensitive to the inclusion of double fixed effects for state and year. Without fixed effects enforced parental involvement laws significantly lower abortions but the effect of whether abortions were paid or not by public funds (Medicaid) is insignificant. Adding fixed effects for state and year causes parental involvement to turn positive – the wrong sign – and insignificant, while the Medicaid funding triples in magnitude and becomes significant. Hotz et al. (1997) conclude that the double fixed effects strategy alone is not sufficient to eliminate all of the endogeneity of state policy. This means that the number of abortions may explain policies rather than policies explaining the number of abortions.

This example shows that using a simple technique and using a method to control for endogeneity produced very different results. Unfortunately it is common in empirical research that results are different depending on the specification of the model. In this case both the simple method and the more sophisticated method produced unexpected and difficult to explain results.

3.3 Instrumental variables

Perhaps the most widely used method to control for endogeneity is the instrumental variables approach. It would be easy to believe that we had controlled correctly for endogeneity if the sophisticated method produced more plausible results than the simple method. Boulier and Rosenzweig (1984) find an improvement of the estimated results by using the more sophisticated method (3SLS) compared to OLS:

> "While none of the statistically significant OLS mating function coefficients shift importantly when the 3SLS (three stage least squares) estimation technique is applied, use of ordinary least squares appears to understate significantly, as predicted, the effect of marital search by women in attracting a "better" mate – indeed, while the 3SLS AMAR coefficient is statistically significant (5 percent level, one-tail test) and positive, the corresponding OLS parameter is insignificant and negative."

But what would we conclude if the simple method produced plausible results whereas the sophisticated method produced totally incredible results? In such a case it may be the case that the instruments are invalid and it seems to us that the method of controlling for endogeneity is very difficult to implement in practice. The problem with implementation is to find a suitable set of instruments. Having bad instruments is like walking on a trail finding a discrepancy between the map and the path of the trail and believing that the map must be right and the trail must be wrong, even if following the map leads straight into a lake. Hotz et al. (1997) mention a paper by Schultz (1985) on the Swedish fertility transition 1860 to 1910 as their best practice example. This paper shows an excellent creative use of instruments. Schultz uses butter prices for the female price of time and rye prices for the male price of time. Pre-industrial butter production was mainly performed by women, while men were working on the fields producing rye[2]. In the 1850s Sweden was a grain exporting country, which nowadays is hard to believe. However, the world market for grain changed drastically, when it became economically feasibly to ship grain from the United States and the Russian steppes to Europe and the Swedish rye was no longer competitive on the European market. This is a truly exogenous variation in the butter to rye price ratio, which increased the value of female time in butter production, giving an incentive to reduce family size in order to have more time for butter production. The use of the butter to rye price ratio is intelligent also because most people in the Swedish 19th century did not earn a wage. They were farmers and for most of their time they were not working for a wage but living off their own production and only selling a marginal output on the market. This marginal output however included butter and cheese. One can also measure potential wages or education rather than actual wages of the mother to measure the opportunity cost of children. Willis (1973) uses wages of husbands predicted at age 40 from Mincer (1974) type earnings functions for husbands's earnings together with wife's education.

A very popular instrumental variable approach is to use data on twins. Twins supposedly and in particular if they are monozygotic have the same genetic equipment. Therefore they have been used for studying the effects of education on earnings while keeping ability constant. In fertility research the birth of twins has been taken as an exogenous variation of quantity of children in order to study the quantity-quality interaction in demand for children. Hotz et al. refer to a paper by Rosenzweig and Wolpin (1980). Another instrument that has been used successfully in determining the transition for a two child family to having a third birth is whether the first two children had the same sex (Angrist and Evans, 1996). A recent study of Greek fertility (Symeonidou and Mitsopoulpos, 2003) however shows that in Greece the transition to a third child is only increased if the first two children are girls not if they are boys. The Angrist and Evans instrument can of course not be used in studies of postponement of maternity where we concentrate on the first birth. The search for instruments is a valuable part of economic research but it will never be the case that there will be instruments found that should always be used in fertility research. Butter and rye prices have nothing to tell us about 21st century fertility in Sweden although they were an intelligent invention to study 19th century fertility. Chapter 3 of this volume (Skirbekk, Kohler and Prskawetz) shows that birth month of a woman within a one year birth cohort, has an effect on birth timing in Sweden. This is because compulsory school starts in August for all children born in a given calendar year and ends in June, 9 years later, and most women plan their start of family formation to begin after school is completed. This finding is in line with earlier findings showing that the probability of a birth while studying is very low (e.g. Blossfeld and Huinink, 1991; Gustafsson, Kenjoh and Wetzels, 2002) and with the findings of chapters 9, Kreyenfeld, chapter 10 Kantorova and chapter 11 Gustafsson and Worku of this volume). The finding of chapter 3, Skirbekk, Kohler and Prskawetz suggests that not only age of the woman in years but also in months may have an effect on birth timing, where the months effect is negative since December born women finish school while 11 months younger than January born women. For most research problems suitable instruments will probably not be available.

4. HAZARD MODELS

Hazard rate models are widely used for the empirical analysis of outcomes of fertility decisions or, more specifically, the timing of births. Modelling the timing of births and analysing its determinants result in a natural way to inference on completed fertility since the latter is essentially the sum of the outcomes of past fertility decisions. Furthermore, using a hazard model does justice to the inherent dynamic nature of the timing of births. Given the popularity of hazard models we review in this section the statistical model in its basic form.

Individual or household level survey data typically contain information on a random sample of all women or households in the population and an increasing number of data sets have information on the complete fertility history. Many women in the survey may still be childless or will have more children than they have at the time of the survey and, moreover, the fertility plans of women from the younger cohorts may differ from the fertility plans of women from the older cohorts for whom we observe completed fertility. These considerations are in particular of importance when examining the relationship between declining (completed) fertility rates and the postponement of maternity of women from the younger cohorts, as observed in most developed countries over the last decades (see Chapter 1). A static model of completed fertility (e.g. Becker, 1960, Willis, 1973), estimated on a sub-sample of older women, is therefore inadequate for making inferences concerning the fertility behaviour of the whole female population. Furthermore, if one wishes to make the link from changes in timing behaviour to changes in completed fertility it is insufficient to only analyse the timing of maternity and one also needs to analyse the timing (spacing) of subsequent births (e.g. Newman, 1983).

The seminal article of Newman and McCulloch (1984) introduces hazard models for the economic analysis of the timing of births. Previously such models have been widely used in the demographic literature and, within the field of economics, for analysing unemployment durations. Lancaster (1990) provides an excellent overview on hazard rate models. Since the influential study of Heckman and Walker (1990) on the timing of births in Sweden many empirical studies using hazard rate models have followed. In this section we outline a basic econometric model often used to analyse the timing of births and discuss estimation issues. Furthermore we briefly discuss the restrictions often imposed in empirical work on this basic hazard rate model, often solely for reasons of computational convenience, and extensions proposed in the literature concerning interrelationships with other decisions of households such as marital and female labour supply decisions, and the econometric problems this introduces.

4.1 A basic hazard rate model for analysing the timing of births

The durations analysed in the economic analysis of the timing of births are the duration from a certain starting point in the lifecycle of women, say the age of 14, age of marriage or the age of schooling completion, until first birth occurs, and the spacing of subsequent births (Newman and McCulloch, 1984). An important extension to this model that has been proposed in the literature is to account for unobserved heterogeneity. Some women would not invest in a long education like some men also do not. Such women have less to lose from early birth timing as argued section 2. But women who are concerned with their career will gain more by postponing. The unobserved heterogeneity 'being career conscious' is then correlated with education which is one of the explanatory variables. Not taking unobserved heterogeneity into account may yield spurious relationships between the timing of births and the economic variables of interest such as education and wages. For this reason Heckman, Hotz and Walker (1985) introduce unobserved heterogeneity in a non-parametric way following the approach of Heckman and Singer (1984). Causal interpretations of the effects of the exogenous explanatory variables, the covariates, however, have to be made with caution since the approach is essentially a random effects approach, i.e. unobserved heterogeneity is assumed to be uncorrelated with the covariates.

In the following we present a basic hazard rate model in continuous time and discuss empirical specification and estimation. We assume that for all women we observe the complete fertility history up to the time of the survey. First some necessary notation is introduced. Let k denote the source state, i.e. the number of children a woman or household has at time t. The hazard rate, i.e. the transition intensity of a departure from state k in a short interval $(t, t + dt)$, given survival to t, is denoted by $h_k(t_k \mid Z, \theta_k)$. We assume that the destination state is always a higher parity $(k + 1)$. Z is a vector of exogenous covariates and the unknown parameter vector is denoted by θ_k. A woman (or household) is denoted by the index i. The probability of being in state k after a duration of t_{ik}, i.e. the so-called survivor function, is given by:

$$S_k(t_{ik} \mid Z_i; \theta_k) = \exp\left\{ -\int_0^{t_{ik}} h_k(s \mid Z_i; \theta_k) \partial s \right\} \tag{25}$$

The survivor function is the probability a woman is still at risk of conceiving at time t_{ik}, hence at risk of a transition from parity k to parity $k + 1$. The contribution to the likelihood function of an observed transition from state k (to $k + 1$) after a duration of t_{ik} in state k is given by:

$$f_k(t_{ik} \mid Z_i; \theta_k) = h_k(t_{ik} \mid Z_i; \theta_k) S_k(t_{ik} \mid Z_i; \theta_k) \tag{26}$$

This likelihood contribution incorporates the information that a woman who transits to a higher parity is at risk of conceiving at the initial parity k. For every woman the last observed spell is essentially still ongoing, hence the contribution to the likelihood function for these incomplete spells is the survivor function (equation (25)). This means that women who have two children are assumed to be at risk of having a third child.

A woman can experience multiple births during the observation period and K_i is the number of children woman i has at the end of the observation period. K_i is not necessarily completed fertility. If the data are a cross section of all women at some given point of time t, younger women may still have more children after the observation period finishes at t. K denotes the maximum number of children in the sample (over all women) that any woman has in the sample. For example if there is one woman who has 8 children and no one who has 9 children $K = 8$. What we observed is a sequence of spells, i.e. birth intervals, for each woman. Of course, for some women we may observe no transitions since they remain childless during the observation period. For notational simplicity we only consider time-constant covariates but this framework can be easily adapted to deal with for time-varying covariates (e.g. Lancaster, 1990). Several contributions to this volume also use time varying variables: Kreyenfeld chapter 9, Kantorova chapter 10 and Gustafsson and Worku chapter 11. The covariates Z_i are decomposed in a vector of observable characteristics X_i and an unobserved individual specific effect v_i. This unobserved individual specific effect could, for instance, be interpreted as the preference of a woman or couple for having children. Other examples of unobserved woman specific effects could be the woman's market career interest or fecundity of the woman and or her husband. The density function of the unobserved heterogeneity is denoted by $g(\nu_i)$. The distribution of the unobserved heterogeneity is unknown and by definition we cannot observe the values for individual women. Collecting all ingredients, the contribution to the likelihood of a woman, indexed by i, with a sequence of spells $\{t_{i0},..,t_{iK_i}\}$ and characteristics X_i and ν_i is given by:

$$L_i\left(\theta \mid t_{i0},..,t_{iK_i},X_i\right)=$$

$$\int_{-\infty}^{\infty}\left(\prod_{s=0}^{K_i-1} f_s\left(t_{is} \mid X_i,\upsilon_i;\theta\right)\right) S_{K_i}\left(t_{iK_i} \mid X_i,\upsilon_i;\theta\right) g(\nu_i)\partial\nu_i \qquad (27)$$

with $\theta = (\theta_0,.., \theta_K)$. A spell is the time elapsed between any two events for example between age 15 and couple formation time or between age 15 and first birth if couple formation time is not studied. The vectors $\theta_0,..,\theta_K$ are the parameters of interest that will be estimated. In this case there is one vector for each parity k and there is one estimated coefficient for each explanatory variable in X_i that may include education of the woman and background variables like social class of the family of origin. The integral in (27) is over all possible values of ν_i. The K_i^{th} spell is an incomplete spell (i.e. a right-censored spell) and all preceding (K_i - 1) spells are completed. This means that we take account of the fact that we do not know if a woman with two children will proceed to have a third child for example.

The log-likelihood for the complete sample of N women is defined as:

$$L(\theta \mid t, X) = \sum_{i=1}^{N} \ln(L_i(\theta \mid t_{i0},..,t_{iK_i}, X_i)) \qquad (28)$$

With $t = \left\{t_{i0},..,t_{iK_i}\right\}_{i=1}^{N}$ and $X - \left(X_1,.., X_N\right)$ and $\theta = \left(\theta_0,.., \theta_K\right)$.

The Maximum Likelihood estimates of the parameters of interest (θ) are given by:

$$\hat{\theta} = \max_{\theta} L(\theta \mid t, X) \qquad (29)$$

This formulation requires a full specification of the density function $g(\nu_i)$. A non-parametric specification would not require that. A popular choice for $g(\nu_i)$ which is a parametric one, is the Gamma distribution and several studies show this may work well (e.g. Newman and McCulloch, 1984). This choice is nowadays supported by most statistical packages. The parameter estimates are, however, known to be sensitive with respect to a specific choice of the density function of unobserved heterogeneity $g(v_i)$. One can use different density functions such as, for instance, a normal distribution (e.g. Lillard, 1993). This, however, required solving numerically the integral that appears in equation (27) since in this case no closed form solution can be found for solving this integral. In this perspective it is noteworthy that simulation-based methods are becoming increasingly popular for solving the integral that appears in equation (27) (Gourieroux Montfort, 1997). However, to avoid the parameter estimates to be affected by the choice of $g(v_i)$ Heckman and Singer (1984) propose the Non-Parametric Maximum Likelihood Estimator. This estimation procedure does not require a full specification of the density function $g(v_i)$ but approximates the distribution function with a discrete distribution with mass points and corresponding probabilities. These mass points and corresponding probabilities, and the number of mass points, are estimated and not fixed a priori. A discussion of the performance of this method can be found in Huh and Sickles (1994). This nonparametric method is successfully used in many areas of applied economic research. A cautionary note we wish to make is that the empirical implementation is not always without problems and it often results in a distribution of unobserved heterogeneity with only two points of support. This means that the unobserved heterogeneity only has two different values, with respect to the timing of births. Furthermore it requires some additional assumptions that are discussed in somewhat more detail below.

4.2 Empirical Implementation

A proportional hazard rate specification is commonly used in empirical research. An important methodological advantage of the proportional hazard rate model is that it allows (non-parametric) identification of duration dependence and the distribution of unobservables in a single-spell framework. In the unemployment literature this received a lot of attention because of the interest in separating genuine duration dependence, i.e. that is if a person who has been unemployed for a long time has been stigmatized, from sorting effect, i.e. the longer unemployed have undesirable (unobserved) characteristics. Elbers and Ridder (1982) discuss identification of a single spell duration model, e.g. the timing of maternity, and Honoré (1993) discusses identification of a multiple spell duration models, e.g. the timing of births. The question is if one can identify and separate effects of duration dependence from unobserved heterogeneity? The proportionality assumption is formalised as follows:

$$h_k(t_{ik} \mid Z_i, \theta_k) = h_k^1(t_{ik} \mid \alpha_k) \times h_k^2(X_i, v_i; \beta_k, \gamma_k) \qquad (30)$$

$h_k^1(.)$ is commonly referred to as the baseline hazard and the individual characteristics are assumed to affect the baseline hazard proportionally through the function $h_k^2(.)$. We introduced a set of parameters $\theta_k = (\alpha_k, \beta_k, \gamma_k)$ to measure the different effects. The dimensions of these parameter vectors depend of course on the functional forms chosen.

The pattern of duration dependence $h_k^1(.)$ is assumed to be the same for all N women. In its simplest form one assumes a continuous monotonic relationship between the time in state k and the baseline hazard, e.g.:

$$h_k^1(t_{ik} \mid \alpha_k) = (t_{ik})^{\alpha_k} \tag{31}$$

It may of course be desirable to allow for a more flexible or a nonparametric baseline specification. The choice of the exact functional form of $h_k^1(.)$ will depend on the available data, for instance one can have monthly or yearly data. If enough data is available one can choose a nonparametric specification and include dummy variables for each duration value.

The proportional hazard specification implies that population heterogeneity affects the baseline hazard in a multiplicative way and is often taken to be of an exponential form, e.g.:

$$h_k^2(X_i, v_i; \beta_k, \gamma_k) = \exp\{X_i \beta_k + \gamma_k v_i\} \tag{32}$$

Explanatory variables, or covariates, included in X_i are for example the years of schooling, wage rates, or birth cohort. In such a conventional specification variables such as schooling or wages are assumed to be exogenous or predetermined variables. The unobserved heterogeneity, the values of v_i are woman-specific and constant over spells. That means that a career conscious woman is always career conscious and a woman with low fecundity always has low fecundity. However, the effects of being career conscious can differ between spells, the $\beta_k : s$ are spell specific. The first parity spell i.e. going from being childless to having the first child can be longer for the career conscious woman whereas the second child may arrive sooner. There are as equation (32) shows different effects (γ_k) for each spell (k). These coefficients corresponding to the effects of unobserved heterogeneity on the hazard rates, γ_k 's, are often referred to as the factor loadings. In order to estimate the γ_k 's they need to be normalized; usually for $k = 0$ one sets $\gamma_0 = 1$. In order to identify the effects of the unobserved heterogeneity the γ_k 's as different from the effects of the observed heterogeneity the β_k 's unobserved heterogeneity has to enter the model in a multiplicative way and in the specification chosen above this means additively in the index. A practical note is that most empirical studies choose to restrict the hazard rates of parity 3 or higher to be equal, apart from a different intercept, because not many women have more than 4 children and, consequently, identification becomes problematic.

As mentioned above, Elbers and Ridder (1982) discuss identification of a single spell duration model, e.g. the timing of maternity, and Honoré (1993) discusses identification of a multi-spell duration model, e.g. the timing of births.[3] The conditions for identification have empirical consequences of which one needs to be aware when specifying which variables are included as covariates in equation (32). Issues such as restricting the analysis to the timing of maternity or including lagged duration dependence when analysing a sequence of births have consequences for the identification of the model outlined above. In case of using a single spell proportional hazard model, when analysing the timing of maternity, one needs to include at least one continuous variable as a covariate in the model in order to separately identify the baseline hazard and the distribution of unobserved heterogeneity. Of course, if one is not interested in identifying these separately and only interested in identifying the effects of the covariates on the timing of maternity one can estimate Cox's proportional hazard model, which allows for a fully flexible baseline hazard. Generally speaking, the multi-spell duration model is identified under less strong assumptions than a single-spell duration model and does not require at least one continuous variable as a covariate. However, when analysing a sequence of births, hence employing a multi-spell duration model, one may for instance be interested in the effects of the duration until first birth on the transition probability of having a second child. In this case one includes lagged duration values and this requires an additional identifying assumption. For instance, that there is at least one continuous explanatory variable included in X_i. For an excellent discussion on the identification of hazard models, and in particular multi-spell duration models, we refer to Van den Berg (2001).

4.3 Restrictions and Extensions

Heckman and Walker (1990) in studying third births in Sweden criticize what they call a 'piecemeal' approach and warn that one cannot safely estimate higher parity transitions without taking lower parity transitions into account but if one estimates only the first transition as in most chapters of this book it is alright. If one does estimate a piecemeal model, when higher order parities and the total family size are of priority interest this may result in inconsistent estimates. This will be the case if there are unobserved time invariant woman-specific effects (unobserved heterogeneity). The likelihood contribution of woman *i*, equation (27), makes it clear that one can indeed not split up the likelihood function in separate 'pieces', unless one is willing to assume there is no unobserved heterogeneity.

Unobserved heterogeneity in Heckman and Walker (1990) in studying third births in Sweden is however motivated by some women being less fecund than others, which is a very small explanation for current day 0, 1, 2, 3 children born to a woman, and nowadays one expects a proportion of women to chose remaining childless or decide to stop conceiving when the desired number of children has been reached. But as pointed out by Hewlett (2002) observed childlessness among career women may not be voluntary. Many high achieving women may have tried to start a family too late according to their biological clock and then fecundity plays an important role again. It is easy to think of variables that have different effects on the hazard between spells and the model outlined above allows for this by allowing for different parameters for each parity, where β_k is different for every k. Such a variable is woman's education because higher educated women may wait longer to have the first birth while waiting a shorter time to have the second birth, compared to low educated women. If the unobserved heterogeneity is career consciousness, two equally educated women can be differently career oriented and the one who is more career oriented may delay first birth more and have second birth sooner because of economics of scale in child raising or in order to cope with the biological clock. But if two equally educated and equally career oriented women arrive at the same optimal timing of births, fecundity may be another unobservable which makes one woman delay first birth more that the other one.

An extension not considered in this chapter is the inclusion of the so-called parity specific stopping probabilities (Heckman and Walker, 1990). Essentially this means that the model explicitly takes into account infecundity together with the decision to stop conceiving once the desired number of children has been reached. Also from a methodological point it may be of importance to allow for parity specific stopping probabilities since one of the assumptions made when using a hazard model is that a transition will occur at some point in time. Applications using these additional features and showing the importance when analysing the timing of births are, for example, Heckman and Walker (1990), Merrigan and St.-Pierre (1998) and Bloemen and Kalwij (2001). However, as for instance discussed in Merrigan and St.-Pierre (1998), infecundity may as well be captured when modelling unobserved hetereogeneity. To be more specific, a mass point of the discrete distribution of unobserved heterogeneity at minus infinity implies a transition probability equal to zero. More explicitly modelling stopping behaviour may require additional information, on say infecundity, that is usually not available in a household survey. Nevertheless, if such information would be available, this would yield a richer empirical framework.

Other desirable extensions to the model outlined in section 4.1 are plentiful, think of marital and female employment decisions, but are severely hindered by the fact the hazard rate model is a nonlinear model. Linear fertility models, such as the model by Willis (1973) who examines fertility and female labour supply, allow for a simultaneous approach or, from a different perspective, allow for instrumental variables estimation. Recent work on fertility and female labor supply using simultaneous estimation of linear models includes Del Boca (2002) and Bratti Chapter 5 in this volume. There is, however, generally speaking, no similar approach available for nonlinear models such as hazard rate models. In the literature several studies have tried to deal with this. Hotz and Miller (1988) and Moffitt (1984) examine the interrelationship between fertility decisions and female employment decisions using (nonlinear) discrete choice models. Such a framework allows for random effects but do not explicitly analyse timing issues. Kalwij (2000) employs a hurdle count data model to analyse the effects of female employment status on the presence and number of children in households in the Netherlands. The hurdle takes explicitly into account the interrelationship between female employment status and timing of first birth. The number of children, once children are present in the household, is modelled conditional on female employment status.

Blau and Robins (1989) examine both the timing of births and transitions on the labour market but implicitly assume there is no simultaneity, conditional on a set of observable variables. In line with Lillard (1993) one can introduce in such models some sort of dependency between the two events via the time-constant unobservables (see e.g. Van den Berg, 1997). This does, however, not allow one to make inferences on how the duration in one event affects the duration in the other event, without making additional assumptions. Having said this, a possible and appealing solution, exploiting the sequence of life events, is presented in the studies of Lillard (1993) and Brien and Lillard (1994) on the simultaneity between marriage duration and fertility timing. Bloemen and Kalwij (2001) also examine both the timing of births and transitions on the labour market but implicitly assume that these processes are interrelated, hence the special case of no interrelationships is not nested in their model. An alternative approach often advocated in the demographic literature (see Section 3) is that one may assume there is a sequence of events that can be exploited, say a woman first completed schooling, finds a suitable partner and marries after some time, and then starts having children. However, from a lifecycle perspective these events are still interrelated and some (implicit) assumptions are needed for consistency of the estimates. A recent study (Holmlund 2004) shows that sisters of teenage mothers, who did not have an early birth also have less education than women on average. This suggests that social class of the family of origin and genetically inherited ability are variables that determine investment in schooling. In the econometric literature a reversed less likely causality has been proposed namely that childminded women will not want to invest in schooling rather than the more likely causality that planned human capital investments come first and birth timing follows. Opportunity costs of wrong birth timing are higher for a woman with career ambitions. Also a woman does not become a teenage mother because she is child minded but this happens because her contraception failed.

A final example to clarify the inherent difficulty in addressing simultaneity issues when analysing the timing of births is the following. One may assume that a woman is at risk of conceiving a child from the age of 14. When interested in the timing of maternity, the duration of interest is the time when the woman turned 14 until the time of conceiving her first child. During this period the woman experiences several other events, such as schooling completion and finding a partner. These outcomes affect the hazard of conceiving a child and this can essentially be analysed in a standard hazard rate model, as described above, by including the outcomes as time varying covariates. Consistency of the parameters of interest depends, however, on the assumption of (conditional) exogeneity of the covariates. In other words, the assumption made is that a woman does not anticipate the outcomes of these events. Whether or not this is a reasonable assumption to make is up to the researcher to assess. Ad hoc solutions often encountered in empirical research involve splitting up the sample in, for instance, married and single women. No need to argue that such sample splits do not solve the inherent econometric problem since one introduces at least one new problem, namely that of an endogenous population split.

The examples given here show the inherent problem a researcher faces, and the methodology applied to deal with this problem, when trying to model the timing of different events that are presumably interrelated. While a standard methodology of dealing with simultaneity in a hazard model is not available, the studies discussed above do provide interesting insights the interrelationships between lifecycle events and stimulate further research in this area.

5. ESTIMABLE STOCHASTIC DYNAMIC DISCRETE CHOICE MODELS

Hotz et al. (1997) view dynamic stochastic discrete choice models as the correct way to analyze life-cycle fertility. Hazard models, as in Heckman and Walker (1990), are reduced form estimates. By using dynamic programming methods it is possible to estimate a structural dynamic model. Hotz et al. (1997, p. 340):

> "This approach attempts to impose more directly the insights of economic theory both to summarize the effect of non-contemporaneous prices and to estimate deeper structural parameters."

Structural models are made with the purpose to allow policy analysis different from reduced form models. The reason life-cycle fertility is not more often studied by this method is according to Hotz et al. (1997) because the method is computationally intensive. Two recent good examples of estimating dynamic programming models are Van der Klaauw (1996) and Francesconi (2002). Van der Klaauw (1996) studies marital choice and labor force participation as jointly determined so that a woman in any given period decides to be in one of four different states: single and working, single and not working, married and working, married and not working. The estimates are used to predict changes in life-cycle patterns of marriage, divorce and employment due to changes in female earnings, (potential) husband's earnings, education, as well as differences by race. Van der Klaauw (1996, p. 228) concludes:

> "The strong interdependence between the gains to marriage and the gains from working, further implies that a female's marital status cannot be considered exogenous to the participation decision."

And further on p. 229:

> "For our sample, ignoring the endogeneity of marital status decisions causes current work response to own and husband's earnings changes to be underestimated by 4% to 17%."

Francesconi (2002) studies the joint decisions of fertility with working full time or working part time, so that in every period a woman chooses between six different states: 1) no birth and not working, 2) birth and not working, 3) no birth and part time work, 4) birth and part time work, 5) no birth and full time work, 6) birth and full time work.

In his conclusions Francesconi emphasizes the difference between part time workers and full time workers (p. 374):

> "The results show that while the disutility of work increases with own experience, i.e. number of years worked full-time which by itself could lead to negative state dependence, the observed persistence in full time employment is due to a large positive own experience effect on full time earnings. The observed lower persistence in part time employment is mainly due to the small own-experience effect on part time earnings."

Further Francesconi draws very precise conclusions about full-time work as against part-time work:

> "Because we estimate a joint model of fertility and labor force participation we can quantify the lifetime utility effect of a work interruption when a child is born. For a woman who withdraws from full time employment for 5 years, the utility decrease of a work interruption from full-time work is about 1.5% per year over a 20-year period, provided that she re-enters the full time employment sector after interruption. Short withdrawals lead to smaller utility losses. But part time work during childbirth and childrearing years does not contribute to a substantial increase in lifetime utility as compared to a work interruption."

Both Van der Klaauw (1996) and Francesconi (2002) reference Wolpin (1984) as the model for this kind of estimable dynamic programming model. Hotz et al. (1997) use the work of Wolpin (1984) to give an intuition about how these types of models work. The model starts with an additively separable life-cycle utility function. In each period the woman's problem is to maximize the expected value of life-cycle utility:

$$\max E_t \sum_{k=0}^{T-1} \delta^k U_{t+k}\left(M_{t+k}, X_{t+k}\right) \qquad (35)$$

where M is the stock of children and X is other consumption, E is the expectations operator, δ is the discount factor. This life-cycle utility function is like the utility functions (2), (5) and (6) in our presentation of received theory above. The formulation (35) also shows that in any period t the remaining expected life-cycle utility is considered. Francesconi (2002) adds more arguments in his life-cycle utility function. In addition to the stock of children and other consumption arguments the utility function includes utility or disutility of part time work, or full time work, the utility of having a birth in time period t and the utility of the educational level. The utility function of Van der Klaauw includes choices about whether or not to work, whether or not to be married and how much to consume each period.

For understanding the intuition of the method we follow Hotz et al. (1997) in using the Wolpin (1984) model with the utility function (35) above. The model assumes a finite life-time horizon. For Van der Klaauw the observed life-time period starts at leaving school and ends when the observation is censored in 1985 or if the woman dropped out of the sample earlier. He studies a specific cohort from the Michigan Panel Study of Income Dynamics (PSID), of women who were aged 12 to 19 in 1968 and 29 to 36 in 1985. For Francesconi the studied part of the life-cycle goes from age at marriage until retirement at age 65, but the option of having a birth in any period stops at age 40. Francesconi (2002) uses data form the National Longitudinal Survey of Young Women (NLS-YW), delimits his analysis on the subset of women who were always married during the observation period. Both studies are thus performed on data from the United States. The utility function (35) is subject to a period-by-period budget constraint in Wolpin's (1984) case:

$$y_t = X_t + cn_t \tag{36}$$

where y is income, X is consumption with a price normalized to unity, n is a dummy variable which is equal to one if the woman had a birth in period t, c is the price of a child in its first year of life. In principle the life-time budget constraint could be as in (7) above, where life-time expenditures must be no larger than life-time income. Such a life-time budget constraint allows for possibilities to borrow and save. For example, by student loans and housing mortgages one can finance current consumption by future incomes and one can also save to finance future consumption by current incomes, such as is the case by saving in retirement pension schemes. Both Van der Klaauw (1996) and Francesconi (2002) make the simplifying assumption following Wolpin (1984) that there is no borrowing or lending. The reasons for this simplification are tractability of the model.

In order to compute utility every period, which is the essence of this methodology, one needs to specify the utility function (35). It is not enough to say that utility depends on consumption and children, as in (35), one also needs to say how it depends on those two arguments. Wolpin (1984) assumes that the utility function is quadratic in the stock of children (M) and other consumption (X):

$$U_t(M_t, X_t) = (\alpha_1 + \xi_t) M_t - \alpha_2 M_t^2 + \beta_1 X_t + \beta_2 X_t^2 + \gamma M_t X_t \tag{37}$$

The second term ξ introduces the stochastic element to the model. This term is assumed to be an independently identically distributed preference shock (i.i.d)[5]. This preference shock is assumed to be known by the decision maker but not by the econometrician. The rest of the procedure is summarized by Hotz et al., p. 340:

> "Assuming that ξ is normally distributed, induces a probit form for the choice of probabilities. The non-stochastic part of the probit is given by the difference in the expected utility of choosing to have or not to have a child in this period. Since for given values of the parameters, these two components can be computed (by backwards recursion), the structural parameters of the economic choice problem – those appearing in the utility function and in the budget constraint – can be estimated by maximizing the implied likelihood."

This method then estimates directly maximum utility subject to the budget constraint, like our theory above tells us to do. The woman is supposed to know what her ξ is, how large her desire to have children is and how much other consumption she is willing to forego in order to fulfil her child wish. The econometrician estimates the ξ which fulfils a similar role as the residual term in an ordinary least squares regression. In Francesconi's case three stochastic variables are estimated and the women are estimated to belong to one of three groups based on their values on the stochastic variables. The intuitive interpretation of this procedure is that it corresponds to the error terms in an ordinary least squares regression. You would group together women with large positive error terms, women with small error terms in another group and women with negative error terms in a third group. How does the econometrician estimate the parameters of the utility function? The method is backward recursion. It starts at the end of the observation period, in Van der Klaauw's case in 1985 and in Francesconi's case in 1991. You must have given values for the parameters to start with. You estimate the last period parameters first separately, by a simple method, and then use these parameters in a maximum likelihood estimation period-by-period backwards. But the interpretation is forward looking. Francesconi (2002, p. 344):

> "The state at any age t contains all the relevant history of choices that enter the current utility as well as the realizations of the three shocks up to t."

The estimable stochastic dynamic programs is an impressive contribution. As is often the case with sophisticated methods, this method puts large demands on the data. There must be complete panels of income, earned every year by husband and wife. A particular demand is to use variables for potential husbands during periods when the woman is single. In Francesconi's case there also has to be complete histories of whether the woman worked part-time or full time or did not work in any given year. Further you need complete birth histories, which is not so difficult to get because birth histories, different from income histories, can accurately be collected retrospectively since everyone knows the birthday of their children. In Van der Klaauw's case you need also complete marital histories, which for the cohort that he is studying, until 1985, is perhaps accurate. The marital history data is also becoming more difficult to get at because of unmarried cohabitation. People may in surveys not remember and thus not give the accurate dates of moving together and moving apart again. Such information may be easier to get for periods when such behaviour required registration as marriage and divorce. Register data sets have the advantage of accuracy in many respects, earnings are from tax files, and there are large numbers of observations because they come from registers of the whole population. However, these register data, i.e. Naz, Anti-Nilsen and Vagstad (chapter 12 of this volume), do not register unmarried cohabitation, which for many couples has substituted for marriage, and there are also many children born to couples in unmarried cohabitation particularly in Nordic countries.

Neither Francesconi (2002) nor Van der Klaauw (1996) discuss timing of events and have nothing to say about postponement of maternity, which is the focus of this volume. Although the 'estimable stochastic dynamic programs' explicitly take every period of the expected life-time utility into account they do not focus on timing. The method estimates the increase in lifetime utility by having a birth in any particular period, but the empirical results are not presented in a form that one can draw any conclusion about timing of maternity. Kalwij (1999), when assessing the goodness of fit of a structural model explaining female labour force participation and the timing of birth in the Netherlands, concludes that his structural model is not capable of accurately explaining the timing of births. A further shortcoming from an economic modelling point of view is the omission of savings decisions of households. Savings are at the core of economic theory of household decisions and, as argued in Chapt 1 of this volume, consumption smoothing motives may explain the postponement of maternity. Liquidity constraints or precautionary savings may, for instance, play a role. Some empirical evidence on this is presented in Browning and Ejrnaes (2002) for the UK and Kalwij (2003) for the Netherlands who both conclude that households save to deal with financial consequences of having children.

6. INSTITUTIONS AND POLICY ANALYSIS

While economic theory of fertility as outlined in section 2 above is general enough to be taken as a guideline for all geographic regions and all time periods this is not true for empirical applications. Policy evaluations therefore apply to changes over time in one country (Ermisch, 1988, 1990). For example Francesconi (2002) treats part-time work and full-time work as two separate sectors of the economy. Such treatment is plausible for the United States and the United Kingdom, but not for Sweden and the Netherlands, where workers have a legal right to shorten work hours in any job and then increase work hours again. In Sweden this right is since 1974 available for parents who have children aged less than 8 years. And the shorter work week is 30 hours which classifies as part-time work according to international standards, where 35 hours or more is full-time work. In the Netherlands since 2000, any worker for any reason may shorten weekly work hours in any job, and an employer who objects has the burden of proof that such shortening of work hours would damage his business. Working part-time in the Netherlands or Sweden may therefore be expected to have less career damaging effects than is the case in the United States or in Britain. Indeed, Gustafsson, Kenjoh and Wetzels (2003) show that whereas there are hourly wage penalties for working part-time in Germany and Britain, this is not the case in Sweden and the Netherlands. This example shows that the practice of much econometrics is unjustified, in ignoring institutional knowledge and treating research results as if they are everywhere applicable and make believe that the country studied does not matter. Having estimated a structural model and used only exogenous variables for explanations is not enough. For example Francesconi (2002) finds that a woman can better take a labor force interruption and return to full-time work than continue to work part-time. But this result is obtained for American women who were at least 40 years old by 1995. In the USA part-time jobs are low level jobs. Therefore such an advice is of no value for a Swedish or Dutch 25-year old woman in 2005, who considers how to combine her child wish with her career planning.

One of the most important and most cited contributions of policy analysis is Esping-Anderson (1990, 1999). Esping-Anderson emphasizes that the three worlds of welfare capitalism: Sweden, Germany and the United States - also labelled the 'Social Democrat', the 'Conservative Christian Democrat' and the 'Liberal' models - have developed from different historical ideas and concepts and have different logics. A similar policy change across the three different countries therefore cannot be expected to result in the same outcomes, because this policy change will interact with other institutional characteristics in each country. Also the time of a policy change within a country matters for the same reasons. This approach to policy analysis works by comparing institutional changes in different countries. It is important to have solid institutional knowledge about the countries studied and the effects of policy changes can be analyzed by studying outcomes between countries. The approach is international comparative and the names of the countries studied are essential contributions to the understanding. Gustafsson and co-authors have contributed to this line of research (for example: Gustafsson 1981, 1994, Gustafsson and Stafford 1994, Gustafsson, Kenjoh and Wetzels 2003). This approach is interdisciplinary because it draws from research by political science, sociology and history in addition to economics and econometrics. This line of research questions the common practice among economists to regard a policy change as exogenous and having an expected similar effect across time periods and across countries. Rather policy changes are results of changes that take place in society. One example is the introduction of separate taxation of earnings for husband and wife introduced in Sweden in 1971. This change was introduced when 50% of married women were labor force participants because more votes could be gained by a tax system that benefits the two-earner family rather than a tax system that benefits a one-earner family (Gustafsson 1992, Elvander 1974). In quantitative analysis one does not find a jump in female labor force participation after the introduction of separate taxation in 1971 nor does one find a change in the slope for a dummy variable interacted with time after 1971 (Schettkat 1987, Gustafsson 1996). In spite of this separate taxation has a positive effect on female labor force participation as is clear from an analysis Gustafsson (1992) where labor supply of married women in Germany and Sweden was estimated and then tax systems of each country were programmed and the labor supply of women predicted if they had had the simulated after tax wages and husband's incomes of the tax system of the other country. The family based tax system of Germany if applied on the Swedish couples would decrease labor force participation from 80% to 60% among Swedish women, whereas the individual based separate tax system of Sweden if applied to the German couples would increase German women's labor force participation from 60% to 70%.

The transition of the Czech Republic from a state socialist economy into a market economy is such a big shift, which makes it reasonable to expect different responses to similar variables before and after (chapter 10, Kantorova, in this volume). While high education was attractive also in the state socialist Czechoslovakia it did not to the same extent have the connotation of investment in human capital as in the post 1990 market economy and we may expect other fertility responses before 1990 than after 1990. Analyzing the difference in response by a separate model for the state socialist period and compare the estimates to those of a similar model for the post 1990 period seems like the most relevant research strategy. Similar considerations apply to the study of East Germany during the German Democratic Republic as compared to the post 1990 period of reunified Germany (chapter 9, Kreyenfeld in this volume). This line of research has been criticized for often omitting an explicit model. Econometric policy analysis expects to find exogenous variation in the proxies for the price and income concepts appearing in the theories. It would not be enough like in Kantorova's case to say that institutional changes make us hypothesize that longer education after 1990 will delay motherhood because of investment in human capital considerations, whereas for the state-socialist period longer education hardly delayed motherhood because student mothers had access to low cost child-care and couples with children had preferential treatment on the housing market. The econometrician expects one model to be formulated of both periods and the policy changes to be captured by price variables. We should have measures of child-care costs and availability and housing costs and availability and wages of women and men which can be used together with educational information to estimate effects of human capital investments before and after transition.

Kantorová in chapter 10 compares the two time periods and draws the conclusion that the economic transition caused postponement of maternity. She shows, that the educational difference in timing of maternity observed in the West European and North American market economies begin to appear in the Czech Republic after the transition but were virtually absent before. There are good explanations for why this would be the case. However based on her results we can not quantify the individual components of the change like changes in child-care caused postponement by half a year, changes on the housing market caused another half a year and widening wage differential between men and women caused redistribution of caring tasks to women which resulted in another half a year postponement and larger returns to human capital caused more effects on the labor market which resulted in another half a year postponement of maternity. Such research is of course a possible extension if data becomes available but in our view the comparison of the two time periods give reasons to interpret the change in the educational effects.

Does one need an economic theory of fertility as outlined in section 2 above for working on institutions? Economic theory helps to identify which institutional changes are important and what effects those changes would have on prices and incomes. Economic theory is therefore used both to formulate hypotheses and to interpret results. Women want equality. They want husbands who are actively involved in parenting tasks and they do not want to lose their career. An overwhelming political argumentation along these lines is analysed and well documented for all western countries (Sainsbury ed, 1994). Also some high achieving women who do not have children have not made this choice voluntarily. In many cases they regret not having started a family in time before infecundity makes it impossible (Hewlett, 2002).

Often econometric papers do not comment on the implications of the results. Comments about the results are limited to discuss if the model fits the data, how large possible biases are and what methods have been applied in order to decrease the effects of biases. One study that combines econometric rigor with a solid knowledge of the institutional environment and political discussions on the topic is Ghysels (2003), who studies time use of couples. Policy advice requires knowledge of institutions. Increasingly knowledge of institutions combined with reviews of econometric work form a basis for policy advice. One recent example is Boeri, Del Boca and Pissarides (2005).

7. CONCLUSION

An ideal empirical model for an economic analysis of the timing of parenthood, and subsequent births, is directly related to a theoretical economic model and uses exogenous variation in all past, current and expected future prices to identify effects on the choice of when to have a child, hence a structural model. This would yield clear interpretations of results that are of importance for policy recommendations. Of course, such results are conditional on the validity of the economic model. When formulating and estimating a lifecycle fertility model one is restricted by the variables available in the data and has to deal with complex issues such as, for instance, simultaneity with other household decisions. Taking into account explicitly all theoretical considerations would rapidly result in a model that is no longer feasible to estimate. For this reason assumptions have to be made to get to a statistical model that is feasible to estimate and be able to draw conclusions. This usually results in a reduced form model in which one approximates the costs and benefits of children and the way these affect the choice of when to have a child. For instance using educational levels of the woman as a proxy for the opportunity costs of having children.

Once a specific model is estimated several omissions, perhaps due to data limitations, may yield biased estimates of the parameters of interest. If some variables that should be included in the analysis have not been included could result in an *omitted variables bias*. This occurs when the omitted variable is correlated with both the explanatory variables and timing of births. For example in a study of timing of maternity failing to include information on husband's income would result in an omitted variables bias concerning the effects of female wages. For example if one finds a negative effect of female wages on fertility when male wages are not included and if this effect disappears when we add male wages then we have an example of omitted variable bias in the first case. This is what is found in chapter 12 Naz, Nilsen and Vagstad for wife's and husband's education. In this volume chapters 11 by Gustafsson and Worku and chapter 12 by Naz, Nilsen and Vagstad include husbands' characteristics but use selected samples of only married women. A similar case is made in Kalwij (2003) concerning the strong relationship with household income and wealth. Empirical studies on fertility decisions usually ignore assets holdings of households and Kalwij (2003) shows that ignoring household wealth results in an overestimation of the income effect.

Failing to take account of differences in 'taste for children' has also been considered to result in biased estimates of the parameters of interest, in particular of the pattern of genuine duration dependence. The solution to this problem suggested by Heckman and Walker (1990) has been to model unobserved heterogeneity in addition to the observed heterogeneity which is taken account of by the included explanatory variables. Working with a select sample results in *selectivity bias*. If for example the sample is restricted to only include married and cohabiting women in order to have information on husbands characteristics a selectivity bias is introduced. Some econometric techniques to take care of sample selection bias rely on instrumental variables techniques. Amuedo-Dorantes and Kimmel chapter 7 in this volume is an application of these techniques. Another solution to the selection over time has been to model the whole birth history jointly. Heckman and Walker (1990) model the timing of first, second and higher parity births jointly, in line with the basic hazard model specified in section 4 of this chapter. In this volume although using a different method chapter 4 by O'Donogue and O'Shea study both the decisions to marry and the decisions to enter parity 1, 2 etc. and they are able to decompose the fertility decline into its constituent explanations.

Decisions that may be thought of as taken jointly, should be estimated jointly, like the decision to marry or cohabit, the decision to have a child the decision to educate oneself and the decision to supply labour to the market. Failing to do so may result in spurious relationships or, when assuming that the other decision is exogenous with respect to the fertility decisions, may results in *simultaneity bias*. For instance, economic theory as outlined in this chapter shows that labour force participation decisions and fertility decisions may be taken simultaneously. Jointly modelling labour supply and fertility decisions has been done by Willis (1973), Moffit (1984), Kalwij (2000), Bloemen and Kalwij (2001), Francesconi (2002) and in this volume in chapter 5 by Bratti. Lillard (1993) and Van der Klaauw (1996) model fertility and marital decisions jointly.

Some researchers argue that only by estimating a structural model one can say something about how policy changes will affect people's behaviour because then we obtain estimates on how a change in a certain price will change the utility of a certain choice made by an individual. Structural fertility models have been estimated by Wolpin (1984), Van der Klaauw (1996) Kalwij (1999) and Francesconi (2002). Clearly, such an analysis is conditioned by the assumptions on households maximizing an intertemporal separable utility function using rational expectations, like we showed in the theoretical section. For example the models we referred to in the section on structural discrete choice models (Wolpin 1984, Van der Klaauw 1996 and Francesconi 2002) all assume no liquidity constraints, and that there are costs for the child only in its first year of life. Moreover, from a policy perspective these structural models ignore the *institutional structure* of the particular country studied and the particular time period. In this volume chapters 9 by Kreyenfeld, 10 by Kantorová and 11 by Gustafsson and Worku are instead focusing on the institutional setting when interpreting their results from reduced form estimations and de la Rica and Iza in chapter 6 analyse the effect of a specific institutional variable namely the large growth of fixed term contracts on particularly the youth labour market in Spain. All the chapters in this volume focus on various aspects of the timing of parenthood. None of the chapters estimate a full structural model as outlined in this chapter. Structural models can also be partial like studying savings behaviour around first birth as is done in chapter 8 by Kalwij in this volume.

A researcher will always have to make choices that imply introducing some biases while solving others. Even the most structural models make choices leaving out some simultaneity, using a select sample, ignoring the institutional setting as has been shown in this chapter. The methodological choices made by authors in this volume are well motivated although each chapter, and indeed any research contribution, suffers from a number of methodological shortcomings while solving some. As methodological contributions in econometrics develop and new software becomes available applied economists improve their econometric tools when it helps answer their research question.

NOTES

[1] In STATA, fixed effects estimation and random effects estimation is available. Both of these can be described by equation (24). If there is correlation between the state dummies and the (X_{st}) 's policy variables etc. varying by state and year, then the fixed effects estimation is the correct procedure. Instead if there is no correlation between the state dummies and the year and state specific policy variables etc., then one can use random effects models. The advantage of random effects models is that you can identify the effects of a time constant explanatory variable. But if there is correlation as described above then the random effects procedure would produce biased estimates. STATA provides normal and gamma distributions. See the command 'frailty', p. 359, STATA 7, 2001.

[2] Actually industrialization of the dairy industry in Sweden by the use of separator technology turned this previously female occupation into a totally male occupation as women were not accepted into the engineering schools necessary to qualify for the job (Sommestad 1992).

[3] Identification of a model means that if we have two different variables that both depend on the same explanatory variables it is difficult to disentangle what we have estimated as in the simple supply and demand model for a marketed good:

$$Q_D = \alpha_1 + \beta_1 P$$
$$Q_S = \alpha_2 + \beta_2 P$$

where the effect of the price P on supply is expected to be positive $\beta_2 > 0$ and the effect of P on demand is expected to be negative $\beta_1 < 0$. If we are able to estimate both β_1 and β_2 we are estimating a structural model but we are not going to be able to identify those two different effects if we do not have access to more information. If for example the marketed good is ice cream and we know that more ice-cream is demanded on a sunny day we may add a dummy variable for rain so that:

$$Q_D = \alpha_1 + \beta_1 P + D, \qquad \text{where } D = 1 \text{ if it rains.}$$

The variable D is then identifying the model or equivalently D is used as an identifying restriction. In the model on birth with unobserved heterogeneity the discussion on identification refers to the question whether one can identify separately the baseline hazard and the distribution of unobserved heterogeneity.

REFERENCES

Amuedo-Dorantes, C. and Kimmel, J., USA: Can the Family Earnings Gaps be Reduced by Postponing Maternity?, chapter 7 of this volume.

Angrist, J., 2002, How Does Sex Ratio Affect Marriage and Labor Markets? Evidence from America's Second Generation, *The Quarterly Journal of Economics*, 997-1038.

Angrist, J. and Evans, W.N., 1996, Children and Their Parents' Labor supply: Evidence from Exogenous Variation in Family Size, *The American Economic Review*, 88(3), 450-477.

Becker, G.S., 1960, *An Economic Analysis of Fertility*, pp. 209-231 in Universities National Bureau Committee for Economic Research (ed.), Demographic and Economic Change in Developed Countries. Princeton, N.J., Princeton University Press.

Becker, G.S., 1973, A theory of marriage: Part I, *The Journal of Political Economy*, Vol. 81, No. 4, pp. 813-846.

Becker, G.S., 1981, 1994, (1st, 2nd ed.), *A Treatise on the Family*, Harvard University Press.

Becker, G.S. and Lewis, H.G., 1973, On the Interaction between Quantity and Quality of Children, *Journal of Political Economy*, 81: S279-S288.

Bergstrom, T.C., 1997, A Survey of Theories of the Family. In: Rosenzweig, Mark R. & Stark, Oded (eds.), *Handbook of Population and Family Economics*, Elsevier, Amsterdam.

Bergstrom, T. and Lam, D., 1989, The Effects of Cohort Size on Marriage Markets in Twentieth Century Sweden. In: *The Family, the Market and the State in Industrialized Countries*, Oxford University Press, Oxford.

Blank, R., George, C. and London, R., 1994, State Abortion Rates: the Impact of Policy, Provider Availability, Political Climate, Demography and Economics, *working paper* no. 4583 (NBER, Cambridge).

Blau, D.M. and Robins, P.K., 1989, Fertility, Employment, and Child-Care Costs, *Demography*, 26 (2), 287-299.

Bloemen, H. and Kalwij, A., 2001, Female Labor Market Transitions and the Timing of Births: A Simultaneous Analysis of the Effects of Schooling, *Labour Economics* (8) 5, pp. 593-620.

Blossfeld, H.P. and Timm, A., (ed.), 2003, *Who Marries Whom? Educational Systems as Marriage Markets in Modern Societies*, Kluwer Academic Publishers.

Blossfeld, H.P. and Huinink, J., 1991, Human Capital Investments or Norms of Role Transition? How Women's Schooling and Career Affect the Process of Family Formation, *The American Journal of Sociology*, Vol. 97, No. 1, pp. 143-168.

Boeri, T., Del Boca, D. and Pissarides, Ch. (eds.), 2005, *Women at Work an Economic Perspective. A Report for the Fondazione Rodolfo Debenedetti*, Oxford, Oxford University Press.

Boulier, B.L. and Rosenzweig, MR., 1984, Schooling, Search, and spouse Selection: Testing Economic Theories of Marriage and Household Behaviour, *The Journal of Political Economy*, Vol. 92, Issue 4, 712-732.

Bratti, M., 2004, Italy: Female Labor Force Participation and Marital Fertility, chapter 5 of this volume.

Brien, M.J. and L.A. Lillard, 1994, Education, Marriage, and First Conception in Malaysia, *The Journal of Human Resources*, 29, 4, pp. 1167-1204.

Browning, M. and M. Ejrnaes, 2002, *Consumption and Children*, working paper no. 06, Centre for Applied Microeconomics, University of Copenhagen.

Cigno, A., 1991, *Economics of the Family*, Oxford, Clarendon Press.

Cigno, A. and Ermisch, J., 1989, A Micro-Economic Analysis of the Timing of Births, *European Economic Review*, 69: 318-328.

De Cooman, E., Ermisch, J. and Joshi, H., 1987, The Next Birth and the Labour Market: A Dynamic Model of Births in England and Wales, *Population Studies*, 41: 237-268.

De la Rica, S. and Iza, A., 2004, Spain: Fixed-term Jobs and the Entry into Marriage and Maternity, chapter 6 of this volume.

Del Boca, D., 2002, The effect of Childcare and Part-time Work on Participation and Fertility of Italian Women, *Journal of Population Economics*, 15: 549-573.

Elbers, C. and Ridder, G. (1982). 'True and Spurious Duration Dependence: The Identifiably of the Proportional Hazard Model', *Review of Economic Studies*, Vol. 49, pp. 403-09.

Elvander, N., 1974, Skattepolitik 1945-1970. En studiei partiers och organisationers funktioner, Stockholm: Rabén och Sjögren.

Ermisch, J.F., 1988, Econometric Analysis of Birth Rate Dynamics in Britain, *Journal of Human Resources* 23: 563-576.

Ermisch, J.F., 1989, Purchased Child Care, Optimal Family Size and Mother's Employment, *Journal of Population Economics*, 2: 79-102.

Ermisch, J.F., 1990, European Women's Employment and Fertility Again, *Journal of Population Economics*, 3: 3-18.

Ermisch, J.F., 1990, Family and Household as Objects *of Political Action,* in: Birg, H. and Mackensen, R. (eds.), *Demografische Wirkungen politischen Handels*, Frankfurt/Main, Campus Verlag.

Ermisch, J., 2003, *An Economic Analysis of the Family*, Princeton University Press.

Esping-Andersen, G., 1999, *Social Foundations of Postindustrial Economics*, Oxford: Oxford University Press.

Esping-Anderson G., 1990, *The Three Worlds of Welfare Capitalism*, Polity Press.

Francesconi, M., 2002, A joint Dynamic Model of Fertility and Work of Married Women, *Journal of Labor Economics*, Vol. 20, No. 2.

Ghysels, J., 2003, *The Work and Care Game: An Empirical Analysis of Household Decision Making in the European Union*, Doctoral Dissertation, Universiteit Antwerpen.

Gourieroux, C. and A. Montfort, 1997, *Simulation-based Econometric Methods*, Core Lecture Series, Oxford: Oxford University Press.

Green, W.H, 2003, (5th ed.), *Econometric Analysis*, Prentice Hall.

Grossbard-Shechtman, S.A., 1984, A Theory of Allocation of Time in Markets for Labor and Marriage, *Economic Journal*, Vol. 94, pp. 863-83.

Grossbard-Shechtman, S.A., (ed.), 2003, *Marriage and the Economy: Theory and Evidence from Advanced Industrial Societies*, New York and Cambridge, Cambridge University Press.

Gustafsson, S.S., 1992, Separate Taxation and Maried Women's Labor supply. A Comparison between West Germany and Sweden, *Journal of Population Economics*, 5: 61-85, pp. 61-85.

Gustafsson, S.S., 1996, Tax Regimes and Labor Market Performance, In: Schmid, G., O'Reilly J. and Schömann K., *International Handbook of Labor Market Policy and Evaluation*, Edgar Elgar, Cheltenham, UK.

Gustafsson, S.S., 2001, Optimal Age at Motherhood: Theoretical and Empirical Considerations on Postponement of Maternity in Europe, *Journal of Population Economics*, 14: 225-247.

Gustafsson, S.S. and Stafford, F., 1994, Three Regimes of Childcare: the United States, the Netherlands and Sweden, *In: Blank, Rebecca (ed.) Social Protection versus Economic Flexibility: Is there a Trade-off?*, Chicago: NBER and Chicago University Press, pp. 333-363.

Gustafsson, S.S. and Wetzels, C., 2000, Optimal Age for First Birth: Germany, Great Britain, the Netherlands and Sweden, in: Gustafsson, S.S. and Meulders, D. (eds.), *Gender and the Labor Market. Econometrics Evidence of Obstacles to Achieving Gender Equality*, London, MacMillan Press Ltd.

Gustafsson, S.S., Kenjoh, E., and Wetzels, C., 2003, Employment Choices and Pay Differences between Nonstandard and Standard Work in Britain, Germany, the Netherlands and Sweden, In: Housenam S. and Osawa M. (ed.), *Nonstandard Work in Developed Economies: Causes and Consequences*, W.E. Upjohn Institute for Employment Research , Kalamazoo, Michigan.

Gustafsson, S.S., and S. Worku., 2004, Education, Assortative Mating and the Duration to Couple Formation and First Birth in Britain and Sweden, Chapter 11 of this Volume.

Harmon, C. and I. Walker, 1995, Estimates of the Economic Return to Schooling for the United Kingdom, *The American Economic Review*, Vol. 85, no. 5, pp. 1278-1286.

Heckman, J.J., Hotz, V.J. and J.R. Walker, 1985, New Evidence on the Timing and Spacing of Births, *American Economic Review*, 75, 179-184.

Heckman, J.J. and B. Singer, 1984, A Method for Minimizing the Impact of Distributional Assumptions in Econometric Models for Duration Data, *Econometrica*, 52, 2: 271-320.

Heckman, J.J. and J.R. Walker, 1990, The Relationship Between Wages and Income and the Timing and Spacing of Births: Evidence from Swedish Longitudinal Data, *Econometrica*, 58, 1411-1441.

Hewlett, S.A., 2002, *Baby Hunger: The New Battle for Motherhood*, Atlantic Books.

Holmlund, H., 2004, Estimating Long Term Consequences of Teenage Childbearing-A Test of the Siblings Approach, Paper presented at the 2004 meeting of the European Society for Population Economics, Bergen Norway.

Honoré, B.E., 1993, Identification Results for Duration Models with Multiple Spells, *Review of Economic Studies*, 60, pp. 241-246.

Hotz, V.J., Klerman, J.A. and Willis, R.J., 1997, The Economics of Fertility in Developed Countries, In: Rozenzweig M.R., and Stark O., (eds.), *Handbook of Population and Family Economics*, Vol. 1A, Amsterdam: Elsevier.

Hotz, V.J. and K.I. Miller, 1988, An Empirical Analysis of Life-Cycle Fertility and Female Labor Supply, *Econometrica*, 56, 91-118.

Huh, K. and R.C. Sickles, 1994, Estimation of the Duration Model by Nonparametric Maximum Likelihood, Maximum Penalized Likelihood, and Probability Simulators, *The Review of Economics and Statistics*, 4, 683-694.

Joshi, H.E., 1990, The Opportunity Cost of Childbearing: An Approach to Estimation Using British Data, *Population Studies*, 44: 41-60.

Joshi, H.E., Paci, P. and Waldfogel, J., 1999, The Wages of Motherhood: Better or Worse?, *Cambridge Journal of Economics* 23: 543-564.

Joshi, H.E. and Davies, H., 2002, Women's Incomes over a Synthetic Lifetime, in: Ruspini, E. and Dale, A. (eds.), *The Gender Dimension of Social Change. The Contributions of Dynamic Research to the Study of Women's Life Courses*, Bristol, Policy Press.

Browning, M., 1992, Children and Household Economic Behavior, *Journal of Economic Literature*, 30: 1434-1475.

Kalwij, A, 1999, *Household Consumption, Female Employment and Fertility Decisions*, Ph.D. Dissertation, CentER for Economic Research, Tilburg University.

Kalwij, A., 2000, The Effects of Female Employment Status on the Presence and Number of Children, *Journal of Population Economics*, 13, pp. 221-239

Kalwij, A., 2003, Female Employment and Fertility Decisions: an Analysis of the Effects of Household Financial Wealth, *Applied Economics Quarterly*, Volume 49, Issue 3, pp. 231-252

Kalwij A., 2004, Consumption and Income Around the Time of Births in the Netherlands, chapter 8 of this volume.

Kantorova, V., 2004, Education and Entry into Motherhood in the Czech Republic During State-Socialism and the Transition Period 1970-1997, chapter 10 of this volume.

Kreyenfeld, M., 2004, Family Formation in East and West Germany Before and After Unification, chapter 9 of this volume.

Lancaster, T., 1990, *The Econometric Analysis of Transition Data*, Cambridge University Press.

Lam, D., 1988, Marriage Markets and Assortative Mating with Household Public Goods, *Journal of Human Resources*, 23: 462-487.

Lillard, L., 1993, Simultaneous Equations for Hazards: Marriage Duration and Fertility Timing, *Journal of Econometrics*, 56, 189-217.

Malthus, T.R., 1798, *An Essay on Population*, Everyman's library, London.

Maynard, R. and A. Rangarajan, 1994, Contraceptive Use and Repeat Pregnancies Among Welfare Dependent Mothers. *Family Planning Perspectives* 26: 198-205.

Merrigan, P. and Y. St.-Pierre, 1998, An econometric and Neoclassical Analysis of the Timing and Spacing of Births in Canada from 1950 to 1990, *Journal of Population Economics*, 11, 29-52.

Mincer, J., 1963, Market Prices, Opportunity Costs and Income Effects, In: Chirst C. et al. (ed.), *Measurement in Economics: Studies in Mathematical Economics in Honour of Yehuda Grunfeld*, Stanford University press, Standford.

Mincer, J., 1974, *Schooling, Experience and Earnings*, New York: Columbia University Press.

Moffitt, R.A., 1984, Profiles of Fertility, Labor Supply, and Wages of Married Women: A Complete Life-Cycle Model, *Review of Economic Studies*, 51 (2), 263-278.

Naz, G., Nilsen, O.A, and Vagstad, S., 2004, Education and Completed Fertility in Norway, chapter 12 of this volume.

Newman, J.L., 1983, Economic Analyses of the Spacing of Births, *The American Economic Review*, Vol. 73, No. 2, pp. 33-37.

Newman, J.L. and C.E. McCulloch, 1984, A Hazard Rate Approach to the Timing of Births, *Econometrica*, 52, 939-961.

O'Donogue, C. and O'Shea, E., 2004, Explaining the Fertility Decline in Ireland, chapter 4 of this volume.

Ono, H., 2002, Women's Economic Standing, Marriage Timing and Cross-National Contexts of Gender: The Case of Japan, US and Sweden, *Working Paper*, University of Michigan, Ann Arbor, USA.

Plug, E. and W. Vijverberg, 2003, Schooling Family Background and Adoption: Is it Nature or is it Nurture? *Journal of Political Economy*, 111, 611-641.

Rosenzweig, M. and Wolpin, K., 1980a, Testing the Quantity–Quality Fertility Model: the use of Twins as a Natural Experiment, *Econometrica*, 45:1065-1015.

Sainsbury, D., (ed.) 1994, *Gendering Welfare States*, London: Sage Publications.

Schettktat, R., 1987, *Erwerbsbeteiligung und Politik-Theoretische und Empirische Analyse von Determinanten und Dynamic des Arbeitsangebots in Schweden und der Bundesrepublik Deutschland*, Edition Sigma, Berlin.

Schultz, T.P., 1985, Changing World Prices, Women's Wages and the Fertility Transition: Sweden 1860-1910, *Journal of Political Economy*, 93: 1126-1154.

Skirbekk, V., Kohler, H.P, and A. Prskawetz, The Marginal Effect of School Leaving Age on Demographic Events. A Contribution to the Discussion on Causality, Chapter 3 of this volume.

Sommestad, L., 1992, *Fraan Mejerska till Mejerist*, Academic Dissertation, Department of History, University of Uppsala, Sweden.

Symeonidou, H. and Mitsopoulpos, G.P., 2003, The Timing of the First, Second and Third Childbirths in Greece, *Working paper*, National Centre for Social Research (EKKE), Athens.

Van den Berg, G.J., 1997, Association Measures for Durations in Bivariate Hazard Rate Model, *Journal of Econometrics*, Vol.79 (2), 221-245.

Van den Berg, G.J., 2001, 'Duration models: Specification, Identification, and Multiple Durations'. In: Heckman, J.J., Leamer, E. (eds.), *Handbook of Econometrics*, Vol. V. North-Holland, Amsterdam.

Van der Klaauw, W., 1996, Female Labor Supply and Marital Status Decisions: A Life Cycle Model, *Review of Economic Studies*, 63:199-235.

Wetzels, C. (diss.), 1999, 2001, *Squeezing Birth into Working Life: Household Panel Data Analyses Comparing Germany, Great Britain, Sweden and the Netherlands*, Aldershot, Ashgate Publishing Ltd.

Willis, R.J., 1973, A new Approach to the Economic Theory of Fertility Behaviour, *Journal of Political Economy*, March/April, Part 2, S14-S64.

Wolpin, K., 1984, An Estimable Dynamic Stochastic Model of Fertility and Child Mortality, *Journal of Political Economy*, 92:852-874.

Chapter 3

THE MARGINAL EFFECT OF SCHOOL LEAVING AGE ON DEMOGRAPHIC EVENTS. A CONTRIBUTION TO THE DISCUSSION ON CAUSALITY

VEGARD SKIRBEKK, HANS-PETER KOHLER AND ALEXIA PRSKAWETZ

1. INTRODUCTION

The age at first birth has increased in Sweden from 24.4 (1975) to 27.9 (2000) years (Council of Europe 2001). This trend has been shared with many other European and developed countries (Council of Europe 2001). In Norway, for instance, the mean age at first birth increased from 25.6 (1990) to 26.9 (2000), while in Denmark, women's age at first birth increased from 26.9 (1960) to 29.7 (2000).

The increases in women's age at first birth took place parallel to the expansion of education that resulted in young adults, and in particular women, spending more time in the school or university system and graduating at older ages. For example, the average duration of schooling, including primary, secondary and tertiary education, for Swedish women aged 25 and older increased during 1975 to 2000 by almost 3 years (Skirbekk et al. 2004). This phenomenon and its potential relation to fertility and fertility-related behaviors in early adulthood inspired considerable research interest, including many analyses about the effect of increased education on the timing and quantum of fertility and marriage.

Earlier investigations typically compare individuals with different educational attainment. This means that the individuals compared do not only differ in terms of the school leaving age, but also with other characteristics associated with different educational attainment (such as preferences, abilities and wealth) that are likely to influence fertility patterns irrespective of the school leaving age.

In the current study we utilize an exogenously determined change in the age at graduation from compulsory school[1] across birth months, and examine the impact from this variation on the timing of fertility and cumulated fertility. This approach allows us to overcome the problem of unobserved heterogeneity (i.e. the fact that education and fertility decisions are caused by common unobserved individual

Siv Gustafsson and Adriaan Kalwij (eds.), Education and Postponement of Maternity, 65–85.

characteristics) that has hampered previous attempts to measure the effects of variations in the school leaving age on fertility.

Exploiting the fact that an individual's birth month determines the age when graduating from compulsory schooling, our findings suggest an 11 months difference in the school leaving age does have a strong impact on the timing of first and second child, but is not related to the cumulated fertility.

2. SURVEY OF THEORY AND RESEARCH FINDINGS ON EDUCATION AND FERTILITY

Age at finishing school is an important determinant for the age at first child and other demographic events in early adulthood, as most women do not have children while being enrolled in education (Blossfeld and Huinink 1991). An important reason why individuals tend to finish education before entering parenthood is that young adults sequence their events in adulthood according to rigid scripts, where having completed educational careers typically precedes childbearing (Corijn 1996; Marini 1984).

Kohler et al. (2002) argue that the fertility postponement of the more educated is caused both by higher socio-economic costs of having children as well as social interaction effects that lead to postponement of childbearing. Further, Kohler et al. argue that delayed childbearing is an important causal factor towards reducing completed fertility, an argument which is supported by other studies (Bumpass et al. 1978; Kohler et al. 2001; Morgan and Rindfuss 1999; Rindfuss et al. 1996). Lutz and Goujon (2001), for instance, show that more educated women have lower fertility in most regions of the world, although the negative relation between education and total fertility is stronger in developing countries than in developed countries.

This effect of education on the timing and quantum of fertility is consistent with theoretical predictions. For instance, Becker (1991), Oppenheimer (1988), Heckman and Walker (1990) and Gustafsson (2001), along with many other studies, argue that (a) more schooling increases a woman's opportunity costs of having children, in particular as a result of higher wages for more educated women, and (b) a postponement of childbearing and lower completed fertility constitute a rational response of women (and couples) to these changes in opportunity costs due to increased education. Further, societal norms and individual preferences often imply that women are expected to finish education before establishing their own family, which means that increases in the educational length will delay the onset of childbearing.

In addition to the above factors, the effect of the educational expansion on fertility patterns has been reinforced during the second demographic transition, with increased focus on self-realisation, and a lowered importance of traditional values (van de Kaa 1987; Lesthaege 1998; Lesthaege and Meekers 1986).

3. METHODOLOGICAL CONSIDERATIONS IN STUDIES ON THE RELATION BETWEEN EDUCATION AND FERTILITY

Studies on the effect of the age of exiting education on fertility usually base their analysis on comparisons of the fertility patterns of subgroups of women with different educational degrees. A common problem with most of these studies is that women who differ in terms of educational attainment, also differ with respect to preferences, abilities, family background, wealth levels, and other characteristics associated with school attainment (see for example Barret and Depinet 1991). For example, a woman's educational attainment is likely to affect the marriage partner she will seek (Vandberg 1972), which again influences her fertility behavior (Merrigan and St. Pierre 1998).

Moreover, attending higher education is also likely to affect women's values and attitudes towards childbearing, and education is likely to have also ideational effects on fertility. Finally, societal and cultural change rendering late and low fertility, including childlessness, more acceptable may also affect the fertility patterns of women with high education differently than women with low education.

One attempt to overcome the problem induced by selectivity in abilities and preferences is a study by Kohler et al. (2001). They compare monozygotic (MZ) twins – that is, a pair of individuals that share identical biological endowments as well as the same parental background and related socialization experiences – and analyze the impact of delayed childbearing on completed fertility. The twin experiment allows Kohler et al. to control for unobserved heterogeneity, such as labor market opportunities, preferences, ability, etc., by focusing on the within-MZ twin pair differences in the timing and quantum of fertility. Nevertheless, despite the substantial merits of this twin approach, individuals may differ according to attitudes, values, marriage and labor market experiences that are caused by individual-specific experiences and are not shared by both MZ twins in a pair. For instance, matching in the marriage market, partner characteristics and related aspects of household bargaining can systematically differ even between MZ twins. To the extent that these aspects have an important influence on fertility, within MZ twin studies are not fully able to control for unobserved heterogeneity.

Other econometric approaches to adjust for the endogeneity problems associated with education in analyses of fertility behavior (e.g., Neiss et al. 2002; Retherford and Sewell 1989), often need to rely on strong assumptions in order to identify "causal influences" of education on fertility patterns. From a methodological point of view, therefore, the role of educational attainment as an explanatory variable in models of fertility behavior is highly disputed, and many criticisms of directly including education in the analyses of fertility are related to the heterogeneity of individuals and the endogeneity of education. While some alternative methods have been proposed in the literature to account for this endogeneity problem, the solutions are often not fully satisfactory. In the current study, we therefore propose a simple and intuitive way based on the relation between birth month and school enrollment to study the marginal causal effect of age at finishing compulsory education on the timing of first childbirth. In particular, we are able to establish these causal effects because the school entrance cut off age in combination with a woman's birth month determines her age of entering – and due to a relatively rigid school system – also her age of graduating from compulsory school. This exogenous variation in the age at graduation then avoids the endogeneity and unobserved heterogeneity problems that are typically associated with studies of the effect of variation in the graduation age on fertility.

4. HOW BIRTH MONTH RELATES TO SCHOOLING AND DEMOGRAPHIC OUTCOMES

Much research has been carried out, investigating the role of birth month on various human characteristics and life course events. These include the influence of birth month on the risk of suffering from schizophrenia and the effect on the offspring's sex ratios (Sham et al. 1992; Nonaka et al. 1987). Doblhammer and Vaupel (2001) find a relation between season of birth and mortality, by studying people older than 50 years in Denmark, Austria and Australia. Those born in autumn, both in the Northern and the Southern Hemisphere, were found to live the longest and the spring born the shortest. The strongest impact was observed in Austria, where autumn borns outlived spring borns by 0.6 years. In Denmark and Australia, longevity differences between spring and autumn borns amounted to 0.3 and 0.35 years, respectively.

Angrist and Krueger (1991) investigated how individuals' birth quarter affects their schooling and earnings. They show among American men from the 1920-1949 cohorts that those born in the first quarter of the year obtain less education and earn less than those born in the three other quarters. The authors attribute these small, but statistically significant differences to compulsory schooling laws that allow individuals to drop out from school after a given age. The drop out age is reached after a lower schooling amount for those born early in the year; which has the effect that those born in the first months of the year receive less schooling[2].

Angrist and Krueger's study provoked several follow-up papers that point to various weaknesses in their analysis. Bound and Jaeger (1996) show that the link between season of birth and educational/labor market success can at least partially be explained by other factors than schooling regulations. Studying American white male citizens born 1840-75, a period long before compulsory schooling laws came in effect, they find summer borns had a higher income than those born in the winter season. They also show that the relation between education and birth quarter has decreased gradually for the 1920-1940 birth cohorts in the US, but that the relation between private income and birth quarter was strengthened in the same period, implying that the birth quarter effect is caused by an unobserved factor, rather than compulsory schooling laws.

Another weakness with the Angrist and Krueger study, which utilizes the fact that those born early in the year earn less since they can drop out after a shorter schooling period, is that it may only be valid for a small group of selected individuals who would like to drop out of school at an age as young as they are allowed to. Angrist and Krueger (1991, p. 992) suggest that compulsory schooling laws made a difference for the schooling length for about 10% of the students in 1980. Since the majority of students, regardless of birth quarter, however, do not drop out of school at the youngest age allowed, the compulsory schooling laws are irrelevant to the majority's educational attainment and wage levels.

Our analyses of the marginal effect of school leaving age on the timing and quantum of fertility have been inspired by the above approach of using the birth month as a "natural experiment" that determines the age at entering and graduating from compulsory school. Moreover, many aspects of the Swedish school system make Sweden even more suitable for these analyses than the U.S.

A normal Swedish school year starts at the end of August and lasts until the beginning of June the next year. Compulsory school starts for almost all children in the year they turn 7, lasts for nine years and is finished in June the calendar year the pupils turn 16 (or $n+9$ if they started at the age of n). Moreover, in contrast to the U.S., the Swedish school system does not allow individuals to drop out after a certain age, but requires completion of a compulsory school length. The Swedish school system therefore requires children to stay in school until a certain *grade* is reached, in contrast to the compulsory school attendance laws in the US, which permit children to exit school only when a certain *age* is reached. Graduation from compulsory school thus occurs when children are 15.5 to 16.5 years old. Graduation at younger ages is virtually impossible (exceptions are the very few cases of early enrollment), and graduation at older ages is rare since very few students repeat classes and/or enter school at a later age. Upon completing compulsory school after the 9th grade, pupils can choose whether they would like to go on to a vocational or academic program in upper secondary school, which normally lasts three years.

When compulsory education is completed, children born in January will be 11 months older than children born in the preceding December. This differential age at graduation thus provides exogenous variation to identify the effect of educational enrollment on demographic behaviors because those born during December and the following January live their childhood and early adulthood during virtually the same time period. Any period influences on education or fertility, such as variation in the returns to education, economic up- or downswings, or changes in family policy, affect these individuals almost identically. Moreover, at graduation from compulsory education, women born in December and January differ in their age, but not in the level of human capital: in both cases, the women have completed 9th grade education and face decisions about further options within the educational system or entering vocational training. Since many women extend schooling beyond 9th grade, and there is little or no possibility to "catch-up" within the school system, the difference in the age at graduation also extends to the age at graduation from upper secondary school, 12th grade, and potentially also to the age at graduation from post-secondary schooling among women who continue education. For women who pursue higher education, therefore, the month of birth is likely to have an effect on the age at graduation substantially beyond the 9th grade.

5. DATA DESCRIPTION

Our data is collected from Swedish administrative registers.[3] Our original dataset consists of 891,066 women born 1946-62, who are observed until the end of 1999. The data extracted from the Swedish registration system provides detailed individual-level information for these cohorts on fertility, marriage and education that is registered on a monthly basis. Women from these cohorts have finished most of their childbearing by the end of the observation period, and the sample is therefore well suited for investigations relating to the timing of fertility.

In our analyses, we do not consider immigrants, which reduces the number of individuals in the dataset by 27,761 individuals. We also drop one woman who is reported to have her first child in 1897, although she was born in 1960. This leaves the dataset with 863,304 women.

The dataset includes information on dates of various demographic events (child birth, marriage, divorce, death, emigration and immigration) and economic variables (income, public study benefits). For our analysis we used the following set of variables: date of woman's birth and age when she received a child (in months), as well as information on educational attainment. The fertility by parity is reported in Table 3-1 for four groups of cohorts: 1946-1949, 1950-1954, 1955-1958 and 1959-1962. As can be seen from the table, the share of childless women has increased for the younger cohorts. Further, the share of women with 1 or 2 children have declined as well for women born 1955-1958 and 1959-1962, although this may be due to right-censoring at the end of the observation period.

Table 3-1. Women by Child Parity, 1946-1962 Cohorts

	1946-1949	1950-1954	1955-1958	1959-1962
0	12.97%	14.25%	15.48%	17.44%
1	15.79%	14.96%	13.53%	13.28%
2	44.06%	41.84%	40.07%	40.74%
3	20.47%	21.34%	22.56%	21.12%
4	5.07%	5.66%	6.18%	5.62%
5+	1.64%	1.95%	2.18%	1.8%

Source: Swedish Administrative Registers, Own Calculations.

To test our hypothesis on the marginal effect of school leaving age on the timing of first birth, we utilize the cut off date (January 1st) that determines the year of school entrance age in the Swedish school system. In particular, children in Sweden enter school in the calendar year they turn 7 years old, with school beginning in August of that year.[4] The effect of the Swedish cut off date therefore is that in each grade – and in particular also at the time of school graduation from compulsory school – children born in January will be 11 months older than children born in December. This age difference will also be propagated to those who pursue higher secondary education after compulsory schooling since the secondary school system provides few opportunities to "catch up" the age difference resulting from the enrollment cut-off date.

6. DESCRIPTIVE RESULTS

6.1 Age at first birth

The age at first birth has increased from about 23.8 years to 26.3 years for the birth cohorts 1946 to 1962. The youngest cohorts, in particular those born 1959-62, are right censored at the age of 37, and further childbearing in these cohorts is likely to result in an even higher mean age at first births in the youngest cohorts. Moreover, in addition to this general trend towards delayed childbearing across cohorts, there exists a systematic pattern in the timing of first births across birth months. As seen from Figures 3-1 and 3-2, the woman's age at first childbirth is higher for those born early in the year relative to those born late in the year. In spite of the *increase* in the age at first birth for subsequent cohorts, we observe a *decrease* in the age at birth within each cohort. The largest difference between any two successive calendar months in the mean age at first birth is 4.9 months and occurs between women born in December and women born in the following January (see also Skirbekk et al. 2004). That is, 4.9/11 = 45% of the increase in the age at graduation from school that occurs between individuals who are of virtually the same age but belong to different school cohorts is not caught up in early adulthood and still reflected in the age at first birth. This effect is striking because the first birth occurs on average 9 years after graduating from compulsory school and 5.5 years after graduating from highest education attained.

Regression results for the effect of birth month on the age at first birth are given in Table 3-2. These regressions also include birth year dummies to control for the secular increase in the age at first birth across cohorts. The dummies for different birth months (January is the reference category) reveal the effect of school enrollment and graduation on the timing of fertility. In particular, the analyses reveal a difference in the age at first birth between January and December borns of the *same* birth cohort (and hence also school cohort) of 3.1 months. Combining the coefficients of the birth year and birth month dummies further reveals that the biggest difference between two consecutive birth months occurs – as already indicated above – between women born in December and women born in the following January, that is, between women who are basically of the same age but belong to different birth cohorts. For instance, the difference in the timing of first birth between women born in December 1946 and January 1947 is estimated in Table 3-2 as 3.09 + 1.16 = 4.25 months, and the difference in the timing of first birth between women born in December 1955 and January 1956 is estimated as 3.09 + 2.77 = 5.86 months.

Figure 3-1. Woman's Birth Month and Age at Birth of First Child, By Cohort

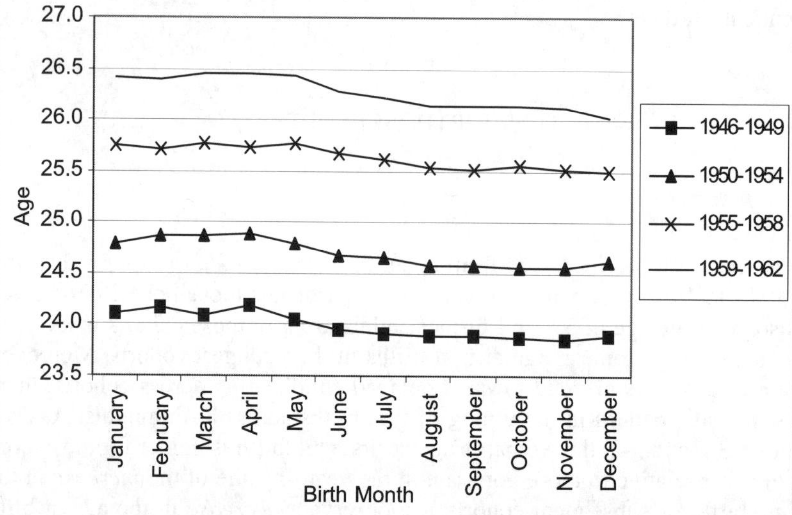

Source: Swedish Administrative Registers, Statistics Sweden

Figure 3-2. Woman's Age at First Childbirth Relative to December Borns

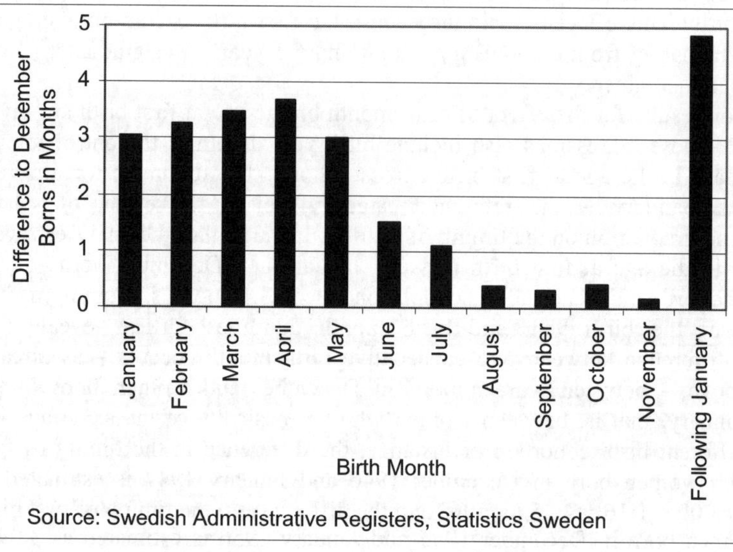

Source: Swedish Administrative Registers, Statistics Sweden

Table 3-2. Dependent Variable: Mother's Age at First Birth (Measured in Months, Reference Category: Born January 1946)

		Coefficient	*Std. Dev.*
Constant		287.84	*0.35* **
Mother's Birth Month	February	0.20	*0.35*
	March	0.34	*0.33*
	April	0.54	*0.33*
	May	-0.14	*0.33*
	June	-1.60	*0.34* **
	July	-2.01	*0.34* **
	August	-2.75	*0.34* **
	September	-2.85	*0.34* **
	October	-2.85	*0.35* **
	November	-3.11	*0.35* **
	December	-3.09	*0.35* **
Mother's Birth Year	1947	1.16	*0.37* **
	1948	1.58	*0.37* **
	1949	3.70	*0.38* **
	1950	6.05	*0.38* **
	1951	8.33	*0.39* **
	1952	10.03	*0.39* **
	1953	11.99	*0.39* **
	1954	14.36	*0.39* **
	1955	16.86	*0.39* **
	1956	19.63	*0.39* **
	1957	22.91	*0.39* **
	1958	25.67	*0.39* **
	1959	28.11	*0.40* **
	1960	28.60	*0.40* **
	1961	29.57	*0.40* **
	1962	28.58	*0.40* **
N = 721861	R^2 (adjusted) = 0.0178		

*** = Significant at $p < 0.01$ Level, ** = Significant at $p < 0.5$ Level, * = Significant at $p < 0.1$ Level

This evidence supports our hypothesis that those who are born early in the year are older when they have children than those born late in the year since they graduate from school at a higher age. In particular the sharp age difference between those who are born in December and those who are born in the following January implies a strong effect of the school entrance cut off date laws and the resulting variation in the age at entering and graduating from compulsory school on the timing of first births. Though the birth date of these women differs only by one month, the school entrance cut off date implies that they belong to two different school cohorts and that their age at finishing compulsory – and potentially also upper secondary and tertiary – education differs by 11 months. An important conclusion from these results therefore points towards the additional importance of the *duration* since leaving school, rather than biological age alone, in determining the timing of demographic events in early adulthood.

In addition (as observed in Figures 3-1, 3-2, and Table 3-2) the largest difference *within* every birth cohort is found between April and November borns. A plausible reason for this is that women from the higher social classes, who are typically older when they have children, tend to be born in spring; while women born in autumn tend to come from the lower social classes.[5] Consequently, the net effect of the school entrance cut off date would be a decline in the age at first birth for women born later in the year, but with a peak in spring and a through in autumn. Therefore, the seasonality difference in social class, which we can not fully capture with the available control variables, would lead to a sharp decrease in the first birth ages in the summer months.

Differences in human capital attainment of those born in different months of the year could influence the timing of demographic events, as a higher educational attainment implies a later graduation age. In order to investigate this hypothesis, we regress the effect of the birth month on educational level. These analyses show a weak, but statistically significant association between birth months and the probability of completing a tertiary education (Table 3-3). On average, those who are born in the first month of the year attain about 1/12 of a school year more education than those born in December.

This effect of birth month on educational attainment is likely to be due to the *relative class age* effect: Those who are oldest in class are more self-confident, resulting in an increased probability of attaining higher education (see for example Plug 2001).

Table 3-3. Probability of Attaining Any Tertiary Education for Women. Logistic Regression Results (Odds Ratio)

		Any Tertiary Education
Mother's Birth Month	January	1.020 *
	February	1.053 ***
	March	1.046 ***
	April	1.057 ***
	May	1.043 ***
	June	1
	July	0.978 **
	August	0.944 ***
	September	0.969 ***
	October	0.960 ***
	November	0.953 ***
	December	0.953 ***
Mother's Birth Year	1946	1
	1947	1.084 ***
	1948	1.148 ***
	1949	1.255 ***
	1950	1.306 ***
	1951	1.320 ***
	1952	1.359 ***
	1953	1.352 ***
	1954	1.361 ***
	1955	1.387 ***
	1956	1.344 ***
	1957	1.348 ***
	1958	1.326 ***
	1959	1.271 ***
	1960	1.253 ***
	1961	1.253 ***
	1962	1.209 ***

*** = Significant at $p < 0.01$ Level, ** = Significant at $p < 0.5$ Level, * = Significant at $p < 0.1$ Level

In order to control for the potential effect of higher educational attainment of those born early in the year on the above findings, we also disaggregate our sample according to educational attainment (Figure 3-3). As observed from this figure, the effect of the birth date remains: even within each educational category, women who are born in the first months of the year are older when they have their children than those who are born later in the year.

Figure 3-3. Woman's Birth Month and Age at First Child, by Educational Level

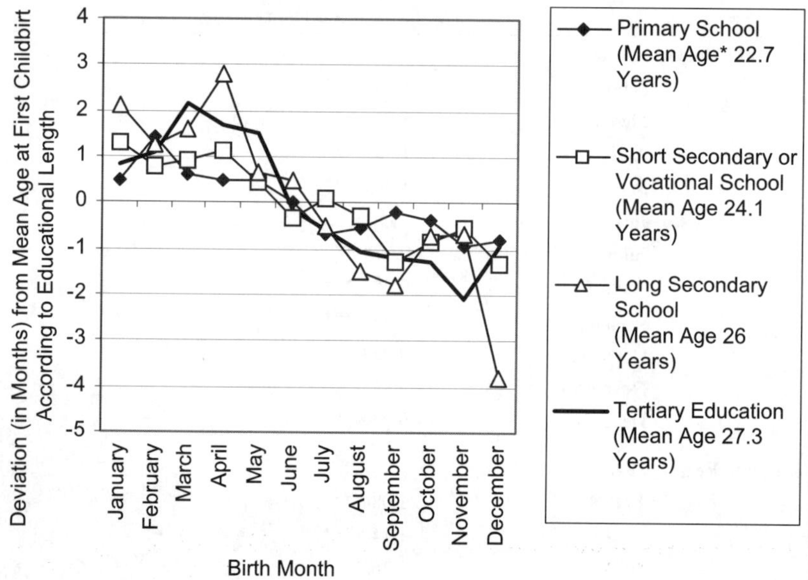

* The term "Mean Age" refers to average age at first birth for women by educational level.

Source: Swedish administrative registers, Statistics Sweden

Moreover, the impact of birth month tends to be even stronger for higher levels of education: the difference between January-December borns is greater for women with long secondary schooling as compared to those with short secondary school, and greater for those with short secondary school relative to those with primary school. One potential reason for this effect is the fact that the duration between school leaving age and demographic events is shorter for those with an older school leaving age. Consequently there is less time left for an attenuation of the impact of the higher graduation age for those born early in the year on ages at experiencing demographic events in early adulthood.

Although the timing of demographic events for tertiary educated women (short college, bachelor and postgraduate degrees) still supports the cut off date hypothesis – January borns are older than December borns – this difference seems to be of a smaller magnitude than those for women with secondary education, though university educated are older when they graduate. However, tertiary schooling comprise a large variety of studies with more variation in the graduation age which is likely to decrease the effect of the school entrance cut off date, in contrast to primary and secondary education. Further, women with tertiary education, unlike those with shorter education, usually study together with individuals from different age groups, and not only with individuals born in their own calendar year. This means that the social influence will come from several age groups, and not just individuals born in the same year, which explains the weakening of the school entrance cut off date effect for the university educated relative to secondary graduates.

6.2 Age at second birth

Similar to the age at first birth, the age at second birth has increased over the period studied (Figure 3-4 and 3-5). For the cohorts born from 1946 to 1962, the age at second birth has increased from 27.2 years to 29 years. Similar to the findings of the first birth, the effect of being born later in the year – and having a younger school leaving age – is a younger age at second birth. Results from a regression analysis of the impact of birth month on the age at second childbirth is given in Table 3-4. The regression includes, as in our previous analyses, dummies for birth month and birth year, where the latter are included to adjust for the trend of higher childbearing ages.

Figure 3-4. Woman's Birth Month and Age at Birth of Second Child, By Cohort

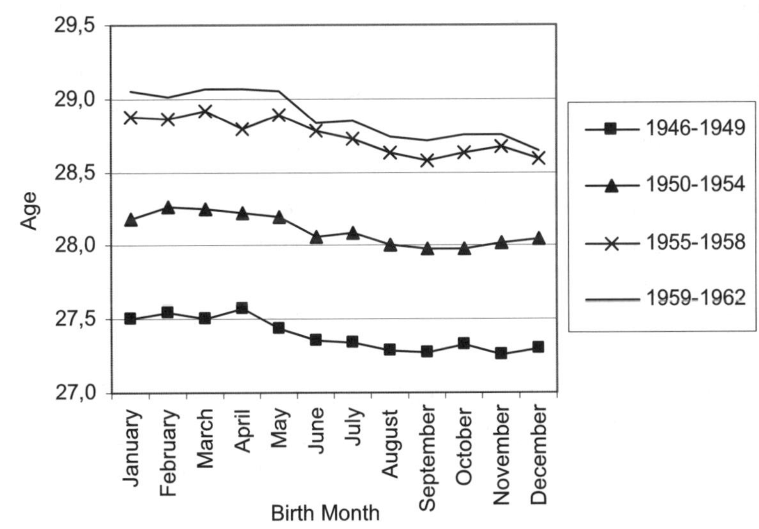

Source: Swedish Administrative Registers, Statistics Sweden

Table 3-4. Dependent Variable: Mother's Age at First Birth (Measured in Months, Reference Category: Born January 1946). All Women who Had a Second Child

		Coefficient	*Std. Dev.*
Constant		327.44	*0.36* ***
Mother's Birth Month	February	0.20	*0.35*
	March	0.43	*0.34*
	April	0.18	*0.34*
	May	-0.15	*0.34*
	June	-1.67	*0.35* ***
	July	-1.77	*0.35* ***
	August	-2.80	*0.35* ***
	September	-3.09	*0.35* ***
	October	-2.73	*0.36* ***
	November	-2.67	*0.36* ***
	December	-2.97	*0.36* ***
Mother's Birth Year	1947	2.29	*0.38* ***
	1948	3.48	*0.38* ***
	1949	5.84	*0.39* ***
	1950	7.41	*0.39* ***
	1951	10.10	*0.40* ***
	1952	11.52	*0.40* ***
	1953	13.17	*0.40* ***
	1954	14.88	*0.40* ***
	1955	16.74	*0.40* ***
	1956	18.01	*0.40* ***
	1957	20.15	*0.40* ***
	1958	20.94	*0.40* ***
	1959	22.14	*0.40* ***
	1960	20.97	*0.41* ***
	1961	20.45	*0.41* ***
	1962	18.52	*0.41* ***
N= 601684	R^2 (adjusted)=0.0304		

*** = Significant at p < 0.01 Level, ** = Significant at p < 0.5 Level, * = Significant at p < 0.1 Level

Figure 3-5. Woman's Age at Second Childbirth, Difference to December Borns in Months

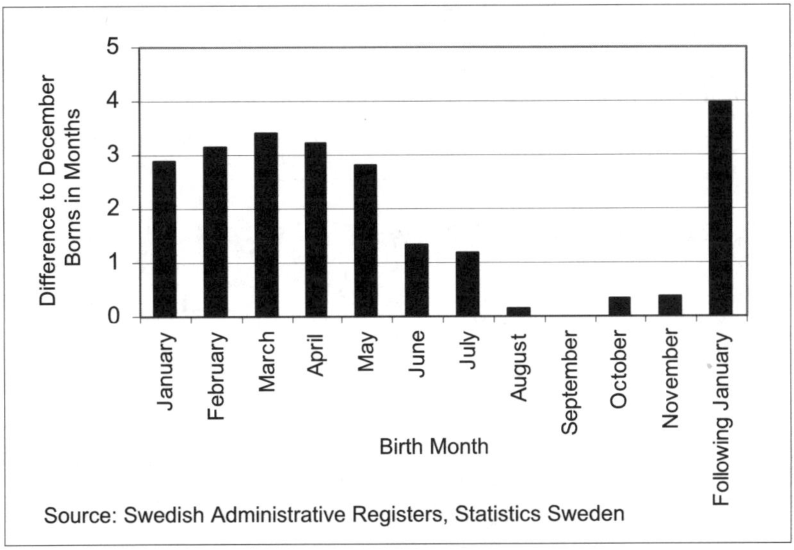

The pattern of the age at second birth is very similar to the one found for the age at first birth. Women born in January have their second child when they are 3 months older than those born in December the same calendar year. The largest difference between any two subsequent birth months is also found between those born in December and the following January, where January borns are 4 months older (Figure 3-5).

Our results for second births therefore show that the effect of birth month and school enrollment, resulting from the January 1st cut-off date for school enrollment in Sweden, has remarkably persistent effects that affect not only the timing of the first, but also the timing of the second births. While the effect is somewhat weaker at the second birth, which is not surprising given that second births occur at an older age, the effect continues to be remarkably strong: 4/11 = 36% of the age-difference at graduation from compulsory school is perpetuated to the age at second birth.

In addition, as shown in Figure 3-6, there is no clear relationship between age at school exit (mother's birth month) and the *duration* between first and second child. The duration from first to second childbirth is thus relatively independent from the mother's month of birth: A later initiation of childbearing translates into a later timing of subsequent births. Put differently, our results lend evidence to the hypothesis that Swedish women follow tight demographic scripts in terms of sequencing of first and second births in relation to the age at finishing compulsory – and potentially also upper secondary and tertiary – education.

There is, however, a trend towards a shorter duration between first and second child for younger cohorts, which can be attributed to the "speed premium" policy[6] that awards financial incentives for relatively short inter-birth intervals, and right censoring of the younger cohorts, as some women are likely to have had a second child after the end of the observation period. This trend, however, does not influence the within-year differences in the timing of births.

Figure 3-6. Duration from Birth of First to Second Child

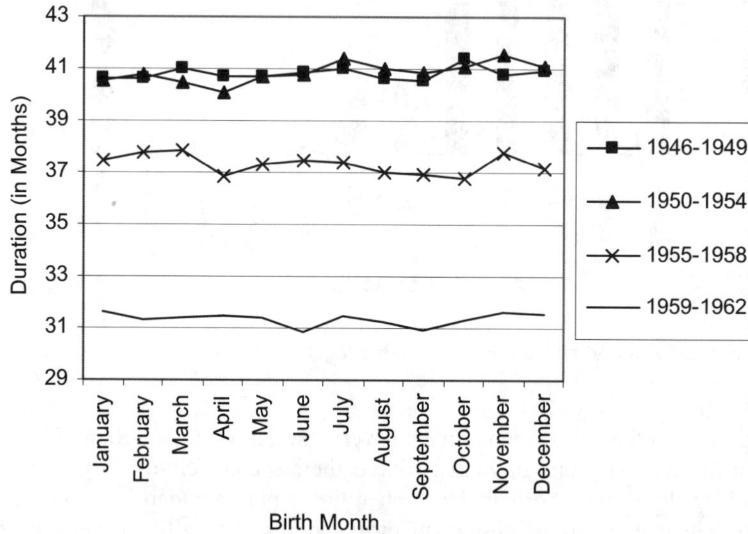

Source: Swedish Personal Registry, Own Calculations

6.3 Completed fertility

The relation between birth month and women's completed fertility is given in Figure 3-7 and 3-8. These figures show a relatively stable pattern of children within cohorts, which suggests that birth month and age at school graduation do not have strong effects on completed (or almost completed) fertility. Hence, the effect of birth month and age at school graduation affects primarily the timing, but not the quantum, of fertility. In addition, there is also quite a stable relation in the birth month pattern across different cohorts, with the exception occurring in the last months of the youngest cohorts. This is likely due to censoring, since the youngest cohorts in the dataset have not ended their reproductive career by the end of our observation period (December born women of the 1962 cohort have just turned 37 at the end of the observation period on Dec 31, 1999). Therefore, the lower fertility for the 1959-1962 cohorts is at least partially likely to be due to right-censoring. In

Figure 3-8 we eliminate this effect of right-censoring by studying fertility only up to age 37, that is, up to an age that is observed for all cohorts in our data, and we see that all birth month effects then disappear.

Figure 3-7. Cumulated Fertility at The End of The Observational Period (31.12.1999)

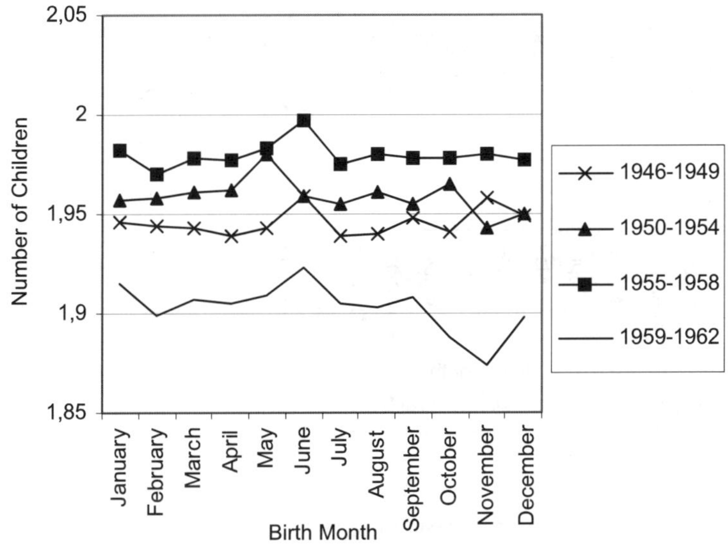

Source: Swedish Administrative Registers, Statistics Sweden

In summary, we conclude based on the above descriptive analyses that completed fertility is not related to the month of birth. In contrast to the timing of the first and second birth, where our analyses demonstrate clear and strong effects due to birth month and school enrollment, the quantum of childbearing (completed fertility) is not sensitive to birth month and age at graduation from compulsory education.

Figure 3-8. Cumulated Fertility at Age 37

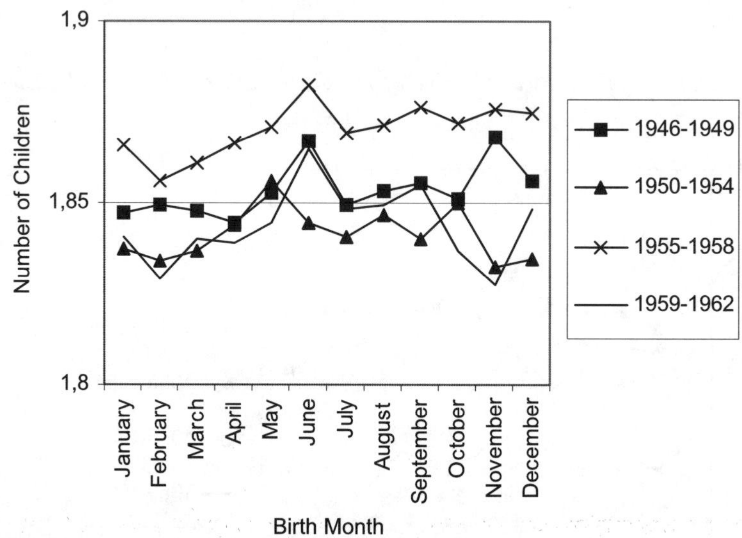

Source: Swedish Administrative Registers, Statistics Sweden

7. CONCLUSION

In this chapter we analyze the effect of birth month on fertility, utilizing the fact that Swedish school enrollment regulations imply a variation in the age at entering and graduating from compulsory education that varies across birth months, with the biggest age difference in school graduation occurring between women born in December and women born in the subsequent January. Our analyses find that a 11 months difference in the age of leaving compulsory education between women born in December and the following January causes a difference of 4.9 months in the age at first birth and of 4 months in the age at age at second birth.

The main advantage of our approach based on birth month is that it overcomes many of the problems that have hampered earlier studies on the relation between education and timing or quantum of fertility. Consistent with earlier investigations, our analyses find that an older age at graduation from compulsory school translates into a later timing of fertility. In contrast to earlier studies, however, we do not find that a higher age at entrance into motherhood results in a lower fertility outcome.

In summary, this finding is important because it demonstrates the causal effects of the age at graduation from compulsory school on the timing of demographic events in early and late adulthood. Our findings clearly show that birth month, in combination with the school entrance cut off date, has important causal effects on the timing of first and second births, without affecting the quantum of fertility. Similar effects have also been shown with respect to the timing of marriage (Skirbekk et al. 2004). A striking aspect of these results is that a one-month difference in the month of birth affects the age of graduation from compulsory school by 11 months, and that this affects the timing of demographic events, which follow several years after compulsory education. For example, the first birth occurs on average 8 to 10 years after the graduation from compulsory schooling after the 9th grade, and the second birth occurs on average about 10-12 years after graduation from compulsory school.

The strong impact of the graduation age on the timing of first and second childbirth also suggests that individuals space and sequence events in adulthood according to relatively rigid schemes. In this context, graduation from compulsory school – and potentially also upper secondary or tertiary education – is an important event that usually precedes family formation. Moreover, marginal variations in the timing of school graduation have strong causal effects on the timing of fertility that extend many years after completing education.

In addition to identifying this important influence of birth month and age at graduation, our results also emphasize the importance of social age that is defined as the mean age of a woman's school cohort. In particular, our analyses suggest that individuals tend to experience demographic events at the same time as those with a similar social age represented by their peers in the school cohort, rather than in synchronization with persons who are of the same biological age, and women who are born early or late in a calendar year adjust their timing of fertility ages towards the mean age of their school cohort (for further discussions, see Skirbekk et al. 2004).

ACKNOWLEDGEMENTS

The authors would like to thank Gunnar Andersson, Marilyn Brandl, Gabriele Doblhammer-Reiter, Jan Hoem, Birgitta Lidholt, Ingrid Lindskog, Jonathan MacGill, Michaela Kreyenfeld and the Max Planck Institute for Demographic Research. Vegard Skirbekk acknowledges the financial support provided through the European Community's Human Potential Programme under contract HPRN-CT-2001-00234. A companion paper on this research theme has been published in Demography, 2004, vol. 41(3):547-568.

NOTES

[1] We use the terms "school leaving age", "age at graduation", "school exit age" and "school completion" as synonyms that refer to the age at leaving *compulsory school* education, or higher educational levels when stated.

[2] Cut off birth dates in the US differ from the 01.09 to the 01.01, according to State. An overview of American state-specific school cut off dates is found in Angrist and Krueger (1992).

[3] The Swedish data from administrative registers was made available through a cooperation of the Max Planck Institute for Demographic Research, Rostock and Statistics Sweden, Stockholm.

[4] A small proportion of the pupils enter school at another age than when they turn 7. More than 97% for all 7 or 8 year olds are in school, for the cohorts we are looking at, and this is usually either when children start school at the age of six or when they delay school entrance to the year they turn eight. The proportion of all female pupils who entered school at the age of six, constitutes 1.6-2 % of all

six year old females in 1960, 1963, 1966 and 1969, which are the years where there are data available (Statistisk Tidsskrift 1962 and Statistiska Meddelanden 1964, 1968, 1970). The percentage who first started going to school at the age of eight, is not explicitly given, although the differences between the share of the 7 year old population in comparison to the 8 year old female population is small, indicating that very few postponed school entrance. The population share of the 8 year olds in school is only up to 2.4 percentage points higher than that of 7 year olds. The birth month of the individuals who pre- or postponed school entrance is unknown.

[5] This phenomenon has been reported by Smithers and Coopers (1984) who showed that more non-manual workers were born in spring while more manual workers were born in autumn.

[6] The speed premium refers to Swedish laws that allow parents (typically women) to maintain the income compensation during parental leave if a next child arrives within a fixed period of time. In 1980, this period was set to 24 months while it was extended to 30 months in 1986. For the effect of the speed premium on the timing of demographic events, see Andersson (2002).

REFERENCES

Andersson, G. 2002, Fertility Developments in Norway and Sweden Since the Early 1960s, *Demographic Research*, Vol. 6, No. 4, pp. 65-86.

Angrist, J. and Krueger, A.B. 1991, Does Compulsory School Attendance affect Schooling and Earnings, *Quarterly Journal of Economics*, Vol. CVI, No. 4, pp. 979-1014.

Angrist, J.D. and Krueger, A.B. 1992, The Effect of Age at School Entry on Educational Attainment: An Application of Instrumental Variables With Moments From Two Samples, *Journal of the American Statistical Association*, No. 87, pp. 328-336.

Barrett, G.V. and R.L. Depinet 1991. A Reconsideration of Testing for Competence Rather than for Intelligence, *American Psychologist*, Vol. 46, No. 10, pp. 1012-1024.

Becker, G. 1991, *A Treatise on the Family*. Harvard University Press.

Blossfeld, H.-P. and Huinink, J. 1991, Human Capital Investments or Norms of Role Transition? How Women's Schooling and Career Affect the Process of Family Formation, *American Journal of Sociology*, No. 97, pp. 143-168.

Bound, J. and Jaeger, D. 1996, On the Validity of Season of Birth as an Instrument in Wage Equations: A Comment on Angrist and Krueger's "Does Compulsory School Attendance Affect Schooling and Earnings?", *NBER WP* 5835.

Bumpass, L.L., Rindfuss, R.R. and Janosik, R.B. 1978, Age and Marital Status at First Birth and the Pace of Subsequent Fertility, *Demography*, Vol. 15, No. 1, pp. 75-86.

Council of Europe 2001, *Recent Demographic Developments in Europe*, Council of Europe Press, Strasbourg.

Corijn, M. 1996, *Transition into Adulthood in Flanders. Results From the FFS.* NIDI/CBGS Publications, Den Haag.

Doblhammer, G. and Vaupel, J.W. 2001, Life Span depends on Month of Birth, *Proceedings of the National Academy of Sciences*, Vol. 98, No. 5, pp. 2934-2939.

Gustafsson, S. 2001, Optimal Age at Motherhood. Theoretical and Empirical Considerations on Postponement of Maternity in Europe, *Journal of Population Economics*, No. 14, pp. 225-247.

Heckman, J.J. and Walker, J.R. 1990, The Relationship between Wages and Income and the Timing and Spacing of Births: Evidence From Swedish Longitudinal Data, *Econometrica*, No. 58, pp. 1411-1441.

Kohler, H.P; Skytthe, A. and Christensen, K. 2001, The Age at First Birth and Completed Fertility Reconsidered: Findings from a Sample of Identical Twins, Max Planck Institute for Demographic Research, Working Paper *WP-2001-006*.

Kohler, H.P., Billari, F.B. and Ortega, J.A. 2002, The Emergence of Lowest-Low Fertility in Europe During the 1990s, *Population and Development Review*, Vol. 28, No. 4, pp. 641–680.

Lesthaeghe, R. and Meekers, D. 1986, Value Change and the Dimension of Familism in the European Community, *European Journal of Population*, No. 2, pp. 225-268.

Lesthaeghe, R. 1998, On Theory Development. Application to the Study of Family Formation, *Population and Development Review*, No. 24, pp. 1-14.

Lutz, W. and Goujon, A. 2001, The World's Changing Human Capital Stock: Multi-State Population Projections by Educational Attainment, *Population and Development Review,* Vol. 27, No. 2, pp. 323-339.

Marini, M.M. 1984, The order of Events in the Transition to Adulthood, *Sociology of Education*, 57, pp. 63-84.

Merrigan, P and St. Pierre, Y. 1998, An Econometric and Neo-Classical Analysis of the Timing and Spacing of Births in Canada from 1950 to 1990, *Journal of Population Economics*, 11, pp. 29-51.

Morgan, P.S. and Rindfuss, R.R. 1999, Re-examining the link of Early Childbearing to Marriage and to Subsequent Fertility, *Demography*, Vol. 36, No. 1, pp. 59-76.

Neiss, M., Rowe, D.C. and Rodgers, J.L. 2002, Does Education Mediate the Relationship Between IQ and Age of First Birth? A Behavioral Genetic Analysis, *Journal of Biosocial Science*, 34, pp. 259-275.

Nonaka, K., Nakamura, I., Shimura, M. and Miura, T. 1987, Secondary Sex ratio and the Month of a Mother's birth - a Hypothesis of Sex-Ratio-Decreasing Factors, *Progress in Biometeorology*, 5, pp. 51-60.

Oppenheimer, V.K. 1988, A Theory of Marriage Timing, *American Journal of Sociology*, 94, pp. 563-591.

Plug, E.J.S. 2001, Season of Birth, Schooling and Earnings, *Journal of Genetic Psychology,* 22, pp. 641-660.

Retherford, R.D. and Sewell, W.H. 1989, How Intelligence Affects Fertility, *Intelligence*, 13, pp. 169-185.

Rindfuss, R., Morgan, P. and Offutt, K. 1996, Education and the Changing Age Patterns of American fertility, 1963-1989, *Demography*, 3, pp. 277-290.

Sham, P.C., O'Callaghan, E., Takei, N., Murray, G.K. Hare, E.H. and T.M. Murray 1992, Schizophrenia Following Prenatal Exposure to Influenza Epidemics Between 1930 and 1960, *British Journal of Psychiatry*, 160, pp. 461-466.

Smithers, A.G. and Cooper, H.J. 1984, Social Class and Season of Birth, *Journal of Social Psychology*, 124, pp. 79-84.

Skirbekk, V., Kohler, H.-P. and Prskawetz, A. 2004, Birth Month, School Graduation and the Timing of Births and Marriages, *Demography*, Vol. 41, No. 3.

Statistik Tidsskrift 1962, *Elevernas Ålder Höstterminen 1960 : Age Distribution of Pupils in Different Sections of the Educational System.* Stockholm: Statististics Sweden.

Statistiska Meddelanden 1964, *Elevernas Ålder Höstterminen 1963 : Age Distribution of Pupils.* Stockholm: Statististics Sweden.

Statistiska Meddelanden 1968, *Elevernas Ålder Höstterminen 1966 : Age Distribution of Pupils.* Stockholm: Statististics Sweden.

Statistiska Meddelanden 1970, *Elevernas Ålder Höstterminen 1969 : Age Distribution of Pupils.* Stockholm: Statististics Sweden.

Van de Kaa, D.J. 1987, Europe's Second Demographic Transition, *Population Bulletin,* 42, pp. 389-432.

Vandberg, S.G. 1972, Assortative Mating, or Who Marries Whom?, *Behavior Genetics*, Vol. 2, No. 2-3, pp. 127-157.

Chapter 4

EXPLAINING THE FERTILITY DECLINE IN IRELAND

CATHAL O'DONOGHUE AND EAMON O'SHEA

1. INTRODUCTION

Ireland is a country that has experienced massive economic and social transformations over the last three decades of the twentieth century. During this period the country has moved from a poor agricultural country, with traditional family structures to the Celtic Tiger with the highest growth rates in Europe, an economy where although agriculture is still important, has been superseded by high technology and financial service industries. Family structures also have changed enormously with earlier marriage rates, the legalisation of divorce and of focus here sharply falling birth rates.

Traditionally Ireland has been characterised by a high fertility rate. In 1965, the total fertility rate (TFR), in Ireland was about 4 compared with an EU15 average of about 2.7 (Eurostat, 2002). In the last number of decades, as in most other western countries, the birth rate has fallen in Ireland, so that the TFR by 1995 was 1.82, rising slightly over the remainder of the last decade to 1.98 in 2000. The size of the decline in the TFR over this period was very similar to Southern European countries, but falling however from a higher base. Although Ireland, even after this decline has a high fertility rate compared with other countries in Europe, it's fertility rate is not high compared with "New World" countries such as Australia, the USA, Canada and New Zealand. In this chapter we consider some of the reasons for this decline in fertility in Ireland.

In Table 4.1 we describe some of the main demographic trends in fertility between 1965 and 2000. Part of the reason for the decline in fertility is that people are having smaller families; accounting for less than 43% of births in 1965, first and second births have risen to over 71 per cent in 2000. In 1965 over 40% of births were fourth or later children (in fact one third were fifth order or higher), while by 2000 this accounted only for about 12% of births. As Fahey (2001) acknowledges, this signifies a trend away from a distinctly Irish pattern of low marriage rates and exceptionally high marital fertility. The move away from the large traditional family is also evidenced by the rapid increase in extra-marital births observed in Ireland

Siv Gustafsson and Adriaan Kalwij (eds.), Education and Postponement of Maternity, 87–112.

from about 2% of births in 1970 rising slightly to 5% in 1980. This proportion trebled to 15% in 1990 and doubled to over 30% of total births in 2000. While data on births within cohabiting partnerships is limited, there is some evidence that many of the first births occurring outside of marriage are followed later by the marriage of the parents (see Fahey, 2001).

Figure 4.1 Age-Specific Fertility Rate 1965-94

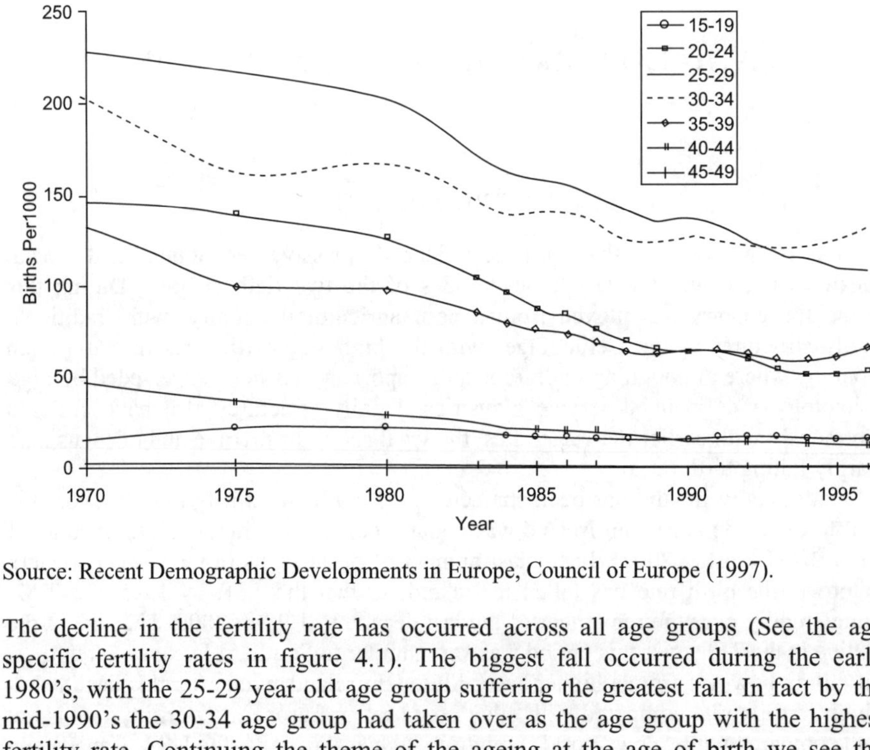

Source: Recent Demographic Developments in Europe, Council of Europe (1997).

The decline in the fertility rate has occurred across all age groups (See the age specific fertility rates in figure 4.1). The biggest fall occurred during the early 1980's, with the 25-29 year old age group suffering the greatest fall. In fact by the mid-1990's the 30-34 age group had taken over as the age group with the highest fertility rate. Continuing the theme of the ageing at the age of birth we see the fertility rate of the 35-39 age-group also passing out that of the 20-24 age group which until 1990 had been higher. The remaining age groups have lower and slightly falling fertility rates, with a slight increase in the under 20 age group due to the rise in unmarried births. The shift in the order of importance of the fertility of different age groups can be seen in the increase in Table 4.1 of the mean age at first birth. Stable at 25.5 until 1985, the mean age at first birth rose by over two years in 2000 to 27.8. Comparing period with cohort effects, we see the earlier decline in mean at first birth to a low of below 25 for the cohort 45-55 before rising for later cohorts. However the rise highlighted by the period effect has been recent and so it has not been captured in the cohort effect yet.

Table 4.1. Period and Cohort Fertility Statistics for Ireland

Period	1965	1970	1975	1980	1985	1990	1995	2000
TFR (Ireland)	4.03	3.93	3.40	3.23	2.47	2.11	1.84	1.98
TFR (EU-15)	2.72	2.38	1.96	1.82	1.60	1.57	1.42	1.47
% of First Order Births	23.5	27.2	30.7	29.2	29.7	33.4	36.4	40.8
% of Second Order Births	19.2	21.5	24.4	24.4	25.9	27.8	30.1	30.1
% of Third Order Births	16.1	16.5	17.3	19.3	18.8	18.6	18.2	17.4
% of Fourth and higher Order Births	41.1	34.8	27.7	27.2	25.6	20.1	15.2	11.7
Births Outside Marriage	2.2	2.7	3.7	5.0	8.5	14.6	22.3	31.2
Mean Age At First Birth			25.5	25.5	26.1	26.6	27.3	27.8
Birth Cohort			1935	1940	1945	1950	1955	1960
Completed Fertility			3.4	3.3	3.3	3.0	2.7	2.4
Mean Age At First Birth				25.3	24.9	24.8	25.1	25.8
% Childless			4.0	5.0	6.0	9.0	13.0	15.0
% With Number of Children: 1			18.0	15.0	12.0	13.0	9.0	11.0
% With Number of Children: 2			10.0	14.0	17.0	19.0	22.0	27.0
% With Number of Children: 3			21.0	23.0	26.0	27.0	27.0	26.0
% With Number of Children: 4+			47.0	43.0	40.0	34.0	28.0	22.0

Source: European Social Statistics: Demography (Eurostat, 2002)·

Similarly the size of the completed fertility also follows the period effect at a lag for the same reason. We do not see a decline in the fertility rate for pre-1955 cohorts, while the completed fertility rate of the last cohort considered (1960-1965) at 2.4 is still high and much higher than the TFR. Amongst cohorts we see a tripling of the childless rate from 4% for the 1935 cohort to 15% for the 1960 birth cohort. There has also been a decline in completed family size from 47% of the 1945 cohort having 4+ births to 22% of the 1935 cohort. By 2000 two children had become the modal group resulting from the decrease of families with three or more children, but also from the decline of families with only one child from 18% for the 1935 to only 9% of the 1955 cohort having only one child.

An interest of many economists (for example, Walker, 1995) has been to assess the impact of public policy changes on demographic characteristics. Ireland has an Anglo-Liberal Welfare state that has a predominately means tested system of benefits, including family related benefits such as one parent family benefits (introduced in the 1970's) and in-work benefits paid to low-income families with children (introduced in the 1980's). During the 1980's there was a move away from child related tax instruments, such as child and caring related tax allowances to a small universal family benefit. Resources targeted at this instrument have consistently remained about 1% of GNP. For much of the period of interest, the income tax system was an optional joint system, where families could pool the allowances and tax bands of both spouses to reduce the income tax burden. There are no state instruments for childcare and for much of this period formal childcare was fairly limited in Ireland. Overall tax-benefit policy has had relatively low support for children during periods of higher fertility. Therefore the tax-benefit policy environment in Ireland is unlikely to have had a strong effect.

The policy reform with the likelihood of having the strongest effect has been the belated liberalisation of contraceptive laws. Until the 1973 Supreme Court judgement, the use of artificial contraception methods was illegal. This judgement ruled that the importation of contraceptives for personal use was legal. The 1979 Family Planning Act made contraceptives available on prescription through pharmacists and the 1985 Act removed the requirement to seek authorisation from doctors. In 1993, remaining restrictions on their sale were removed. Abortion remains illegal in Ireland, however significant numbers travel to the UK for this procedure. The liberalisation of the contraceptive laws in Ireland during the 1980's coincided with the period of the largest fall in the TFR, allowing fertility to be controlled more easily as preferences for large families fell over that period (Fahey, 2001).

The period since Ireland joined the European Union in the early 1970's has seen large economic changes. While the late 1990's have seen high growth rates, much of the period of Ireland's fertility decline has occurred during periods of high unemployment. The male unemployment rate (see Figure 4.2c) rose from about 6% in the early 1970s to a peak in 19% in the mid 1980's falling during the 1990's to 4% in 2000. The upward trend in unemployment coincided with the biggest decline in fertility (Figure 4.2a), while the unemployment peak coincided with the lowest birth rate, followed by a rise in fertility rates again as unemployment rates dropped, corresponding with Ahn and Mira's (1999) finding of pro-cyclical fertility. Unemployment has in part been concentrated amongst young workers (15-24) who have had in the period an unemployment rate of about 50% higher than the average. This is likely to have influenced marriage and fertility decisions, reducing overall fertility rates delaying the fertility of the 20 to 30 age group.

At the same time education levels have been rising, resulting in an increase in the age leaving education from about 16 for women born in 1940's to 18 for those born in the early 1970's. Rising education levels tend to reduce fertility for two reasons (a) because being in education is in general incompatible with having children and (b) rising education levels as we see below, increase the cost of having a child due to the opportunity cost associated with increased wages and participation rates. In Table 4.2 we decompose the impact of changes in both education levels and marriage rates on the fertility rate. The table reports for different education and marital groups the change in the group specific fertility rate, the group as a percentage of the population and the proportion this group makes to the population fertility rate.

Figure 4.2 Births, marriage, male unemployment and female labour force participation rates over the period 1971-2001

(a) Birth Rate per 1000 people 1971-2001

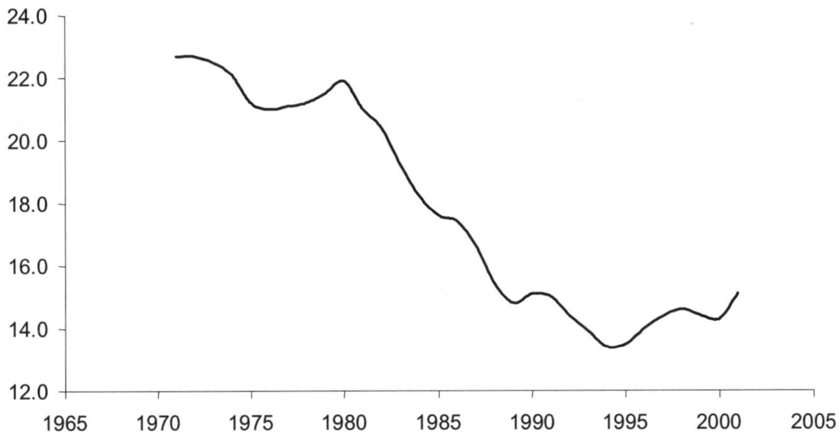

(b) Marriage Rate per 1000 people 1971-2001

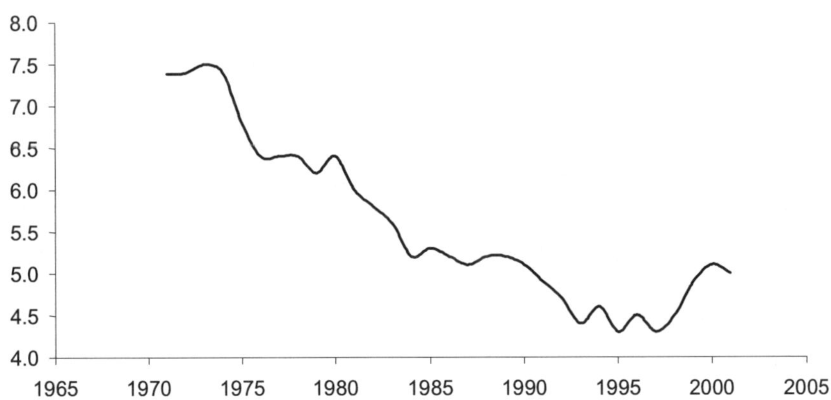

(c) Male Unemployment Rate 1971-2001

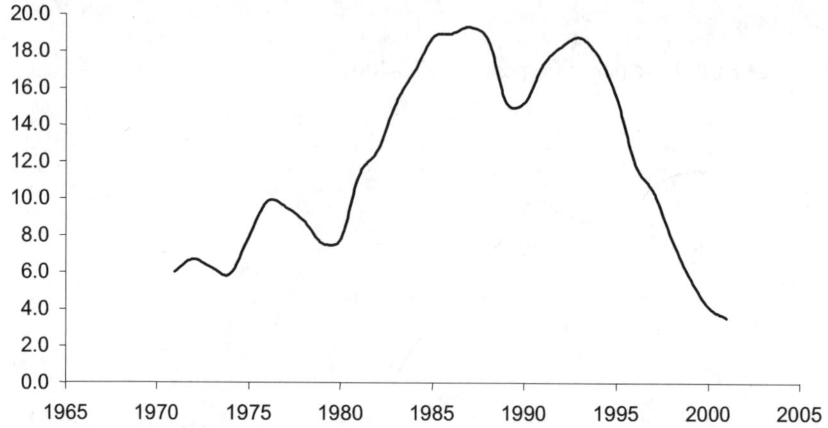

(d) Female Labour Force Participation Rate 1971-2001

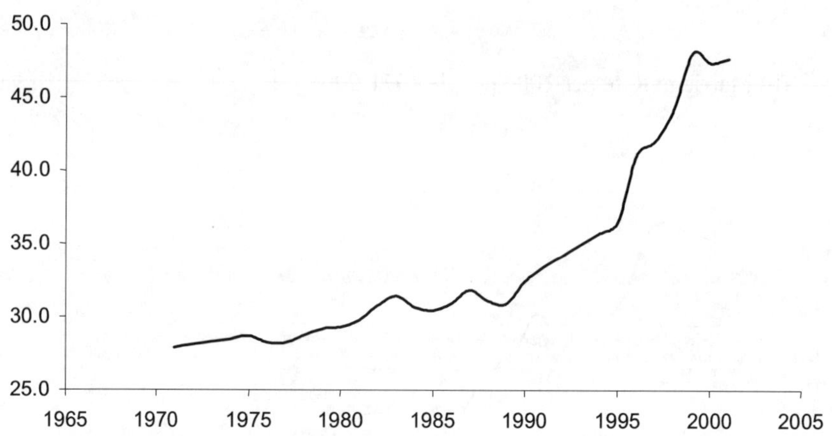

Sources: Statistical Yearbook (CSO: 1975-1997), The Trend of Employment and Unemployment (CSO: 1979-1988), Statistical Bulletin (CSO: 1979-2002), Labour Force Survey (CSO: 1979-2001).

Table 4.2 highlights the upward shift in education levels of women aged 20-45 over the two decades (columns P), with the proportion of upper secondary educated women moving from 20.6% in 1972 to 37% in 1992 and university educated women from 9.6% to 15.1%. We must note however that these numbers are 5 year moving averages to smooth the sample results, where the year reported is the middle year of the 5 year period. Higher educated women have the lowest fertility rates. However lower educated women have seen the largest decline. It is in part the fall in this group as a proportion of the population numbers that drives the overall fertility decline as this group falls from over 50% of the married women in 1972 to about a third in 1992. However the birth rate of these women has more than halved (21.3 to 9.7), so that the change in their behaviour has had a greater impact on the overall decline. This has especially been the case for third and later births with falls in the birth rate of 50%-60%.

Upper secondary and university-educated women have increased by 90% (20.6% to 37.1%) and 55% (9.6% to 15.1%) respectively over the period as a percentage of the population aged 20-45. While the birth rate of the lowest educated women has halved, the decline has been lower for higher educated women. However the decline in the birth rate for the higher educated women has been counter-balanced by their increasing share of the population, so that the births from these groups as a percentage of the size of the population has risen in the case of upper secondary educated women and remained constant for university educated women. This combined with a fall in the over all birth rate has seen births as a share of total births rise for higher educated women.

The primary cause of the fall in overall birth rate for higher educated women has been fall in the birth rate of women with higher order births, with other orders remaining constant or falling slightly. The fall for fourth and higher order births has been similar to that of lower educated births. As a share of the population the number of higher educated women with 1 and 2 births and married upper secondary educated women with 3 births at the start of the year have matched the general rise in the population of individuals with these education levels.

Until recently, fertility has occurred primarily within marital unions, therefore trends in marriage will have an influence on overall fertility. Historically, marriage rates in Ireland have tended to be low and age at marriage high by international standards (Coleman, 1992). High average fertility rates therefore were driven largely by exceptionally high, marital fertility rates in Ireland (Walsh, 1968). However as marriage rates increased (average age at marriage fell) during the economic expansion of the 1960's and the early 1970's, this disguised in the total TFR, a fall in the fertility rate of married women (the non-marital fertility rate has been quite low). The marriage rate fell back again during the recession of the 1980's, and early 1990's, following (or driving) the trend in fertility before increasing again in the late 1990's economic boom, resulting in a stabilisation of the TFR (see Figure 4.2b). In Table 4.2 from survey data we see that although the proportion of the fertile population fell by 10% from the peak in 1977 to 1992, the birth rate for this group decreased by 45%. Therefore the fertility decline of this group has had a stronger effect on total fertility than the compositional shift in the population.

Table 4.2. Birth Rate[a] and Population Composition According to Birth Order and Education Level of Married Women

	First Birth[b]		Second Birth[b]		Third Birth[b]		Fourth and Later Births[b]		Married Women			All Women		
	R[c]	B[d]	R[c]	B[d]	R[c]	B[d]	R[c]	B[d]	R[c]	P[e]	B[d]	R[c]	P[e]	B[d]
Lower Sec. and below														
1972	25.9	19.5	31.7	15.8	19.7	14.1	15.2	23.3	21.3	50.8	73.1	16.7	69.8	77.5
1977	27.0	21.3	32.8	13.7	18.2	12.5	12.9	18.6	19.8	50.8	67.4	16.4	64.4	71.1
1982	24.3	5.8	29.2	13.4	15.7	15.5	11.2	24.2	16.5	46.5	60.8	14.6	59.4	66.7
1987	21.0	14.1	22.6	9.1	11.1	7.6	8.6	19.1	12.5	41.2	51.1	11.0	54.1	58.9
1992	18.8	7.4	19.6	10.6	9.0	12.3	5.9	12.9	9.7	33.5	43.1	8.5	47.8	50.5
Upper Sec.														
1972	21.2	5.3	28.4	3.9	19.6	2.0	15.1	3.7	21.0	12.7	14.9	13.0	20.6	15.2
1977	22.5	9.1	30.8	8.1	12.6	2.1	10.9	2.7	18.1	15.2	21.9	11.4	24.3	22.3
1982	22.6	7.6	29.9	8.0	14.6	5.8	8.0	2.4	17.8	16.6	24.0	10.8	28.9	24.4
1987	22.5	11.8	26.9	6.6	12.7	7.4	6.5	4.7	16.5	20.7	30.6	11.0	32.8	31.9
1992	21.0	8.2	27.9	10.7	12.3	7.1	6.1	5.2	14.7	22.7	31.2	9.8	37.1	38.2
University														
1972	19.2	1.9	31.5	1.4	11.7	0.8	15.9	2.8	17.8	5.4	6.9	10.0	9.6	7.3
1977	18.4	1.4	34.3	2.0	11.1	0.9	13.0	1.6	18.0	5.7	5.9	10.1	11.2	6.6
1982	18.2	2.4	27.5	3.9	11.0	2.0	10.4	0.6	15.6	6.7	8.9	9.4	11.7	8.9
1987	19.0	1.5	22.4	3.8	7.4	1.2	8.1	2.7	13.3	7.2	9.2	7.4	13.2	9.2
1992	16.0	3.6	25.7	3.0	9.2	3.5	5.9	1.2	13.6	7.9	11.3	7.5	15.1	11.3
All														
1972	24.1	26.6	31.0	21.2	18.9	16.9	15.2	29.8	21.0	68.8	94.9	15.3	100	100
1977	24.6	31.7	32.4	23.7	16.2	15.5	12.6	22.9	19.3	71.7	95.2	14.5	100	100
1982	22.7	15.7	29.3	25.3	14.9	23.3	10.6	27.2	16.8	69.9	93.7	12.9	100	100
1987	21.4	27.4	24.3	19.6	11.1	16.3	8.2	26.5	13.8	69.0	90.9	10.5	100	100
1992	19.3	19.2	23.9	24.3	10.3	22.9	6.0	19.3	12.0	64.2	85.6	8.9	100	100

Source: O'Donoghue and O'Shea (2004).

Notes.

a. Birth Rates - Five-Year Moving Average from the Living in Ireland Survey (1994). The year reported is the middle year of the 5 year period, so 1972 is the average of 1970-1974.

b. Parity specific birth for *Married* Women.

c. R – group specific fertility rate.

d. B – the percentage of total births in the population.

e. P – the percentage of the female population aged 20-45.

Cultural influences also play a role in the demand for children and have been historically used an explanation for higher fertility rates in Ireland (Walsh, 1973). Ó'Gráda and Walsh (1995) find some evidence that although this influence has declined, the high proportion of Catholics in the population still has an effect.

The purpose of this chapter is to consider the various influences on the fertility rate in Ireland with a view to explaining fertility decline in the country in recent decades. The socio-economic context influences the fertility decision in a number of different ways. Increases in schooling levels and wage rates for women, allied to changes in female labour force participation rates will affect fertility rates. More highly educated women are also more likely to have higher wages and so have higher foregone earnings when having children. Male employment is also likely to be important in explaining fluctuations in fertility and marriage through income effects and on the formation of expectations. High levels of economic uncertainty, linked to unemployment and/or job instability, affects expectations about the future, which, in turn, is likely to have an impact on both marriage and fertility.

In the next section, we consider the theoretical background to economic explanations of fertility behaviour, describing the economic model of fertility used in this chapter and the data used. Section 3 describes the data used. In section 4 we estimate empirical models of married fertility by birth order separately for only demographic characteristics, the additional impact of women's work related characteristics and also additionally male wages. In section 5, utilising the empirical models estimated in section 4, we consider the driving factors behind the fertility decline. Section 6 concludes.

2. THE MODEL

Fertility is a dynamic process over the life-course and, as such, is best examined within the framework of dynamic, sequential theories of life-cycle fertility. These theories should include consideration of life-cycle consumption, life-cycle labour supply, human capital accumulation, institutional models and stochastic models of human reproduction (Hotz et al. 1997).

In this chapter we utilise a variant of Walker's (1995) and Del Bono's (2001) models of fertility. Our life-cycle model depends upon the utility from consumption (x_t) and utility from children both from the number of children (n_t) and from the quality of these children (q) at times t across the lifetime from 0 to T. The number of children (n_t) at time t depends upon the fertility at different points in time.

The model assumes no bequest motive and assumes that consumer preferences are inter-temporally and contemporaneously strongly separable. At time t discounted future utility is:

$$U_t = \sum_{s=t}^{T} \delta_s \left[v(n_s q) + u(x_s) \right], \tag{1}$$

where $\delta_t = \left(\frac{1}{1+r}\right)^{-(t-1)}$ is the rate of time preference, r the interest rate and $v(\ )$ and $u(\ )$ are strictly increasing and concave functions.

At each time t the mother has a time endowment scaled to 1 divided into labour market activity h_t and childcare $f(n_t)$. Childcare depends upon the age of each child, where a child at age j requires ϕ^j proportion of the year of care. Summing over the number of children in a family at time t, total childcare demanded is:

$$f(n_t) = \sum_{j=0}^{M} \phi^j b_{t-j}, \tag{2}$$

Hence

$$1 = f(n_t) + h_t = \sum_{j=0}^{M} \phi^j b_{t-j} + h_t \tag{3}$$

and so

$$h_t = 1 - \sum_{j=0}^{M} \phi^j b_{t-j} \tag{4}$$

where M is the age of adulthood or independence of the child from their parents. The quality of the child is assumed to depend upon the total monetary expenditure to produce child services $g(n, q)$ and is defined as the sum of direct expenditures times the quality index $m_t^j q_t$ plus childcare costs c_t^j (that in turn depend upon the hours worked – both vary with the age of the child j)

$$g(n,q) = \sum_{j=0}^{M} m_t^j q b_{t-j} + h_t \sum_{j=0}^{M} c_t^j b_{t-j} \tag{5}$$

Total income at time t is the mother's income from labour yf_t and the husband's income from labour ym_t.

Economic uncertainty provides an incentive to delay decisions that imply long-term commitments such as children and it provides an incentive to invest in education and human capital. Individuals may form expectations about the future on the basis of current information on income and jobs (Del Boca, 1999; Bettio and Villa, 1998). Therefore job stability is an important influence on preference formation and so generations faced with current poor employment prospects are likely to have lower fertility. Evidence from Ahn and Mira (1999a) for Spain suggests that unemployment and a lack of stable jobs among young men has forced couples to delay their marriage and childrearing leading to a very low fertility rate in that country. When young adults do not have confidence in the ability of the economy to deliver jobs and income they are less willing to consider marriage or having children. Conversely, a strong labour market is likely to increase both marriage and childbearing with positive effects of male income and male employment on fertility (Hotz and Miller, 1988; Heckman and Walker, 1990).

We incorporate economic instability in our model through the inclusion of the unemployment rate u_t at each time t. Hence expected male earnings are $ym_t \times (1-u_t)$. As most working age males work full-time in Ireland, we assume that fathers work full-time, ignoring labour supply effects. We allow female labour supply (h_t) to vary. Hence total female labour income at time t is labour supply times the wage rate (w_t):

$$yf_t = h_t w_t \tag{6}$$

The wage rate of the woman depends in turn upon the human capital accumulation k_t from on the job experience (h_t) and schooling (s_t) at time t and the market rental rate of human capital ω_t:

$$w_t = \omega_t k_t = \omega_t.\exp\left(\mu_0 + \mu_1 \sum_{j=1}^{t-1} h_j + s_t\right) \tag{7}$$

Where p_t is the price of the composite good x_t and δ_t is the discount rate the life-cycle budget constraint for the family can be defined as:

$$\sum_{t=1}^{T}(p_t x_t + g(n_t q))\delta_t = \sum_{t=1}^{T}(ym_t + h_t w_t)\delta_t \tag{8}$$

It is often argued that more generous social policies in the form of family income transfers and childcare provision can have a positive effect on fertility rates within countries. Estimating the impact of these institutional costs on the decision to have children is difficult, however, given the intractable nature of most of the empirical data in this area. Attributing costs is also often impossible in respect of childcare costs in a world where women tend to combine family, voluntary, private and state services. Walker (1995) did however attempt to quantify the impact of public policy on the budget constraint and the fertility decision. However given the limited child related social policies pursued in Ireland, we ignore the impact of public policy the definition of our budget constraint.

The optimisation problem therefore becomes

$$\underset{b_t, x_t, q_t; t=1...T}{Max} \sum_{t=1}^{T} \delta_t [v(n_t q) + u(x_t)] \tag{9}$$

subject to the budget constraint

$$\sum_{t=1}^{T}(p_t x_t + g(n_t q))\delta_t = \sum_{t=1}^{T}(ym_t(1-u_t) + h_t w_t)\delta_t$$

This model is optimised in O'Donoghue and O'Shea (2003). The expression π_t derived and represents the present value of a childbearing in period t:

$$\pi_t(q) = \sum_{k=0}^{T-t} m_{t+k}^{k} q \delta_{t+k} + \sum_{k=0}^{T-t} h_{t+k} c_{t+k}^{k} \delta_{t+k} - \sum_{k=0}^{T-t} \phi^k \delta_{t+k} \sum_{l=0}^{M} c_{t+k}^{l} b_{t+k-l}$$
$$+ \sum_{k=0}^{T-t} \phi^k w_{t+k} \delta_{t+k} + \sum_{k=1}^{T-t} h_{t+k} \left(\mu_1 \sum_{l=0}^{j-1} \phi^l b_{t-l} \right) w_{t+k} \delta_{t+k} \tag{10}$$

The terms can be described as follows:

- Quality adjusted direct expenditure for the child at different ages until aged M.
- Direct childcare expenditure for the hours worked by the mother for each of the dependent years.
- The reduction in non-parental childcare expenditure for other children due to having more than one child.
- The cost of parental childcare for the child.
- The foregone human capital due to rearing the child.

Where $V_t = \sum_{j=t}^{T} \delta_j v'(n_j q)$ and $v'(\ )$ is the derivative of $v(\ )$ with respect to b_t ., the following expression relating to the inter-temporal decision is derived.

$$\frac{V_{t+1}}{V_t} = \frac{\pi_{t+1}(q)}{\pi_t(q)} \tag{11}$$

This describes how fertility is allocated across the life-cycle, conditional on the pattern of earnings over the life-cycle and upon the quality of child demanded. This expression relates the price a woman is willing to pay to transfer fertility between periods, while the right hand side of the equation is the price available in the market to transfer fertility between years.[1]

How do the different terms impact on the decision to have a birth? As per Becker and Lewis (1973), the higher the quality of the child, the higher the shadow price of the child. The demand for child services is regarded as a normal good, and so higher income (say of the father ym_t) will cause demand for child services to increase. Becker (1960) postulates that the income elasticity of quality is likely to be substantially higher than the income elasticity of the number of children. Therefore as family income rises, the demand for quality is likely to increase at a faster rate than quantity and so because higher quality increases the shadow price of a child, there may be a negative relationship between income and number of children. However because quality depends upon a positive quantity, the income elasticity of demand for the first child is likely to be positive, whereas the demand for later children is likely to be negative.

Economic models of fertility behaviour predict that increases in educational attainment and wage rates for women would lead to increases in their labour supply. The impact of the increased labour supply impacts on the shadow price of a child through the second term due to the cost of childcare, resulting in reduced fertility (Becker and Lewis, 1973; Willis, 1973). However the existence of more children, through the third term in the shadow price reduces the price. Del Bono (2001) attributes this to positive economies of scale in childcare.

There is a positive correlation between investment in schooling and investment in on the job training as seen by the fact that age-earnings curves are steeper for higher educated, further increasing wages for educated women (Gustafsson, 2001) and thus increases the opportunity cost of having children increases in the short term, the opportunity caring for them (in shadow price term 4) and in the long term due to lower human capital (in shadow price term 5).

3. DATA

In this chapter we utilise the 1994 *Living in Ireland* Survey, the Irish component of the European Community Household Panel Survey, to investigate the strength of the different forces on fertility trends. The Survey contains substantial cross-section information on employment and demographic characteristics in 1993-1994. The 1994 wave also contained additional retrospective information on fertility, partnership formation, parental history and employment status that we use to decompose the effects on fertility since 1970. The event history data allows us to utilise variables that describe the duration in a number of dimensions; since last birth, marriage, and since leaving education.

O'Donoghue and O'Shea (2003) compare the validity of the main dependent variables recorded in the survey with similar figures in official statistics published by the Central Statistics Office. Overall the survey captures the decline observed in the official statistics, but the decline is observed to be smoother than the sharp decline observed in official statistics.

In this chapter, we are interested in the relationship between labour market histories and fertility. It would have been desirable to have historical panel data or at least detailed employment recall event history data. However the retrospective employment history data available is imperfect. Nevertheless in the majority of cases it was possible to identify full histories. For a minority of cases (8.5% of women and 3.5% of their spouses), some imputations were necessary.[2] For simplification purposes and because recall information is expressed in years, spells have been rounded to nearest year.

In this chapter we focus on marital births as during the period we are focusing on, non-marital births accounted only for a small proportion of all births. In the original sample of women, we produce a panel data set of 25 years from 1970-1994 comprising a total of 58938 observations for 3235 married women. In the subset of women whose histories we can identify, we have 38803 observations for 3043 married women, while in the subset whose spouse's history we can identify, we have 31027 observations for 2237 married women.[3]

Because of potential error generated through our imputation mechanism in addition to the recall error associated with this type of data, we utilise duration in employment rather than actual employment status at a point in time as an explanatory variable. As this is an aggregate measure, it is likely to be more accurate than current employment status.

Fertility levels in our model depend upon potential female wage rates and male earnings. However as we only observe wage levels in 1994, we need to simulate the history of wages. We regress 1994 wages on 1994 characteristics and then simulate potential wages for each person each year based upon the characteristics of that year.[1] In both cases, we use a standard earnings equation to estimate female wage rates and male earnings, utilising the Heckman procedure to account for sample selection bias (Heckman, 1979). In the earnings equation, we use education level and employment experience. The "Heckman" method adjusts the coefficients in the model in order to account for any selection bias associated with the fact that we only observe earnings for those who work. This is done through the use of an extra variable in the earnings equation, known as the inverse Mills ratio λ, generated from a (probit) selection equation. We define the inverse Mills ratio as

$$\lambda = -\frac{\phi(bx)}{\Phi(bx)}, \tag{12}$$

where $\phi(bx)$ is the normal probability density function, $\Phi(bx)$ is the normal cumulative distribution function and bx is the probability value of being in work as predicted from the selection equation. In addition to education and experience, duration of marriage as well as parental and spouse characteristics are used for identification. Coefficients for this model are reported in O'Donoghue and O'Shea (2003). Because simulated earnings depend upon 1994 earnings levels, the predicted earnings will only capture changes in earnings levels due to shifts in education and employment patterns and not wealth changes due to productivity gains generally in the economy. We would therefore expect the impact of these variables to be underestimated.

In our models of fertility we utilise a logit model where the dependent variable is the existence of a particular birth order in a year for the population at risk during the year. So for the first birth order equation, the population at risk is married women who have not had a child before. The model allows us to examine the impact of changing population characteristics on the period parity specific fertility rate. We limit our study to married women as non-marital fertility rates for much of the period of this data were very small and so sample sizes would be small. Unlike many other economic demography papers, we chose to use the logit model because of the alternative use for these models forming the basis of the fertility module of a dynamic microsimulation model.

---

[1] The explanatory variables used in the models include: education levels and duration in work, duration in work^2. The selection equations include in addition for identification, parental education levels, duration married.

4. EMPIRICAL RESULTS

In this section we report the results of our empirical model of fertility by birth order (first, second, third and later births). In Table 4.3 we describe a set of logit models of first marital births as in the marriage model. We consider a number of variants of the model. Model A considers simply the impact of demographic characteristics. Model B introduces the impact of the opportunity cost of having a child, including female labour market variables (wage rate and experience). Model C introduces the income effect due to the husband's income, while model D introduces the influence of uncertainty through the age and education level specific unemployment rate. In model E, we interact time with a number of the variables to investigate the stability of the estimates over time.

In the first variant we consider only the impact of demographic variables. The probability of having a birth increases with duration since leaving education, to a peak before declining and as it does with duration since marriage. The interaction term between duration since finishing education and duration since marriage (the product of the two variables) is negative, accounting for the fact that duration since marriage and education overlap. The time and time-squared terms are significant and are respectively negative and positive indicating a falling fertility rate that gets less steep with time.

In equation (B) we consider the opportunity cost of fertility. The coefficient of the female potential wage rate is significant and negative, indicating that women with higher potential wages are less likely to have a child. The percentage of time since leaving education spent in work, another measure of existing and a proxy for future human capital of a woman is also significantly negative. Therefore, in general, women with higher human capital are less likely to have a first birth at any point in time. From above their wage enters the shadow price increasing the short-term cost of caring for children and increasing the opportunity cost of human capital foregone from child rearing. The coefficients on the other variables are robust to the changed specification.

In model (C), we consider the impact of the spouse's earnings. Adding male potential earnings has a positive sign and is significant, indicating a positive income effect as child services are normal goods. Therefore other things being equal, families that are more able to afford a child are more likely to have a child. In model (D) we introduce the impact of uncertainty due to unemployment through the use of an age and education level specific male unemployment rate. We find that this variable is negative and significant at the 90% level, indicating that if husbands with a particular age and education level face a higher unemployment rate, they face higher uncertainty and so on average have lower fertility rates.

Table 4.3. Logit Model of First Birth for Married Women[a]

Model	A[b]		B		C		D		E	
	Coef	p	Coef	p	Coef	p	Coef	p	Coef	p
Dured	0.117	**	0.110	**	0.107	**	0.104	**		
Dured[c]-1970's									0.118	**
Dured-1980's									0.105	**
Dured-1990's									0.083	**
Dured Squared	-0.007	**	-0.007	**	-0.006	**	-0.006	**	-0.006	**
Durmarr[c]	0.073	**	0.066	**	0.070	**	0.066	**		
Durmarr[c]-1970's									0.106	**
Durmarr-1980's									0.133	**
Durmarr-1990's									0.150	**
Durmarr Squared	-0.001	**	-0.001	**	-0.001	**	-0.001	**	-0.001	**
Durmarred	-0.002	**	-0.002	**	-0.002	**	-0.002	**		
Durmarred-1970's									-0.009	**
Durmarred-1980's									-0.003	**
Durmarred-1990's									-0.002	**
Female Wage			-0.015	**	-0.033	**	-0.019	**		
Female Wage-1970's									-0.027	**
Female Wage-1980's									-0.013	**
Female Wage-1990's									-0.017	**
Work%[c]			-0.907	**	-0.842	**	-0.917	**		
Work%-1970's									-0.744	**
Work%-1980's									-1.220	**
Work%-1990's									-1.101	**
Male Earnings					0.0003	**	0.0002	**	0.0002	**
Unemployment Rate							-0.887	*	-0.797	
Time	-0.095	**	-0.062	**	-0.059	**	-0.063	**	-0.060	
Time Squared	0.002	**	0.001	*	0.001	*	0.002	**	0.002	
Constant	-0.233		0.195		0.570	*	-0.009		0.239	
No. of Observations	5538		5538		5538		5538		5538	
Pseudo R2	0.0347		0.0464		0.0477		0.0484		0.0545	

Source: Author's Calculations based on retrospective data 1970-1994 from the Living in Ireland Survey, 1994.

Notes:

a. Parental education, Cohort and education participation dummies are not reported.
b. Equations: A-Demographic; B-Substitution Effect: Female Labour Market; C - Income Effect: Male Earnings; D - Risk; E - Time Variance.
c. Variables: Dured Duration since leaving education; Durmarr- Duration since marriage; Work% - Percentage of Work History in Work.
d. p - p value for coefficient - ** Significant at 5% level, * significant at 10% level.

The objective of this chapter is to consider the determinants of the decline in fertility in Ireland. Therefore in model (E), we consider the stability of our parameter estimates in different time periods, interacting decade with the duration and opportunity cost variables. The coefficients are generally significant. The coefficients on the duration variables are confusing as the coefficients on duration since education rise with time and the coefficients on duration since marriage fall over time. The net effect of these parameter changes is to capture the effect that the duration until first birth has been increasing with time. Although there has been a compositional shift from lower educated to higher educated (who tend to have lower durations from completion of education to first birth), which should tend to reduce the duration from education, for women of all educational backgrounds there has been increasing duration to first birth (See O'Donoghue and O'Shea 2004). Although the coefficients on female wage rates are not significantly different from each other, the coefficients on experience have become stronger after the 1970's, indicating the higher average opportunity cost of having a child due to rising education levels.

In Table 4.4 we describe models of second and higher order marital births. We consider only "final" variants of these models here. For second births, the impact of duration since education on fertility rises and then declines due as before to the positive coefficient and negative square coefficient. Duration since marriage becomes negative once duration since last birth is introduced. As before it is difficult to interpret the separate coefficients in isolation. Combining them, the net effect for a given duration since last birth, is that in the 1970's probabilities of a second birth were higher earlier, but fell more rapidly over time than in later decades. In the 1990's the decline in the probability of birth declined at a faster rate over time than in the 1980's, due to the large fall in the second birth rate later in the period. For third and later births, the net impact of the duration coefficients is similar for the 1980's and 1990's, but that the probability of a birth is lower for each duration than in the 1970s. In each case the probability of a birth rose and then fell with duration since last birth. However this effect fell in each case between the 1970's and 1990's. For fourth and later births the number of children also has a positive effect, so that the more children, the higher the probability of having another child.

The opportunity cost of having a child as captured by potential wage and work history has a partially significant effect on second, third and later births. For second births potential females wages is significant (at the 90% level) only for those with upper secondary education. Work experience does not have a separate significant impact on this decision. This is not surprising however as the impact of human capital is incorporated in the wage education interactions. For third order births, female wage rates have negative coefficients but not significant. Experience however falls just outside the 90% significance level. Finally for later births female wage is found to be significantly negative.

Table 4.4. Logit Model of Second, Third and Later Births for Married Women[1]

Model	Second Birth		Third Birth		Fourth and Later Births	
	Coef	p[c]	Coef	p	Coef	p
Dured[b]-1970's	0.062	**	0.092	**	0.083	**
Dured-1980's	0.051	*	0.077	**	0.107	**
Dured-1990's	0.071	**	0.106	**	0.082	**
Dured Squared	-0.002	**	-0.003	**	-0.003	**
Durmarr[b]-1970's	0.001		-0.203	**	-0.146	**
Durmarr-1980's	-0.085	**	-0.224	**	-0.175	**
Durmarr-1990's	-0.080	**	-0.224	**	-0.052	
Durmarr squared	0.001	**	0.002	**	0.001	**
Durmarred-1970's	-0.011	**	-0.003		-0.002	
Durmarred-1980's	-0.001		0.000		0.000	
Durmarred-1990's	-0.003	*	0.000		-0.004	*
Durbirth[b]-1970's	0.654	**	0.545	**	0.436	**
Durbirth-1980's	0.578	**	0.566	**	0.426	**
Durbirth-1990's	0.591	**	0.484	**	0.347	**
Durbirth squared	-0.053	**	-0.045	**	-0.040	**
Number of Previous Children[2]		**		**	0.019	**
Female Wage (Univ)	-0.012		-0.008			**
Female Wage (UpSec)	-0.016	*	-0.004			**
Female Wage (LoSec)		**	-0.010			**
Female Wage		**		**	-0.008	**
Work%[b]	-0.089		-0.264			**
Male Earnings (Univ)	0.00042	**	-0.00001			**
Male Earnings (UpSec)	0.00029	**	-0.0001		-0.0002	**
Male Earnings (LoSec)		**		**	-0.0002	**
Average Unemployment Rate	-1.119	**	-1.554	**	-0.215	
Time	-0.033		-0.023		-0.046	
Time Squared	0.000		0.000		0.000	
Constant	-0.829		-1.595	*	-0.418	
Number of observations	4713		7082		13677	
R2	0.0723		0.0901		0.0936	

Source: Author's Calculations based on retrospective data 1970-1994 from the Living in Ireland Survey, 1994.

Note:

a. Parental education, Cohort and education participation dummies are not reported.
b. Variables: Dured Duration since leaving education; Durmarr - Duration since marriage; Work% - Percentage of Work History in Work; Durbirth - Duration Since Last Birth.
c. p - p value for coefficient- ** Significant at 5% level, * significant at 10% level.

For second order births the coefficient on male earnings is positive, indicating the importance of the income effect as in the case of first order births. We interact male earnings with education level because although those with higher earnings at the same education level have higher fertility rates, it is not necessarily the case across the population as a whole. For third and higher births, the sign changes on this variable. For third births, the variable is not significantly different from zero, but for later births it is significantly negative for those with upper secondary education levels and lower. This result tallies with the quality term in the theoretical model as advocated by Becker and Lewis (1973), where wealthier families will have a higher income elasticity of quality than of number of children and so may have higher expectations of the standard of living for their children and invest more in their child.

Uncertainty has been found to have a significantly negative effect for second and third order births. During times of higher unemployment, families will not have extra children. Noticeably for fourth and later births, the time variables are more significant than for second and third order births. This may explain the fact that for later births the unemployment rate variable becomes insignificant as it follows closely the time path of the decline in fourth and higher order fertility. Excluding time as an explanatory results in the unemployment rate having a significant impact.

5. DECOMPOSITION OF TRENDS

In the previous section we estimated empirical models that describe factors that influence fertility in Ireland. In this section we consider how compositional shifts in the population combined with the behaviour captured by the models combine to produce the fertility decline in Ireland.

5.1 Compositional Trends

In Table 4.5 we report summary statistics for three decades of the explanatory variables used in the models for the different order births. We must note that the summary statistics describe the characteristics of the at-risk population (i.e. married women without a child at the start of the year) rather than those who actually have a child. The statistics therefore include the impact of individuals, who although at risk never have a child of that order. The increase in childless women will influence the duration variables. We do not however discard right-censored individuals.

We notice that the average age of the group at risk of a first birth increased by 3.5 years as the duration since completing education and since marriage has risen from the 1970's to the 1990's due to the postponement of maternity. As the fertility rate tends to decline with duration, the increase in the average duration contributes to the overall fertility decline. The same is true for those at risk of later order births. The average age for later births group passed 40, which is close to the end of the normal fertile years when fertility is reduced. The slight fall in the average number of children causes fertility to run in the opposite direction due to the positive coefficient in Table 4.4.

Turning to the education level of women in this group, we notice that the proportion of women at risk of a first birth with a upper secondary education doubles and with a large increase in university education. This increase in education levels resulted in a rise in the female potential wage rate and proportion of life in work. As the coefficients on these variables are significantly negative, net impact of the increase in the opportunity cost of a child has been to reduce fertility. The overall education level of the later birth groups is lower than that for those at risk of first births because (a) they are older and (b) because educated women are less likely to reach the position of being at risk of having a later order birth because of lower fertility rates for each birth order. The increase in the education level also has been lower than for first order births. As a result the potential wage rate and the resulting opportunity cost of having another birth is lower. Combined with a lower coefficient on potential wage means that the impact of the opportunity cost is low relative to first births.

Male potential earnings in general rise over time, combined with the positive coefficient, tending to increase fertility for first and second order births but reducing fertility for later order births. The economic climate facing all groups as measured by the male age/education-specific unemployment rate deteriorated over the period resulting in increased uncertainty. Increased uncertainty combined with the negative coefficient reduced fertility.

Table 4.5. Summary Statistics by Decade for Married Women

	First Birth[a]			Second Birth[a]			Third Birth[a]			Fourth and Later Births[a]		
	1970	1980	1990	1970	1980	1990	1970	1980	1990	1970	1980	1990
Sample Size	2165	2297	1076	1740	1959	1014	2394	2967	1721	4201	6611	2865
Duration since leaving education	9.3	10.5	11.8	11.2	12.5	13.9	13.7	16.1	17.0	17.5	19.6	21.0
Duration since marriage	2.5	4.7	8.4	4.8	6.7	10.0	7.6	10.6	11.5	11.6	14.3	15.9
Duration since last birth				2.5	3.7	4.4	3.5	5.4	5.8	3.4	4.9	6.0
Number of Previous Children Squared										20.0	18.8	17.7
Female Hourly Wage Rate	5.3	5.7	6.1	4.8	4.9	5.5	5.0	5.2	5.4	4.5	4.6	4.5
Percentage of Potential Work History in Work	0.72	0.89	0.91	0.564	0.682	0.768	0.488	0.528	0.613	0.368	0.399	0.420
Male Potential Monthly Earnings	1103	1181	1256	1287	1205	1218	1155	1234	1282	1139	1188	1268
Average Unemployment Rate	0.068	0.100	0.138	0.050	0.098	0.157	0.043	0.089	0.152	0.035	0.090	0.165
University Educated	0.127	0.161	0.200	0.098	0.107	0.144	0.113	0.149	0.145	0.066	0.081	0.086
Upper Secondary Educated	0.286	0.443	0.514	0.235	0.374	0.449	0.214	0.311	0.406	0.183	0.218	0.300
Age	28.6	30.0	32.1	28.5	29.6	31.4	31.2	33.3	34.4	37.4	39.9	40.5

Source: Author's Calculations based on retrospective data 1970-1994 from the Living in Ireland Survey, 1994.

Note: a. The first birth group consists of married women aged 20-45 who have had or could have a first birth. In other words the group consists of all women who either have no child or have their first child in year; the group at risk of having a first birth.

5.2 Decomposition

We now try to assess the importance of these compositional trends in driving the decline in fertility. As the impact of explanatory variables in logit models cannot be decomposed as in the case of OLS regression models, we instead decompose the impact of the explanatory variables on the underlying variable representing the propensity to have a child. The logit model is

$$p = \frac{\exp(XB)}{(1+\exp(XB))} \tag{13}$$

The underlying latent variable we consider is

$$Y = \ln\left(\frac{p}{(1-p)}\right) = XB = \sum_j b_j x_j \tag{14}$$

This model is linear and so can be decomposed and retains the same order of preferences as the logit model.

In order to examine the importance of the explanatory variables in explaining the fertility decline, we take the average for the population in 1970 and again in 1994 and apply them to the equations in Tables 3 and 4. The components $b_i x_i^{70}$ and $b_i x_i^{94}$ represent the contribution of variable i to the propensity of the event in respectively 1970 and 1994. The contribution of each variable i to the overall change in propensity is:

$$\Delta Y_i = \left(b_i x_i^{94} - b_i x_i^{70}\right) / \left(\sum_J b_j x_j^{94} - \sum_J b_j x_j^{70}\right) \tag{15}$$

In Table 4.6, we report the results for different order birth rates. Because the effects of many variables are confounded with each other, we combine variables into groups, described in the footnote to the table. The decomposition shares sum to 100%.

Overall the most important effect on first births has been the increased labour market position and earnings of women with the resulting increase in the opportunity cost of having a child. Although the opportunity cost of a child increases for all birth order groups, we noticed above that variables relating to the opportunity cost were less significant than for first order births. In our decompositional analysis, the effect is that female labour market characteristics and thus opportunity cost are noticeably less important than for first order births, indicating that the opportunity cost for later births is lower. This may be explained by the fact that once a decision has been made to have a child then the woman incurs the opportunity cost of caring for children and the cost of foregone future earnings due to lower human capital. More time spent caring for children reduces the level of human capital at later ages, reducing the potential wage and thus reducing the opportunity cost of caring for a child. Extra children require proportionally less parental care as indicated by the third term in shadow price of children that captures economies of scale in caring for children. This may explain that the highest gap in parity specific birth rates between women of different education levels, found in Table 4.2 is for first births. The gap for later births is not as high.

For first order births, the next most important impact is the postponement of maternity, however it must be noted that this effect also captures the rise in childless women. The duration variables are more important for later order births as rising durations for earlier order births reduce the time available for further births.

The income effect as represented by male potential earnings is relatively small and is outweighed by the postponement of maternity and the increase in the opportunity cost of children. As above the sign of the effect changes from increasing to reducing fertility for third and higher order births supporting our hypothesis that the income effect translates into a demand for higher quality for higher order births. We noted above that the earnings definition used is limited, being based upon 1994 earnings. We might expect the strength of this effect to increase if we had access to time specific earnings.

Table 4.6. Decomposition of Percentage change in Female Fertility Propensity 1970-1994[a]

	Birth			
	1	2	3	4+
Duration since Marriage/Education[b]	28.7	17.8	29.9	16.2
Duration Since Last Birth[c]	0.0	25.0	32.8	29.3
Cumulative Number of Children	0.0	0.0	0.0	1.6
In education	0.6	0.0	0.0	0
Female Labour Market[d]	41.0	10.6	2.8	0.6
Husbands Potential Earnings[e]	-4.0	-5.0	4.6	2.2
Uncertainty due to Unemployment[f]	6.4	9.0	11.5	1.3
Education Level of Father of Women[g]	0.4	2.5	0.7	0.3
Time	19.3	28.8	24.9	50.4
Cohort	7.5	11.3	-7.2	-1.8

Source: Author's Calculations based on retrospective data 1970-1994 from the Living in Ireland Survey, 1994.

Notes:

a. The propensity of each event is considered for average characteristics in 1970 and 1994. Each row represents the change in the contribution to the change in the propensity of each category as a percentage of the overall change in propensity.
b. Duration - Duration since Education squared; Duration since Marriage, Duration since Marriage squared and interactions between duration married and since education.
c. Duration Since Last Birth - Duration since Birth, Duration since Birth squared.
d. Female Labour Market - Combination of Expected Female Wage, Proportion Career in Work.
e. Husband's Labour Market -Husband's Potential Earnings.
f. Average unemployment rate of men with the same education level and the same 5-year age band as the husband of the women.
g. Father's Education - Dummies indicating the level of education of the father of the women sampled.

Increased uncertainty due to deterioration of economic conditions is also a factor rising in importance with birth order until the third order group. The effect however is relatively modest for the fourth order group.

The general time trend and cohort effects are quite important especially for the highest order group, contributing the most in explaining the lower fertility in 1994 in comparison to 1970. The lack of influence of other explanatory variables for the latter group mirrors the finding in Table 4.2 that the fertility levels and decline have been similar across different education groups. Increased availability of contraception over this period may have allowed people to manage their fertility better. This combined with changing cultural patterns that have reduced preferences for large families (Fahey, 2001) together with an underestimated income effect that causes an increased demand for quality (not fully captured by this model due to the reliance on 1994 based variables) are forces that may be captured by the time trend.

6. CONCLUSIONS

To conclude, in this chapter we have described the trend in birth rates in Ireland over the period 1970–1994. Although there has been a fall in the married population, this compositional shift has been less important than the change in fertility behaviour amongst married women over the period. For first order births the most important impact on fertility has been the increase in the opportunity cost of having a child due to the impact of rising education levels of women on potential wage rates and labour market participation. This effect was smaller for later order births indicating economies of scale in having more children. Decisions to delay or postpone maternity have led to a fall in the birth rate. Over time, women are delaying having children after education, behaviour that is supportive of the career motive hypothesis. The substitution effect due to the increased cost of a child is more important than the income effect. The income effect has a positive impact on lower order fertility, changing signs for later birth orders supporting the hypothesis that the income elasticity of quality is higher than for quantity. This means that families that are more able to afford a child are more likely to have one, but that for higher order births wealthier families may prefer to substitute away from extra children to put more investment in their existing children. Rising uncertainty due to higher male unemployment rates has also had an impact on the fall in the fertility rate. The general time trend is relatively important in explaining the trend, especially for higher order births, capturing other cultural and behavioural shifts in Ireland over the period.

The period after years covered by this analysis, has been marked by a stabilisation and recovery of the fertility rate in Ireland (See Fahey, 2001). Fahey highlights that continuing increases in the female labour market participation rate has not resulted in a convergence to European fertility rates but instead to fertility rates observed in the "New World" countries. He argues that the increasing cost of children has limited family size, due to a decline in higher order births but that the income effect and the reduced uncertainty of income of the Celtic Tiger has dominated when making decisions about first or second children. He also highlights the impact of cultural factors citing the fact that desired number of children in Ireland as measured by the European Values Survey were the highest of all European countries, so despite the convergence of economic characteristics to European averages, Irish people have more children and wish to have more children than elsewhere in Europe.

ACKNOWLEDGEMENTS

This chapter is based upon empirical analyses carried out by Cathal O'Donoghue as part of his PhD at the London School of Economics, forming the fertility module of his Life-cycle Income Analysis Model (LIAM). He gratefully acknowledges financial assistance from the Postgraduate Fellowship of the Economic and Social Research Institute, Dublin. This chapter was partially written while Cathal O'Donoghue was a SAGE Visiting Fellow at the London School of Economics. He gratefully acknowledges the hospitality provided. The chapter uses data from the 1994 Living in Ireland Survey, made available by the Economic and Social Research Institute, Dublin. We have benefited from comments from seminar participants in Galway and at SCHOLAR in Amsterdam and in particular Siv Gustafsson. The authors are responsible for all remaining errors.

NOTES

[1] See Walker (1995) for a more detailed discussion of the properties of this relation.

[2] See O'Donoghue and O'Shea (2003) for a description of this process. Checks were considered to assess the degree of bias introduced by the different samples. We find that results are robust to this process.

[3] Further observations are available for the years before marriage. These are not reported here.

REFERENCES

Ahn, Namkee and Mira, Pedro. "Job Bust, Baby Bust?: Evidence from Spain". *Journal of Population Economics* (vol. 14, 2001): 505-521.

Ahn, Namkee and Mira, Pedro., "A note on the Changing relationship between Fertility and Female Employment Rates in Developed Countries", Documento de Trabajo 99-09, FEDEA, Spain, 1999.

Becker, G., "An Economic Analysis of Fertility" in Demographic and Economic Change in Developed Countries. Universities National Bureau Conference Series 11. Princeton N.J.: Princeton University Press, 1960.

Becker, G. and H. Lewis., "On the interaction between the Quantity and Quality of Children", Journal of Political Economy, (Vol. 81, 1973): S279-S288.

Bettio, F. and P. Villa., "A Mediterranean perspective on the breakdown of the relationship between female participation and fertility", Cambridge Journal of Economics, (vol. 22, 1998): 137-171.

Coleman, D.A. "The Demographic Transition in Ireland in International Context" in Goldthorpe, J. and C. Whelan (eds.), The Development of Industrial Society in Ireland, Proceedings of the British Academy, Vol. 79. London: British Academy, 1992.

Del Bono, E, "Estimating Fertility Responses to Expectations: Evidence from the 1958 British Cohort". Paper presented to the Conference of the European Society of Population Economics, Athens, June, 2001.

Eurostat. European Social Statistics: Demography. Luxembourg: Eurostat, 2002.

Fahey, T. "Trends in Irish Fertility Rates in Comparative Perspective", Economic and Social Review (vol. 32, no. 2, 2001).

Gustafsson S. "Optimal age at motherhood. Theoretical and empirical considerations on postponement of maternity in Europe", Journal of Population Economics, (vol. 14., 2001)225-247.

Heckman, J. "Sample selection bias as a specification error", Econometrica, (vol. 47, 1979): 153-161.

Heckman J. and J. Walker. "The Relationship between Wages and Income and the Timing and Spacing of Births: evidence from Swedish Longitudinal Data", Econometrica, (vol. 58, 1990): 1411-1441.

Hotz V., J. Klerman, and R. Willis. "The Economics of Fertility in Developed Countries" in Rosensweig, M and O. Stark (eds.), Handbook of Population and Family Economics, (1997): 275-347.

Hotz V. and R. Miller. "An Empirical Analysis of Life Cycle Fertility and Female Labour Supply", Econometrica, (vol. 56, no. 1, 1988): 91-118.

O'Donoghue C. "Redistribution over the Lifetime in the Irish Tax-Benefit System: An Application of a Prototype Dynamic Microsimulation Model for Ireland", Economic and Social Review, (vol. 32, No. 3, 2002).

O'Donoghue C. and E. O'Shea, "Explaining the Fertility Decline in Ireland", Department of Economics Working Paper, National University of Ireland Galway, 2003.

O'Donoghue C. and E. O'Shea., "Decomposing the Impact of Increased Education Levels on the Fertility Decline in Ireland", Department of Economics Working Paper, National University of Ireland Galway, 2004.

Ó'Gráda C. and B.M. Walsh. "Fertility and Population in Ireland, North and South", Population Studies, (vol. 49, 1995): 259-79.

Walker, J.R. "The Effect of Public Policies on Recent Swedish Fertility Behaviour", Journal of Population Economics, (vol. 8, 1995): 223-251.

Walsh, B.M., Some Irish Population Problems Reconsidered, General Research Series No. 42, Dublin: The Economic and Social Research Institute, 1968.

Walsh B.M. Religion and Demographic Behaviour in Ireland, Dublin: Economic and Social Research Institute, 1973.

Willis J. (1973), "A New Approach to the Economic Theory of Fertility Behaviour", Journal of Political Economy, (vol. 81, 1973): S14-S64.

Chapter 5

FEMALE LABOUR FORCE PARTICIPATION AND MARITAL FERTILITY IN ITALY

MASSIMILIANO BRATTI

1. INTRODUCTION

Italy has very low female labour force participation (LFP hereafter) and fertility rates. Both phenomena have recently drawn the attention of many researchers and policy makers since they are likely to have very important economic consequences. On the one hand, low fertility rates, well below the population replacement level, have caused a progressive ageing of the Italian population, and the social contributions paid by current workers are becoming insufficient to finance the pensions of retired workers, causing huge problems of sustainability of the current pension system. On the other hand, unlike other European countries, in Italy female labour force participation rates are increasing very slowly, and this fact contributes to exacerbating the problem of the progressive lack of manpower related to population ageing.

Some of the causes for the low LFP and fertility of Italian women that have been put forward are related to the specific characteristics of the Italian labour market and the Italian welfare system (see Del Boca, 2002b). As to the low female participation (in 1999 more than one out of two women were out of the labour market), it is often stressed that the Italian labour market is heavily regulated and characterised by high levels of employment protection and rigidity. According to an OECD (1999) study Italy ranks[1] between 3rd-5th out of 15 countries as to strictness for individual dismissal, 2nd-3rd as to strictness for collective dismissals, 2nd for strictness of temporary employment regulation and 3rd for overall employment protection.[2] The hiring system and the very strict firing rules have negative effects especially on the employment rate of particular segments of the labour market, such as young, female and old workers and also contributes to the high long-term unemployment rate. Moreover, part-time work, which may contribute to reconcile family and market work is scarcely diffused in Italy compared to other countries.[3] Eurostat (1999) reports that in 1998 in Italy only 10.1% of employed women worked part-time. The

Siv Gustafsson and Adriaan Kalwij (eds.), Education and Postponement of Maternity, 113–145.

Italian welfare system, in the taxonomy of Esping-Andersen (1990), is a "conservative regime" in which the State, the market, and other institutions, typically the family and the church, share responsibility for citizens' welfare. In such regimes, women are traditionally the main responsible for child rearing and are only marginal to the labour market. The system of provision of public child care is characterised in Italy by constraints in terms of both number of hours of care provided and number of places available (see Del Boca 2002c). As documented by Del Boca (2002b) public child care is also the only form of formal child care that is likely to be affordable by many families: in the Italian Survey of Households Income and Wealth (*Indagine sui Bilanci delle Famigli Italiane,* ISHIW hereafter) 1993 data the monthly costs were about € 229 and € 110 for private and public child care, respectively, related to children aged 0-2. As to the low fertility rates of Italian women some possible economic causes may be related to the high cost of child rearing.[4] The institutional rigidities reported above contribute to make it difficult to conciliate family with market work and might push women to withdraw from the labour market in the case of child birth, which has therefore high

Figure 5.1. Average years of education per woman aged more than 14 in some European countries

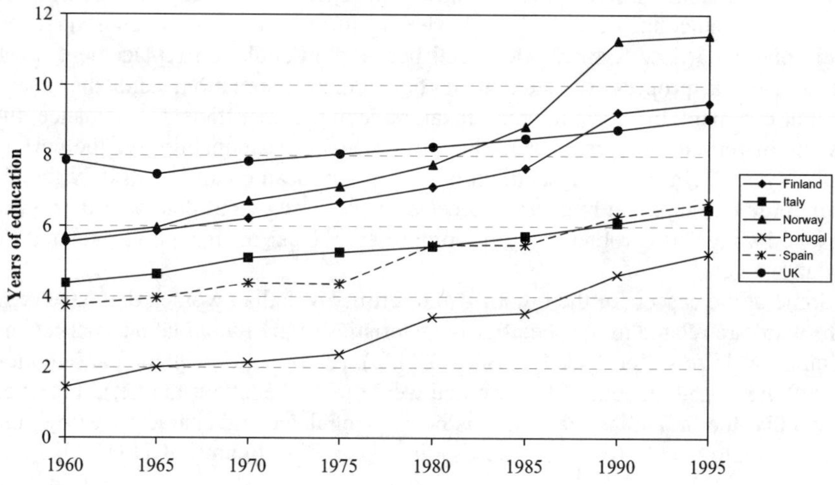

Source: Barro and Lee (2001).

Figure 5.2. Average years of education per woman aged more than 14 in some European countries

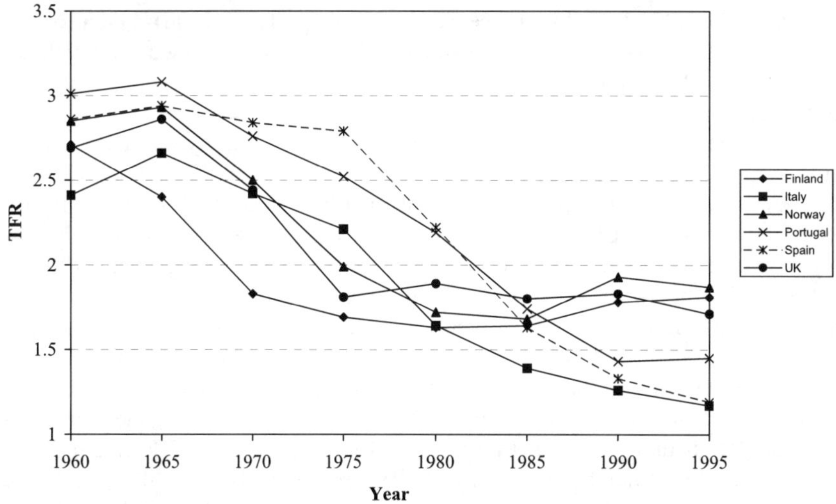

Source: World Bank (2000). Total Fertility Rates are the number of births per woman at fecund ages.

Figure 5.3. Female Labour Force Participation (LFP) rate in some European countries

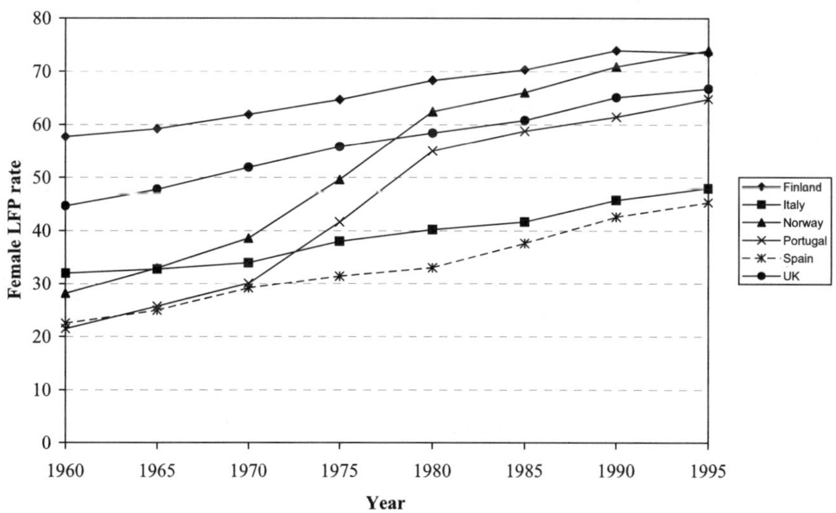

Source: World Bank (2000). Female LFP rates are computed by dividing female labour force by the female population aged between 15 and 64.

opportunity costs (in terms of forgone earnings). The direct costs are also important in Italy where youth unemployment rates are very high, and children tend to acquire independence at older ages compared to other European countries. For instance, according to the ISTAT Multipurpose Survey 1998 (ISTAT, 1998) 29% (16%) of Italian males (females) aged 30-34 resided with their parents (see Giannelli and Monfardini, 2000). All these direct and indirect costs might contribute to the lower fertility observed in Italy.

Besides the institutional factors, which have been largely discussed in the literature, individuals' personal characteristics are likely to affect both LFP and fertility. A major determinant is probably women's education. While the positive effect of education on LFP is a general result of neoclassical models of labour supply (since education increases employability and wages), the sign of the effect of education on fertility is less clear. In fact, although the analysis of time-series data at country level commonly shows that increasing education is correlated with a higher female LFP and a lower fertility, the negative correlation between education and fertility is weaker when comparing time series-cross section data related to different countries. For example, some countries with low average years of education in the female population in 1995, such as Spain (6.68), Italy (6.98) and Portugal (5.22), also have very low total fertility rates (TFRs), respectively 1.19, 1.17 and 1.49, whilst countries with higher average years of education have relatively higher

Figure 5.4. Women's education, fertility and labour force participation: some possible interactions

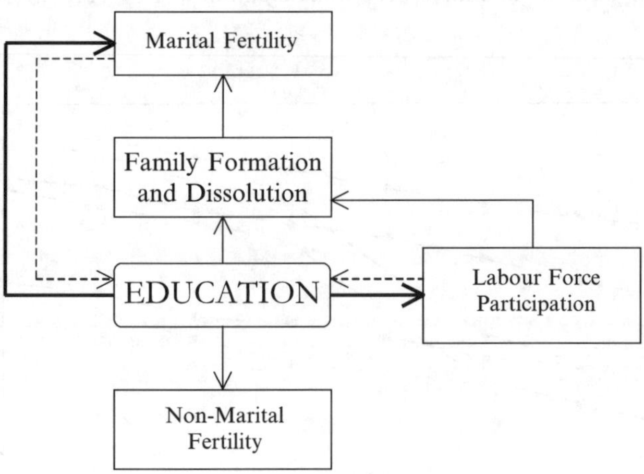

Notes: In the present chapter we focus only on the interactions shown by bold or dotted arrows.

TFRs, such as Finland or Norway (where average years of education and TFRs are 9.50 and 1.81, 11.41 and 1.87 in 1995, respectively).[5]

Theoretical models of fertility also do not offer unambiguous predictions for the sign of the effect of education. For this reason in the current chapter we seek to explore the effect of education on LFP and fertility using micro-level cross-section data for Italy. Indeed, cross country-time series data may not be ideal for testing the implications of economic models of female fertility and LFP, due to problems of aggregation and the different institutional frameworks that characterise different countries (such as child care and contraception availability and costs, which are difficult to control for) as well as the same country over time. For example, the negative effect of education on fertility reported in time series studies may be only a spurious correlation and driven by the positive correlation between education and some other unobserved factor operating at the macro level, which is not controlled for, such as the increasing availability of contraception. Therefore, the use of micro-level data can contribute to reducing the risk of omitting relevant factors, it helps to control for potential endogeneity of some explanatory variables of interest and is more in line with micro-level theoretical models of LFP and fertility, which are widespread in the fields of labour and population economics and by which econometric analysis is often motivated.

However, the relationship between education and fertility is a complex one and the total effect of education may act through several channels. Figure 5.4 shows that education may influence fertility both indirectly by affecting the age at marriage, and other aspects of marriage such as its duration,[6] and directly through its effect on marital fertility. Moreover, marital fertility may affect marriage duration while the expectation of family dissolution may influence fertility, LFP and the investment in human capital.[7] Last but not least, education may be in part endogenous: strong preferences for market work may induce women to invest more in education and perhaps to have a lower fertility (these effects operating through preferences are shown in the figure by dotted arrows). In macroeconomic studies of female fertility and LFP, it is difficult to isolate the different effects of education on marriage formation and dissolution, marriage duration and marital fertility. Hence, the estimated effect is a total effect that does not shed light on the way in which education affects both fertility and LFP.

For this reason, the present chapter focuses on married women's LFP and fertility decisions using household survey micro-data, i.e. it analyses the interactions shown by bold arrows in Figure 5.4.

The outline of the chapter is as follows. In the following section we review some of the insights into the effect of education offered by dynamic theoretical models of fertility and LFP. Section three summarises the findings of previous empirical work relating to Italy. Section four describes the data and the variables used in the empirical analysis, the econometric model and the main results. Section five concludes.

2. EDUCATION, LABOUR FORCE PARTICIPATION AND MARITAL FERTILITY, INSIGHTS FROM LIFE-CYCLE THEORETICAL MODELS

Theoretical models of LFP and fertility can be divided into *life-time static models* and *life-cycle dynamic models*. The former are mainly concerned with the study of completed fertility while the latter enable the analysis of a greater number of issues, such as the timing and spacing of births. In the present section we illustrate the insights into the role of education offered by some theoretical *life-cycle dynamic models* of fertility and LFP, since we are interested in both completed fertility and fertility *tempo*.[8]

In a recent survey of theoretical and empirical work on the optimal age at motherhood Gustafsson (2001) describes three theoretical models in detail: Happel et al. (1984) , Cigno (1991) and Walker (1995). We focus here on the predictions of these models regarding the effect of education, while the interested reader can find their detailed description either in Gustafsson (2001) or in the original articles.

Happel et al. (1984) emphasise *consumption smoothing* as the main determinant of fertility timing. In their model, individual utility is separable into consumption and the 'effective' number of children (a combination of quantity and quality of offspring). Under the perfectly imperfect capital market (PICM) assumption, i.e. individuals cannot borrow against their future incomes, the husband's (exogenous) earnings profile matters for fertility timing since women give birth in a time interval in which the income of the primary earner is relatively high.

According to the model, the wife's earnings depend on pre-marital work experience and when she gives birth she retires from the labour market for a fixed exogenous number of periods, during which job skills are subject to depreciation or obsolescence. Happel et al. (1984) do not explicitly consider formal education; however its effect can be roughly likened to that of a higher stock of pre-marital work experience (i.e. human capital), which increases the probability of a delayed first birth. The reason is that when pre-marital work experience is high the probability of total skill loss during child rearing is less, and the latter is the sole case in which an early birth is preferred to a late birth in the model.

Cigno (1991) and Walker (1995), instead, emphasise the *career planning motive* as the main determinant of LFP and fertility behaviour.

In Cigno (1991) parents derive utility from consumption and 'effective' children. Parents have a positive discount rate and capital markets are perfect. In the model a higher stock of pre-marital human capital determines a lower completed fertility and early child births. This is due to the income effect, because parents discount the utility derived from offspring. As Gustafsson (2001) observes, this prediction is at odds with the Happel et al. (1984) result. The differences are due to the fact that in the latter model there was a positive rate of depreciation of human capital (and women better endowed with human capital were less at risk of losing their job skills) and no discounting was assumed. However, Cigno (1991) also maintains that women with a steeper earnings profile have a slower fertility *tempo*, i.e. they postpone child births. Cigno and Ermisch (1989), for instance, find that women in semi-skilled or manual occupations (who have a relatively flat earnings profile) have earlier child births than do women in more skilled clerical occupations.

Of course, the probability of entering skilled occupations depends, among other things, on women's education. The reason for this effect is that a withdrawal from the labour market has a current opportunity cost, the wage, and a future opportunity cost, the capital loss due to the potential job experience forgone. For a steep earnings profile the current cost is relatively lower when a woman is young, while the future cost decreases with age (since there are less years of work activity left). Furthermore, the age pattern of the total opportunity cost depends on the shape of the earnings profile. Gustafsson (2001, p. 241), for instance, observes that if it is concave the capital loss due to a later birth is very much smaller than that due to an early child birth. To summarise, in Cigno's (1991) model education may have a two-fold effect. If education increases only the size of life-cycle wealth but does not alter the earnings profile, highly educated women are likely to give birth early in the marriage, while if education alters only the earnings profile but not life-cycle wealth, namely makes it steeper, women have an incentive to postpone fertility. Finally, if education changes both the size of life-cycle wealth and the earnings profile, the sign of the net effect on fertility timing cannot be predicted theoretically and must be addressed empirically.

Walker (1995) specifies a dynamic model in which parents derive utility from children and consumption and have intertemporally and contemporaneously strongly separable preferences, and capital markets are perfect. In Walker's model parents are strongly motivated to have children early in the life-cycle since children produce a recursive flow of utility also for all periods following the birth event, which is discounted at a positive rate of time preference (unlike in Happel et al. 1984). Walker does not consider the effect of pre-marital human capital in his model, although he does consider the effect of different wage profiles and maintains that changes which make the profile steeper reduce the *tempo* of fertility (with the same level of completed fertility), while changes which flatten the earnings profile tend to delay fertility. The reason is that during a period of increasing wages, *ceteris paribus*, women have an incentive to give birth early in the life-cycle, when the opportunity cost of their time is relatively less. The difference of results with respect to Cigno (1991) is due to the recursive structure of the utility of fertility and to the different specification of the wage function, which is not linear but convex in work experience. This means that the current wage forgone by giving birth and caring for children is much lower when an individual is relatively younger. In the model an increase in wealth tends by the cumulative nature of the utility flows to reduce the *tempo* of fertility too. Therefore, since highly educated women generally experience both higher life-cycle wealth and a steeper wage profile (see Murphy and Welch, 1992) the prediction of the model is that an increase in women's education induces them to give birth sooner.

Blackburn et al. (1993) study the interactions between fertility timing, wages and human capital accumulation. The authors consider a dynamic model in which women make their human capital investment decision conditional on their preferences with regard to the timing of their first birth. The model shows that if the discount rate is greater than the economy growth rate of wages for workers who do not invest in human capital, then individuals who prefer an early child birth are less likely to invest in human capital. This model therefore reverses the direction of the causality, which now runs from preferences for fertility timing to women's education, suggesting a potential endogeneity problem for women's education neglected by other models.

In conclusion, different theoretical models stress different factors and motives as the main determinants of LFP and fertility behaviour and sometimes generate opposite predictions about the effect of education which rely heavily on the assumption made. Therefore, the question of the effect of education on LFP, fertility *quantum* and fertility *tempo* must be addressed empirically.

3. FERTILITY AND LABOUR FORCE PARTICIPATION IN ITALY: PAST EMPIRICAL RESEARCH

Although there are several empirical studies which investigate female labour supply and labour market participation in Italy conditioning on 'child services' variables[9] (the 'standard approach' as defined by Browning, 1992), we review here only recent empirical work using an approach similar to ours, i.e. studies which jointly model and estimate female LFP and marital fertility behaviour in Italy (the 'purist approach', in Browning 1992).

Some recent contributions are:

Colombino and Di Tommaso (1996), who estimate a simultaneous model of female marital fertility and LFP using a sequence of cross-sections of micro data form the waves 1987, 1989 and 1991 of the ISHIW. Their sample includes women aged between 18 and 40. They find that cohort effects are not significant whereas wage effects are strong and significant. They use a bivariate probit model, which though allowing for correlation between fertility and participation decisions, theoretically implies separability of the lifetime utility function into fertility and leisure, as shown by Weeks and Orme (1999). Colombino and Di Tommaso consider the effect of various measures of unearned income and wealth to investigate income effects. The effect of the regressors included is reported in Table 5.1. Education has a positive impact on women's wage and therefore, indirectly, a positive effect on participation and a negative effect on fertility. Colombino and Di Tommaso do not account for the potential endogeneity of education.

Di Tommaso (1999), who estimates a trivariate model of women's participation, fertility and wages using ISHIW data for the same period as Colombino and Di Tommaso (1996). She uses a sample of women aged 18-40. The results are shown in Table 5.1. Schooling has a positive impact on participation and a negative impact on fertility through the effect on wages. From the technical point of view Di Tommaso's econometric specification is based on the restrictive assumption of separability of the lifetime utility function into leisure and fertility. Education is considered exogenous.

Del Boca (1999), who analyses the effect of market rigidities on the participation and fertility behaviour of Italian married women.[10] She performs cross-section and panel data analyses using data from the ISHIW for the years 1991, 1993 and 1995. Her sample includes women aged 21-45. The preferred model is the fixed effects model, which does not allow estimation of the effect of education. The results are shown in Table 5.1. In the cross-sections education has a positive impact on fertility for the 1991 and 1995 cohorts and a positive impact on participation for all three years. From a technical point of view Del Boca's panel estimation procedure rests upon the assumption of independence of fertility and LFP decisions. In that case, once the unobserved heterogeneity has been eliminated using a fixed effects model, the two logit models for participation and fertility can be estimated separately. However, the author uses two separate logit models for estimation of the cross-sections without accounting for the possible correlation between the two decisions (unlike Colombino and Di Tommaso 1996). This study does not account for the possible endogeneity of education.

With respect to the above studies the current chapter:

1. uses 1993 ISHIW data. The choice of the cohort depends on the availability of the variables used in the econometric specification (in particular data on child care availability by province of residence);[11]
2. considers a flow-fertility variable (a precise definition is given in section 4.3) and by including some interaction terms between years of education and age, we also analyse issues related to the effect of education on fertility timing;[12] Moreover, we use a spline function (with 'knots' at the different educational levels: compulsory, upper secondary and tertiary education) which allows the effect of additional years of education on LFP and fertility to differ across educational levels. This formulation is more general than that which imposes an equal coefficient for all years of education (usually adopted in the literature). In particular, a test for the equality of coefficients across educational levels is rejected;[13]
3. explicitly controls for family background variables that might affect a woman's, or her husband's, preferences towards fertility and LFP, often neglected in past empirical work;
4. uses a multinomial model. A multinomial model is more general than a bivariate one since it accounts for the possible non-separability of the life-cycle utility function into leisure and fertility, as shown in Weeks and Orme (1999). Di Tommaso and Weeks (2000), for instance, in an application of Weeks and Orme (1999) to LFP and fertility decisions on UK data, find that the bivariate probit and logit models, which imply a restrictive form of additive separability across the decisions, are rejected in favour of their multinomial counterparts;
5. estimates a reduced form-purist model, in the language of Browning (1992). In particular, we are interested in the effect of education upon fertility and LFP. Therefore, in the empirical specification we do not include 'child services' variables, which are endogenous, but only their determinants, such as a woman's level of education;[14]
6. accounts for the potential endogeneity of female education by including several possible controls for the 'taste for market work' and testing for the weak exogeneity of education.

Table 5.1. Results of the previous literature on female labour force participation (LFP) and fertility behaviour in Italy

Characteristics	Articles					
	Colombino and Di Tommaso (1996)		Del Boca (1999)		Di Tommaso (1999)	
Data set	ISHIW		ISHIW		ISHIW	
Sample	Women 18-40		Women 21-45		Women 18-40	
Years	1987, 1989, 1991		1991, 1993, 1995		1987, 1989, 1991	
Participation definition	Employment		Employment		Employment	
Fertility definition	One or more children in the household		One or more children aged <2 in the household		One or more children aged <18 in the household	
Econometric technique	Bivariate probit		Fixed effects logit model (panel) and two separate logit (cross-sections)		Bivariate probit	
Variable	Effect					
	P	F	P [(a)]	F [(a)]	P	F
Woman's wage	+	-			+	-
Husband's wage	-	+			-	+
Unearned income	-	no	-	no	+	-
Wealth	+	no			-	+
Family transfers			+	+		
Child care			+	no		
Parents alive			+	+		
Part-time			no	+		
Schooling	+	-	+	no	+	-

Notes: the + and – signs show the direction of the effect of the variables listed on participation (Part.) and fertility (Fert.), 'no' means that the effect is not found significant. [(a)] results for the 1993 cross-section.

4. THE EMPIRICAL ANALYSIS

In the following sub-sections we describe the methodology and the results of the empirical analysis.

4.1. The econometric model

Under standard regularity conditions the dynamic life-cycle models described in section 2 can be solved giving an optimal solution for the choice variables, in particular life-cycle fertility and labour force participation.

We code participation in period t as $L_t = 1$, non-participation as $L_t = 0$, the decision to give birth in period t as $B_t = 1$ and the decision not to give birth as $B_t = 0$ and focus here only on marital fertility. Therefore, we assume that women have already made their maximising choices in their pre-marital period and we condition on those optimal choices.

Focusing on L_t and B_t only and omitting in the notation the other choice variables, the optimal life-cycle plan concerning LFP and fertility can be stated as:

$$P^* = \{(L^*_1, B^*_1), (L^*_2, B^*_2), \ldots, (L^*_T, B^*_T)\} \tag{1}$$

where T is the end of the planning horizon.

In period t the probability of observing $L_t = z$ and $B_t = j$, where $z, j = \{0,1\}$ is the probability that the pair of decisions ($L_t = z$, $B_t = j$) is included in the optimal life-cycle plan, i.e. $\Pr[(L_t = z, B_t = j) \in P^*]$. If we define as V_t the life-cycle utility function evaluated at time t, this probability can be expressed as:

$$\begin{aligned} &\Pr[V_t\{(L^*_1, B^*_1), (L^*_2, B^*_2), \ldots, (L_t = z, B_t = j), \ldots, (L^*_T, B^*_T)\} > \\ &V_t\{(L^*_1, B^*_1), (L^*_2, B^*_2), \ldots, (L_t = h, B_t = k), \ldots, (L^*_T, B^*_T)\}] \end{aligned} \tag{2}$$

$\forall (h,k) \neq (z, j)$. The four different outcomes for (L_t, B_t) can be recoded to obtain a single dependent outcome variable Y_{it}, where the subscript i refers to the individual:

$$Y_{it} = \begin{cases} 1 \text{ if } L_{it} = 0, B_{it} = 0 \text{ (NP, NF)} \\ 2 \text{ if } L_{it} = 1, B_{it} = 0 \text{ (P, NF)} \\ 3 \text{ if } L_{it} = 0, B_{it} = 1 \text{ (NP, F)} \\ 4 \text{ if } L_{it} = 1, B_{it} = 1 \text{ (P, F)} \end{cases} \tag{3}$$

(NP, NF) stands for 'non participation-non fertility', (P, NF) for 'participation-non fertility', (NP, F) for 'non participation-fertility' and (P, F) for 'participation-fertility'.

Now we can define the life-cycle expected utility function as V_{yit}, where t is the current period which we are analysing (since we use in the empirical work cross-section data) and y is one of the four possible outcomes of Y_{it} for the individual i. Adopting a linear specification we have:

$$V_{yit} = X_{it}'\beta_y + \varepsilon_{yit} \tag{4}$$

where X_{it} is a vector of exogenous explanatory variables and ε_{yit} is a random variable unobservable to the econometrician (e.g. differences in tastes). By assuming a Type I extreme-value distribution for ε_{yit} and independence across the ε_y's, the multinomial logit model (MNL model, hereafter) can be derived from utility maximisation (result originally due to McFadden, 1974). In this case the probability of observing $Y_{it} = 1$, for instance, is:

$$\Pr[Y_{it} = 1] = \Pr[V_{1it} = \arg\max_{y} V_{yit}] = \frac{\exp(X_{it}'\beta_1)}{\sum_{y=1}^{4}\exp(X_{it}'\beta_y)}. \quad (5)$$

As equation (2) shows, the value of life-cycle utility at time t is a function of past, current and future choice variables. In the empirical specification we should include only exogenous variables among the regressors if we want to estimate unconditional effects (as in the *purist* approach described in Browning, 1992).

Moreover, we have seen in section 2 that when empirical study is made of married women's LFP and fertility behaviour education cannot be considered an exogenous variable. In fact, it is likely that the form of a woman's preferences, i.e. the relative weights of consumption, offspring and leisure in her life-cycle utility, affects her optimal human capital investment.[15]

4.2. Some possible determinants of female labour force participation and fertility

In the empirical model we include the exogenous or predetermined variables that, acting through preferences or the budget constraint, affect women's marital fertility and LFP. The relevant factors are well summarised in Lehrer and Nerlove (1986) and Dex and Joshi (1999). Here we consider:

Role of the partner. The husband[16] affects a woman's fertility and participation decisions in several ways. If we adopt a unitary model of family, LFP decisions are jointly made by the spouses, as are fertility decisions. This suggests that the husband's labour incomes are endogenous in that setting (in the sense that they are jointly determined with female labour supply). If we adopt a collective model of family (see Chiappori, 1992) labour force and fertility decisions are individually made by each spouse who takes into account her/his non-labour income and the income of her/his partner (since family incomes are shared according to a certain 'sharing rule'). Unfortunately, in this case past non-labour incomes depend on past LFP, fertility and saving behaviour and are likely to be endogenous. We believe that, because of the strong institutional rigidities existing in the Italian labour market (see Del Boca, 2002c, and Del Boca and Pasqua, 2002) where part-time jobs are scarce[17] and women have primary responsibility in child rearing, the hypothesis that family labour supply is jointly determined by the spouses is not adequate: Italian men generally work and have limited degrees of freedom regarding the number of hours worked so that their incomes can be considered as exogenous with respect to female labour supply and fertility decisions.[18] Therefore, a *traditional family model* (see Del Boca, 1997) is probably more suitable to the Italian case:[19] a woman makes her participation and fertility decisions taking into account the fact that she can share some family resources with her partner (and therefore also her partner's incomes). The sign of the impact of husband's income on female fertility cannot be determined theoretically. In models that only account for the quantity of children the expected effect is positive. In contrast, in models accounting also for the demand for quality the effect is generally expected to be negative (see De Tray, 1973, and Becker and Lewis, 1973). Then the question must be addressed empirically. Besides the role of husband's income, we consider other husband-related variables that may affect a woman's LFP and fertility decisions, namely job qualification, branch of activity, education and age. The first three variables are proxies for the husband's permanent income and income profile while the fourth is a proxy for a woman's probability of conception. Moreover, the last two variables may also affect the husband's attitude towards his wife's LFP.

Preferences and cultural factors. We consider the effect of the *gender role model* inherited by a woman from her mother and the attitude of the husband towards his wife's LFP. Namely, we include among the explanatory variables the job qualification and branch of activity of a woman's mother and the fact that her mother in law worked.[20]

Child care. Women have to decide which form of child care to use and how many hours of child rearing to allocate to the market. For this reason we include in the econometric specification some variables related to the availability of external child care, in particular public and informal child care (i.e. child care provided by a woman's parents or parents in law).

Female education. In this chapter we focus on the role of formal education in shaping the participation and fertility decisions of married women. Women's stock of formal education at time t is a predetermined variable. This does not rule out that it could be endogenous: women with a more marked 'taste for market work' could simultaneously invest more in education, and have a higher LFP and a lower fertility.[21] The observed correlation between education, LFP and fertility would in this case be only spurious and driven by a fourth factor: the 'taste for market work'. For this reason in the empirical work we shall account for the possible endogeneity of education by including a wide range of family variables which control for heterogeneity in the 'taste for market work', in the spirit of the *proxying and matching method* (see Blundell et al. 1997), and testing for the weak exogeneity of education.

Easterlin model. Although in section 4.1 we considered LFP and fertility decisions to be the outcomes of maximising behaviour, as observed in Gustafsson (2001), for some time the main rival theory to neoclassical models of fertility was the so called Easterlin model (Easterlin, 1980). For this reason and to avoid a possible model misspecification (due to omitted variables) we also include some variables related to the Easterlin *relative income hypothesis.* In the Easterlin model 'the driving force behind both increased LFP and reduced fertility, is the desire of a large cohort to improve relative economic status, with parental income as a measure of that cohort's material aspirations.' (Macunovich, 1996, p. 95). A survey of the results of works attempting to test the Easterlin *relative income hypothesis* is provided in Macunovich (1996). These studies have usually employed proxies for relative incomes, such as parental occupational status, and the empirical evidence on the validity of the hypothesis is 'mixed'.

4.3. Data Description

The data used are drawn from the 1993 Italian Survey of Household Income and Wealth (ISHIW) of the Bank of Italy. The ISHIW is the most popular source of micro-data for Italy. For a detailed description the interested reader may consult Banca d'Italia (1995) and Filippin (1997). The nature of the ISHIW, which does not include data on fertility and LFP histories, does not allow us to estimate a complete life-cycle model. Hence, we have to rely on cross-sectional data; in particular we use 1993 data. We consider women aged between 21 and 39 cohabiting with their husband or partner, for whom we have information in the data set, and exclude from the sample self-employed women.[22] The sample includes 1,467 women. We choose the same age interval as Del Boca (1999), which is the study closest to ours among those listed in section 3 for the definition of fertility, but discard women in the age class 40-44. This we do since our 'economic model' of participation and fertility can explain only desired fertility, and we want to focus on the ages at which women have a high *fecundability*.[23]

Table 5.2. Observed distribution of the MNL outcomes by level of women's education

Education	(NP, NF)	(P, NF)	(NP, F)	(P, F)
Primary	74.04	19.23	6.25	0.48
Lower Secondary	56.90	33.16	6.90	3.03
Upper secondary	28.96	59.30	4.89	6.85
Tertiary	5.61	80.37	0.00[(a)]	14.02

Notes: the sample includes 1,420 observations. The four LFP and fertility outcomes are: (NP, NF), non participation-non fertility; (P, NF), participation-non fertility; (NP, F), non participation-fertility; (P, F): participation-fertility. [(a)] The fact that this cell is empty is not a problem since we do not consider dummies for education but a continuous variable, namely the years of education.

As already emphasised, our main focus is on the effect of formal education. Since the ISHIW contains information only on the highest educational qualification obtained, we computed the total number of years of education using the years of legal duration of the different educational grades, as follows: primary school (*scuola elementare*) – 5 years; lower secondary school (*scuola media inferiore*) – 8 years; upper secondary school (*scuola media superiore*) – 13 years; tertiary education (*laurea*) – 17 years.[24] Years of education are interacted with four age dummies (21-24, 25-29, 30-34, 35-39) which enable us to study the effect of education on the timing of fertility and LFP, and we use a spline function to account for possible non-linear effects of education (i.e. the effect of the years of education is not constrained to be equal across the different levels of education).

As to the dependent variables, we define participation as employment or unemployment and consider as non-participating those women who replied to the ISHIW that they were housewives.[25] We consider a birth event to be the presence in the family of a child more than one and less than two years old. Our choice depends on the fact that we want to analyse the effect of education and other variables on the decision to give birth and to participate in the labour market. For this reason we consider a flow fertility variable rather than a stock fertility variable. We consider children more than one and less than two years old since we do not know the exact age (number of months) of children aged less than one and we want to avoid considering periods when participation in the labour market is not possible, e.g. in the first months immediately after a child birth.[26] Therefore, we study the issue of fertility and LFP in the period surrounding a birth event. This provides nonetheless useful information on future labour market participation.[27]

In the model we explicitly control for the geographic area of residence, municipality size, husband's income, Easterlin's variables, parents' education, parents' job qualification, parents' branch of activity, husband's education, husband's job qualification and economic branch, husband's age, public child care availability and potential informal child care availability (parents' availability). The rationale for the inclusion of these variables along with their description is given in Appendix 5.A.

When it was possible we preferred to use missing-value dummies rather than discarding observations for which some variables had missing information. Unfortunately, this was not always possible. In fact, for women for whom data on father's or mother's education was missing not all the four MNL outcomes were observed, which caused major problems in the model estimation. Hence, we decided to drop observations with missing data on parents' education (47 observations, 3.2% of the sample).[28] Therefore, the final sample includes 1,420 women (for some descriptive statistics see Table B.1 in Bratti, 2003b). Table 5.2 shows the distribution of the four MNL outcomes by level of women's education: the positive correlation between education and participation is evident, although the data also show a positive correlation between education and fertility for participating women.

4.4. Econometric strategy

In order to assess the effect of education we adopt the following empirical strategy:
1) We include in the model specification a wide range of controls for a woman's family background that may proxy for unobserved heterogeneity in the 'taste for market work' (in the spirit of *the proxy and matching method*, see Blundell et al. 1997);
2) We test for the weak exogeneity of education. In the case of endogeneity of women's education we plan to apply a Non Linear Instrumental Variables (NLIV) estimation strategy, by 'instrumenting' education.

The estimated effect of education in models of women's marital fertility and LFP may be partly spurious. It may be the unobserved individual heterogeneity (e.g.

unobserved preferences for market work) which induces some women to invest more in education and also affects their LFP and fertility decisions later on.[29] One way of controlling for the presence of unobserved heterogeneity (which may affect our estimates) is to include a wide range of family background variables, which are likely to shape a woman's preferences, in the model.[30] We included father's and mother's education, job qualification and branch of activity, which could affect a woman's 'taste for market work'. The full set of estimates of this model are not reported here for the sake of brevity,[31] while the coefficients of the educational variables are listed in Table 5.3.

Table 5.3. Significance of the educational variables in the explanation of female LFP and fertility

Variable[a]	(P, NF)		(NP, F)		(P, F)	
	Coef.	t	Coef.	t	Coef.	t
MNL model with controls for 'taste heterogeneity"						
21-24 * C	0.19	1.38	0.39	2.15	0.52	1.09
21-24 * US	-0.11	-0.46	-0.20	-0.74	0.26	0.68
25-29 * C	0.15	1.43	0.29	2.04	0.73	1.71
25-29 * US	0.18	1.96	0.12	0.85	0.24	1.86
25-29 * T	0.15	0.65	-7.84	-25.49	-0.63	-1.46
30-34 * C	0.14	1.37	0.30	2.05	0.51	1.24
30-34 * US	0.30	3.61	0.05	0.35	0.42	2.89
30-34 * T	0.29	1.28	-7.82	-33.86	0.35	1.24
35-39 * C	0.28	2.66	0.21	1.27	0.51	1.16
35-39 * US	0.19	2.81	-0.02	-0.09	0.36	1.96
35-39 * T	0.87	3.51	-7.19	-13.50	1.14	3.98
'Parsimonious' MNL model						
21-24 * C	0.18	1.28	0.39	2.23	0.38	0.84
21-24 * US	-0.08	-0.35	-0.13	-0.49	0.29	0.75
25-29 * C	0.14	1.30	0.29	2.01	0.63	1.61
25-29 * US	0.18	1.92	0.11	0.77	0.23	1.73
25-29 * T	0.16	0.69	-7.74	-23.32	-0.45	-1.26
30-34 * C	0.13	1.25	0.32	2.12	0.41	1.06
30-34 * US	0.30	3.62	0.02	0.15	0.44	2.99
30-34 * T	0.27	1.17	-7.62	-31.18	0.38	1.40
35-39 * C	0.27	2.54	0.23	1.37	0.44	1.06
35-39 * US	0.19	2.86	-0.03	-0.20	0.36	2.02
35-39 * T	0.88	3.60	-6.90	15.76	1.15	4.18

Notes: the four LFP and fertility outcomes are: (NP,NF), non participation-non fertility; (P, NF), participation - non fertility; (NP, F), non participation-fertility; (P, F): participation-fertility. (NP,NF) is the reference outcome. The sample includes in all cases 1,420 women. The table shows the coefficients of the educational variables.

Since the MNL model uses the maintained assumption of the Independence of Irrelevant Alternatives (IIA), we performed some specification tests to assess the validity of this assumption (see Hausman and McFadden, 1984). All tests (see Table 5.4) concluded that the IIA could not be rejected by our data.

Clearly, even after controlling for possible taste heterogeneity, women's education retains its significance. In order to obtain a 'parsimonious' model we performed some likelihood ratio (LR, hereafter) tests for the different groups of (by age group and level of education) estimated from the MNL model with all controls and the 'parsimonious' MNL model. The estimates of the coefficients of the other regressors can be found in the Appendix B in Bratti (2003b). [(a)] This column shows the coefficients of the interaction variables between age and level of education (C: compulsory, US: upper secondary, T: tertiary, LS: lower secondary is the reference group).

Table 5.4. Hausman test of the independence of irrelevant alternatives

Omitted outcome	Distribution	Test statistic	*p*-value
(NP, NF)	$Chi^2(122)$	-6.29	[(a)]
(P, NF)	$Chi^2(122)$	31.35	1.00
(NP, F)	$Chi^2(122)$	10.45	1.00
(P, F)	$Chi^2(122)$	7.15	1.00

Notes: in all cases the Hausman test shows that the IIA assumptions cannot be rejected. [(a)] Hausman and McFadden (1984, footnote 4) maintain that the fact that the test statistic takes on a negative value can be interpreted as strong evidence against rejecting the hypothesis that the IIA assumption holds.

regressors.[32] The groups of regressors that were not significant at the 10% level, when individually tested, were the variables related to the wife's parental wealth, father's job qualification and branch of activity and husband's education, job qualification and branch of activity. However, when jointly tested the restrictions were not valid, while the model omitting only wife's parental wealth variables, father's job qualification and branch of activity was an admissible reduction of the general model.[33] The estimates of the 'parsimonious' model are shown in Table 5.B1 in Appendix 5.B.

Although the introduction of a wide range of controls to account for unobserved heterogeneity helps to obtain consistent estimates, it does not exclude that the left-out heterogeneity may still be important. For this reason, in the case of the endogeneity of education a Non Linear Instrumental Variables Estimator[34] may be more appropriate. We use as identifying instruments the variables related to a woman's parental wealth and father's job qualification and branch of activity, which the first part of the analysis suggested do not affect women's LFP and fertility, but which might affect their education. Table 5.B2 in Appendix 5.B shows the estimate of the education equation. The instruments turn out to be highly significant in explanation of the number of years of education achieved. Following the suggestions of Bound et al. (1995) we computed a LR test for the joint significance of the identifying instruments. The value is $\chi^2(11) = 52.46$ (p-value: 0.00), which confirms that the instruments are quite good.

In order to test for the endogeneity of education we performed Smith and Blundell's (1986) weak exogeneity test, including the predicted residual from the education equation in our 'parsimonious' MNL model. The predicted residual included in the 'artificial regression' turned out not to be significant ($\chi^2(3) = 0.82$, p-value = 0.84). Hence, we conclude that our data do not allow rejection of the null hypothesis of weak exogeneity of women's education with fertility and LFP (once we control for a number of family background characteristics which might affect women's decision to invest in human capital). This is not an unusual result. Sander (1992), for instance, obtains similar results in his study of the effect of women's schooling on fertility in the United States. For this reason we focus on the estimates of the 'parsimonious' MNL model.

In the light of these results, Table 5.5 shows the predicted probabilities of the four MNL outcomes by level of education and age group computed at the sample average of all the remaining variables using the 'parsimonious' MNL model. Since no married woman in our sample has a university degree at age 21-24 we do not simulate the LFP and fertility behaviour of women with a tertiary education for this age group and consider their probability to give birth and participate as null.

4.5. The effect of education

From Table 5.5, it is clear that education raises the labour force attachment of women, who continue to participate in the labour market even in the period surrounding a birth event. Moreover, better educated women tend to postpone fertility. In what follows we interpret the probability of giving birth as fertility.

Both for women with primary and with lower secondary schooling the probability of giving birth peaks at the ages 21-24 (3.50% and 9.04%, respectively). Highly educated women, i.e. women with upper secondary and tertiary educational levels tend to postpone fertility, which reaches its maximum at the ages 25-29 (12.62%) and 35-39 (6.55%), respectively. For women with primary and lower secondary education fertility decreases monotonically with age, while for tertiary educated women it increases monotonically with age. Women with upper secondary schooling have an inverse-U shaped pattern of fertility with age.

We could interpret the sum of the probabilities of giving birth for the different age groups by educational level as a raw measure of the hypothetical marital fertility at ages 21-39 (24-39 for women with tertiary education). Indeed, assuming that all women get married between age 21 and 24 (between ages 25 and 29 for women with tertiary education) and that their marriages last at least until they are in the age interval 35-39,[35] it is evident that *ceteris paribus*, i.e. for an equal duration of marriage,[36] the marital fertility of women with upper secondary schooling is the highest. A rising pattern of fertility with education is also found by Ben-Porath (1973) and Danziger and Neuman (1989) for Israel, and Moffitt (1984) for the US. Bloemen and Kalwij (2001) using data from the Netherlands find that 'an increase in years of schooling of a woman causes her to schedule births later in life but it does not significantly affect her completed fertility' (p. 593). Rising marital fertility with increasing education may be explained by the prevalence of income over substitution effects at higher levels of education, especially when child care can be purchased in the market (see for example Ermisch, 1989). In that case, in fact, the cost of giving birth for a woman is the lowest between the income and experience lost by withdrawing from the labour market to care for children and the cost of external child care. Highly educated women, therefore, are relatively more likely to work and to use their income to purchase external child care and, given their higher expected amount of life-cycle wealth, they could eventually 'afford' a higher fertility as well. This is what seems to happen in our sample, since women with upper secondary and tertiary schooling are more likely to participate during child rearing. Blau and Hagy (1998), for instance, find for the US a positive effect of the mother's wage rate on the probability of buying external child care and conclude that: 'paid child care arrangements and more formal arrangements are complementary to being employed' (p. 127). Chiuri (2000) using 1993 ISHIW data does not find a positive effect of education on the probability of using external child care. However, the ISHIW data do not include information on the use and the cost of child minders and given the strong restrictions in the places and the timetable available in Italy (see Del Boca, 2002c, and Del Boca and Pasqua, 2002), especially for *crèches*, child minders might be an important form of external child care purchased by highly educated women working full-time with children under the age of two (i.e. in our case). In this respect, although Chiuri (2000), using data from the 1993 ISTAT Survey on Household Consumption (ISTAT, 1995a), states that only 2.5% of households with more than two members and at least one pre-school child had positive expenditures on domestic child care services, she also observes that paid informal child care was relatively more diffused among high income families (to which working women with higher education are more likely to belong).

Table 5.5. Probabilities (%) of the MNL outcomes, by level of education and age-group ('parsimonious' MNL model)

Education	Age	LFP and fertility outcomes					
		(NP,NF)	(P,NF)	(NP,F)	(P,F)	P[(a)]	F[(b)]
Primary (5 years)	21-24	72.07	24.43	3.33	0.17	24.60	3.50
	25-29	76.18	21.04	2.16	0.62	21.66	2.78
	30-34	76.67	20.68	2.45	0.20	20.88	2.65
	35-39	64.41	34.08	1.30	0.20	34.28	1.50
				"Total fertility":			10.44
Lower secondary (8 years)	21-24	57.72	33.24	8.63	0.41	33.65	9.04
	25-29	65.04	26.97	4.43	3.56	30.53	7.99
	30-34	67.06	26.78	5.56	0.60	27.38	6.16
	35-39	44.94	52.74	1.79	0.53	53.27	2.31
				"Total fertility":			25.50
Upper secondary (13 years)	21-24	66.96	25.73	5.25	2.06	27.79	7.32
	25-29	43.74	43.64	5.19	7.42	51.06	12.62
	30-34	34.23	59.82	3.18	2.78	62.59	5.95
	35-39	24.53	72.92	0.83	1.72	74.65	2.55
				"Total fertility":			28.44
Tertiary (17 years)	21-24	-	-	-	-	-	-
	25-29	34.32	64.73	0.00	0.96	65.68	0.96
	30-34	15.55	78.62	0.00	5.83	84.45	5.83
	35-39	0.92	92.53	0.00	6.55	99.08	6.55
				"Total fertility":			13.34

Notes: the four LFP and fertility outcomes are: (NP, NF), non participation-non fertility; (P, NF), participation- non fertility; (NP, F), non participation-fertility; (P, F): participation-fertility. The probabilities of the four MNL outcomes are computed at the sample average values for all variables but education. They may not sum to one because of rounding. "Total fertility" is the sum across age groups of the probability of giving birth by educational level. [(a)]Probability of participation: Pr(P, NF) + Pr(P, F); [(b)] Probability of fertility (i.e. of giving birth): Pr(NP, F) + Pr(P, F).

For women with a university education the fertility rate at ages 21-39 is higher than that of women with primary schooling but lower than that of women with the other two levels of education. Since in Italy it is extremely rare for students to obtain a university degree before age 24, for these individuals the negative effect of a university education on fertility and the fertility postponement might run mostly through the postponement of marriage after the completion of tertiary education.[37]

It is worth noting that what we estimate is only a part of the overall effect of education on fertility. In particular, we estimate the effect of education on marital fertility for the age classes 21-39, conditional on marriage or cohabitation.[38] But as we have seen in Figure 5.4 education may influence also non-marital fertility and fertility before age 21,[39] and marital formation and dissolution. However, since in Italy the nuptiality rate at ages before 21 is very low[40] our estimated effect can be roughly interpreted as the effect of education on marital fertility.

Our findings are not necessarily in contrast with the evidence for the less developed countries (LDCs), which generally shows, instead, that female education has an important negative effect on fertility (see for instance Schultz, 1993). Firstly, if one refers to overall (and not only marital) fertility is clear that education may negatively affect fertility by increasing the age at first marriage. Secondly, even if one considers marital fertility only (see, for instance, Lam and Duryea, 1999) some possible explanations for these apparently contrasting findings are that while in the developed countries is usually assumed that contraceptive methods are largely available and used for family planning, in poor countries, where education is very low, a rise in schooling could affect the use and the effectiveness of contraceptive methods and lead to fewer unwanted births (see Rosenzweig and Schultz, 1985). Moreover, while models for developed countries usually assume an altruistic, or consumption, motive to have children (see Becker, 1981), models for LDCs often stress an egoistic, or investment, motive to have children: the so-called *old-age security hypothesis* (see Cigno, 1991). Therefore, the determinants of fertility may be very different in countries at different stage of development (see Hotz et al. 1997 for the developed countries, and Schultz, 1997, for less developed countries).

We find that especially for women with primary and lower secondary schooling, working in the labour market appears to be scarcely compatible with child rearing. Indeed, in these two educational groups 'fertile' women generally do not participate in the labour market. Moreover, their participation seems to increase at ages 35-39, where their fertility is particularly low. This is hardly surprising given what we have already said about the lack of availability of part-time work opportunities (for the period under study) and the insufficient provision of public (often subsidised) child care in Italy. By contrast, highly educated women appear to be able to reconcile family and work. This is particularly evident for women with tertiary education, for whom the probability of fertility and non participation is null. This could be explained, as we have already said, in terms of both the higher value of time of highly educated women and the possibility to pay for private child care.

Table 5.6. Probabilities (%) of the MNL outcomes, for other explanatory variables

Variable	LFP and fertility outcomes					
	(NP,NF)	(P,NF)	(NP,F)	(P,F)	P[(a)]	F[(b)]
Sample average	46.86	51.30	0.32	1.52	52.84	1.84
Husbands'annual income + 1 million lira (about € 516)	47.23	50.96	0.32	1.49	52.45	1.81
Child care + 1%	44.05	54.23	0.27	1.45	55.67	1.72
Parents not available	62.63	35.25	0.22	1.89	37.15	2.11
Parents available	41.68	56.59	0.35	1.39	57.98	1.73
Mother's job: housewife	46.46	50.47	0.32	2.75	53.22	3.07
Mother's job: low skilled	37.40	62.16	0.28	0.16	62.31	0.44
Mother's job: medium and high skilled	35.34	63.79	0.20	0.66	64.45	0.86
Mother's job: self-employed	70.10	27.68	0.25	1.98	29.66	2.23
Mother in law did not work	50.88	47.33	0.46	1.33	48.66	1.79
Mother in law worked	37.47	60.36	0.13	2.04	62.40	2.16

Notes: the four LFP and fertility outcomes are: (NP, NF), non participation-non fertility; (P, NF), participation- non fertility; (NP, F), non participation-fertility; (P, F): participation-fertility. The probabilities may not sum to one because of rounding. They may not sum to one because of rounding. [(a)] Probability of participation: Pr(P, NF) + Pr(P, F); [(b)] Probability of fertility (i.e. of giving birth): Pr(NP, F) + Pr(P, F).

In general, the probability of LFP rises with education and is particularly high for women with a university education (e.g. it is about 99% in the age group 35-39). Women with tertiary education, for instance, are almost three times more likely to participate in the labour market than women with primary schooling at ages 35-39.

Apart from the exact measures of the estimated effects, we think that the qualitative implications of our analysis are quite clear. Firstly, education raises the LFP of women, especially of women giving births; secondly, for married women aged 21-39 the probability of giving birth increases with years of formal education up to the upper secondary schooling level and then declines; finally, education determines a fertility postponement. The fertility postponement can be explained by some of the economic models reviewed in section 2. For highly educated women an early withdrawal from the labour market is costly both in terms of current opportunity costs (i.e. wages) and future accumulation of human capital (*career planning motive*). Moreover, highly educated women might decide to give birth when their current incomes are relatively higher (*consumption smoothing motive*), which usually happens at older ages given the steeper wage profile for high skilled jobs.

4.6. The effects of other factors

In this section we comment on the effects of other variables discussed in the literature, which turn out to be statistically significant in our empirical analysis and that may be important for economic policy design. They are reported in Table 5.6.

Husband's income. Partner's income is a significant determinant of fertility and participation behaviour. In particular, an increase in husband's annual income by one million of Italian lira (about € 516), decreases the probability of participation by 0.36 percentage points. The sign of the effect is those generally predicted by economic models. Other studies for Italy finding a negative husband's income effect are Colombino and Di Tommaso (1996) and Di Tommaso (1999). By constrast, the effect on fertility is negligible and in the opposite direction to that usually suggested by economic theory (i.e. a positive income effect on fertility).

Child care. One percentage point increase in the ratio of public child care places over the population aged 0-2 raises the probability of participation by 2.85 points whilst it has a very tiny effect on fertility. The interpretation of this effect is, however, problematic as child care availability may be endogenous (see for example Del Boca, 2002c). Since the child care sector typically employs female workers, the positive effect of public child care may in part pick up also the effect of a local environment which offers good employment opportunities to women. A similar effect is observed for parents' availability. Women whose parents are available have a higher probability of participation compared to women who have no access to informal external child care (+20.83%), while the effect on fertility is negligible. This result confirms the importance of informal child care availability for promoting new mother's LFP. Informal and unpaid child care become substitutes for formal child care arrangements when the latter are unavailable or unaffordable. Similar evidence is found by several other papers on Italy such as Del Boca et al. (2003), Marenzi and Pagani (2003) and Bratti et al. (2004), among others.

The positive effect of both public and informal child care on participation can be explained by the fact that women who already have children older than two may in part transfer to relatives and public institutions the "burden" of child rearing, and participate in the labour market. However, our results on child care are difficult to reconcile with a forward-looking model in which women plan fertility according to the availability of low-price child care.

Gender role model and cultural factors. Women whose mother was in a low (high) skilled job are 9.09% (2.14%) more likely to participate and 2.83% (0.42%) less likely to give birth than women whose mother did not work. This suggests that labour force participation may be in part an attitude that a woman inherits from her mother. Women living with a working mother may have developed a particular view of their role in the family. The importance of cultural factors also emerges from the significance of the variable related to the fact that a woman's mother in law worked. As said (see Appendix A), the latter variable may be a proxy for the husband's attitude towards female work in the marketplace. Women whose mother's in law worked are 13.74% more likely to participate and 0.37% less likely to give birth. These findings confirm the traditional character of Italian families, where the husband's opinion on female work appear to have a strong impact on a woman's LFP.

5. CONCLUDING REMARKS

In this chapter we have developed an analysis of female marital fertility (at ages 21-39) and LFP decisions using data from the 1993 Italian Survey of Household Income and Wealth of the Bank of Italy. We had a primary interest in the role of education in shaping labour market and marital fertility decisions and therefore a primary concern about its potential endogeneity. The former has been accounted for by including in the model a wide range of controls (*proxying and matching method*), estimating an education regression and testing for weak exogeneity of education. However, after controlling for a wide range of characteristics of a woman's family and marital background we did not find any residual evidence of endogeneity of education with labour force participation and fertility. Our main findings are the following:

- education increases the job attachment of women, in particular highly educated women also work in the period surrounding a birth event;
- there is some evidence of a *ceteris paribus* rising pattern of marital fertility with increasing education at ages 21-39, except for women with tertiary education, which can be explained in terms of the prevalence of income over substitution effects due to education and by the greater access to external private child care available to highly educated women. The exception related to university educated women is due to their extremely low fertility rate at the ages 21-29, since they tend to postpone marriage and fertility until the completion of full-time education;
- rising education determines a fertility postponement, which can be explained by the *career planning* and the *consumption smoothing motives* emphasised by the theoretical literature.

Our results have important policy implications. For example, policies which aim to increase women's education at least up to the upper secondary level have a positive effect upon LFP and marital fertility. In particular, we expect that the recent increase in the duration of compulsory schooling introduced in Italy will raise future female LFP. Some other interesting results of our analysis concern the effect of informal and public child-care availability, which exert a positive effect on female labour force participation, and of cultural factors, which appear to be particularly strong in Italy. In particular, the fact that a woman's mother in law worked, as a proxy for her husband's attitude towards women's work in the labour market, has a strong positive effect on her labour force participation.

ACKNOWLEDGEMENTS

This paper was originally published in the *Journal of Population Economics*, 2003, vol. 16, issue 3, pp. 525-554 with the title "Female Labour Force Participation and Marital Fertility of Italian Women: The Role of Education". The introduction in this chapter has been partially rewritten while section 4.6 did not appear in the original article. The author (Massimiliano Bratti) wishes to thank Springer-Verlag, which holds the copyright of the original article, for granting him the permission to reprint it in the present book.

NOTES

[1] Rank one means the highest strictness.

[2] For a recent survey on the problems and prospects of the Italian labour market see Dell'Aringa (2003).

[3] As observed by Del Boca (2002b) some causes for its scarce diffusion are the traditional opposition by the unions, which did not want to favour measures that might have contributed to create a dual regime in the labour market and workers with different standards, and the welfare system, where employers' contributions are determined on the basis of the number of employees and not on the quantity of hours worked.

[4] Other causes may be changes in women's preferences, however Colombino and Di Tommaso (1996) do not find support for this hypothesis.

[5] Data on LFP and fertility come from World Bank (2000) and data on education from Barro and Lee (2001).

[6] Smith (1997), for example, finds that the rising earnings of women, which are partly due to increasing educational levels, are a significant determinant of the rising incidence of divorce in Great Britain.

[7] Lillard and Waite (1993), for instance, test the hypothesis that the risk of marital disruption affects marital fertility and that marital dissolution is affected by the presence of children in the family, while Parkman (1992, p. 672) maintains that 'the increase of married women's labour force participation under unilateral divorce is due to the lack of compensation at divorce for reduced human capital based on sacrificed opportunities to acquire and maintain market skills'.

[8] I.e. the distribution of births over the life-cycle. In particular, we use fertility *tempo* to refer to the average time between first marriage and births.

[9] For an empirical survey see Bratti (2003a).

[10] In the published version of the paper, Del Boca (2002c), the author reports only panel data results and results of the pooled OLS for the three cohorts. We prefer to refer to the working paper version since results specific to the 1993 cohort are reported by the author.

[11] Del Boca (1999) uses data on child care availability at the regional level.

[12] Due to the cross-sectional nature of our study, in principle it should not be possible to distinguish between age and cohort effects. This problem is overcome by including in the empirical work some proxies for the individual preferences towards 'taste for market work', which proxy for cohort effects or secular trends. Accordingly, we interpret the effect of the interaction terms between education and age as the impact of education on the timing of fertility and LFP. A likelihood-ratio (LR) test for the equality of the effect of education across age-classes in the MNL model with control for heterogeneity (see section 4.4) was rejected ($\chi^2(21) = 38.99$, p-value = 0.01).

[13] The outcome of the likelihood-ratio test for the 'parsimonious' MNL model (see section 4.4) was $\chi^2(24) = 70.20$, p-value = 0.00.

[14] This means, for instance, that the probability that a woman will give birth in a specific year depends on her desired level of completed fertility and fertility timing (hence on her realised fertility), whose effects are picked up in the empirical specification by their 'first determinants', such as her level of education.

[15] There is also a literature showing that women may increase their level of formal education and LFP as a form of insurance against the risk of separation and divorce. In this case the optimal levels of education and LFP depend also on the characteristics of the marriage (see for instance Parkman, 1992, 1998).

[16] Hereafter, we use the nouns spouse, husband and partner exchangeably.

[17] There is also a literature showing that women may increase their level of formal education and LFP as a form of insurance against the risk of separation and divorce. In this case the optimal levels of education and LFP depend also on the characteristics of the marriage (see for instance Parkman, 1992, 1998).

[18] Hereafter, we use the nouns spouse, husband and partner exchangeably.

[19] Del Boca (1997, p. 76), for instance, finds that the *traditional family model* cannot be rejected using ISHIW 1993 data.

[20] Some researchers in Italy have matched Bank of Italy data with data on hours spent in domestic activities coming from other sources (such as the ISTAT Multiscopo Survey 1987-91 on time use, see ISTAT, 1993a) in order to obtain a proxy for the gender role model prevailing in a specific geographic region. However, we think that such measures are likely to be endogenous, especially for women (this applies also if data on intra-household allocation of time were available at the individual level). In fact, the time devoted to child bearing, for instance, it is likely to be affected by the fact that a woman participates in the labour market. Alternatively, hours of labour supply and child bearing may be jointly determined. Therefore, we preferred to use the fact that a woman's mother worked, since we think that the family (especially in Italy) is the primary social unit that transfers values (such as the 'taste for market work') to an individual and that the parents are the first source of gender role models for individuals.

[21] For a discussion of the endogeneity of education see also Macunovich (1996, pp. 118-119).

[22] Like all the studies reviewed in section 3.

[23] We observe only realised fertility. Although in our economic model realised and observed fertility are equal, in reality they may differ because of problems of infecundity and the effectiveness of contraception. Therefore, we included in the analysis only the ages at which a woman's degree of *fecundability* is relatively high and for which an 'economic model' of fertility and participation, which explains only desired fertility, makes sense.

[24] We dropped individuals without formal education and those with post-graduate qualifications, whose number is very low, in order to avoid spurious results.

[25] Hence, we drop students. Although in the theoretical models it is usually assumed that individuals invest in education at the beginning of the life cycle, as observed by an anonymous referee, especially for women education might happen in slots during life to combine work, children and requalification. This seems not to be a frequent phenomenon in Italy. In fact, in the 1993 ISHIW data only the 0.32% of married or cohabiting women in the age group 21-39 declared to be students. However, this figure might underestimate the true number of women who are engaged in education, since some of the them might be involved in part-time education and consider market work or child rearing as their primary activities.

[26] For the same reason we exclude from the sample women with a child aged less than one, moreover for them giving birth may not be possible.

[27] Previous studies focusing on first birth (Shapiro and Mott, 1979, and Mott and Shapiro, 1983) showed that women who did not enter the labour market within two years after a birth event have a high probability of staying out of the labour market for the rest of their life.

[28] The rate of non-response for other parental variables (such as parents' jobs) is of the same order of magnitude. All regressions use a weight computed by the Bank of Italy which is the inverse of the probability that an individual is included in the sample.

[29] In the model of Blackburn et al. (1993), for example, it is the preference for late childbearing which induces women to invest more in human capital.

[30] This information is provided by the ISHIW at the respondent's age. The same procedure is applied, for instance, by Blackburn et al. (1993).

[31] However, they can be found in Bratti (2003b), Table B.2.

[32] See Table B.3 in Bratti (2003b).

[33] The LR-test gives the following result: $\chi^2(33) = 36.34$, p-value = 0.32.

[34] See Grogger (1990). For some recent developments on its consistency see also Dageneais (1999) and Lucchetti (2002).

[35] This is a measure of period marital fertility, in particular the total fertility of a hypothetical marital cohort with the age-specific marital fertility rates observed in a certain year.

[36] For women with a university degree the hypothetical marriage duration considered is between age 25 and 39.

[37] In 1999 the average age at graduation was 26.7 in 4-5 years undergraduate programs. The percentage of married or cohabiting women with upper secondary school diploma who are university students at ages 21-39 is 1.13% in the 1993 wave of the ISHIW.

[38] As we noted we do not address in this chapter the potential endogeneity of marital status.

[39] Gustafsson et al. (2001), for instance, find that in Britain, Germany, the Netherlands and Sweden combining motherhood and education is not generally chosen by women.

[40] In 1993 the nuptiality rate at age 20 (i.e. number of married women aged 20/number of women aged 20), for instance, was 4.87% (electronic data from ISTAT, Italian National Institute of Statistics).

APPENDIX A: Variables description

The explanatory variables included in the econometric model are:

Broad area of residence. This variable is included to account for regional effects due to differences in the institutional and cultural setting. We consider three broad regions: North, Centre, and South.

Municipality size. We include the number of inhabitants of the municipality in which a woman resides to capture differences in labour market opportunities and child care availability that may exist between municipalities of different size. We consider four possible dimensions: very small (<20 thousands), small (20-40 thousands), medium (40-500 thousands), big (>500 thousands).

Partner's income. We include the net disposable total husband's income (in thousands of Italian lira) to control for pure income effects.

Parents' availability. This variable is a dummy for 'parents' availability' for child care and is included as a proxy for the availability of low cost external child care. We build the variable as follows. For each spouse we check if the province of birth is equal to that of residence, in which case we check if his/her mother is still alive in 1993. If both conditions are satisfied for at least one of the spouses, parents are considered 'available' for the purpose of child care (we assume that parents had not changed their province of residence since the birth of their child, and that they resided in the province in which birth took place). We consider only the mother to account for a possible gender role model (especially for older people). We prefer this variable, which may nevertheless have some drawbacks, to that of parents living in the household, used in other work (see for example Barrow 1999 or Del Boca et al. 2000) since we consider the interpretation of the effect of the latter more problematic. In fact, living with one's own parents is probably non-random. A mechanism of non-random selection might be at work, for example parents could be in bad health (for which we can not control) and the effect on LFP and fertility may be in the opposite direction to that expected. Anyway, our measure nests that used by previous studies even if the effect of self-selection should be less harmful.

'Easterlin variables'. The 1993 wave of ISHIW contains a section on intergenerational information. In particular there is a question on the relative position of the family in terms of accumulated wealth compared to the husband's and wife's families. There are three possibilities: less, equal or more resources.

Parents' education. We consider the educational qualifications of a woman's parents. In particular for the father we consider six educational categories: 1) missing education; 2) no formal education; 3) elementary; 4) lower secondary; 5) upper secondary; 6) university degree. For the mother the last two categories are grouped, since the low number of mothers with a university education caused several problems to the estimation procedure.

Father's job qualification. We consider the following qualifications: 1) not known; 2) blue collar, white collar low (low skilled) or unemployed (we can not consider the unemployed category separately since the cell of the outcome (P, F) is empty); 3) teacher or white collar high (medium skilled); 4) manager, head teacher, university lecturer, professional, entrepreneur (high skilled); 5) self-employed;

Father's branch of activity. We consider the following branches: 1) not known or not applicable; 2) agriculture, hunting, fishing; 3) manufacturing; 4) public administration (PA); 5) other.

Mother's job qualification. We consider the following categories: 1) not known; 2) blue collar and white collar low (low skilled); 3) teacher, white collar high, manager, head teacher, university lecturer, professional, entrepreneur (medium and high skilled); 4) self-employed; 5) not working. Compared to father's education categories 3 and 4 are grouped since only three mothers fall in category 4.

Mother's branch of activity. See the father's branch of activity.

Husband's education. We include four dummies: 1) primary schooling; 2) lower secondary schooling; 3) upper secondary schooling; 4) university degree or more.

Husband's job qualifications. We include 5 dummies: 1) low skilled; 2) medium skilled; 3) high skilled; 4) self-employed; 5) unemployed (for the content of the different categories see father's job qualifications);

Husband's branch of activity. We include five dummies: 1) agriculture, hunting, fishing; 2) building; 3) manufacturing; 4) public administration; 5) other.

Husband's age.

Child care availability. We use data on child care availability, namely places available in public institutions providing child care by province (ISTAT, 1995b), and data on population aged under two by province, from the 1991 Census data (ISTAT, 1993b), in order to build a ratio giving a measure of the 'degree of coverage' of the local potential demand for public child care.

Mother's in law worked. It is a proxy for the husband's attitude towards women's work in the labour market.

APPENDIX B. Further tables

Table 5.B1. 'Parsimonious' MNL model

	(P,NF)		(NP,F)		(P,F)	
Variable	Coef.	t	Coef.	t	Coef.	t
Husband's income	-	-2.17	8.71E-06	0.92	-3E-05	-2.48
Parents available	0.88	3.58	0.86	1.71	0.10	0.21
Public child care	11.56	3.86	-8.49	-1.51	1.12	0.22
Mother's education						
none	-0.08	-0.24	0.08	0.17	-1.82	-2.05
lower secondary	0.32	0.90	-1.69	-2.30	0.62	1.06
upper secondary or higher	-0.50	-0.77	-0.67	-0.56	0.06	0.08
Mother's job						
missing	0.51	0.58	1.70	1.82	0.72	0.42
low skilled	0.43	0.85	0.10	0.11	-2.63	-2.10
medium and high skilled	0.51	0.76	-0.17	-0.11	-1.15	-1.14
self-employed	-1.01	-1.83	-0.65	-0.55	-0.74	-0.62
Husband's education						
Primary	-0.13	-0.46	-0.05	-0.10	-2.11	-1.65
upper secondary	0.33	1.39	-0.29	-0.67	0.13	0.27
degree	0.89	1.58	-0.23	-0.18	0.80	0.96
Husband's job						
medium skilled	-0.11	-0.24	-1.44	-1.43	0.04	0.06
high skilled	-0.57	-2.16	0.09	0.23	-0.30	-0.46
self-employed	-0.67	-1.44	-0.31	-0.37	-0.23	-0.31
unemployed	0.19	0.34	0.70	1.01	-1.38	-1.26
Husband's age	-0.07	-2.14	-0.10	-2.05	-0.04	-0.77
Mother in law worked	0.55	2.41	-0.99	-1.75	0.73	1.84
N. obs.			1420			
Overall p-value			0.00[(a)]			
Pseudo R^2			26.86%			

Notes: (NP,NF) is the reference outcome. The model controls also for area of residence, the municipality size, Easterlin's variables, father's education, mother's sector, husband's sector (see Appendix 5.A). The reference characteristics are: southern residence; medium municipality; father's education: primary school; mother's education: primary school; mother's job: not working; mother's branch: not applicable; 'parents not available'; mother in law did not work; husband's education: lower secondary; husband's job: low skilled; husband's branch: other. [(a)] LR-test for the joint significance of the whole set of regressors included (except the constant).

Table 5.B2. Education equation

Variable	Coef.	t	p-value
North	-0.32	-1.09	0.27
Centre	-0.27	-0.94	0.35
Town: very small	0.05	0.25	0.80
Town: small	-0.26	-1.08	0.28
Town: big	-0.22	-0.85	0.39
Father's education: none	-0.48	-1.51	0.13
Father's education: lower secondary	0.33	1.18	0.24
Father's education: upper secondary	1.12	2.83	0.01
Father's education: degree	2.31	3.61	0.00
Father's job: missing	0.40	0.38	0.70
Father's job: medium skilled	1.36	2.57	0.01
Father's job: high skilled	1.44	2.95	0.00
Father's job: self-employed	1.16	4.44	0.00
Father's branch: missing	0.01	0.02	0.99
Father's branch: agriculture	-0.19	-0.62	0.53
Father's branch: manufacturing	0.52	1.99	0.05
Father's branch: PA	0.61	2.05	0.04
Mother's education: none	-0.56	-1.82	0.07
Mother's education: lower secondary	0.34	1.05	0.30
Mother's education: upper secondary or higher	-0.19	-0.46	0.65
Mother's job: missing	-0.53	-0.47	0.64
Mother's job: low skilled	0.30	0.62	0.54
Mother's job medium and high skilled	0.23	0.35	0.72
Mother's job: self employed	0.54	1.02	0.31
Mother's branch: agriculture	-0.77	-1.38	0.17
Mother's branch: manufacturing	-0.72	-0.94	0.35
Mother's branch: PA	0.86	1.56	0.12
Mother's branch: other	0.59	1.16	0.25
constant	9.37	13.06	0.00
N. obs.		1420	
Overall p-value		0.00[(a)]	
R^2		49.08%	

Notes: the dependent variable is the number of years of formal education. The reference characteristics are: southern residence; medium size municipality; father's education: primary school; father's job: low skilled or unemployed; father's branch: other; mother's education: primary school; mother's job: not working; mother's branch: not applicable. The regression included also all the other family background variables included in the MNL model with controls for heterogeneity (see Table B.2 in Bratti, 2003b). [(a)] LR-test for the joint significance of the whole set of regressors included (except the constant).

REFERENCES

Banca d'Italia. *I Bilanci delle Famiglie Italiane nell'Anno 1993. Supplementi al Bollettino Statistico, Note Metodologiche e Informazioni Statistiche*, Anno V, n. 9. Rome: Banca d'Italia, 1995.

Barro, Robert J., and Jong-Wha Lee. "International Data on Educational Attainment: Updates and Implications". *Oxford Economic Papers* 53(3) (November 2001): 541-563.

Barrow, Lisa. "Child Care Costs and the Return-to-Work Decisions of New Mothers". *Federal Reserve Bank of Chicago Economic Perspectives* 23(4) (fourth quarter 1999): 42-55.

Becker, Gary S. *A Treatise on the Family*. Cambridge (MA): Harvard University Press, 1981.

Becker, Gary S., and H. Gregg Lewis. "On the Interaction between the Quantity and Quality of Children". *Journal of Political Economy* 81(3) (March-April 1973): S279-S288.

Ben-Porath, Yoram. "Fluctuations in Fertility and Economic Activity in Israel". *Demography* 10(2) (1973): 185-204.

Blackburn, McKinley L., Bloom, David E., and David Neumark. "Fertility Timing, Wages and Human Capital". *Journal of Population Economics* 6(1) (1993): 1-30.

Blau, David M., and Alison P. Hagy. "The Demand for Quality in Child Care". *Journal of Political Economy* 106(1) (February 1998): 104-146.

Bloemen, Hans, and Adriaan S. Kalwij. "Female Labor Market Transitions and the Timing of Births: A Simultaneous Analysis of the Effects of Schooling". *Labour Economics*, 8(5) (December 2001): 593-620.

Blundell, Richard, Dearden, Lorraine, Goodman Alissa, and Howard Reed. *Higher Education, Employment and Earnings in Britain*. London: Institute for Fiscal Studies, 1997.

Bound, John, Jaeger, David A., and Regina M. Backer. "Problems with Instrumental Variables Estimation When the Correlation between the Instruments and the Endogenous Explanatory Variable Is Weak". *Journal of the American Statistical Association* 90(430) (June 1995): 443-450.

Bratti, Massimiliano. "Offerta di Lavoro: Partecipazione e Orario di Lavoro". In Claudio Lucifora (ed.), *Mercato, Occupazione e Salari: La Ricerca sul Lavoro in Italia*, pp. 30-57. Milan: Mondadori Università, 2003a.

Bratti, Massimiliano. "Labour Force Participation and Marital Fertility of Italian Women: The Role of Education". *Journal of Population Economics*, 16(3) (August 2003): 525-554.

Bratti, Massimiliano, Del Bono, Emilia, and Daniela Vuri. "New Mother's Labour Force Participation in Italy: The Role of Job Characteristics". *Centre for Household, Income, Labour and Demographic Economics (CHILD) Working Papers* n. 5, Turin, 2004, forthcoming in *Labour*.

Browning, Martin. "Children and Household Economic Behavior". *Journal of Economic Literature* 30(3) (September 1992): 1434-1475.

Chiappori, Pierre-André. "Collective Labor Supply and Welfare". *Journal of Political Economy* 100(3) (June 1992): 437-467.

Chiuri, Maria Concetta. "Quality and Demand of Child Care and Female Labour Supply in Italy". *Labour* 14(1) (March 2000): 97-118.

Cigno, Alessandro, and John Ermisch. "A Microeconomic Analysis of The Timing of Births". *European Economic Review*, 33(4) (April 1989): 737-760.

Cigno, Alessandro. *Economics of the Family*. Oxford: Clarendon Press, 1991.

Colombino, Ugo, and Maria Laura Di Tommaso. "Is the Preference for Children so Low or Is the Price of Time so High? A Simultaneous Model of Fertility and Participation in Italy with Cohort Effects". *Labour* 10(3) (Autumn 1996): 475-493.

CNEL, *Economia della Famiglia e Politiche Sociali*. Documenti CNEL. Rome: Consiglio dell'Economia e del Lavoro, 2000.

Dagenais, Marcel G. "Inconsistency of a Proposed Nonlinear Instrumental Variables Estimator for Probit and Logit Models with Endogenous Regressors". *Economics Letters* 63(1) (April 1999): 19-21.

Danziger, Leif, and Shoshana Neuman. "Intergenerational Effects on Fertility: Theory and Evidence from Israel". *Journal of Population Economics* 2(1): 25-37.

De Tray, Dennis N. "Child Quality and the Demand for Children". *Journal of Political Economy* 81(2) (March-April 1973): S70-S95.

Del Boca, Daniela. "Intrahousehold Distribution of Resources and Labor Market Participation Decisions". In Inga Persson and Christina Jonunug (eds.) *Economics of the Family and Family Policies*. London: Routledge, 65-83, 1997.

Del Boca, Daniela. "Participation and Fertility Behavior of Italian Women: The Role of Market Rigidities". *NYU C.V. Starr Center Working Papers*, New York, 1999.

Del Boca, Daniela. "Do Child Care Costs Affect Labor Supply?". *Centre for Household, Income, Labour and Demographic Economics (CHILD) Working Papers* n. 18, Turin, 2002a.

Del Boca, Daniela. "Low Fertility and Labour Force Participation of Italian Women: Evidence and Interpretations". *OECD Labour Market and Social Policy, Occasional Papers* n. 61, Paris, 2002b.

Del Boca, Daniela. "The Effect of Child Care and Part Time Opportunities on Participation and Fertility Decisions". *Journal of Population Economics*, 15(3) (August 2002c): 549-574.

Del Boca Daniela, Locatelli, Marilena, and Silvia Pasqua. "Employment Decisions of Married Women: Evidence and Explanations". *Labour* 14(1) (March 2000): 35-52.

Del Boca, Daniela, and Silvia Pasqua. Labour Market Participation of Mothers in Italy: Facts, Studies and Public Policies. *Centre for Household, Income, Labour and Demographic Economics (CHILD) Working Papers* n. 4, Turin, 2002.

Del Boca , Daniela, Locatelli, Marilena, and Daniela Vuri. " Child Care Choices by Italian Households" *Centre for Household, Income, Labour and Demographic Economics (CHILD) Working Papers* n. 30, Turin, 2003.

Dell'Aringa, Carlo. "The Italian Labour Market: Problems and Prospects". *Quaderni dell'Istituto di Economia dell'Impresa e del Lavoro* n. 33, Università Cattolica del Sacro Cuore, Milano, 2003.

Dex, Shirley, and Heather Joshi. "Careers and Motherhood: Policies for Compatibility". *Cambridge Journal of Economics* 23(5) (September 1999): 641-659.

Di Tommaso, Maria Laura. "A Trivariate Model of Participation, Fertility and Wages: The Italian Case". *Cambridge Journal of Economics* 23(5) (September 1999): 623-640.

Di Tommaso, Maria Laura, and Melvyn Weeks. "Decision Structures and Discrete Choices: An Application to Labour Market Participation and Fertility". *DAE Working Papers* n. 00-09, University of Cambridge, Cambridge (UK), 2000.

Easterlin, Richard A. *Birth and Fortune: The Impact of Numbers on Personal Welfare*. Chicago: University of Chicago Press, 1980.

Ermisch, John F. "Purchased Child Care, Optimal Family Size and Mother's Employment: Theory and Econometric Analysis". *Journal of Population Economics* 2(2) (1989): 79-102.

Esping-Andersen, Gosta. *The three worlds of welfare capitalism*. Cambridge: Polity Press, 1990.

Eurostat. *Labour Force Survey 1998*. Luxembourg: Office for the Official Publications of the European Communities, 1999.

Filippin, Antonio. "I Bilanci delle Famiglie Italiane in Formato Stata". *Lavoro e Relazioni Industriali* 2 (1997): 177-85.

Giannelli, Gianna C. "Squilibrio nell'Offerta di Lavoro e Rigidità dell'Orario di Lavoro: Un'Analisi Microeconometrica su un Campione Nazionale e un Campione Regionale". *Politica Economica* 13(1) (April 1997): 87-115.

Giannelli, Gianna C. and Chiara Monfardini. "A Nest or a Golden Cage? Family Co-Residence and Human Capital Investment Decisions of Young Adults". *International Journal of Manpower* 21(3-4) (2000): 227-245.

Grogger, Jeffrey. "A Simple Test for Exogeneity in Probit, Logit and Poisson Regression Models". *Economics Letters* 33(4) (August 1990): 329-332.

Gustafsson, Siv. "Optimal Age at Motherhood. Theoretical and Empirical Considerations on Postponement of Maternity in Europe". *Journal of Population Economics* 14(2) (2001): 225-247.

Gustafsson, Siv, Kenjoh, Eiko, and Cecile Wetzels. "The Role of Education in Postponement of Maternity in Britain, Germany, the Netherlands and Sweden". Paper presented at the *15th Annual Conference of the European Society for Population Economics,* 2001.

Hausman, Jerry, and Daniel McFadden. "Specification Tests for the Multinomial Logit Model". *Econometrica* 52(5) (September 1984): 1219-1240.

Happel, S.K., Hill, J.K., and S.A. Low. "An Economic Analysis of the Timing of Childbirth". *Population Studies* 38(2) (July 1984): 299-311.

Hotz, V. Joseph, Klerman, Jacob A., and Robert J. Willis. "The Economics of Fertility in Developed Countries". In: Mark R. Rosenzweig and Oded Stark (eds.) *Handbook of Population and Family Economics. Volume 1A*. Elsevier, Amsterdam, 275-347, 1997.

ISTAT. *Indagine Multiscopo sulle Famiglie 1987-1991. L'Uso del Tempo in Italia.* Rome: ISTAT, 1993a.

ISTAT. *Censimento Generale della Popolazione e delle Abitazioni 20 Ottobre 1991*. Rome: ISTAT, 1993b.

ISTAT. *Indagine sui Consumi delle Familiglie*. Documentazione tecnica. Rome: ISTAT, 1995a.

ISTAT. *Statistiche della Previdenza, della Sanità e dell'Assistenza Sociale, Anni 1992, 1993, Annuario n. 33.* Rome: ISTAT, 1995b.

ISTAT. *Indagine Multiscopo. "Famiglie, Soggetti Sociali e Condizione dell'Infanzia".* Rome: ISTAT, 1998.

Lam, David, and Suzanne Duryea. "Effects of Schooling on Fertility, Labor Supply, and Investments in Children, with Evidence from Brazil". *Journal of Human Resources*, 34(1) (Winter 1999): 160-192.

Lehrer, Evelyn, and Marc Nerlove. "Female Labor Force Behavior and Fertility in the United States". *Annual Review of Sociology* 12 (1986): 181-204.

Lillard, Lee A., and Linda J. Waite. "A Joint Model of Marital Childbearing and Marital Disruption". *Demography*, 30(4) (November 1993): 653-681.

Lucchetti, Riccardo. "Inconsistency of Naive GMM Estimation for QR Models with Endogenous Regressors". *Economics Letters*, 75(2) (April 2002): 179-185.

Macunovich, Diane J. "A Review of Recent Developments in the Economics of Fertility". In: Paul Menchik (ed.) *Household and Family Economics,* 91-150. Boston: Kluwer Academic, 1996.

Marenzi, Anna, and Laura Pagani. "The Impact of Elder Parents on Italian Women's Labour Market Participation", *Università dell'Insubria, Facoltà di Economia Working Paper* n. 18, Varese, 2003 forthcoming in *Rivista di Politica Economica.*

McFadden, Daniel. "Conditional Logit Analysis of Qualitative Behavior". In: Paul Zarembka (ed.) *Frontiers in Econometrics,* 105-142. New York: Academic Press, 1974.

Moffitt, Robert. "Profiles of Fertility, Labour Supply and Wages of Married Women: A Complete Life-Cycle Model". *Review of Economic Studies*, 51(2) (April 1984): 263-278.

Mott, Frank, and David Shapiro. "Complementarity of Work and Fertility among Young American Mothers". *Population Studies* 37(2) (July 1983): 239-252.

Murphy, Kevin, and Finis Welch. "The Structure of Wages". *Quarterly Journal of Economics*, 107(1) (February 1992): 285-326.

OECD. *Employment Outlook.* Paris: OECD, 1999.

Parkman, Allen M. "Unilateral Divorce and the Labor-Force Participation Rate of Married Women, Revisited". *American Economic Review* 82(3) (June 1992): 671-678.

Parkman, Allen M. "Why Are Married Women Working So Hard?". *International Review of Law and Economics*, 18(1) (March 1998): 41-49.

Rosenzweig, Mark R., and T. Paul Schultz. " The Demand and Supply of Births: Fertility and Its Life Cycle Consequences". *American Economic Review*, 75(5) (December 1995): 992-1015.

Sander, William. " The Effect of Women's Schooling on Fertility". *Economics Letters*, 40(2) (October 1992): 229-233.

Schultz, T. Paul. "Returns to Women's Education". In: Elizabeth M. King and M. Anne Hill (eds.) *Women's Education in Developing Countries: Barriers, Benefits and Policies*, 51-99. Baltimore: Johns Hopkins University Press, 1993.

Schultz, T. Paul. "Demand for Children in Low Income Countries". In: Mark R. Rosenzweig and Oded Stark (eds.) *Handbook of Population and Family Economics. Volume 1A,* 349-430. Amsterdam: Elsevier, 1997.

Shapiro, David, and Frank Mott. "Labor Supply Behavior of Prospective and New Mothers". *Demography* 16(2) (May 1979): 199-208.

Smith, Ian. "Explaining the Growth of Divorce in Great Britain". *Scottish Journal of Political Economy* 44(5) (November 1997): 519-544.

Smith, Richard J., and Richard Blundell. "An Exogeneity Test for a Simultaneous Equation Tobit Model with an Application to Labor Supply". *Econometrica*, 54(3) (May 1986): 679-685.

Walker, James R. "The effect of Public Policies on Recent Swedish Fertility Behavior". *Journal of Population Economics* 8(3) (August 1995): 223-251.

Weeks, Melvyn, and Chris Orme. "The Statistical Relationship between Bivariate and Multinomial Choice Models". *DAE Working Papers* n. 99-12, University of Cambridge, Cambridge (UK), 1999.

World Bank. *World Development Indicators 1999 on CD-ROM.* Washington D.C.: World Bank, 2000.

Chapter 6

CAREER PLANNING IN SPAIN: DO FIXED-TERM CONTRACTS DELAY MARRIAGE AND PARENTHOOD?

SARA DE LA RICA AND AMAIA IZA

1. INTRODUCTION

At the beginning of the sixties, north-western Europe started a drastic transformation in the pattern of household formation and reproduction, which was reflected in a pronounced increase in age at first marriage and a clear postponement of entry into maternity. Towards the end of the eighties, these features of behaviour had reached some of the Mediterranean countries, such as Portugal, Italy and Spain. Theoretical life-cycle models of fertility have analyzed the factors that may induce families to change their fertility pattern over their life-cycle (Cigno and Ermisch (1989), Cigno (1991), Walker (1995)). Children entail large costs in terms of time, maternal time costs of mothers which vary over their life cycle, and goods or direct expenditure on children. Therefore, changes in childbearing costs (direct expenditure and opportunity costs) and income over the family life-cycle may result in changes in the timing of maternity (see Hotz et al. (1997)). Women's educational attainment and their participation in the labour market affect childbearing costs (particularly through opportunity costs of childbearing) and household income over their life-cycle differently depending on their educational level. More highly educated women place a higher value on their time in the labour market at each age, given that if they decide to participate in the labour market, they will have higher earnings profiles than less educated women. Since childbearing imposes time, the higher the wages the higher the opportunity cost of childbearing for women (substitution effect). Furthermore, sometimes there is not only a loss in current income but also in their future earnings profile due to the depreciation of women's human capital at work during their temporary absence from the labour force for childrearing. The latter are the costs of children for the mother's career, which constitute the main point in the literature on the career planning motive for postponing maternity (see Joshi (1990,

Siv Gustafsson and Adriaan Kalwij (eds.), Education and Postponement of Maternity, 147–174.

1994, 1998), Dankmeyer (1996), Gustafsson (1996, 2001)). This effect is particularly important for highly educated women.

However, in Spain, postponement of maternity cannot be explained only by a transition from early parenthood by poorly educated women to late parenthood by highly educated ones. The reason is that, even though the distribution of more educated women of fertile age has increased, postponement of parenthood has been observed at all educational levels. Recent empirical research (Ahn and Mira (2001)) stresses the connection between unemployment and fluctuations in marriage and fertility in Spain. They find an empirical link between high and persistent rates of unemployment and a delay in marriage in Spain during the eighties. From an economic point of view, high and persistent unemployment must be viewed as a drop in current and future expected income, and given that children are normal goods, childbearing is expected to be delayed. This issue is particularly important in economics with imperfect capital markets, where households need savings so as to afford the fixed costs imposed by children (Kalwij (1999)).

The aim of this chapter is to find an empirical connection between another particular labour market phenomenon and the delay in marriage and maternity in Spain. The labour market phenomenon we focus on is the huge increase in the use of fixed-term contracts that young Spanish workers in particular have suffered since the mid eighties. This increase has been due to a labour market reform which took place in 1984 and whose main point was that employers were allowed to contract workers on a fixed-term basis even when the nature of the job was not temporary. Since this reform, the vast majority of new contracts in Spain has been and still is on a fixed-term nature. These fixed-term contracts are at least partially responsible for the findings of Gutierrez-Doménech (2002), who looks at Spanish women before and after childbirth, and shows that one third of women who were at work one year before childbearing were unemployed nine months after. Pre-childbirth fixed-term contracts seem to be the main determinant for this "career break job penalty" that Spanish mothers are exposed to.

Our hypothesis is that given that Spanish women with fixed-term contracts are aware of the career break job penalty they are exposed to when they become mothers, some of them, presumably those with higher career prospects, decide to postpone maternity until they get a more stable labour market situation, i.e., until they get an indefinite contract.

We estimate the impact of education and type of contract on the decisions whether to enter into marriage and into motherhood for the nineties, which is when fixed-term contracts were most widely extended. Using the eight waves of the European Household Panel for Spain, we use two empirical approaches: First, a "static" approach, where we estimate the probability of entry into marriage (or cohabitation) and the probability of entry into parenthood by maximum likelihood methods assuming a logistic functional form. The second approach consists of estimating a discrete time duration model for the probability of entering into marriage and into parenthood so as to take into account dynamic aspects of each decision.

Results reveal that for men, the decision whether to get married is strongly negatively affected by holding unstable contracts or not working, relative to when an indefinite contract is held. This is an expected result given the role of men as the main breadwinners in Spanish households. However, for women, results suggest that holding fixed-term contracts is not a deterrent for the decision whether to get married.

With respect to the decision of whether to enter into parenthood, results indicate that for all childless women, either with or with no partner, holding fixed-term contracts delays entry into motherhood relative to the holding of indefinite contracts. The discouragement effect is stronger for women with no partner.

The rest of the chapter is organized as follows: In section 2 we describe the stylized facts regarding the observed delay in entry into marriage and into motherhood in Spain. Section 3 describes the institutional context of fixed-term contracts in Spain. Section 4 is devoted to describing the data. In section 5 we estimate the impact of the type of contracts individuals (men and women separately) hold on entry into marriage, and on entry into parenthood for married or cohabiting women. Section 6 concludes.

2. STYLIZED FACTS – OBSERVED DELAY IN SPAIN

Table 6.1 reports the observed average age at first marriage[1] for males and females in 1985 and 1998, the latter disaggregated by educational level[2]. We also report the observed average age of women at entry into motherhood. Regarding age at first marriage, we can see that from the mid eighties to the late nineties, both men and women delayed marriage by around three years on average, which represents a remarkable postponement in such a short period of time. When we look at entry into marriage for women disaggregated by educational level, we can see, as we stated in the introduction, that postponement of parenthood is observed at all educational levels, although women with only primary education (or less) delay marriage less than two years on average, whereas women with university education delay it for almost six years on average.

With respect to entry into parenthood, the same pattern is observed: Postponement is observed at all educational levels, although it is highest for women with university education and lowest for those with only primary cducation.

Given these stylized facts, the next question we pose is why individuals postpone marriage and parenthood, and why women with university education postpone it for longer than those with only primary education.

As we said in the introduction our hypothesis is that the massive introduction of fixed-term contracts may have played an important role in explaining at least part of this observed postponement from the mid eighties to the late nineties, particularly for women with high career prospects. Unfortunately, we cannot show any descriptive analysis for entry into marriage and into maternity by type of contract for 1985, given that data are not available. However, we can show whether women behave differently concerning their timing for entry into maternity by type of contract in the nineties, which is precisely when fixed-term contracts were more extensively used. This can be done by using pooled data from the European Panel for Households (1984-2001)[3]. This survey, which we also use for the empirical analysis presented below, offers full information concerning every birth each woman has, as well as the age of the mother at each birth. The survey also contains labour market information. Using this data set, we can take the percentage of women that have a first birth by education and by type of contract and see whether the timing concerning these first births is affected by their type of contract or not[4]. Table 6.2 presents these percentages. We can see that, whereas the timing of first births of women with only primary or secondary education is not affected by the type of contract, women with a fixed-term contract and university education tend to delay their first birth more than their counterparts with an indefinite contract[5].

In order to fully understand the changes that the increase in the use of fixed-term contracts has brought about in Spain since the mid eighties, section 3 presents the institutional background of fixed-term contracts in Spain, and a description of the notable increase in their use during this period.

Table 6.1. Average age at first marriage and at first childbirth

Years	1985	1998
Average age at first marriage		
Men	27.03	29.85
Women		
All	24.8	27.79
Primary	24.9	26.4
Secondary	27.8	27.4
University	24.2	30.0
Average age of women at first childbirth		
All	25.8	29,1
Primary		26.0
Secondary		29.8
University		32.9

Source: Spanish Institute of Statistics (INE). Data for men are taken from Basic Demographic Indicators. Data for women, disaggregated by educational level, are taken from the Fertility Surveys of 1985 and 1999 carried out by the Spanish Institute of Statistics. These fertility surveys are done only on women, and hence, no information concerning average age at first marriage for men disaggregated by educational level is provided.

Table 6.2. Percentage of Women at birth of first child by education and type of contract

Contract	Primary		Secondary		University	
	Early stage	Late stage	Early stage	Late stage	Early stage	Late stage
Indefinite	7.22	1.15	6.27	3.00	8.04	4.68
Fixed-term	6.87	1.41	6.22	3.22	5.07	5.03
No work	4.89	0.65	1.86	1.45	3.29	3.17

Source: Pooled data from the European Panel of Households (1994-2001). We understand by early (late) stage when the first birth takes place when the woman is younger (older) than the average age of entry into motherhood (29 years).

3. FIXED-TERM CONTRACTS IN SPAIN

3.1 Institutional background

The basic legal reference point for labour contracts in Spain is the Workers' Statute of 1980 (Estatuto de los Trabajadores, Ley 8/80, March 10). This law considers that the general contracting framework is one of indefinite contracts, with fixed-term contracts assumed to be used only for jobs whose nature is temporary (seasonal jobs, temporary substitution of workers with indefinite contracts, temporary increase in activity, etc.). The essence of this law must be understood in a context where unions, which had been legalized in 1977, were trying to achieve higher job protection for workers, and this meant stability in contracts on the one hand, and high severance payment in case of layoff on the other. These two aims led the Spanish labour market to face the beginning of the eighties, a period of recession, with a workforce the vast majority of which held indefinite contracts with high severance payments in case of dismissal for economic reasons[6]. Some type of flexibility was considered necessary and it is in this context that the reform of 1984 took place. This reform created a new type of fixed-term contract, called an "employment promotion contract". Such contracts would be fixed-term, although the type of job associated with them would not necessary be of a fixed-term nature. These "employment promotion contracts" could be signed for a minimum of six months and a maximum of three years. The contract could not be renewed after three years and the worker had to be either laid off or offered an indefinite contract. If the worker was laid off, the firm could not employ another worker for the same job for at least one year. The indemnities at termination for these types of contracts were negligible[7]. This reduction of firing costs produced an impressive change in the way firms contracted labour from then onwards. In fact, as Güell and Petronglolo (2005) show, from 1986 to 1992, 98 % of new contracts registered at the employment office were "employment promotion contracts".

This reform brought about a striking change in the distribution of employment contracts in Spain. Whereas in 1987 only 15% of all contracts were fixed-term, by 1991 the figure was 33%, and the percentage has remained stable since then [8]. However, given that the situation of workers that already held indefinite contracts was unaffected by this reform, by the beginning of the nineties academic experts started to advise against the pervasive effects of these fixed-term contracts (see Segura et al. (1991), Bentolila and Dolado (1994), and Jimeno and Toharia (1993)). In particular, they advised against the creation of a segmented labour market with two types of job, good (indefinite) ones and bad (fixed-term) ones, given that workers with fixed-term contracts might be led to hold unstable, relatively unprotected (in terms of severance payments) and poorly paid jobs, whereas workers with indefinite contracts enjoyed high protection and also higher wages[9].

These perceptions gave rise to the reforms of 1994 and 1997. The spirit of both reforms was to enhance indefinite contracts to the detriment of fixed-term ones, while reducing firing costs of the former. In 1994 the general applicability of fixed-term contracts was virtually eliminated, except for specific groups of workers (older than 45, disabled and long-term unemployed). In addition, firing procedures were restructured in an attempt to reduce them[10]. Finally, the 1997 reform created a new type of indefinite contract, with lower severance payment in case of unfair dismissal (33 days' wage per year worked in the firm for workers younger than 30 or older than 45) and gave fiscal incentives to firms that contracted workers in this form over the first two years of the contract (reductions of employers' social security contribution by 40 percent or by 60 percent for contracting workers over 45 or disabled under indefinite contracts[11]). Recent empirical studies find a positive effect of the reform of 1997 on the hiring of workers (particularly young workers) on an indefinite basis, but the overall impact of these reforms has been found to be rather small (see Kugler et al. (2002)).

In summary, we can see that whereas in the early 1980s workforce adjustment was in general terms considered rigid, during the eighties and nineties the Spanish pattern was to search for more flexibility. However, this flexibility is only achieved at the margins, i.e., for workers signing new contracts, given that severance payments for workers that were already in the labour market holding indefinite contracts before the reform was introduced were unaffected, and therefore they were and are still highly protected against job loss.

3.2 Fixed-term contracts in Spain

Table 6.3 presents the change in the average use of fixed-term contracts for different groups of population and for different periods of time. There is a striking increase in the use of fixed-term contracts, particularly among the youngest group of population. It can also be seen that the trend was strongly increasing until the beginning of the nineties and since then has remained stable. Finally, the incidence is higher among women than among men, and higher for women without higher education.

Another important feature of fixed-term contracts in Spain is the transition from them to other types of contract. Hernanz (2002) shows that during the nineties, annual transitions of female workers from fixed-term jobs were distributed as follows: 13% of them transferred to an indefinite job, 18% went to unemployment, 9% left the labour force, and 60% of them remained in fixed-term job. Moreover, as Güell and Petrongolo (2005) show, the transition from no-work to an indefinite job is almost always done through a fixed-term contract, given that 98% of new contracts registered at the employment office are "employment promotion contracts", which implies that transition from non-employment to indefinite employment is very unlikely. Hernanz (2002) shows that age and more importantly, tenure in the firm clearly facilitates the transition from short-term to indefinite contract. On the other hand, working in small firms and in blue-collar occupations makes this transition more difficult. Finally, having a fixed-term job is basically a temporary status, and therefore there does not seem to be a "fixed-term job" trap.
Through a cohort analysis, she reveals that the percentage of fixed-term contracts decreases a great deal with individuals' age.

Table 6.3. Incidence of Fixed-term Contracts (%)

Years	1987	1990	1998
Average	15,6	29.8	32.9
By educational attainment			
Primary or less	18.0	33.8	35.9
Secondary	19.0	39.1	35.5
University	9.6	20.3	22.9
By age			
16-24	36.2	73.9	73.1
25-34	15.4	37.9	41.2
35-49	9.5	19.1	20.7
By gender			
Males	14.4	27.8	32.1
Females	18.4	34.2	34.4

Finally, holding a fixed-term contract relative to an indefinite one has important effects regarding future prospects for women that become mothers. In Spain, mater nity leave provisions for women workers envisage 16 weeks, and the legal coverage is 80% of wages. In principle, this provision is applicable regardless the type of contract. However, given that a very important proportion of fixed-term contracts are of six month duration, most women with fixed-term contracts that are going to give birth cannot make use of this provision, given that employers do not have any incentive to renew or make indefinite the contracts of women that are giving birth, and therefore are likely to be absent from work for 16 weeks for maternity leave. Therefore, women with fixed-term contracts that become mothers are much more likely to become non-employed after the birth than women with pre-birth indefinite contracts. Moreover, once they have become non-employed, if they want to return to work the career break job penalty they are exposed to is very high given that they have to go through fixed-term contracts again before getting a stable situation.

4. THE DATA

As mentioned in the introduction, the data we use are the eight waves of Spanish data from the European Household Panel (ECHP 1994-2001). ECHP is a survey based on a standardized questionnaire that involves annual interviewing of a representative panel of households and individuals in each country regarding issues such as income, health, education, demographics and employment characteristics. The total duration of the panel is 8 years (1994-2001). Approximately 130,000 adults aged 16 years and over were interviewed in the 12 EU Member States at that point[12]. Other countries, like Austria, Finland and Sweden joined the project later, so full data are not available for them.

The most remarkable characteristics of ECHP are its multidimensional coverage of a range of topics, the standardised methodology across countries, and the panel design so as to study changes over time at the micro level. In order to provide representative cross-sectional pictures over time, ECHP follows up those persons who move or form a new household. At any time the survey covers all persons cohabiting with any of the original sample person in the same household[13].

This database has advantages and drawbacks that have to be mentioned. Among the advantages we must note that, at least for Spain, it constitutes the only existing database with a panel structure that can be used for labour market issues. Moreover, the period under analysis seems very suitable for the aim of this chapter, given that the nineties is the period when fixed-term contracts had the greatest impact in the Spanish labour market. Furthermore, extensive information concerning partners' labour market situations, in particular their types of contract, is available. Such information is clearly relevant in order to learn about the (in)stability of the labour situation of the household, given that although female labour force participation is increasing at a high pace, Spain is still mainly a male breadwinner system, and hence the labour market situation of the partner is likely to play an important role for decisions such as entry into maternity.

But the European Household Panel also has disadvantages which it is important to take into account. The biggest drawback is that the panel is very short, so we cannot follow individuals throughout their fertile adult life, which would be the best way to proceed in order to look at the factors determining postponement of marriage and parenthood. Moreover, there is no retrospective information regarding the labour market situation before or around marriage or parenthood for those who got married or had their first child before 1994. Therefore, we must estimate the factors underlying the probability of marriage and of entry into maternity from a short span of each individuals' fertile period, amounting to eight years at most.

Our samples to estimate the impact of fixed-term contracts on postponement of marriage and parenthood are the following: For the analysis of the determinants of marriage, we take all individuals (men and women separately) who at the time of the first interview have never been married and are not cohabiting. These individuals either do not change their situation while they are observed, or get married at some point during the observation period. The latter are removed from the sample once marriage takes place. For the analysis of the determinants of parenthood, we use two different samples. The first one takes all childless women with or without a partner at the time they are first observed. The second sample is restricted to childless women who have a partner. In the two samples, childless women (restricted to those who have a partner or not) either have their first child during the observation period or remain childless. The former are removed from the sample when they have their first child, while the others remain in the sample throughout the observation period. For the two empirical exercises, we take individuals between 20 and 40 years old at the time of their first interview.

We take two approaches to estimate the probability that each of the events (marriage and parenthood) takes place: The first is a "static" approach, which consists of estimating the factors underlying the probability that any of the events will take place at any period under observation. We estimate by maximum likelihood methods using the whole data as a pooled sample[14]. In order to estimate the impact of education and type of contract on postponement of marriage and parenthood, we have considered three different stages at which events (marriage and motherhood) may take place: (i) An earlier stage of the fertile cycle, when individuals are younger than 25 years of age; (ii) an average stage, when individuals are between 25 and 31; and finally, (iii) a later stage, when individuals are older than 31[15]. By doing this, we can analyze postponement of marriage and parenthood by looking at the effects of the explanatory variables, in particular, education and type of contract, at the particular age-interval at which marriage and parenthood take place.

The second approach consists of estimating duration models for each of the events. In these models we estimate the factors underlying the probability of a single individual (childless women) of getting married (of having a first birth) during the current period, given that she has remained single (childless) up to that moment. The variables affecting the hazard are the same as those included in the static approach, basically education and labour market status[16]. We also include age as a regressor, and therefore, what we measure from this duration analysis is the probability that the events (marriage and parenthood) will take place controlling for age[17]. Consequently, duration analysis does not measure postponement precisely, given that for instance, if more educated women are less likely to marry (or have a first child) at earlier ages but more likely to marry at later ages, on average we might see no net effect of education on the probability of marriage (maternity). However, this would be a clear case of postponement, which would not be captured with duration analysis. The advantage of duration analysis with respect to the "static" approach is that it takes into account the dynamic aspects of the two decisions, namely, entry into marriage and entry into maternity, and it can be seen how each of the decisions changes when some of the explaining factors change. Hence, for the analysis of postponement the two approaches must be seen as complementary.

Tables 6.4 and 6.5 present mean values of the variables to be included in the empirical analysis. Table 6.4 presents the means of the sample of single individuals (men and women) by educational level and type of contract[18], and the percentage of marriages that takes place for the whole sample as well as for each age interval. It can be seen that there are very few marriages at the earliest stage (20-24 years), whereas marriages seem to be concentrated more in the third age interval. Regarding the type of contract, it is interesting to note that the percentage of indefinite contracts increases with the age of individuals, whereas the percentage of fixed-term contracts only decreases when individuals are older than 31.

*Table 6.4. Descriptive Statistics – (%) Individuals never married at the time of the first interview**

	Males				Females			
Age intervals	All	20-24	25-31	>31	All	20-24	25-31	> 31
Educational level								
University	26.5	17.3	34.9	28.0	31.9	21.4	44.0	29.9
Secondary	32.5	44.2	27.3	18.1	34.2	52.5	26.2	19.1
Primary	41.0	38.7	37.6	53.7	33.9	26.1	29.8	51.0
Type of contract								
Indefinite	27.7	15.1	31.6	46.1	20.6	10.1	21.7	34.7
Fixed-term	23.8	21.9	26.4	20.6	18.2	14.4	23.8	15.8
No work	48.5	62.9	41.8	33.2	61.2	75.5	54.5	49.5
% Marry	3.5	0.6	4.7	6.7	6.5	1.1	8.4	11.9
N.obs.	10525	4211	4229	1430	9647	3646	2690	1321

* This sample includes all individuals who are observed to be single (never married) and with no partner at their first interview. Some of them remain in the same situation throughout the observation period and others get married (or cohabit) at some point during that time. The latter are removed from the sample as the event has already taken place.

In order to give a more precise idea of the age at which marriages take place by education and by type of contract, we present Figures 6.1-6.4, where we depict the percentages of first marriages at each age by education (figures 6.1 and 6.3) and by type of contract (figures 6.2 and 6.4)[19]. Regarding education, we can see that for women (figure 6.1), those with only primary or secondary education marry earlier than the more highly educated. With respect to men, figure 6.3 reveals that the more educated tend to marry later, an effect that is observed until the age of 33.

With respect to the type of contract, figure 6.2 reveals that women with ndefinite contracts present higher percentages of first marriage than those with a fixed-term contract and for non-workers, although differences are not very significant.

Finally, figure 6.4 shows that the percentages of marriages among non-working men are the lowest at all ages, which is consistent with men being the main breadwinner of the household in Spain. Comparing men with fixed-term contracts with those holding indefinite ones, there does not seem to be important differences concerning them until the age of 30, but from this age on, the percentage of marriages between workers with indefinite contracts are higher than those with fixed-term contracts.

Figure 6.1. Percentage of first marriage at each age by education – Women

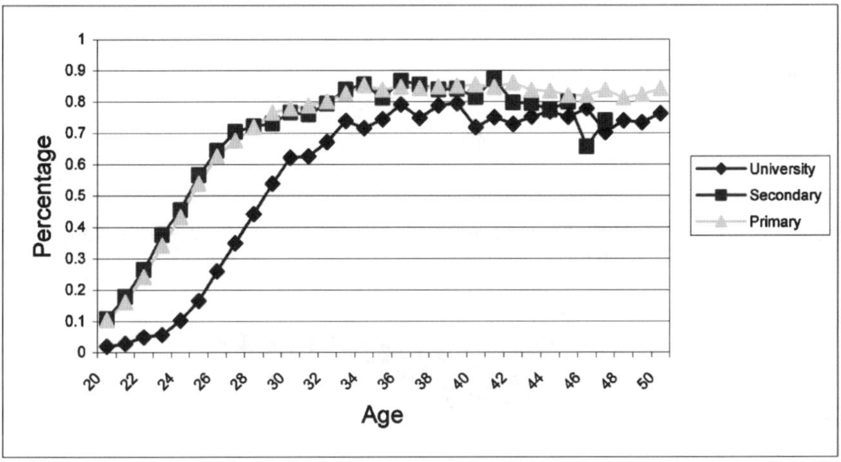

Figure 6.2. Percentage of first marriage at each age by type of contract – Women

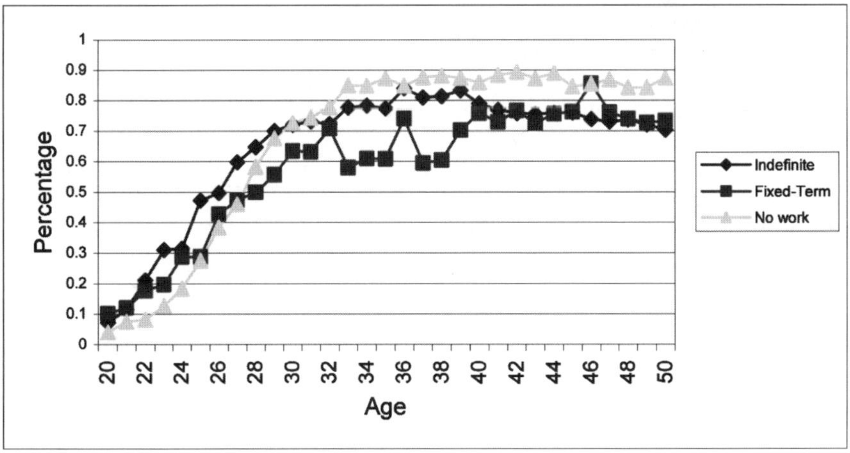

Figure 6.3. Percentage of first marriage at each age by education – Men

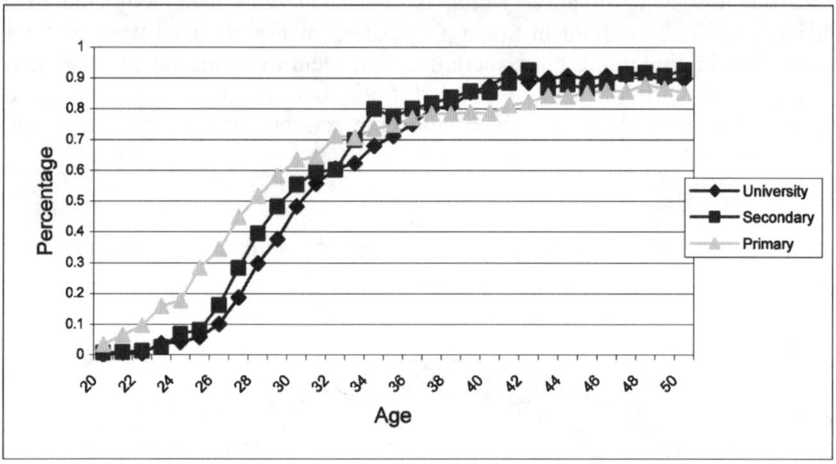

Figure 6.4. Percentage of first marriage at each age by type of contract – Men

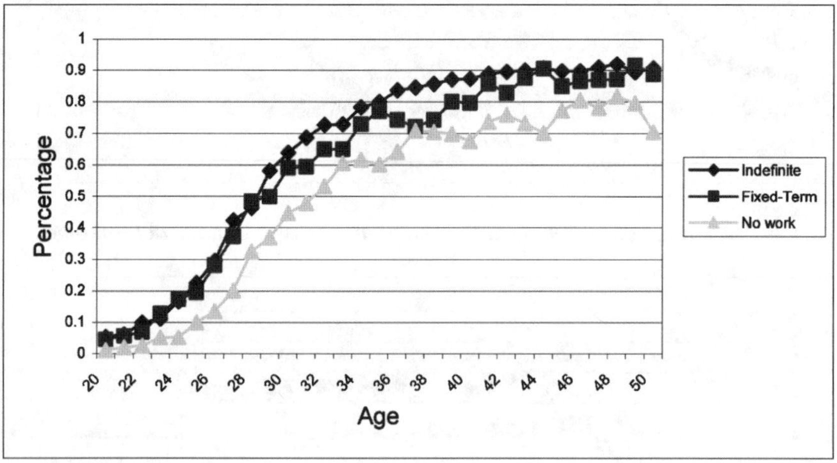

*Table 6.5. Descriptive statistics *–(%). Women childless at the time of the first interview*

	Sample A: All childless Women				Sample B: Childless Women with Partner*			
Variables	All	20-24	25-31	>31	All	20-24	25-31	>31
Educational level								
University	38.8	20.7	45.7	42.3	34.0	17.2	34.2	36.2
Secondary	31.9	53.4	26.8	20.2	24.8	32.4	25.1	22.4
Primary	29.1	25.9	27.3	37.4	41.2	50.3	40.6	41.5
Women' type of contract								
Indefinite	29.3	19.3	26.9	44.5	38.0	30.4	37.1	41.7
Fixed-term	20.6	15.6	24.5	17.7	20.3	28.4	21.5	15.7
No work	50.1	65.1	48.6	37.7	41.7	41.2	41.4	42.6
Husband's type of contract								
Indefinite	—	—	—	—	66.2	61.6	64.3	71.6
Fixed-term	—	—	—	—	22.8	25.8	25.9	16.5
No work	—	—	—	—	10.9	12.6	9.8	11.9
% 1st birth	3.9	1.0	5.2	3.4	10.2	4.0	13.3	6.6
% Partner	29.5	9.1	34.9	38.1	—	—	—	—
N.obs	8452	2128	4215	1757	1563	151	840	472

* This sample includes all women who have a partner and are childless at their first interview. Some of them remain childless throughout the observation period, whereas others enter into parenthood. The latter are removed from the sample given that the event has already taken place.

Table 6.5 presents the means of the most relevant variables for the samples used to estimate the determinants of entry into maternity. As mentioned above, we use two samples for this analysis: Sample A, which consists of all women who are childless at the time of the first interview, with or without partner, and Sample B, comprising women who are childless at the time of the first interview but have a partner at that time. The second sample is a sub-sample of Sample A, and as expected, the women in Sample B are on average older (and hence less educated) and the percentage of non-working women is higher than in Sample A for all ages except the youngest interval, where many of the women included in sample B who have no partner may be still studying, and therefore, are out of the labour force. For the two samples, we can see that the percentage of indefinite contracts increases with age. For sample B, we can see that most husbands of women over 24 have indefinite contracts.

To give a better idea of the age at which women enter into maternity by education, type of contract and husband's type of contract in our samples, we present figures 6.5-6.9, where we depict the percentages of first childbirths at each age by education and type of contract[20]. Figures 6.5 and 6.6 present the percentage of first childbirths at each age by education (figure 6.5) and by type of contract (figure 6.6) for Sample A, whereas figures 6.7-6.9 present the percentages of first childbirths at each age by education (figure 6.7), type of contract (figure 6.8) and partner's type of contract (figure 6.9) for Sample B.

Figure 6.5. Percentage of first children born at each age by education – All women

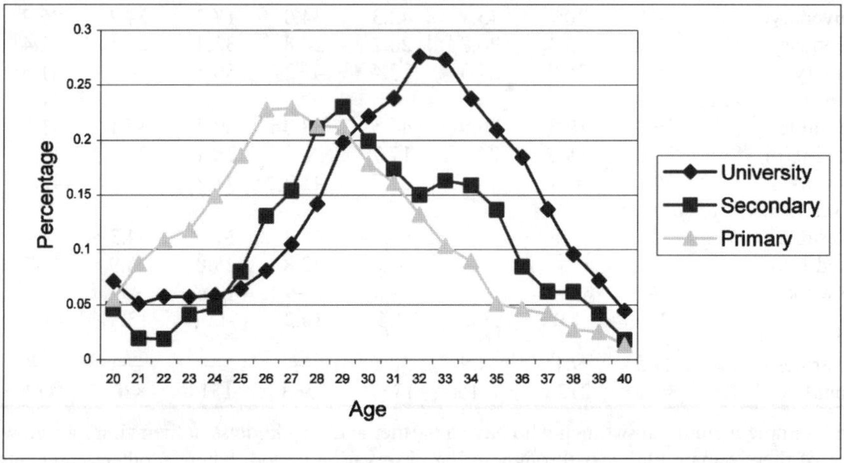

Figure 6.6. Percentage of first children born at each age by type of contract – All women

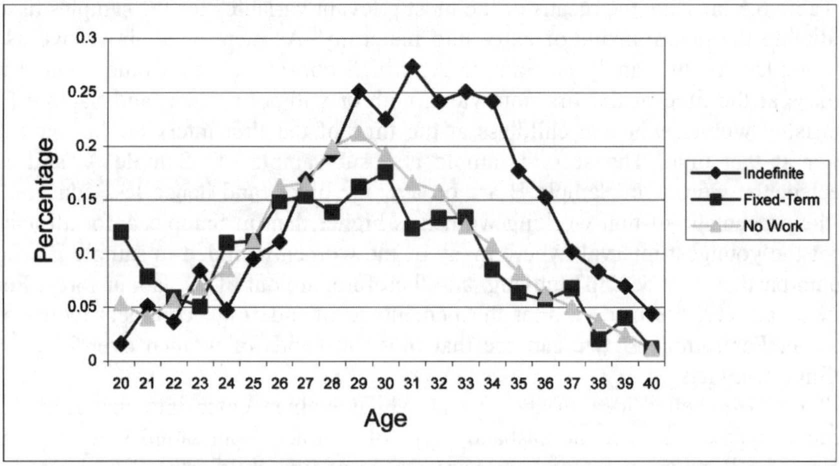

Regarding education, we can see that the less educated women are, the earlier they have their first child, and this is particularly clear for the sample of all women. In fact, for the sample of women with partner (figure 6.7), we do not appreciate clear differences concerning the timing of first birth by education.

Regarding the women's type of contract, it is interesting to see that women with fixed-term contracts present lower percentages of first childbirths at all ages, except for the very young ones (younger than 27) than those with indefinite contracts, regardless whether they have a partner or not (figures 6.8 and 6.6). Finally, for women with partner, figure 6.9 does not reveal a different pattern in the timing of first childbirths depending on the partner's type of contract.

Figure 6.7. *Percentage of first children born at each age by education – Women with Partner*

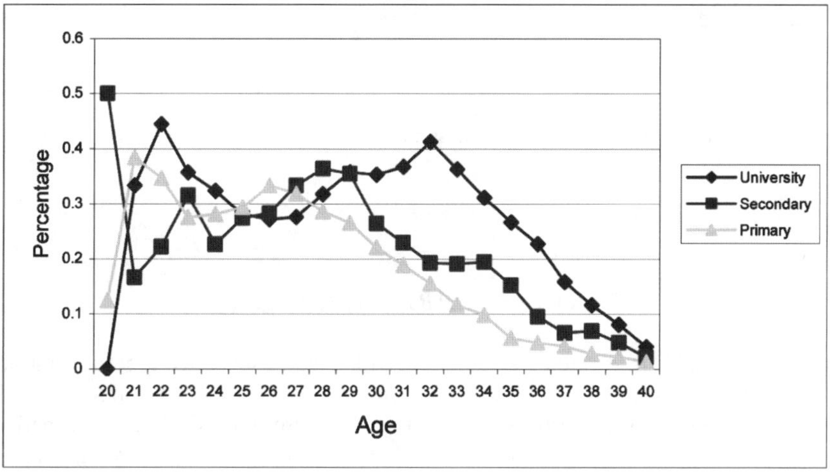

Figure 6.8. Percentage of first children born at each age by type of contract – Women with Partner

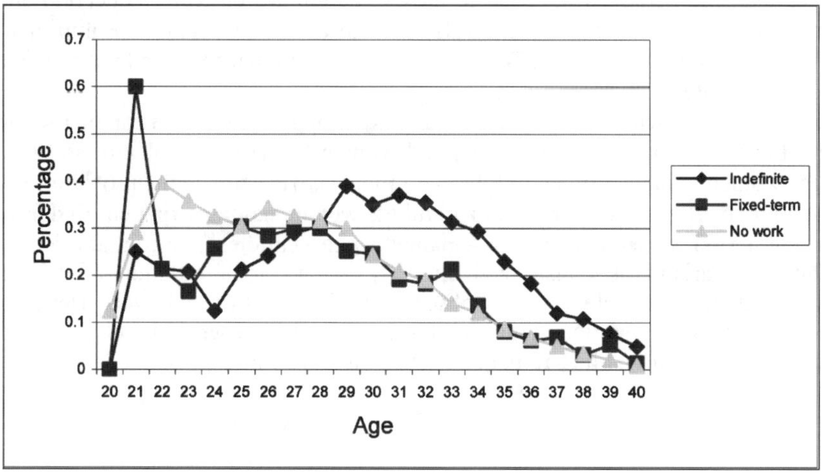

Figure 6.9. Percentage of first children born at each age by Partner's type of contract – Women with Partner

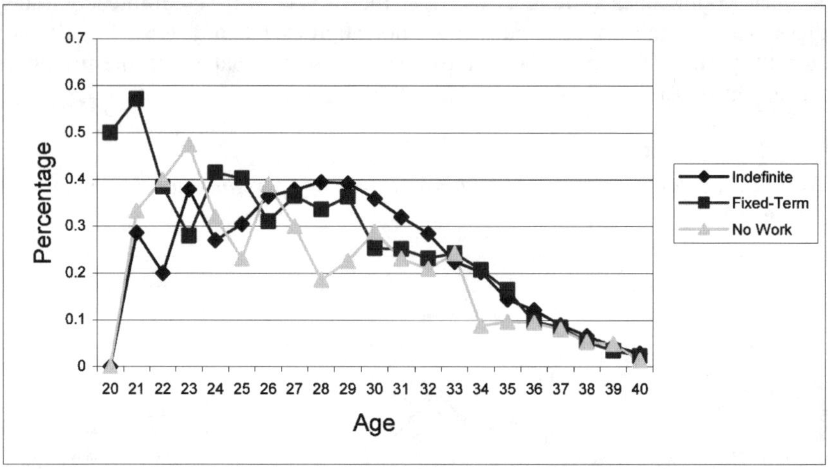

5. ECONOMETRIC APPROACH

To learn the impact of variables such as education and especially type of contract on getting married and on having a first child, we must isolate the effect of each variable in a multivariate estimation setting. We use two different estimation procedures: The first consists of a "static" approach, estimating by maximum likelihood the probability that non-cohabiting men and women will get married (or cohabit) at different age intervals. For the determinants of entry into maternity, we estimate the probability that childless women will have a first child also at different age intervals. The variables included in the estimation are basically education and labour market status. Using age intervals, we can appreciate better the impact of these variables on postponement. We use a logistic functional form and use the data as a pooled sample.

The second approach consists of estimating duration models which can be used to explain the factors that lead single men and women to marry or cohabit, and lead childless women to have a first child. In these models, we estimate the probability of a single individual getting married (of a childless women having a first child) during the current period, given that she has remained single (childless) up to that moment. The duration variable is constructed annually, so we treat duration (T_i) as a continuous random variable which is observed at discrete time intervals. Defining T_i as the length of remaining single (childless) period for each individual i and considering a proportional hazard parameterization[21], we can express the hazard rate

$$\theta_i = \lambda(t)\exp\left[x_i(t)'\beta\right]$$

whereas its corresponding discrete counterpart can be defined as

$$h_i(t) = 1 - \exp\left[-\int_t^{t+1}\lambda(s)\exp\{x_i(s)'\beta\}ds\right]$$
$$= 1 - \exp\left[-\exp\{\gamma(t) + x_i(t)'\beta\}\right]$$

where

$$\gamma(t) = \left\{\int_t^{t+1}\lambda(s)ds\right\}$$

captures the duration dependence non-parametrically. We assume that $x_i(s)$ is constant for $t \leq s < t+1$. The likelihood is exclusively a function of $h_i(s)$ given that both the density function (contribution to the likelihood of individuals with complete duration) and the survivor function (contribution to the likelihood of censored observations) can be expressed in terms of $h_i(t)$. So, defining d_i as the observed duration for each individual and c_i as an indicator variable that takes the value of one if the observation is complete and zero if it is censored, the likelihood function of an individual i can be written as[22]:

$$L_i = \left[h_i(d_i)\prod_{t=1}^{d_i-1}[1-h_i(t)]\right]^{c_i}\left[\prod_{t=1}^{d_i}[1-h_i(t)]\right]^{(1-c_i)}$$

However, following Jenkins (1995) we can treat each exit or continuation in each period as a single observation. So, each individual makes as many contributions to the model as the periods for which she remains in the risk group, treating the model as a sequence of binary choice equations defined on the surviving population at each duration. Define y_{it} as an indicator variable that takes the value of 0 for all spells except the exit year, where y_{it} takes the value of one. Using this indicator variable expression the former equation can be re-written as

$$L_i = \prod_{t=1}^{d_i}\left[\frac{h_i(t)}{1-h_i(t)}\right]^{y_{it}}\prod_{t=1}^{d_i}[1-h_i(t)]$$

6. RESULTS

Before we present the results, a word must be said concerning the endogeneity of some of the explanatory variables, in particular education and type of contract, for estimating the determinants for forming a family. Women who do receive higher education are likely to behave differently from less educated women regarding childbearing (they might require more quality for their children which would decrease quantity (Becker and Lewis (1973)), or we might think that due to their higher attachment to the labour force, their preferences for children might be lower (Francesconi (1998)). However, for the "static" approach, instruments are very difficult to find, given that it is not easy to find variables that affect the level of education individuals finally reach and do not directly affect the decision to form a family. For the "dynamic" approach, the difficulty of estimating duration models with endogenous variables is formidable. Given these restrictions and the fact that the impact of education is not the main issue of this chapter, we have not controlled for the likely endogeneity of it, although we are aware that results might be affected by this issue.

Regarding the type of contract, it is clear that labour force participation is endogenous for fertility. However, for workers an indefinite contract is always preferred to a fixed-term one. Fixed-term contracts do not present any advantage for the worker over indefinite ones. The latter are more stable, better paid and the number of hours worked in each type of contract is basically the same. Therefore, any worker would choose an indefinite contract if he/she could choose between them. This fact suggests that, for workers, the type of contract is exogenous. However, considering the whole population, it is clear that some individuals might choose not to work and this might be correlated with preferences for entering into parenthood. Given, as before, the difficulty of estimating duration models with endogenous variables, and the lack of instruments for labour force participation for the "static" estimation, our approach has been to estimate the model for all individuals in the first place, and only for workers in the second place, and to compare whether the impact of the different variables changes to a large extent or not.

6.1 The decision whether to get married

Tables 6.6 and 6.7 present the results derived from the empirical analysis concerning the decision whether to get married. In table 6.6 we present the results derived from the "static" approach, where we estimate by maximum likelihood methods and assuming a logistic functional form the probability of getting married at any point of time during the observation period. The dependent variable, getting married, takes the value of one when a previously unmarried individual (man or woman) gets married at a particular point of time during the observation period. It takes the value of zero for all other cases. Each individual is included in the sample up to the moment of his/her first marriage. All variables related to education and to type of contract are interacted with the three age intervals. Estimations have been done separately for men and women. Table 6.7 presents the estimation of the probability of getting married from a discrete time duration model[23].

Table 6.6. Probability of Getting Married (or cohabiting) – Logit Estimation Dependent variable = 1 if Marry or Cohabit; 0: Otherwise*

	Males				Females			
	All		Workers		All		Workers	
Variables[a]	Coef	|z|	Coef.	|z|	Coef	|z|	Coef.	|z|
Education (ref. Primary)								
20-24*U	-2.47	2.44	—	0.01	-0.67	1.93	-0.60	2.12
25-31*U	-0.14	0.95	-0.01	0.32	0.28	1.96	0.47	2.06
>31*U	0.13	0.62	0.08	2.57	-0.16	0.78	-0.21	0.73
20-24*S	-1.92	3.67	-1.34	0.57	-1.52	4.55	-1.52	2.75
25-31*S	-0.18	1.12	0.10	0.14	0.07	0.41	0.39	1.63
>31*S	0.06	0.26	-0.04	0.14	-0.09	0.40	-0.36	0.99
Type of contract (ref: Indefinite)								
20-24*FT	-0.79	2.34	-0.76	2.24	-0.23	0.61	0.14	0.34
25-31*FT	0.12	0.81	0.001	0.01	0.46	2.76	0.37	2.15
>31*FT	-0.38	1.51	-0.39	1.51	-0.14	0.52	0.05	0.19
20-24*NW	-1.81	4.22	—		-0.29	1.17	—	
25-31*NW	-0.58	3.75	—		0.05	0.35	—	
>31*NW	-1.15	4.31	—		-0.08	0.44	—	
N. obs.	8951		4972		7436		3463	

Notes: [a] This column shows the coefficients of the interaction variables between age and level of education (U: University, S: Secondary, Primary is the reference group), and between age and type of contract (FT: Fixed-Term, NW: No Work, Indefinite is the reference group).
* Estimations also include 6 region dummies, and for the estimations with only workers, in addition to these, 8 dummies for occupation.

*Table 6.7. Hazard Estimation for the Probability of Getting Married**

	Males				Females			
	All		Workers		All		Workers	
Variables	Coef.	|z|	Coef.	|z|	Coef.	|z|	Coef.	|z|
Age	-0.01	0.99	-0.02	1.38	-0.01	1.09	-0.05	3.94
Education (ref. Primary)								
University	-0.23	1.87	-0.18	1.08	0.03	0.27	-0.01	0.05
Secondary	-0.40	3.00	-0.15	1.00	-0.42	3.12	-0.16	0.77
Type of contract (ref: Indefinite)								
Fixed-Term	-0.23	1.88	-0.25	2.03	0.21	1.46	0.06	0.41
No work	-1.09	8.04	—		-0.30	2.23	—	

* Estimations also include 6 region dummies and 7 year dummies, and for the estimations with only workers, in addition to these, 8 dummies for occupation

6.1.1 Men

From table 6.6 the first result to note is that men with university or secondary education tend to delay marriage up to the second or third stage more than those with only primary education. If we consider only working men, however, the probability of marriage for workers with university education is higher than for workers with primary education at the oldest age interval. From the duration analysis presented in table 6.7, results indicate that, controlling for age, more highly educated men present lower probabilities of getting married.

Concerning the type of contract, results indicate that postponement is particularly stronger for non-workers than for those with an indefinite contract. Moreover, we can see that the lack of a job clearly discourages marriage even at the later stage of life (over 31 years). This is quite an expected result, given that the man is generally the main breadwinner of the household in Spain. However, we also observe some postponement of marriage for those with a fixed-term contract relative to those with an indefinite contract (the latter result is not statistically significant when only workers are considered). From the duration analysis presented in table 6.7, results indicate that non-workers are highly discouraged from marrying, and having a fixed-term contract lowers the probability of getting married in comparison with having an indefinite one.

In summary, men with fixed-term contracts (and of course those not working) are less likely to get married than those with indefinite contracts.

6.1.2 Women

The factors underlying the probability of marriage for women differ to some extent from those found for men. From table 6.6 we can see that the probability of getting married for women with university studies is lower than for women with only primary studies at earlier ages but higher in the medium age interval. This effect is even stronger when we consider only working women. The fact that women with university studies are less likely to marry at earlier ages but are more likely to marry in the medium age interval than women with only primary studies is likely to be the reason why we cannot find a negative effect of university studies with respect to the decision whether to get married from the duration analysis, depicted in table 7. However, controlling for age, we find that women with secondary studies are less likely to marry than those with only primary studies.

Regarding the type of contract, holding fixed-term contracts is no more likely to delay or discourage entry into marriage than holding indefinite ones, contrary to what we found for men. However, non-working women seem to marry less than their counterparts with an indefinite contract.

In summary, we can conclude that highly educated women postpone marriage more than less educated ones, and that fixed-term contracts do not seem to be a greater deterrent for marriage for women than indefinite ones.

6.2 The decision whether to enter into parenthood

Tables 6.8 and 6.9 present the results for the estimation of the probability of entry into parenthood for those women who are observed to be childless at the first interview. Table 6.8 displays the results derived from a "static" maximum likelihood estimation where the dependent variable, having a first child, takes the value of one when a childless woman has her first child at any point of time during the observation period. Table 6.9 presents the results derived from the estimation of a discrete time duration model. Both estimations are presented for all women who are childless at the time of the first interview, with or without a partner (Sample A) and for all women that are childless at the time of the first interview and have a partner at that time (Sample B)[24].

6.2.1 All childless women (with or without partner)

Table 6.8 reveals that highly educated women delay entry into maternity for longer than less educated ones. This is consistent with the career prospects motive for postponing maternity. Highly educated women earn high labour income, and this raises an important substitution effect if they have to drop out of the labour force after giving birth for childrearing. From the duration analysis presented in table 6.9, we can see that, controlling for age, having higher than primary education decreases the probability of having a first child.

Concerning the type of contract, the probability of having a first birth is much higher for women at any age interval with an indefinite contract than for those with a fixed-term one or for non-workers. The fact that the probability of having a first child is significantly lower for fixed-term and non workers than for their counterparts with indefinite contracts indicates that the discouragement effect of an unstable (or no) contract is permanent. These findings are consistent with the duration analysis results presented in table 6.9. Controlling for age, the probability of having a first child is significantly lower for women with fixed-term contracts and for non-workers than for women with indefinite contracts.

Therefore, it can be concluded that for women, unstable contracts (or no contract at all) discourage entry into maternity relative to their counterparts with indefinite contracts.

6.2.2 Childless women with partner

If we restrict our sample to women who have a partner, the factors affecting entry into motherhood change to some extent. Contrary to the results found before, the delaying effect of education on entry into maternity disappears, even when we consider only working women. This indicates that married (or cohabiting) women are more likely to give up their career prospects than women without a partner.

Regarding the type of contract, non-workers do not delay entry into maternity more than those with indefinite contracts, contrary to what we found for the whole sample of women. This is again understood if we take into account that most married non-working women that are out of the labour force do not expect to work. For them, there is no reason to delay maternity, given that households value their offspring and the longer they can enjoy them, the better. However, we find that fixed-term contracts delay entry into motherhood more than indefinite contracts. Therefore, even for women with partners, fixed-term contracts tend to delay motherhood until a stable job is secured.

Finally, with respect to the partner's type of contract, tables 6.8 and 6.9 reveal that women whose partner has a fixed-term contract postpone entry into motherhood longer than when they have an indefinite one. The effect of a non-working partner is not significant for postponement but this is probably because our sample contains very few non-working partners (less than 10%).

In summary, results concerning the decision whether to enter into parenthood indicate that on average, childless women with fixed-term contracts, whether or not that have a partner, delay entry into motherhood longer than those with indefinite contracts. This is particularly strong when we do not restrict the sample to childless women who have partners.

Table 6.8. Probability of having a first birth – Logit Estimation –Dependent Variable: 1: Have a first child; 0: Otherwise*

	Sample A: All childless women				Sample B: Childless women with Partner			
	All		Workers		All		Workers	
Variables[(a)]	Coef.	|z|	Coef.	|z|	Coef.	|z|	Coef.	|z|
Education (ref: less than university)								
20-24*U	-0.60	1.44	-1.89	2.59	-0.60	0.54	—	
25-31*U	-0.53	3.4	-0.82	3.59	-0.06	0.26	0.08	0.23
> 31*U	-0.33	1.50	-0.73	2.51	0.25	0.78	-0.12	0.27
20-24*S	-2.07	3.90	-2.27	3.77	-1.42	1.33	—	
25-31*S	-0.28	1.68	-0.02	0.08	0.33	1.28	0.54	1.45
>31*S	0.06	0.23	-0.62	1.59	0.21	0.53	0.31	0.63
Type of contract (ref: Indefinite)								
20-24*FT	-1.16	2.2	-1.04	1.96	-0.31	0.38	0.48	0.56
25-1*FT	0.09	-0.16	0.88		-0.32	0.95	-0.41	1.21
>31*FT	2.22				-0.16	0.39	-0.15	0.35
20-24*NW	-1.40	3.88	—		-0.4	0.05	—	
25-31*NW	-0.15	1.00	—		0.38	1.68	—	
> 31*NW	-0.65	2.76	—		-1.03	2.67	—	
Partner's type of contract (Ref: Indefinite)								
20-24*FT	—		—		-1.09	0.98	—	
25-31*FT	—		—		-0.51	1.85	-0.73	1.68
>31*FT	—		—		0.36	0.94	0.36	0.75
20-24*NW					—		—	
25-31*NW					-0.09	0.25	-0.33	0.58
>31*NW					-1.07	1.45	-0.68	0.90
N. Obs.	8452		4221		1392		779	

Notes: [(a)] This column shows the coefficients of the interaction variables between age and level of education (U: University, S: Secondary, Primary is the reference group), and between age and type of contract (FT: Fixed-Term, NW: No Work, Indefinite is the reference group).
* Estimations also include 6 region dummies, and for the estimations with only workers, in addition to these, 8 dummies for occupation.

Table 6.9. Hazard Estimation for the Probability of Having a First Child.

	Sample A: All childless women				Sample B: Childless women with partner*			
	All		Workers		All		Workers	
Variables	Coef.	|z|	Coef.	|z|	Coef.	|z|	Coef.	|z|
Age	-0.09	0.87	-0.02	1.52	-0.04	2.22	0.01	0.48
Education (ref. Primary)								
University	-0.36	2.78	-0.69	3.21	0.10	0.53	-0.14	0.42
Secondary	-0.45	3.11	-0.32	1.69	0.04	0.17	0.13	0.45
Type of contract: (ref: Indefinite)								
Fixed-term	-0.36	2.38	-0.41	2.70	-0.42	1.82	-0.40	1.69
No Work	-0.62	4.66	—		-0.09	0.53	—	
Partner's Type of Contract (ref: Indefinite)								
Fixed-term	—		—		-0.25	1.25	-0.30	1.07
No work					-0.44	1.54	-0.62	1.44

* Estimations also include 6 region dummies and 7 year dummies, and for the estimations with only workers, in addition to these, 8 dummies for occupation.

7. CONCLUSION

The aim of this chapter is to find an empirical connection between the striking increase in the use of fixed-term contracts and the delay in marriage and maternity in Spain. Holding a fixed-term contract increases uncertainty about the future and prevents workers from having a stable labour market situation. In this context, individuals may feel inclined to postpone the decision to form a family until their labour market situation becomes more stable. Using the eight waves of individual information from the European Household Panel for Spain, we estimate empirically the impact of the type of contract on postponement of marriage and maternity in Spain. We use two empirical approaches: First, a "static" approach, where we estimate the probability of entry into marriage (or cohabitation) by maximum likelihood methods assuming a logistic functional form. The second approach consists of estimating a discrete time duration model for the probability of entry into marriage and into parenthood so as to take into account the dynamic aspects of the two decisions.

Results reveal that for men, the decision whether to get married is strongly negatively affected by holding unstable contracts or not working, in comparison to holding an indefinite contract. This is an expected result given the role of men as the main breadwinners in the Spanish households. However, for women, results suggest that holding fixed-term contracts does not imply a deterrent for the decision whether to get married.

With respect to the decision of whether to enter into parenthood, results indicate that for all childless women, either with or with no partner, holding fixed-term contracts delay entry into motherhood in comparison to indefinite contracts. The discouragement effect is stronger for women with no partner, as expected.

The lesson to be learned from this study is that the labour market reform that took place in Spain in 1984, i.e., the creation of a new type of contract, called "employment promotion contract" , not only created a segmented labour market, but also delayed men's decision concerning when to get married, and women's decision concerning when to enter into motherhood. This postponement of marriage and maternity is at least partially responsible for the overall fall in fertility rates in Spain in the late nineties.

ACKNOWLEDGEMENTS

We are grateful to the Review of Economics of the Household for allowing us the reprinting of the paper titled "Career Planning in Spain: Do Fixed-Term Contracts Delay Marriage and Parenthood?", Review of the Economics of the Household, (2005), vol. 3, pp. 49-73. Financial support from Spanish Ministry of Education and Science (SEC2003-04826, SEC2003-12510), University of the Basque Country (UPV00035.321-13511) and FBBVA is gratefully acknowledged.

NOTES

[1] In the remainder of the chapter, marriage must be understood as either getting married or forming a stable union.

[2] Unfortunately, we cannot present the average age of entry into marriage for men disaggregated by educational level given that such information for women is taken from the Fertility Surveys that the Spanish Institute of Statistics carried out in 1985 and in 1998. In these surveys, however, only women are interviewed, so information concerning men is not provided.

[3] We do not use data from the Fertility Survey of 1999 to describe average entry into motherhood by type of contract because the number of observations is too small.

[4] Average age at motherhood by type of contract is heavily affected by the fact that women (and in general, individuals) with indefinite contracts are much older than those with fixed-term contracts and than non-workers. In particular, from ECHP the average age of women with indefinite contracts is 35, that of women with temporary contracts 30 and that of non-working women 29. Thus, average age at motherhood does not allow us to see whether women time the birth of their first child differently according to their type of contract.

[5] This is very clear if we look at the percentage of women with university education at birth of first child if they have an indefinite contract (8.04) comparative to those with a fixed-term contract (5.07) at their early stage. However, this difference is not so clear when looking at the late stage, which is reasonable given that the biological ending of the fertile cycle plays a much more important role at this later stage.

[6] If the dismissal was considered "fair", the worker had the right to receive 20 days' wages per year of tenure. If considered "unfair" by the labour court, which happened very frequently, the worker would be awarded 45 days' wage per year of tenure. For more details, see Toharia and Malo (1999).

[7] For more details on severance payments associated with fixed-term and indefinite contracts, see Güell and Petrongolo (2005) and Segura et al. (1991).

[8] See Toharia (1996) for a picture of the trend in fixed-term contracts from 1987 to 1995.

[9] De la Rica (2004) estimates that for 1995, the adjusted wage gap between workers with indefinite and fixed-term contracts who work in the same occupation within the same firm is around 11% for men and 9% for women.

[10] For more details, see Toharia and Malo (1999).

[11] The current contribution of employers to social security is 24% of wages.

[12] The Member States at the beginning of this project were Belgium, Denmark, France, Germany, Greece, Ireland, Italy, Luxemburg, Netherlands, Portugal, Spain and the United Kingdom.

[13] More information on the panel can be found in the Website: http://forum.europa.eu.int/irc/dsis/echpanel/info/data/information.html.

[14] The panel structure of the data would allow us to reduce a large part of unobserved individual heterogeneity (that which is invariant with time, such as tastes for marriage and for children) by introducing unobserved fixed effects into the estimation. However, estimation by fixed effects requires there to be individual within-time variation in the variables included in the analysis, and observations with no within-time variation are dropped from the estimation. In fact, given the very scarce within-time variation of the variables included in the empirical analysis, such as education and type of contract, if we use fixed effects, we lose about two thirds of the observations. Given the very few individuals who seem to experience within-time variation, we are afraid that these few individuals are not representative of the whole sample.

[15] Minor changes in these periods do not make for significant changes in the empirical analysis.

[16] In the empirical analysis we also control for region.

[17] Ideally, we would like to take an homogeneous group of individuals (at least of similar age) to carry out the estimation of duration models for each of the events. This would rule out a significant part of unobserved heterogeneity. However, unfortunately, the size of the panel is rather small, and restricting individuals by age, or making groups by individual ages would leave us with too few observations. All we do is control for age and other observables in the estimation, but unfortunately we cannot restrict the sample further. This is another reason why doing the "static" complementary approach is important, given that it looks at the occurrence of the events at different stages of the fertile cycle.

[18] Concerning the type of contract, we have proceeded as follows: salaried workers with an indefinite contract and the self-employed are assigned to indefinite contracts. We have included the latter with the category of indefinite contract because they are not tied to a fixed term contract, as the others are, and this is precisely the point we stress when we make the distinction between indefinite and fixed-term contracts. Salaried workers employed in a training regime are assigned to fixed-term contracts. The category of non-workers includes all those who are unemployed, family help with no pay, out of the labor force or work less than 15 hours a week (the latter are less than 5 percent).

[19] For expositional purposes, in the figures, we have not replaced those individuals for whom the event (marriage or birth of first child) has taken place. The effects are basically the same than replacing them, but these are smoother and can be appreciated better.

[20] As before, for expositional purposes, in the figures we have not replaced those individuals for whom the event (birth of first child) has taken place.

[21] The proportional hazard is a very commonly used parameterization due to its advantages. On the one hand, it does not impose any restriction on β , and it guarantees the non-negativity of the hazard rate. On the other hand, the estimation and inference of these models is rather direct (see Kiefer (1988)).

[22] We have not included a term reflecting unobserved heterogeneity with a Gamma mixture distribution given that our samples are not random, but conditioned on variables like age, marital status and child status.

[23] In the estimation of duration models, we originally also included interactions between type of contract and education, but given that they were not significantly different from zero for men or for women, we did not include them in the final estimations.

[24] In the estimation of the duration model for the probability of entry into parenthood, we also introduced interactions between education and type of contracts. However, they were not significantly different from zero, so we did not include them in the final estimations.

REFERENCES

Ahn and Mira (2001), Job bust, baby bust? Evidence from Spain, *Journal of Population Economics*, 1, pp. 505-522.

Becker, G.S. and H.G. Lewis (1973), "On the interaction between quantity and quality of children", *Journal of Political Economy,* 81, pp. s143-s288.

Bentolila, S. and J. Dolado (1994),"Labour flexibility and wages: Lessons from Spain", *Economic Policy,* pp. 54-99.

Cigno, A. and J. Ermisch (1989), "A Microeconomic Analysis of the timing of births", *European Economic Review,* 33, pp. 737-760.

Cigno, A. (1991), Economics of the Family, Clarendon Press, Oxford.

Dankmeyer, B. (1996), "Long-Run Opportunity-Cost according to Education of the Mother in the Netherlands" *Journal of Population Economics,* 9, pp. 349-361.

De la Rica, S. (2004), "Wage gaps between workers with indefinite and fixed-term contracts: The impact of firm and occupational segregation", *Moneda y Crédito,* Vol. 219, 43-69.

Francesconi, M. (1998), "A Joint Dynamic Model of Fertility and Work of Married Women", *Journal of Labour Economics,* 20 (2), pp. 336-380.

Guell, M. and B. Petrongolo (2005), "How binding are legal limits? Transitions from temporary to permanent work in Spain", forthcoming in *Labour Economics.*

Gustafsson, S.S.C. Wetzels, J.D. Vlasblom and S. Dex (1996), "Women's Labour Force Transitions in connection with childbirth: A Panel Data comparison between Germany, Sweden and Great Britain", *Journal of Population Economics,* 96 (3), pp. 223-246.

Gustafsson, S. (2001), "Optimal age at parenthood: Theoretical and empirical considerations on postponement of maternity in Europe", *Journal of Population Economics,* 14:225-247.

Gutierrez-Domenech, M. (2002), "Employment penalty after Motherhood in Spain", CEP Discussion Paper, Centre for Economic Perfomance, LSE CEPDP0546 (2002).

Hernanz, V. (2002), *El trabajo temporal y la segmentación: Un estudio de las transiciones laborales,* PhD Dissertation, Universidad de Alcalá.

Hotz, V.J., J.A. Klerman and R.J. Willis (1997), "The Economics of Fertility in Developed Countries", in M.R. Rosenzweig and O. Stark, eds., *Handbook of Population and Family Economics* (Elsevier, Amsterdam), pp. 275-347.

Instituto Nacional de Estadística.-Banco de datos TEMPUS.

Jenkins, S. (1995), "Easy estimation methods for discrete-time duration models", *Oxford Bulletin of Economics and Statistics,* 57(1): 129-138.

Jimeno, J.F. and L.Toharia (1993), "The effects of fixed term employment on wages: Theory and evidence from Spain", *Investigaciones Economicas*, 17, pp. 475-494.

Joshi, H.(1990), "The Cash Alternative Costs of childbearing: An approach to estimation using British Data", *Population Studies,* 44, pp. 41-60.

Joshi, H. (1994), "The foregone earnings of Europe's mothers", in Ekert-Jaffé O (ed), *Standards of living and families: Observation and Analysis,* John Libbey, London 101-134.

Joshi, H. (1998), "The opportunity costs of childbearting: More than mother's business", *Journal of Population Economics,* 11, pp. 161-183.

Kalwij, A.S. (1999), "Female Employment and Fertility Decisions: an Analysis of the Effects of Household Financial Wealth" mimeo, *Institute of Economics and Statistics, University of Oxford.*

Kiefer, N.M. (1988),"Economic Duration Data and Hazard Functions", *Journal of Economic Literature, vol. XXVI,* pp. 646-679

Kugler, A., J.F. Jimeno and V. Hernanz (2002),"Employment consequences of restrictive permanent contracts: Evidence from Spanish Labour Market Reforms", Discussion Paper, no. 657.

Segura, J., F. Duran, L. Toharia and S. Bentolila (1991), Colección Economía y Sociología del Trabajo, Ministerio de Trabajo y Seguridad Social, Centro de Publicaciones, Madrid.

Toharia, L. (1996), "Empleo y paro en España: Evolución, situación y perspectivas", *Ekonomiaz,* 35, pp. 36-67.

Toharia, L. and M. Malo (1999), "The Spanish experiment: pros and cons of the flexibility at the margin", chapter 11 of , Ed. Esping-Andersen and M. Regini, Oxford University Press.

Walker, J. (1995), "The effect of public policies on recent Swedish fertility behaviour", *Journal of Population Economics*, 8. pp. 223-251.

Chapter 7

THE FAMILY EARNINGS GAP AND POSTPONEMENT OF MATERNITY IN THE UNITED STATES

CATALINA AMUEDO-DORANTES AND JEAN KIMMEL

1. INTRODUCTION

One of the stylized facts in the United States from the past thirty years has been the declining rate of first births before age 30 for all women and the increase rate of first births after age 30 among women with four-year college degrees (Martin 2000). Accompanying this trend is the rising education level of mothers. This trend of older, more educated first-time mothers mirrors the overall trends observed in Western European countries. However, in the United States, these trends have occurred within a fairly stable total fertility rate, allowing the country to maintain a fertility rate approximately equal to the replacement rate since approximately 1990. In contrast, Western European countries have suffered declines in their total fertility rates, with some countries' rates at 1.3 or 1.4. What factors contribute to the US' maintenance of replacement rate fertility? We hypothesize that the link between motherhood and wages might play a role in fertility delay in the United States, and also might suggest an explanation for differing fertility rates internationally

The economic theory of fertility serves as a starting point for our discussion. The Becker fertility model (Becker 1985) posits that consideration of opportunity costs drives the fertility decision. That is, Becker's model assumes that, when women consider maternity, they consider their "next best alternatives," with a focus on labor market opportunities. In this framework, as women become more educated, they may reduce their fertility due to the rising opportunity cost of motherhood. In addition to the opportunity cost argument, Becker also describes a quantity-quality trade-off; i.e., as mothers' education rises, their demand for higher quality children rises (quality per child), also resulting in reduced fertility rates. While this model has broad appeal and does seem to explain some of the fertility changes that have occurred in the past century, the model is not successful in explaining the trend completely and in particular, it fails one critical test. In particular, if mothers in the

Siv Gustafsson and Adriaan Kalwij (eds.), Education and Postponement of Maternity, 175–206.

US and overseas both are experiencing increased human capital levels, why have the Western European countries suffered significant fertility declines while the US has not?[1]

Described more fully, in this chapter we posit that the relationship between motherhood, wages, and fertility delay might differ among countries, resulting in different fertility outcomes.[2] While our empirical research focuses on the United States, we speculate about our findings' implications for the question noted above. Using U.S. data, we contribute to this debate by re-formulating the fertility timing decision in the framework of a career-oriented woman's effort to minimize the so-called motherhood wage gap. Because education plays a role both in fertility decisions and in family pay gap outcomes, it is likely that education provides the link between these two factors. We find that college-educated mothers actually experience a wage boost compared with college-educated non-mothers, and this wage boost is enhanced by their postponement of motherhood. As explained in more detail in the final section of the paper, we speculate that, in the process of searching for family-friendly employers, college-educated mothers simultaneously are identifying those firms most likely to be friendly to women and to encourage their advancement within the firm.

A better understanding of the observed changes in fertility and the timing of childbearing are of interest and concern to researchers and policy-makers alike for four reasons. First, fertility rates below replacement rates serve as a threat to the long-term survival for any society as the impact of an aging population and reduced economic growth reverberates throughout the economy. Second, with rapidly aging (on average) populations, the ability to provide costly support services to the non-working elderly becomes more uncertain. Third, as women delay fertility, they face declining fecundity in their thirties and forties. Consequently, more families face increased medical expenditures as they confront this natural consequence of aging, a cost that is passed on to society in higher overall medical expenditures and rising health care costs. Furthermore, more women are remaining childless although their preferences are otherwise, merely as a result of delaying fecundity. Finally, because these fertility (as well as marriage trends) vary substantially by education, the resulting impact on family structure produces a rising unequal income distribution in the United States, with an increasingly marginalized population of "have-nots" characterized by poor education, low marital rates, and high rates of single parenthood (Ellwood and Jencks, 2001).

The popular media has also entered the discussion of these trends, most recently with the book titled *Creating a Life: Professional Women and the Quest for Children*, by labor economist Sylvia Ann Hewlett (2002). Hewlett describes the difficulties faced by educated women, including job market problems, mate-finding problems, and fecundity problems resulting from delayed childbearing. Most relevant for this research is her conclusions that the "costs" associated with motherhood are lower for younger first-time mothers than older first-time mothers.[3] Her argument is a convincing one were such choices made in a static framework, but not so convincing when one considers that fertility/employment decisions somewhat early in life affect wage levels and wage growth throughout a working lifetime.

That is, if bearing children early in life scars a woman's career advancement and earnings potential for a lifetime, then the decision-making process must consider the full lifetime costs and benefits of early versus late motherhood. In other words, the potential effects on the motherhood wage gap (and overall career success) arising from the timing of first birth must also be considered. By delaying fertility, educated women leave time for a career to take off, allowing for a less-disruptive maternity period following this career build-up. How rational are these women? Are they making this decision to delay fertility in order to build up formal and on-the-job human capital in their twenties? If so, the fertility timing decision becomes more complicated, given the conflicting goals of career success and motherhood.

In the next two sections of this chapter, we describe in further detail trends in fertility and education, and their link to estimates of the motherhood wage gap. Next, in section IV, we discuss the conceptual framework and empirical methodology of our study. Section V then follows with a description of our data. We present and explain our findings in section VI, and our conclusions follow in Section VII.

2. FURTHER TRENDS IN FERTILITY AND EDUCATION

Aggregate and detailed fertility trends in the United States changed dramatically in the past century. In 1960, the fertility rate per 1000 women in childbearing age was at a high of 120, and by the year 2000 this rate had fallen to 67. Described using total fertility rates (i.e., the number of births that a hypothetical woman is estimated to experience throughout her childbearing years if she follows current fertility patterns), this rate fell from 2.48 per mother in year 1960 to 2.13 in the year 2000.[4] Additionally, over the same time frame, the mother's age at first birth was rising: in 1970, 19 percent of first births were to women aged 25 or older; by 2000 this percentage had increased to over 50 percent. These changes are related intricately to simultaneous changes in women's work, education and marriage patterns. The most interesting change is the average age at first birth for first-time mothers, which has risen from 21.8 in 1960 to 24.2 in 1997. Next, looking at age at first birth, one also sees substantial variation by educational attainment. Less-educated women are much more likely to experience the first birth in their twenties, while more educated women are more likely to experience that first birth in the thirties. Additionally, the wage gap between mothers and non-mothers varies substantively by education, with more educated women experiencing a smaller penalty associated with motherhood. Descriptive evidence to support this conclusion can be found in Schmidt's (2002) study of unmarried mothers. She finds that less-educated unmarried mothers earn only 75 percent, on average, of their non-mother counterparts while the comparable percentage for more-educated unmarried mothers is 95 percent (p. 5). While these figures relate only to never-married mothers, they indicate that the motherhood wage penalty for all mothers is likely to be smaller for better-educated mothers.

Martin (2000) examines the growing trend of delaying fertility beyond the age of 30, and finds that the women underlying this aggregate trend are more educated women. He argues that fertility delay is a consequence of career building demands and the high costs of quality child care, with both factors becoming less insurmountable as the woman's career progresses and earnings grow. As a consequence, "... especially for college-educated women, the competition between work and family roles in the early adult years causes births to be consigned to the later adult years" (pg 523).[5]

Martin's focus is on delay of first birth beyond age 30, and so he also presents statistics concerning childlessness at age 30. He finds that in the time period 1990 to 1995, fifty-six percent of women with four-year college degrees were still childless at age 30, while only 17 percent of those women with less than a high school education were childless at age 30. Both of these percentages were higher than in previous periods. Next, Martin examines the incidence of first birth after age 30 for college-educated women and finds that childlessness falls from the late 1970s to the early 1990s from 65 percent to 49 percent. That is, while more educated women remain childless at age 30, they are becoming more likely to experience a late birth, thereby compensating at least in part for that earlier delay in fertility. He concludes "Conflicts between women's work and family lives reduce fertility in early adulthood for all women, and especially for college-educated women. Yet I find a compensating increase in family formation rates after age 30 only for women with four-year college degrees" (p. 523). Chen and Morgan (1991) also find that the likelihood that childless women age 30 and over will experience a first birth has increased over time. They also note that a large racial gap persists in the timing of first birth.

Rindfuss et al. (1996) examine the link between fertility delay and education levels in the time period 1963 to 1989. First, they note the rising incidence of college completion for women, increasing from 12 percent in 1970 to 23 percent in 1990. Second, they conclude that there is an increasing educational difference in fertility timing, partially due to substantial time pressures for higher educated women early in their career development[6] Finally, they assert that the trend in further delay in fertility by higher educated women results in ever-growing inequality experienced by children of lesser-educated parents and better-educated parents.[7]

There is also theoretical evidence to support this connection. Gustafsson (2001) examines the optimal age of motherhood from both theoretical and empirical standpoints. Her theoretical research identifies women's career planning as the primary explanation for postponement of maternity. This implies that the delay of fertility will be most beneficial for career-oriented women, who are also likely to be relatively better educated (See also Iyigun 2000). This theoretical contribution is extended by Caucutt et al. (2002), who develop an equilibrium search model of marriage, divorce, and child investment that permits differences in the timing of fertility. They find that labor markets produce incentives for fertility delay and that these incentives can explain the motherhood wage gap as well as fertility trends in the past 40 years.

Blackburn et al. (1990) examine the fact that mothers who have delayed fertility until their thirties tend to earn higher wages using a lifecycle model of fertility timing and human capital investment. They find that the increased wages for "late" mothers are driven by greater formal human capital investments (p. 24). They do not, however, address the issue of whether higher educated women can improve their earnings potential by delaying fertility.

In summary, this literature suggests a strong connection between fertility delay and education, although the explanations are not clear. We address this issue in a more rigorous way in the following section.

3. THE FAMILY EARNINGS GAP AND ITS POTENTIAL LINK TO CHANGING FERTILITY PATTERNS

On average, women with children earn less than women without children, even when various relevant productivity characteristics are controlled for. This so-called family earnings gap (alternatively, motherhood wage gap) has been discussed in the labor economics literature for many years, originally as a by-product of comparisons between married and single working women, and the more broad comparison of wages across sex. Early literature examining the sex wage gap proffered the explanation that marriage and childbearing altered the earnings capacity differentially by sex. For example, Becker (1985) suggests that some portion of the wage gap observed between single and married mothers arises from the choice by married mothers to work in less intensive and more convenient jobs (p. S54). Of course, married men are not typically observed making such trade-offs.

Typically, estimates of the motherhood wage gap are obtained from estimates of linear log wage equations estimated with a sample of working women, with a variety of right hand side regressors, including demographic and productivity characteristics, sometimes job characteristics, and variants of motherhood status measures (such as a 0-1 dummy variable for being a mother, two 0-1 dummy variables for having one child and having 2 or more children, and the total number of children of the mother). Hill (1979) was one of the first to use such a model to examine the effect of motherhood on wages. She uses one wave of the PSID and, while she finds a 7 percent motherhood wage penalty for white women when productivity characteristics are excluded, the motherhood wage penalty nearly disappears when they are added into the regression. She finds that the driving factor in the wage differences is intermittent work for mothers. In fact, she concludes that "the number of children is a good proxy variable for differential work history and labor force attachment for white women" (p. 591).

Future work focused further on disentangling the effects of marital status and motherhood status on women's wages. Korenman and Neumark (1992) provide a nice review of this marriage, fertility, and wage literature and find little evidence of a direct motherhood wage penalty. Nonetheless, they explain that the existing literature suffers from econometric deficiencies that may have led to unreliable findings. They rely on the NLS-YW[8] and estimate several different versions of wage equations, using both cross-sectional and panel data methods, OLS and instrumental variable methods. Their work represents the first econometrically rigorous examination of the motherhood wage gap. They address the following problems: endogeneity of experience, tenure, marriage, and motherhood; unobserved heterogeneity; and the importance of employment selection. Their results fail to reject the exogeneity of marriage and motherhood, but reject the exogeneity of tenure and experience. It is likely that they reach this finding regarding motherhood because they do not differentiate the wage gap by education levels, which may alter the results of such exogeneity tests. Additionally, they use an instrumental variable approach that relies on the same set of instruments for a heterogeneous set of potentially endogenous regressors. Interestingly, they do not find the employment sample selection correction to be important but, again, this may be because they are not focusing in differences by education. We expect this selection to vary in importance by education level, as suggested by Neal (2001). Finally, they find that implementing appropriate panel data methods to model heterogeneity is important. Regarding specific estimates of the motherhood wage gap, their results vary tremendously by specification and estimating technique. Most often, however, they find no significant effect on wages of having a first child, but rather large effects from the second child (in the neighborhood of a 10 to 20 percent penalty). Interestingly, implementing panel data methods eliminates this effect, but their methods rely on just two time periods of data, possibly resulting in unreliable estimates. Their instrumental variable estimates lead to their conclusion that working continuously following childbirth will not eliminate the motherhood wage gap.

The literature that follows Korenman and Neumark (1992) utilizes somewhat less technical approaches, although the bulk continues to implement panel data techniques. Perhaps the most prominent of this more recent (post Korenman-Neumark) literature on this topic are the papers by Waldfogel (1997, 1998a, 1998b). Waldfogel takes a rather straightforward approach to the question and finds that the motherhood wage gap is in the area of 8 percent per child. More precisely, her fixed effects results suggest a wage penalty of 4.6 percent for the first child and 12.6 percent for two or more children. She uses the NLSY and requires that each woman have a recorded wage early in the panel and late in the panel. Her research also attempts to link the wage gap to policy, and finds that women who have access to family leave upon childbirth are more likely to return to their pre-childbirth employer and, consequently, receive a wage boost that partially offsets the motherhood wage penalty (75 percent of the wage penalty is eliminated).

Budig and England (2001) compare the motherhood wage gap between married and unmarried mothers using the NLSY. They implement a fixed effects regression approach to address the likelihood of unobserved heterogeneity in their sample. They do not correct their regressions for selection into employment but state that "if women for whom the motherhood wage penalty would be the worst are the most likely to remain out of the labor force, our models will underestimate the motherhood penalty" (p. 213). They suggest that their fixed effects method helps to net out the potential endogeneity of marital status. They also discuss the likely endogeneity of childbearing, and suggest that it is the improper modeling of this endogeneity that could lead to mistaken conclusions regarding the existence or magnitude of a motherhood wage gap (p. 210). Their motherhood control is a variable for total number of children, and they find the wage gap to range between 3.7 percent and 7.3 percent, depending on the list of control variables. Their primary contribution to this literature is two-fold: first, their article presents a very nice discussion of the reasons for interest in this topic as well as a detailed verbal interpretation of their findings. Second, they include a comprehensive set of controls for experience and tenure with the current employer, distinguishing between full-time and part-time years. They note, as a side issue, that they fail to find decisive evidence of differential wage penalties by the mother's skill level. They explain that their findings fail to support the hypothesis that the motherhood wage gap is explained by reduced work effort.

Anderson et al. (2002a) address one specific explanation offered for reduced wages for mothers; that is, reduced work effort. They use the NLS-YW in a panel framework and find no evidence that reduced work effort is at the root of the wage gap. They estimate the wage gap at 3 percent for the mothers with one child and at 6 percent for mothers of two or more children. They posit that the wage gap is largely caused by high costs of flexible work schedules for women holding medium office jobs with standard work hours. Anderson et al. (2002b) examine specifically the existence of educational differentials in the wage gap, with an additional focus on differences based on timing of return to work following childbirth. Their cross-sectional results suggest that the highest educated workers experience the largest motherhood wage penalties, possibly because it is for those workers that intermittent work can be the most costly. However, when they implement a fixed effects model, the results vary widely depending on the particular list of regressors. When they include experience, the wage gap for white college-educated mothers with more than one child is 15 percent. In some specifications, white college educated mothers actually enjoy a wage boost.[9]

How do estimates of the motherhood wage gap compare to such gaps in other developed countries? Todd (2001) examines the link between educational attainment and the family pay gap for five industrialized countries, and finds that the nature of the gap differs across countries.[10] She shows that for the United States and Canada, better-educated mothers experience a very small (nearly non-existent) wage penalty, leading her to conclude "high educational attainment acts as a 'shock absorber'," at least in those two countries. Harkness and Waldfogel (forthcoming) also present an international comparative study, with a focus on seven industrialized nations.[11] They find notable differences across countries in the family pay gap, with the largest gap in the United Kingdom and the smallest in the Nordic countries. They also find a link between the magnitude of the family pay gap in a specific country and that country's gender wage gap. They suggest that some portion of these differences might be due to differences in family-friendly policies in the workplace.

What does the existing wage gap literature say about the role of fertility timing? Three papers from the wage gap literature address this issue and serve as useful lead-ins to our research. Chandler et al. (1994) test the link between marriage and fertility delay and earnings and find that there is an association between delay and enhanced earnings. They define birth delay as the difference between actual age at first birth and predicted age at first birth; therefore, delay of fertility is defined in a static framework and is not very useful in addressing the larger issue of the gradual but steady increase in age at first birth that has occurred over many years. In addition, the authors do not address selection or endogeneity issues, nor do they control for education level in their analyses. Following a similar approach, Drolet (2002) examines the link between fertility timing and the motherhood wage gap using Canadian data from the 1998 Survey of Labour and Income Dynamics. She relies primarily on cross-sectional data but also incorporates a two-period model in some of her analyses, and she conducts her analysis separately for three different cohorts of women. She finds that compared to those mothers with early first births, delayed mothers experience 6% higher wages; in fact, she finds no statistically significant difference in wages between late mothers and non-mothers. She does not examine a potential link between educational attainment and this reduction of the motherhood wage gap.

Most relevant for our project is recent work by Taniguchi (1999). Taniguchi looks separately at two issues: the impact on the motherhood wage gap of fertility delay, and the importance of education on this wage gap. She uses data from the NLSYW to determine how much of the gap can be eliminated by delaying fertility. She relies on the total number of children as her measure of motherhood, making it somewhat difficult to place her findings within the broader literature. To approach this question, she sets up three categories of fertility timing: teenaged birth, birth from 20-27, and birth at age 28 or later. In her baseline results, she estimates the wage gap to be approximately 2.5% to 3%, in the range of Budig and England's (2001) result, which relied on the same measure of motherhood. Looking at fertility delay, she estimates the wage gap separately by age at first birth and shows that late mothers experience a very small (and not statistically significant) wage gap.

Separate from the fertility timing concern, Taniguchi estimates the wage gap by education, and consistent with Todd (2001) and Anderson et al. (2002b), finds that the wage gap declines as education rises. In fact, she finds that college-educated mothers experience a wage boost. However, by addressing the two issues (fertility timing and education) separately, it is not possible to interpret the source of the reduced wage gap because, as described earlier, fertility delay goes hand in hand with increased education.[12]

Our research contributes to the existing literature in three ways. First and most importantly, by isolating the role that fertility timing plays in the determination of wages, separately from the role of education, we are able to address the specific question posed by Ellwood and Jencks concerning the reasons for fertility delay by higher-educated women. Recall that fertility delay is primarily a phenomenon of the higher educated. Thus, we provide separate estimates of the wage effects for college-educated childless women, college-educated mothers, and college-educated mothers who delay fertility. Second, for completeness, we also produce direct estimates of the effect of fertility delay for less educated mothers. Third, we discuss these findings in the context of international differences in fertility rates to suggest explanations for these differences.

4. METHODOLOGY

Our empirical model is based on a standard underlying utility-maximization model that conceptually supports the notion that a reduction of utility might result from motherhood if that status burdens the mother with restricted labor market choices. In the spirit of human capital theory, we model women's labor earnings as a function of personal characteristics (*P*), such as educational attainment; family characteristics (*F*), such as whether they are mothers and age at first birth; job related characteristics (*J*), such as tenure, work experience, and occupation; and a set of regional dummies (*R*) and yearly dummies accounting for macroeconomics factors, such as regional unemployment rates. In addition, given our focus on working women and the differential role of women's educational attainment on their decision to work (Neal 2001), our wage regressions correct for the sample selection bias incurred when focusing on working respondents. In particular, we include the inverse Mill's ratio (λ) derived from the predictions of a probit model of the likelihood of being working among the aforementioned regressors as follows:

$$\ln w_{ijt} = \alpha_i + \beta_1' P_{it} + \beta_2' F_{it} + \beta_3' J_{ijt} + \beta_4' R_t + \beta_5' \lambda_{ijt} + \varepsilon_{ijt} \quad (1)$$

In addition to the respondent's personal, family, and regional characteristics included in the wage regression, the selection model for being working includes information on the highest grade completed by the respondent's mother and father, as well as a dummy variable indicative of whether the respondent lived with her parents by age 18. These three regressors are excluded from the wage regression as determinants of the respondent's current hourly wage other than through her educational attainment, which we already control for. Additionally, the selection model for being working includes years of schooling, whereas the educational attainment information included in the wage regression is captured by dummy variables reflecting the highest grade completed by the respondent. The results from estimating two selection models for being working, one using a dummy variable for motherhood and the other one distinguishing between mothers with one child versus mothers with two or more children, are contained in Table A in the appendix.[13] Finally, in accordance with the results from the Breusch and Pagan Lagrangian multiplier and the Hausman specification tests,[14] the wage regressions are estimated using fixed-effects to account for unobserved personal characteristics affecting women's earnings.[15]

5. DATA AND DESCRIPTIVE ANALYSIS

We use data from the National Longitudinal Survey of Youth (NLSY79), a representative survey of individuals between the ages of 14 and 21 as of December 31,1978. Due to modifications in the survey design implemented over the years, the 2000 wave of the NLSY79 contained information on 8,033 individuals, of whom 4,113 were women[16] In order to use the most information possible, we work with an unbalanced panel dataset on women from the 19 rounds of the NLSY79.[17] We restrict our sample to person-year observations for which information is available regarding education, employment, fertility, and other regression variables. In addition, we deflate hourly wages using the CPI index and restrict our sample to individuals reporting hourly earnings between $1 and $100.[18]

Table 7.1 describes the variables used in the analysis and provides a summary of their means and standard deviations for the year 2000. On average, the working women in our sample are 39 years of age. Reflecting the over-sampling of minorities present early in the NLSY's survey design, thirty percent of the women are African American and 19 percent Hispanic. Approximately 21 percent of women have completed four years of college and the average years of education for the entire sample of working women is 13.3. Fifty-eight percent of women are married and a total of 83 percent are mothers by the year 2000 (fifty-seven percent of women have more than one child and 24 percent only one child). Approximately 10 percent of women in the sample delayed fertility until their thirties.[19] Twenty-seven percent of these working women held part-time jobs, with 36 percent in professional/managerial occupations and 24 percent in clerical services. On average, their hourly wage as of the year 2000 was $8.23 in 1982-1984 dollars, and the majority of them (75 percent) lived in urban areas.

Tables 2 through 5 further describe our sample and motivate our analysis. To begin with, Table 7.2 checks on the existence of a statistically significant motherhood wage gap by women's educational status. The break-up by educational attainment category is of interest since it reveals how the motherhood wage gap is only present among college-educated women at a descriptive level. Consequently, it is not surprising to find in Table 7.3 that college-educated mothers are the ones postponing childbearing to a greater extent, possibly with the intention of reducing the motherhood wage gap. significantly more than their female counterparts who do. However, this seems to be the case for all mothers regardless of their educational attainment. At any rate, the distinction by educational attainment allows us to put wage differences between early and late college-educated mothers in perspective. While the largest nominal wage difference is found among college-educated early and late mothers (approximately $4/hr 1982-1984 dollars), the leading wage gap in percentage terms is found between early and late mothers with less than a high school education. Early mothers with less than high school earn approximately 42 percent less than their late counterparts. In contrast, the wage differential between early and late college-educated mothers is about 30 percent.

Because individual level heterogeneity may be at the source of the observed wage differences between working mothers who delay childbearing and other working-women, we look at a sample of women who were childless at age 25, and compare the wages, at that point in time, of women in the group who delay childbearing to those of women who remain childless. According to the figures in Table 7.5, future mothers earned approximately 50 cents more (a statistically significant difference) than their childless counterparts even before the future mothers ever had children, suggesting the importance of modeling heterogeneity. Nonetheless, it is interesting to note the lack of a statistically significant difference when further distinguishing by women's educational attainment, possibly due to the small samples used in these restricted comparisons.

Table 7.1. Variables, Means, and Standard Deviations in the Year 2000

Variable Name	Variable Description	Means	S.D.
Demographic Characteristics			
Age	Age of respondent	39.0743	2.2449
Hispanic	Race dummy	0.1860	0.3891
Black	Race dummy	0.3020	0.4592
Other Race	Race dummy	0.5121	0.4999
Educational Attainment			
Years of Education	Completed years of schooling	13.2754	2.3763
Less than High School	Educational attainment dummy	0.0826	0.2753
High School	Educational attainment dummy	0.4443	0.4970
Some College	Educational attainment dummy	0.2630	0.4403
College	Educational attainment dummy	0.2101	0.4074
Family and Household Characteristics			
Married	Marital status dummy	0.5808	0.4935
Motherhood	Equal to 1 if woman is a mother	0.8264	0.3788
One Kid	Equal to 1 if woman has one child	0.2422	0.4285
Two Kids or More	Equal to 1 if woman has two plus	0.5717	0.4949
Delayed Motherhood	Equal to 1 if woman delayed motherhood after age 30	0.0962	0.2949
Adults in HH	Number of adults in household	1.7806	0.7960
Family Resources	(Previous Year Family Income–Respondent's Labor Income)	15890.78	22678.77
Mother's Highest Grade	Mother's highest grade completed	10.8158	3.1209
Father's Highest Grade	Father's highest grade completed	10.8206	3.8568
Live with Parents by Age 18	Equal to 1 if respondent lived with parents at age 18	0.6065	0.4886
Work-related Characteristics			
Working	Equal to 1 if woman works	1.0000	0.0000
Part-time Job	Equal to 1 if woman works part-time	0.2746	0.4464
Tenure	Tenure in weeks	298.3043	292.1734
Work Experience	Work experience in weeks	35.1235	34.3159
Real Hourly Wage	Real hourly wage in 1984-1986 dollars	8.2302	6.2559
Professional & Managers	Occupation dummy	0.3560	0.4790
Sales	Occupation dummy	0.0884	0.2840
Clerical	Occupation dummy	0.2366	0.4251
Craftsmen	Occupation dummy	0.0221	0.1471
Operatives	Occupation dummy	0.0741	0.2620
Laborers	Occupation dummy	0.0275	0.1635
Farm	Occupation dummy	0.0084	0.0911
Services	Occupation dummy	0.1864	0.3895

Table 7.1 – Continued

Variable Name	Variable Description	Means	S.D.
Local and Regional Characteristics			
Urban	Dummy for living in urban area	0.7554	0.4741
High Unemployment Rate	Dummy equal to 1 if respondent lives in high unemployment area	0.0548	0.2276
North East	Regional dummy	0.1476	0.3548
North Central	Regional dummy	0.2390	0.4265
South	Regional dummy	0.4229	0.4941
West	Regional dummy	0.1905	0.3927

Table 7.2. Motherhood Wage Penalty by Women's Educational Attainment

By Motherhood Status	Mean Hourly Wages	Standard Error	Difference in Means	t-statistic
All Women:				
Childless Women	6.5235	0.0270	0.4288	11.9826***
Mothers	6.0947	0.0235	-	-
Women with Less than HS:				
Childless Women	4.4100	0.0751	0.0253	0.2989
Mothers	4.3847	0.0390	-	-
Women with HS:				
Childless Women	5.4524	0.0311	0.0172	0.4343
Mothers	5.4352	0.0243	-	-
Women with Some College:				
Childless Women	6.6317	0.0556	-0.1041	-1.4402
Mothers	6.7358	0.0461	-	-
Women with College:				
Childless Women	8.9748	0.0630	-1.4082	-10.2179***
Mothers	10.3831	0.1226	-	-

Notes: *** signifies statistically different from zero at the 1 percent level or better, **signifies statistically different from zero at the 5 percent level or better and *signifies statistically different from zero at the 10 percent level or better.

Table 7.3. Average Age at First Birth for All Mothers and by Mothers' Educational Attainment

By Educational Attainment	Mean Age at First Birth		Standard Deviation	
All Mothers	20.9641		4.1567	
By Educational Attainment	Mean Age at First Birth	Standard Error	Difference in Means	t-statistic
Mothers With Less than HS	18.3227	0.0257	-	-
Mothers With HS	20.6295	0.0223	2.3067	67.8454***
Mothers With Some College	22.4394	0.0428	4.1167	82.4927***
Mothers With College	26.3244	0.0595	8.0017	1.2e+02***

Notes: tests are carried out using women with less than HS as the reference category. *** signifies statistically different from zero at the 1 percent level or better, **signifies statistically different from zero at the 5 percent level or better and *signifies statistically different from zero at the 10 percent level or better.

Table 7.4. Wage Premium Associated With Late Motherhood by Mothers' Educational Attainment

By Delayed Motherhood	Mean Hourly Wages	Standard Error	Difference in Means	t-statistic
All Mothers:				
Non-Delayed Motherhood	5.9165	0.0224	-4.7590	-21.9380***
Delayed Motherhood	10.6754	0.2158	-	-
Mothers with Less than HS:				
Non-Delayed Motherhood	4.3682	0.0389	-3.1253	-3.4472***
Delayed Motherhood	7.4935	0.9058	-	-
Mothers with HS:				
Non-Delayed Motherhood	5.3934	0.0244	-2.2593	-11.7810***
Delayed Motherhood	7.6527	0.1902	-	-
Mothers with Some College:				
Non-Delayed Motherhood	6.6117	0.0443	-2.3692	-6.7628***
Delayed Motherhood	8.9809	0.3475	-	-
Mothers with College:				
Non-Delayed Motherhood	9.7875	0.1245	-4.1680	-10.1590***
Delayed Motherhood	13.9555	0.3909	-	-

Notes: *** signifies statistically different from zero at the 1 percent level or better, **signifies statistically different from zero at the 5 percent level or better and *signifies statistically different from zero at the 10 percent level or better.

Table 7.5. Wage Differences Between Childless Women and 'Late' Mothers Before Birth by Educational Attainment

By Motherhood Status	Mean Hourly Wages	Standard Error	Difference in Means	t-statistic
All Women:				
Childless Women	5.9672	0.1772	-0.5175	-2.3410**
'Late' Mothers	6.4847	0.1321	-	-
Women with Less than HS:				
Childless Women	4.1713	0.4233	0.2842	-0.5340
'Late' Mothers	3.8871	0.3226	-	-
Women with HS:				
Childless Women	5.8785	0.2456	-0.4404	-1.1052
'Late' Mothers	6.3189	0.3138	-	-
Women with Some College:				
Childless Women	6.1327	0.2523	-0.1945	-0.3323
'Late' Mothers	6.3273	0.5283	-	-
Women with College:				
Childless Women	7.7528	0.3425	0.0980	-0.2078
'Late' Mothers	7.6547	0.3245	-	-

Notes: *** signifies statistically different from zero at the 1 percent level or better, **signifies statistically different from zero at the 5 percent level or better and *signifies statistically different from zero at the 10 percent level or better.

In sum, given the descriptive evidence of a wage premium associated to delaying motherhood regardless of mothers' educational attainment, we proceed to examine how postponing childbearing may affect the motherhood wage gap by women's educational attainment. However, since the descriptive evidence in Table 7.2 and Table 7.3 revealed the exclusive significance of a motherhood wage gap and the corresponding largest childbearing delay taking place among college-educated women, we will place special emphasis on college-educated women.

6. THE MOTHERHOOD WAGE GAP AND ITS REDUCTION WHEN POSTPONING CHILDBEARING

6.1. Pooled OLS Estimates

As the earlier literature examining the motherhood wage gap, we first estimate the motherhood wage gap without differentiating by women's educational attainment with the intent of providing a benchmark comparison. The results from these regressions using a motherhood dummy as well as two dichotomous variables indicating the presence of only one child and of two or more children are shown in

Table B in the appendix. As in much of the earlier literature, we estimate these two regressions using pooled OLS and without any correction for either sample selection or individual level heterogeneity. As previous studies, we find that mothers earn approximately 6 percent less than their childless counterparts, with the motherhood penalty for mothers with more than one child approximately doubling that of mothers with only one child.

While of interest, these simple regressions do not distinguish by women's educational attainment nor do they account for the timing of motherhood. As discussed earlier, accounting for the timing of motherhood is of importance since labor market interruptions typically following childbearing may have a more adverse affect early on in women's careers. The analysis by educational attainment further allows us to put our findings for college-educated mothers in a broader context. Without a comparison to other groups of mothers with different levels of educational attainment, it is hard to assess the extent to which college-educated mothers constitute a particularly interesting case.

How does the motherhood wage gap vary when by women's educational attainment? Does delaying childbearing reduce the motherhood wage gap borne by women? And, if so, how does this reduction compare by women's educational attainment? Is this reduction the largest among college-educated women? Table 7.6 expands the earlier literature estimations, allowing us to address these questions. As in Table B, we use two different measures of motherhood (a 0-1 motherhood dummy variable and then measures of one child and two or more children) every time that we progressively improve the empirical approach so as to appropriately account for sample selection and heterogeneity.

Model (1) and model (2) in Table 7.6, both of them controlling for the timing of childbearing and distinguishing by women's educational attainment, constitute our benchmark specifications. However, given the robustness of our results to alternative specifications of the number of children, we focus our discussion on the model specification using the motherhood dummy variable. In addition, we provide a summary of the wage effects found from our regressions in Table 7.6 and discussed herein in Table 7.7.

Table 7.6. Coefficients and Standard Errors (in parentheses) of Real Hourly Wage Regressions

Independent Variables	Model (1): Pooled OLS	Model (2): Pooled OLS	Model (3): Pooled OLS & Selection	Model (4): Pooled OLS & Selection	Model (5): FE & Selection	Model (6): FE & Selection
HS	0.1059***	0.1066***	0.0579***	0.0592***	0.0096	0.0058
	(0.0121)	(0.0121)	(0.0159)	(0.0159)	(0.0246)	(0.0250)
Some College	0.1953***	0.1936***	0.1191***	0.1192***	-0.0008	-0.0072
	(0.0129)	(0.0129)	(0.0172)	(0.0172)	(0.0287)	(0.0292)
College	0.3763***	0.3730***	0.2736***	0.2743***	0.1174***	0.1002***
	(0.0133)	(0.0134)	(0.0187)	(0.0187)	(0.0343)	(0.0347)
Mom	-0.0747***	-	-0.0701***	-	-0.0948***	-
	(0.0134)		(0.0187)		(0.0248)	
One Kid	-	-0.0638***	-	-0.0581***	-	-0.0948***
		(0.0165)		(0.0223)		(0.0273)
Two Kids or More	-	-0.0979***	-	-0.0869***	-	-0.1475***
		(0.0149)		(0.0213)		(0.0290)
Mom*HS	-0.0048	-	0.0168	-	0.0041	-
	(0.0142)		(0.0185)		(0.0245)	
Mom*Some College	0.0241	-	0.0574***	-	0.0669***	-
	(0.0153)		(0.0196)		(0.0266)	
Mom*College	0.0461***	-	0.0968***	-	0.1224***	-
	(0.0166)		(0.0207)		(0.0273)	

Table 7.6 – Continued

Independent Variables	Model (1): Pooled OLS	Model (2): Pooled OLS	Model (3): Pooled OLS & Selection	Model (4): Pooled OLS & Selection	Model (5): FE & Selection	Model (6): FE & Selection
One Kid*HS	-	0.0033	-	0.0202	-	0.0064
		(0.0178)		(0.0231)		(0.0277)
One Kid*Some College	-	0.0438**	-	0.0784***	-	0.0824***
		(0.0193)		(0.0247)		(0.0298)
One Kid*College	-	0.0361*	-	0.0699***	-	0.1121***
		(0.0209)		(0.0260)		(0.0307)
Two Kids or More*HS	-	-0.0050	-	0.0161	-	0.0016
		(0.0158)		(0.0205)		(0.0280)
Two Kids or More*Some College	-	0.0118	-	0.0467**	-	0.0715**
		(0.0172)		(0.0219)		(0.0304)
Two Kids or More*College	-	0.0612***	-	0.1226***	-	0.1547***
		(0.0191)		(0.0238)		(0.0318)
'Late' Mom	0.2264**	0.2104**	0.1772	0.1522	0.0179	0.0065
	(0.0940)	(0.0943)	(0.1115)	(0.1121)	(0.1137)	(0.1135)

Table 7.6 – Continued

'Late' Mom*HS	-0.0749	-0.0718	-0.0021	0.0031	0.0762	0.0816
	(0.0980)	(0.0983)	(0.1162)	(0.1168)	(0.1177)	(0.1175)
'Late' Mom*Some College	-0.1125	-0.1213	-0.0647	-0.0687	0.0242	0.0198
	(0.0973)	(0.0976)	(0.1150)	(0.1157)	(0.1171)	(0.1169)
'Late' Mom*College	-0.0120	-0.0041	0.0164	0.0344	0.1107	0.1171
	(0.0967)	(0.0971)	(0.1144)	(0.1151)	(0.1168)	(0.1166)
Lambda	-	-	0.0867***	0.0850***	0.0282***	0.0233**
			(0.0117)	(0.0121)	(0.0108)	(0.0111)
No. of observations	45,247	43,956	31,417	30,662	31,417	30,662
F statistic	773.97	676.14	530.99	466.19	215.84	191.50

Notes: *** indicates significance at the 1 percent level, ** indicates significance at the 5 percent level, and * indicates significance at the 10 percent level. All regressions include a constant term, age, age squared, race, marital status, dummy indicative of any adults in the household, work experience, work experience squared, tenure, tenure squared, occupation dummies, urban residence, high unemployment rate area, and regional dummies.

According to model (1), we find that mothers earn approximately 7 percent less than their childless counterparts. However, postponing childbearing beyond age 30 can effectively eliminate this motherhood wage gap, with late mothers earning 15 percent more than childless women and up to 23 percent more than women who do not delay motherhood. How do the motherhood wage gap and the premium to delaying childbearing vary by women's educational attainment? According to the estimates in Table 7.7 for model (1), the motherhood wage gap (that is, the wage difference between childless women and mothers) appears to be the largest among women with a high school education (8 percent wage gap), followed by women with some college (5 percent wage gap) and women with a college degree (3 percent wage gap). In contrast, it is interesting to note that the premium to delaying childbearing is the largest for college-educated women, explaining their highest average age at first birth (Table 7.3). Indeed, relative to mothers who choose not to delay childbearing, late mothers enjoy a wage premium of approximately 15 percent if they have a high school education, 11 percent if they attended some college, and up to 21 percent if they received a college degree.

6.2. Accounting for Sample Selection

How do these findings change when we account for the sample selection incurred when focusing on working women? This is done in models (3) and (4) in Table 7.6. As reflected by the coefficient on the inverse Mill's ratio, there is a significant degree of sample selection bias in our study. Furthermore, accounting for sample selection reduces the payoff to educational attainment and lowers the average premium to delaying childbearing for all mothers from 23 percent (in model (1) – Table 7.7) to approximately 18 percent (in model (3) – Table 7.7). The distinction by women's educational attainment once more reveals interesting differences. To start, despite the practically unchanged motherhood wage gap for all women, the motherhood wage gap is reduced among educated women. In particular, mothers with a high school education experience a drop of 2 percentage points (from 8 percent to 6 percent), mothers with some college reduce their motherhood wage penalty from 5 percent to 1 percent, and college- educated mothers actually receive a wage premium of up to 3 percent (from their previous motherhood penalty of 3 percent). As we discuss in more detail in the final section of the paper, one explanation for this wage boost among college-educated mothers may involve unobserved job quality. How is the wage premium associated to delaying childbearing affected by the correction for sample selection? As noted earlier, the overall premium is reduced; although, once more, there are noticeable differences by women's educational attainment. In particular, the wage premium to postponing motherhood is actually increased from 15 percent to 20 percent among mothers with a high school education, whereas it remains unchanged among mothers with some college. In fact, it is only among college-educated mothers that accounting for the selection incurred when focusing on working women reduces the premium to delaying childbearing from 21 percent to 19 percent. Once more, the differential effect that accounting for the employment selection plays on the wage premium associated to the postponement of motherhood among college-educated women underscores the importance of work related characteristics (both observed and unobserved) for the wage effects of motherhood and the timing of motherhood among this group.

6.3. Accounting for Sample Selection and Individual Level Heterogeneity

In order to purge out from the previous wage effects the potential role played by women's unobserved heterogeneity, we re-estimated models (3) and (4) using a fixed-effects panel data technique. This is done in model (5) and model (6) in Table 7.6. Accounting for individual level heterogeneity erases the statistical significance of much of the educational attainment dummy variables and reduces the payoff to a college degree to approximately 10-12 percent, depending on the model specification. Similarly, the magnitude of our estimate for the sample selection correct term λ drops substantially once unobserved heterogeneity is controlled, suggesting that controlling unobserved individual heterogeneity captures much of the individual unobservable characteristics correlated with being employed. In contrast, looking at the wage effects for model (5) in Table 7.7, accounting for individual fixed-effects increases the motherhood wage penalty to approximately 9 percent, whereas it further reduces the premium to delaying childbearing to about 2 percent. How does accounting for individual women's heterogeneity affect the motherhood wage gap and the premium to delaying childbearing by women's educational attainment? As in the previous cases, the distinction by women's educational attainment reveals some significant differences masked in the overall averages for all women. For instance, while the motherhood wage gap widens for mothers with less than a college-education (with the penalty increasing from 6 percent to 8 percent in the case of mothers with a high school education, and from 1 percent to 3 percent for their counterparts with some college), the wage boost received by college-educated mothers remains unaltered (at 3 percent). Nonetheless, the premium to delaying childbearing is reduced for all women, regardless of their educational attainment. In particular, as hypothesized from their highest age at first birth in Table 7.3, the largest premium to postponing motherhood is observed among college-educated women, who earn approximately 13 percent higher wages than their counterparts choosing not to delay childbearing.

Table 7.7. Comparison of Wage Effects by Educational Attainment (Coefficients and F-statistics of Joint Significance)

Group Category	Computation	Model (1)	Model (3)	Model (5)
Mothers	Mom	-0.0747***	-0.0701***	-0.0948***
		(30.84)	(13.98)	(14.66)
'Late' Mothers	(Mom + 'Late' Mom)	0.1517***	0.1071***	-0.0769***
		(17.87)	(8.06)	(7.53)
Women with HS:				
Childless Women	HS	0.1059***	0.0579***	0.0096
		(76.65)	(13.26)	(0.15)
Mothers	[HS + Mom + (HS*Mom)]	0.0264***	0.0005***	-0.0811***
		(158.19)	(27.82)	(20.27)
'Late' Mothers	[HS + Mom + 'Late' Mom + (HS*Mom) + (HS*'Late' Mom)]	0.1779***	0.1797***	0.0130***
		(100.76)	(22.76)	(12.57)
Women with Some College:				
Childless Women	Some College	0.1953***	0.1191***	-0.0008
		(230.53)	(48.20)	(0.00)

Table 7.7: – Continued

Mothers	[Some College + Mom + (Some College*Mom)]	0.1447*** (323.20)	0.1064*** (76.46)	-0.0287*** (6.34)
'Late' Mothers	[Some College + Mom + 'Late' Mom + (Some College*Mom) + (Some College*'Late' Mom)]	0.2586*** (201.26)	0.2189*** (51.76)	0.0134*** (4.10)
Women with College:				
Childless Women	*College*	0.3763*** (798.53)	0.2736*** (213.15)	0.1174*** (11.72)
Mothers	[College + Mom + (College*Mom)]	0.3477*** (854.99)	0.3003*** (218.34)	0.1450*** (19.63)
'Late' Mothers	[College + Mom + 'Late' Mom + (College*Mom) + (College*'Late' Mom)]	0.5621*** (553.92)	0.4939*** (160.43)	0.2736*** (20.96)

Note: *** indicates significance at the 1 percent level, ** indicates significance at the 5 percent level, and * indicates significance at the 10 percent level. Women with less than HS are used as reference category.

Summarizing, once we correct for the sample selection biases incurred when focusing on working women as well as for their individual level heterogeneity, mothers earn approximately 9 percent less than childless women; however, by postponing motherhood, late mothers receive a wage premium of 2 percent over their counterparts choosing not to delay childbearing. More interestingly, these figures substantially differ by women's educational attainment and, to a greater extent, for college-educated women. Through their higher educational attainment, college-educated mothers is the only group who effectively eliminates the motherhood wage gap and, instead, receives a wage boost of 3 percent relative to childless college-educated women. That is, the motherhood wage penalty converts to a wage boost for college-educated women. Furthermore, by postponing childbearing, college-educated mothers further raise their earnings to an average wage premium of 13 percent relative to college-educated women who do not delay motherhood. This is the largest premium to fertility delay across all educational attainment groups. Hence, the possibility of wage enhancement may provide an explanation for the observed postponement of childbearing among highly educated women.

7. SUMMARY AND POLICY IMPLICATIONS

In developed countries during the latter years of the last century, women, and particularly mothers, have improved their education levels. In addition to this rising education level, the age at first birth has been steadily increasing. Despite this seeming mirroring of fertility trends, overall total fertility rates vary substantially among developed countries, with a high of near-replacement rate fertility in the US (a total fertility rate of 2.1), and a low of the Czech Republic of 1.1. Most European countries lie somewhere in between, but considerably below replacement rates. In this chapter, we focus on the role that fertility timing might play in mothers' wages in the United States.

A growing literature addresses the existence and magnitude of a motherhood wage gap, i.e., a difference between the wages of mothers versus non-mothers that cannot be explained by productivity characteristics. This so-called family pay gap has been estimated to be in the range of 5 percent to 10 percent, with the bulk of the literature in the mid-portion of that range. This gap estimate is an average across all education levels. We contribute to this literature by disentangling the origins of this gap based on the mother's education and her age at first birth. In particular, the analysis of the motherhood wage gap as well as the potential premium to delaying childbearing by women's educational attainment allows us to put the findings for college-educated women in perspective.

Our findings are two-fold. First, we find that only in the case of college-educated women, mothers do not experience a wage penalty; in fact, they enjoy a wage boost. We estimate this wage boost to be approximately 3 percent in our Model (5)—full model with sample selection and heterogeneity corrections. This finding goes well beyond the elimination of the wage penalty for higher-educated women presented by Taniguchi (1999) and Todd (2001), which Todd explained as evidence that higher education can serve as a "shock absorber" to mitigate or even eliminate the negative effects of motherhood. In our results, college-educated mothers actually earn more than their college-educated counterparts, even when fertility timing is controlled. This suggests that something is going on beyond what we can observe in our data, particularly relating to job quality, as noted by Waldfogel (1998) and Harkness and Waldfogel (forthcoming). Waldfogel focuses on the Family and Medical Leave Act (FMLA)[20], asserting that the availability of maternity leave tends to reduce the magnitude of the motherhood wage gap. An extension of this notion is that if higher education and fertility delay serve as proxies for "good jobs," then it is conceivable that such workers might exhibit wage boosts rather than wage penalties.

What might be some of the factors behind our first result that college-educated mothers experience a wage boost (in comparison to college-educated non-mothers)? There must exist some relevant unobserved factors accounting for this result. Most importantly, we do not observe enough information regarding job characteristics to determine, for equal wage jobs, which jobs might be considered "good jobs" versus "bad jobs." Jobs that are "good" might provide family-friendly benefits (such as flexible work hours or occasional work from home) that diminish any negative wage effects of childbearing, while also providing other good benefits like job training and job flexibility. Training will enhance job growth, while flexibility is likely to serve as a perk that reduces turnover amongst better workers. Additionally, college-educated mothers might match with employers that display an interest and history in promoting women. These characteristics cannot be measured in the data but would clearly be important to wage growth. It is possible that when mothers seek job matches that best accommodate work/family responsibilities, they are also inadvertently identifying jobs with other positive benefits. That is, the availability (and observability) of family-friendly policies might serve as a signal of job quality in a broader sense. Additionally, employers who provide the most generous family-friendly policies are also likely to be the most motivated to attract and retain female employees. As a consequence, these family-friendly policies might also signal a less discriminatory workplace.

Our second major finding relates to fertility timing. Once more, by comparison to mothers with different educational attainment levels, we find that college-educated mothers who postpone childbearing are the ones enjoying the largest premium relative to their counterparts who choose not to delay motherhood. In particular, college-educated mothers who delay first birth until age 30 or beyond earn higher wages, once observed productivity factors are controlled, than their counterparts who do not postpone motherhood. This further wage boost is estimated to be approximately 13 percent. The result of this finding is the reformulation of our hypothesis regarding college-educated mothers' motivation for delaying fertility. Rather than an attempt to reduce the family earnings gap, it can be considered an effort to accrue the maximum benefit to their formal human capital investment, which is hampered if fertility is not delayed. For college-educated mothers, there is a penalty for interrupting early career human capital investment (see, for example, Martin 2000). Family-friendly policies also play a role here because it is the most senior employees who have the most access to such benefits, particularly in the form of job flexibility.

Overall, these findings reinforce the concern voiced by Ellwood and Jencks (2001) and Rindfuss et al. (1996), who worried that a differential wage gap by education (which now we see can be increased by delaying fertility) will contribute to growing inequality between families with less-educated adults and families with better-educated adults. One policy suggestion is that extension of family-friendly policies down the job quality "pipeline" is warranted. That is, less-educated workers might benefit from better accommodation of work/family conflicts. Left alone, employers often are motivated to implement family-friendly policies for their most valuable employees, who are likely to be the better-educated mothers. Additionally, college-educated women who do not have children might consider seeking jobs that provide quality family-friendly benefits under the assumption that such employers will also provide other less readily observed benefits—like job training and potential for advancement, and also might offer a more female-friendly work environment.

The second policy concern relates to the link between fertility delay and fertility foregone. For college-educated mothers, delaying fertility has clear benefits. As described extensively in the earlier parts of the paper, there is the social concern, at least in the United States, with maintaining current fertility rates while the percentage of mothers with college degrees is growing. This begs the question: how might policy be devised to make it beneficial for college-educated women to begin childbearing earlier? Worded differently, what is it precisely about late childbearing that is so beneficial for college-educated women? One answer might be job flexibility. Once workers reach a level of seniority in the office, productivity is not tied so closely with "face time." Therefore, the professional repercussions of maternity leaves, for example, are not so great given that some portion of the job can be performed from home or with short visits to the office. A second suggestion is to improve family leave policies, making it more affordable and modifying the leave to permit the possibility of a gradual return to work. Given that current leave policy guarantees only unpaid leave, it might be the case that only more senior employees can afford a family leave and a gradual return to work following the leave. A final suggestion reiterates that made by Martin (2000), who noted that more-educated parents tend to desire higher quality childcare, which can be quite expensive. For these mothers, delaying fertility and therefore experiencing sufficient wage growth to afford higher quality care might be necessary. Any policy that assists in the purchase of high quality care (even for families with what most would consider comfortable incomes) might be warranted.

How can these findings for the United States inform the debate regarding fertility decline in Western Europe? Recall that Todd (2001) showed that European mothers with a college education still incur a substantial motherhood wage penalty. Clearly, advanced education does not serve well as a shock absorber to mitigate the negative wage effects of motherhood for them. Because European mothers experience their first births at somewhat older ages than in the United States, this fertility delay must be captured in Todd's (average) regression result, suggesting that further research would find that delay does not benefit European college-educated mothers as it does their US counterparts. The reason for this might be drawn from disentangling the separate effects of education and income on fertility. Recall that according to Nichols (2003), higher education is associated with reduced fertility while higher income is associated with higher fertility. Because the wage-dampening effects of motherhood are not experienced by US college-educated mothers, they experience higher incomes along with their higher education levels. Thus, the two opposing effects are balanced and overall fertility is stable. For European mothers, higher education is not accompanied by higher income so the fertility-depressing effects of higher education are not countered by the fertility-enhancing effects of higher income; thus their fertility rates fall.

To answer this question regarding international differences more fully, more research is needed. More specifically, what is needed is a comprehensive review of international differences in wage returns to high levels of education, then a comparison of the family earnings gap by country, and estimates of the effect of fertility delay on this gap. Finally, with this information in hand, one could discuss more rigorously our hypothesis that differences in the family earnings gap experienced by college-educated mothers helps to explain some portion of differing total fertility rates among developed countries.

ACKNOWLEDGEMENTS

A different version of this chapter is published in the Review of Economics of the Household under the title 'The Motherhood Wage Gap for Women in the United States: The Importance of College and Fertility Delay' (2005, Volume 3, Number 1, pp. 17-48) and we thank the publisher for granting permission to reprint it.

NOTES

[1] One factor that we will not discuss in any detail in this chapter is the role of immigration. The United States enjoys relatively high immigration rates, and on average, immigrants have higher fertility rates, contributing to the US' maintenance of replacement rate fertility.

[2] In the concluding section, we also will discuss an additional explanation that relies on disentangling the effects of wages and income. Here, rising wages push fertility downward but high income (or living standards) has the opposite outcome. (See Nichols, 2003)

[3] Also see Crittendon (2001) for further popular media discussions of the costs of motherhood.

[4] Fertility rates actually increased in 1999 and 2000, with total fertility rates in the year 2000 rising above replacement rates (the rate necessary to keep total population stable) for the first time in 30 years (*National Vital Statistics Reports* 2002). Also, as explained by Rindfuss et al (1996), the bulk of the fertility decline occurred in the early 1960s. Between 1963 and 1989, the overall fertility rate remained fairly stable at about 1.9.

[5] Behrman et al. (1999) provide evidence that improvements in health over time might be more important than rising educational levels in explaining differences in fertility across world regions.

[6] According to Murphy and Welch (1990), on the job human capital investment and therefore wage growth occurs disproportionately in the early years of a worker's life.

[7] Rindfuss et al. (1996) also observe that while the total fertility rate for college-educated women (at 1.5) falls below the overall rate of 1.9, the college rate exceeds the total rate in many entire countries. Looking at detailed age-specific fertility rates, there have been dramatic differences by age levels. Looking at the percentage changes from 1973 to 1988: ages 15-19: -10 percent, 20-24: -7 percent, 25-29: 1 percent, 30-34: 33 percent, and 35-39:26 percent.

[8] Their cross-section results rely on 1,207 working white women in 1982; their longitudinal results use two years of data: 1980 and 1982, resulting in a sample of 911 women.

[9] The analysis in this does not correct for employment sample selection, which could contribute to the differential but inconsistent findings by education.

[10] The five countries she studies are Canada, the United States, Germany, the Netherlands, and Sweden.

[11] The seven countries they study are Australia, Canada, the United Kingdom, the United States, Germany, Finland, and Sweden.

[12] Two other potential drawbacks of her research are somewhat outdated data (Waldfogel (1997) notes that the motherhood wage gap is rising), and a mis-specified wage equation. She uses observed hours of work on the right hand side of the wage equation, thereby producing measurement error that it is highly correlated with measurement error in the dependent variable. Extending her findings, Chiodo and Owyang (2003) present a nice theoretical explanation for the differences in the importance of marriage on wages by sex.

[13] Both models correct the standard errors for clustering at the individual level.

[14] The results from these tests are available from the authors upon request.

[15] At this point, it is worth noting other econometric issues potentially complicating the analysis of wage differences as specified above. The latter refer to the potential endogeneity of wages and two of our variables of interest: the motherhood and delayed motherhood dummies. Women's motherhood and timing of motherhood are likely to depend on the existence and size of a motherhood or an early motherhood wage penalty. For a careful account of these problems, please see Amuedo-Dorantes and Kimmel (2003).

[16] Earlier waves of the NLSY79 included a sample of 1,280 military youths and a supplemental sample designed to over sample civilian Hispanic, black and economically disadvantaged non-black and non-Hispanic youth. However, these two samples were mostly dropped in 1985 and in 1991, respectively.

[17] In particular, NLSY79 survey respondents were interviewed yearly between 1979 and 1994. Beginning with the 1994 interview, interviews are only scheduled to take place biennially. Because of the unbalanced nature of the panel, we calculate robust standard errors to account for the resulting heteroscedasticity that may affect our estimation.

[18] The CPI for all urban consumers, not seasonally adjusted, with base period 1982-1984, was retrieved from http://www.bls.gov/cpi/home.htm.

[19] We chose the age of 30 as representative of the delayed motherhood since the average age at first birth of college-educated women is 26.32 years, with a standard deviation of 4.05 years. Also, this is the age cut-off used by other researchers (see Martin (2000), for example).

[20] The FMLA was passed in the United States in 1993, and allows (in addition to other sorts of leave) eligible new mothers to take up to 12 weeks of unpaid leave while retaining their same jobs.

APPENDIX

Table 7.A. Probit Model for Being Working

Independent Variables	Model (A.1) Coefficient (S.E.)	Model (A.2) Coefficient (S.E.)
Years of Education	0.1214***	0.1134***
	(0.0073)	(0.0075)
Mom	-0.7810***	-
	(0.0292)	
One Kid	-	-0.6978***
		(0.0309)
Two Kids or More	-	-0.9418***
		(0.0360)
Family Resources	-3.82e-06***	-3.71e-06***
	(3.03e-07)	(2.96e-07)
Mother's Highest Grade	0.0124***	0.0140***
	(0.0061)	(0.0062)
Father's Highest Grade	0.0024	0.0017
	(0.0045)	(0.0046)
Live with Parents by Age 18	0.0379***	0.0319***
	(0.0276)	(0.0280)
No. of observations	49609	48247
Wald Chi2(19)	2268.84	2204.22
Prob > chi2	0.0000	0.0000

Notes: *** indicates significance at the 1 percent level, ** indicates significance at the 5 percent level, and * indicates significance at the 10 percent level. The regressions include a constant term, as well as controls for age, age squared, race, marital status, dummy indicative of any adults in the household, urban residence, high unemployment rate area, and regional dummies.

Table 7.B. Coefficients and Standard Errors of Real Hourly Wage Regressions Exclusively Focusing on the Impact of Motherhood

Independent Variables	Model (B.1): Pooled OLS	Model (B.2): Pooled OLS
	Coefficient (S.E.)	Coefficient (S.E.)
HS	0.1049***	0.1073***
	(0.0067)	(0.0069)
Some College	0.2125***	0.2104***
	(0.0075)	(0.0078)
College	0.4064***	0.4030***
	(0.0086)	(0.0088)
Mom	-0.0570***	-
	(0.0046)	
One Kid	-	-0.0348***
		(0.0053)
Two Kids or More	-	-0.0866***
		(0.0056)
No. of observations	45262	43968
F statistic	963.77	908.78
Prob > F	0.0000	0.0000

Notes: *** indicates significance at the 1 percent level, ** indicates significance at the 5 percent level, and * indicates significance at the 10 percent level. All regressions include a constant term, age, age squared, race, marital status, dummy indicative of any adults in the household, work experience, work experience squared, tenure, tenure squared, occupation dummies, urban residence, high unemployment rate area, and regional dummies.

REFERENCES

Anderson, Deborah J., Melissa Binder, and Kate Krause. 2002a. "The Motherhood Wage Penalty Revisited: Experience, Heterogeneity, Work Effort and Work-Schedule Flexibility," *Industrial and Labor Relations Review* .

___________. 2002b. "The Motherhood Wage Penalty: Which Mothers Pay It and Why?" *American Economic Review* papers and proceedings (May) 92 (2): 354-358.

Apps, Patricia F. and Ray Rees. 2001. "Fertility, Female Labor Supply and Public Policy," IZA Discussion Paper No. 409 (December).

Averett, Susan. 2002. "Fertility, Public Policy, and Mothers in the Labor Force," in *The Economics of Work and* Family, edited by Jean Kimmel and Emily P. Hoffman, Kalamazoo: W.E. Upjohn Institute, pp. 105-32.

Becker, Gary S. 1985. "Human Capital, Effort, and the Sexual Division of Labor." *Journal of Labor Economics* 3(1, Pt. 2): S33-S58.

Behrman, Jere, Suzanne Duryea, and Miguel Szekely. 1999. "Decomposing Fertility Differences Across World Regions and Over Time: Is Improved Health More Important than Woman's Schooling?" IDB-OCE Working Paper No. 406 (September).

Blackburn, McKinley L., David E. Bloom, and David Neumark. 1990. "Fertility Timing, Wages and Human Capital." NBER Working Paper No. 3422, August.

Bruni, Frank. 2002. "Persistent Drop in Fertility Reshapes Europe's Future," *New York Times*, December 26, 2002.

Budig, Michelle J. and Paula England. 2001. "The Wage Penalty for Motherhood," *American Sociological Review* 66: 204-225.

Caucutt, Elizabeth M., Nezih Guner, and John Knowles. 2002. "Why do Women Wait? Matching, Wage Inequality, and the Incentives for Fertility Delay." *Review of Economic Dynamics* 5: 815-855.

Chandler, T.D., Y. Kamo, and J.D. Werbel. 1994. "Do Delays in Marriage and Childbirth Affect Earnings?" *Social Science Quarterly* 74 (4): 838-853.

Chen, Renbao, and S.Philip. Morgan. 1991. "Recent Trends in the Timing of First Births In the United States," *Demography* 28: 513-533.

Chiodo, Abbigail J. and Michael T. Owyang. 2003. "Marriage, Motherhood and Money." *The Regional Economist* (April), pp. 5-9.

Crittendon, Ann. 2001. *The Price of Motherhood: Why the Most Important Job in the World is Still the Least Valued.* New York: Henry Holt and Company.

Drolet, Marie. 2002. "Wives, Mothers, and Wages: Does Timing Matter?" unpublished manuscript, Statistics Canada, No. 186.

Ellwood, David T. and Christopher Jencks. 2001. "The Growing Differences in Family Structure: What Do We Know? Where Do We Look for Answers?" Manuscript prepared for the New Inequality Program supported by the Russell Sage Foundation (August), 99 pgs.

Galor, Oded, and David N. Weil. 1995. "The Gender Gap, Fertility and Growth." Centre for Economic Policy Research (CEPR) Discussion Paper No. 1157, August.

Datta Gupta, Nabanita, and Nina Smith. 2002. "Children and Career Interruptions: The Family Gap in Denmark," *Economica* 69 (276): 609-29.

Graham, Mary E. and Julie L. Hotchkiss. 2002. "A Systemic Assessment of Employer Equal Employment Opportunity Efforts as a means of Reducing the Gender Earnings Gap," *Cornell Journal of Law and Public Policy* 12 (1): 169-201.

Gustafsson, Siv. 2001. "Optimal Age at Motherhood. Theoretical and Empirical Considerations on Postponement of Maternity in Europe," *Journal of Population Economics* 14: 225-247.

Harkness, Susan, and Jane Waldfogel. Forthcoming. "The Family Gap in Pay: Evidence from Seven Industrialized Countries." *Journal of Labor Research*, previously circulated as CASE paper 30, Centre for Analysis of Social Exclusion, London School of Economics, London, England.

Hewlett, Sylvia Ann. 2002. *Creating a Life: Professional Women and the Quest for Children.*

Hill, Martha. 1979. "The Wage Effects of Marital Status and Children." *Journal of Human Resources* 14: 579-94.

Hotz, V. Joseph, Susan Williams McElroy, and Seth Sanders. 2002. "Teenage Childbearing and its Life Cycle Consequences: Exploiting a Natural Experiment," unpublished manuscript.

Iyigun, Murat F. 2000. "Timing of Childbearing and Economic Growth," *Journal of Development Economics* 61(1): 255-69.

Jacobsen, Joyce P., James Wishart Pearce III, and Joshua L. Rosenbloom. (2002). "Measuring the Effects of Childbearing on Labor Market Outcomes," unpublished manuscript.

Korenman, Sanders, and David Neumark. 1992. "Marriage, Motherhood, and Wages." *The Journal of Human Resources* 27 (2): 233-55.

Martin, Steven P. 2000. "Diverging Fertility Among U.S. Women Who Delay Childbearing Past Age 30." *Demography* 37(4): 523-33.

Murphy, Kevin, and Finis Welch. 1990. "Empirical Age-Earnings Profiles," *Journal of Labor Economics* 8(2): 202-29.

Mullin, Charles H. and Ping Wang. 2002. "The Timing of Childbearing Among Heterogeneous Women in Dynamic General Equilibrium," NBER Working Paper # 9231 (October).

Neal, Derek. 2001. "Is the Measured Black-White Wage Gap Among Women Too Small?" (University of Chicago), NBER, November.

Neumark, David, and Sanders Korenman. 1992. "Marriage, Motherhood, and Wages," *Journal of Human Resources* 27 (2): 233-55.

Nichols, Austin. 2003. "Fertility, Human Capital, and Wages," unpublished manuscript, University of Michigan.

Population Council. 1999. "Demography: Birth Delays Skew Developing World's Fertility Figures," *Population Briefs* 5 (3) (September):http://www.popcouncil.org/publications/popbriefs;pb5(3)_2.html.

Rindfuss, Ronald R., Philip S. Morgan, and Kate Offutt. 1996. "Education and the Changing Age Pattern of American Fertility: 1963-1989." *Demography* 33(3): 277-90.

Schmidt, Lucie. 2002. "Murphy Brown Revisited: Human Capital, Search and Nonmarital Childbearing Among Educated Women," unpublished manuscript (University of Michigan), March.

Taniguchi, Hiromi. 1999. "The Timing of Childbearing and Women's Wages," *Journal of Marriage and the Family* 61: 1008-1019.

Todd, Erin L. 2001. "Educational Attainment and Family Gaps in Women's Wages: Evidence from Five Industrialized Countries," Luxembourg Income Study Working Paper No. 246, January.

Waldfogel, Jane. 1997. "The Effects of Children on Women's Wages," *American Sociological Review* 62: 209-17.

___________. 1998a. "The Family Gap for Young Women in the United States and Britain: Can Maternity Leave Make a Difference?" *Journal of Labor Economics* 16: 505-545.

___________. 1998b. "Understanding the "Family Gap" in Pay for Women with Children," *The Journal of Economic Perspectives* 12 (1): 137-56.

Chapter 8

HOUSEHOLD CONSUMPTION, SAVING AND EMPLOYMENT AROUND THE TIME OF BIRTHS IN THE NETHERLANDS

ADRIAAN KALWIJ

1. INTRODUCTION

This chapter examines household consumption, income, saving and employment around the birth of children. For this purpose I exploit a panel of Dutch households over the period 1987-1993. The empirical analysis tests the hypothesis of excess sensitivity of consumption with respect to (predicted) income changes, and analyzes the role of children and female employment in this relationship. The results provide insights in the consumption smoothing motive for postponing maternity, as discussed in Chapter 2 of this book, and the validity of the Rational Expectations Permanent Income Hypothesis. Descriptive statistics show that with the arrival of children households, on average, experience a fall in income, reduce consumption and save less. The empirical results show that women leaving employment after having given birth is the principle channel through which children reduce household income. This reduction in income causes consumption to decrease with the arrival of children.

The lifecycle relationship between household consumption and income is important in the determination of aggregate saving in an economy, which determines economic growth. To gain insights in household consumption and savings decisions, many studies have investigated the empirical observation that consumption and income have similar so called hump-shapes over the working life. See, for example, Lester Thurow (1969), Keizo Nagatani (1972), Martin Browning, Angus Deaton and Margaret Irish (1985), Christopher Carroll and Lawrence Summers (1991) and Martin Browning and Mette Ejrnaes (2002). These highly correlated hump-shapes of lifecycle income and consumption are often referred to as consumption 'tracking' income over the lifecycle or excess sensitivity of consumption with respect to

Siv Gustafsson and Adriaan Kalwij (eds.), Education and Postponement of Maternity, 207–224.

(expected) income changes (Majorie Flavin, 1981, Annamaria Lusardi, 1996, Rob Alessie and Annamaria Lusardi, 1997). In a standard lifecycle model of consumer behavior (see, for example, Robert Hall, 1978) households take into account (expected) future streams of income when making consumption decisions and consumption plans are only affected by unanticipated income shocks. Household consumption tracking income is at odds with this prediction and therefore many studies are concerned with reconciling this empirical observation by extending a standard life cycle model. Examples are allowing for liquidity constraints (Thurow, 1969, Stephen Zeldes, 1989), a precautionary motive (Nagatani, 1972), or non-separabilities between labor supply and consumption (James Heckman, 1974). I refer to Browning and Ejrnaes (2002) for an excellent discussion of these explanations.

One explanation for the hump-shape of consumption over the lifecycle that received much attention in the literature builds on the observation that the lifecycle consumption pattern appears to display a similar pattern to that of the size of the household. Roughly speaking, household consumption appears to increase when children are present in the household and to decrease when children leave the parental home. Studies such as Orazio Attanasio and Martin Browning (1995) and Orazio Attanasio and Guglielmo Weber (1995) argue that once controlled for the effect of children on consumption most of the hump-shape for consumption is removed. It appears, however, that not all of the hump-shape is removed and one still needs some kind or precautionary saving motive to reconcile the data with a rational expectations model (e.g., Pierrre-Oliver Gourinchas and Jonathan Parker, 2002). Browning and Ejrnaes (2002) go one step further and, based on a long series of cross-sections of the UK Family Expenditures Survey, argue that family composition can account for the hump-shape pattern in lifecycle consumption found in quasi-panel data. Their analysis is based on a model in which forward looking households save for future consumption needs and possible falls in income as a consequence of having children. As they discuss, this is in line with the empirical evidence in Adriaan Kalwij (2003) who shows that, for a sample of Dutch young couples, savings rise before births and decline thereafter. James Smith and Michael Ward (1980) reach a similar conclusion using US panel data over the period 1967-1970. Smith and Ward (1980) and Kalwij (2003) do not explicitly examine the issues of a precautionary motive or if household consumption tracks income. Browning and Ejrnaes (2002) test for a precautionary motive by testing for non-linear age effects in adjusted consumption series and find no evidence for this. Without explicitly testing for it, they conclude that adjusted consumption does not track income at the beginning of the lifecycle.

Given the importance the presence of children play in explaining the relationship between consumption and income, gaining detailed insight in what happens around the time of births is crucial for understanding this demographic explanation put forward in the literature. Most previous studies use cross sectional data to examine in detail the relationship between consumption and children (e.g., Patricia Apps and Ray Rees, 2001, and Browning and Ejrnaes, 2002). When using cross-sectional data one has to assume that one can compare households with and without children. While one can do this in very sophisticated ways, this may still influence the results if these households are inherently different in their consumption behavior since, for instance, some households will remain childless (planned or unplanned). One way around this problem is to exploit panel data as has been done in, for example, Smith and Ward (1980). This makes it possible to follow the same households over time and compare their consumption before and after children have arrived in the household. This chapter also takes this approach and exploits panel data. To be more specific, the contribution to the literature of this chapter is that it describes in detail household consumption, income, saving and employment around the birth of children and tests in the empirical analysis for excess sensitivity of consumption with respect to income changes. Furthermore I examine the effects of children and employment on household income. For these purposes I employ a panel of Dutch households over the period 1987-1993. The main advantage of these data is that households are followed over a considerable length of time which makes it possible to compare the same household for several years before and after they have children. A consequence of this approach is that the sample has to be restricted to households for whom I observe first birth during the observation period since I need to know if childless households will have children.

This chapter shows that with the arrival of children households, on average in the Netherlands, experience a fall in income, reduce consumption and save less. The empirical results show that women leaving employment after having given birth is the principle channel through which children reduce household income. This result is in line with the conclusions of Smith and Ward (1980). Also in line with Smith and Ward (1980) is our finding that this reduction in income causes consumption to decrease with the arrival of children. The results suggest that a 1% reduction in household income yields a 0.62% reduction in household consumption. This finding is in contrast with the conclusion of Browning and Ejrnaes (2002) that consumption does not track income once controlled for children but is in line with, for instance, Lusardi (1996) who reports significant excess sensitivity of consumption to predictable income growth.

The outline of this chapter is as follows. Section 2 outlines the economic and statistical model. Section 3 discusses the data and provides a picture of households' financial situation around the time of births. Section 4 analyzes consumption changes using an Euler equation. Section 5 summarizes the main findings.

2. THE ECONOMIC MODEL: HOUSEHOLD CONSUMPTION AND FERTILITY DECISIONS

Households may anticipate on the financial consequences of having children, such as an increase in expenditures on child-related goods, and today's contraceptive methods enable them to schedule having children when it is most convenient. In other words, households may simultaneously decide on their fertility and consumption plans. This section presents a theoretical framework that incorporates household consumption and fertility decisions. For this purpose I explicitly model fertility decisions in a lifecycle model of consumer behavior that is used in many studies to examine household consumption and saving decisions (e.g., Hall, 1978). I refer to Martin Browning and Annamaria Lusardi (1996) for an overview of the theoretical and empirical models of household saving and consumption decisions.

I assume that at the beginning of a period the household makes consumption and fertility decisions in such a way that an intertemporal separable lifetime utility function is maximized. I denote the consumption in period t by C_t, the fertility decision by b_t, and $U_t(.)$ is the intratemporal household utility function. Using a value function notation, this decision problem of the household at time t can be written as follows:

$$V_t(A_t, B_t) = \max_{\{C_t, b_t\}} U_t(C_t, B_t) + \frac{1}{1+\delta} E_t[V_{t+1}(A_{t+1}, B_{t+1})], \qquad (1)$$

$$\text{s.t.} \quad A_{t+1} = (1+r)A_t + Y_t - C_t, \qquad (2)$$

$$B_{t+1} = \sum_{s=1}^{t} b_s, \qquad (3)$$

$$A_T \geq 0, \qquad (4)$$

$$C_t \geq 0, \qquad b_t \in \{0,1\}, \qquad (5)$$

Y_t is household income, r is the interest rate, δ the rate of time preference and T the length of life. The value function, $V_t(A_t, B_t)$, is a function of the household assets (A_t) and the number of children (B_t) that are known to the household at the beginning of period t. The fertility decision is denoted by b_t and is equal to 1 if the woman gives birth to a child at the end of period t and 0 otherwise. E_t is an expectation operator to take into account future uncertainties. Equation (2) is the well-known budget constraint. The irreversibility of fertility decisions is formalized by equation (3). Equation (4) imposes a constraint on household wealth at time T to ensure that lifetime household consumption is less or equal to lifetime household income plus initial household wealth. Furthermore, we assume that the intratemporal utility function is of the following additive form:

$$U_t\left(C_t, B_t\right) = U_t\left(C_t\right) + U_t\left(B_t\right). \tag{6}$$

Equation (6) does not imply that the marginal utility of consumption does not depend on the number of children since I will allow the parameters of the utility function to depend on predetermined variables.

The fact that there is both a continuous and a discrete decision variable makes equations (1)-(6) a non-standard optimization problem. Important for this study is that, based on fundamental results of Ariel Pakes (1994), one can show that the Euler equation for consumption still holds, albeit conditional on the optimal fertility choices:

$$E_t\left[\left(\frac{1+r}{1+\delta}\right)\frac{\partial}{\partial C_{t+1}^{b_{t+1}}} U_{t+1}^{b_{t+1}}\left(C_{t+1}^{b_{t+1}}\right)\right] = \frac{\partial}{\partial C_t^{b_t}} U_t^{b_t}\left(C_t^{b_t}\right). \tag{7}$$

Where $C_t^{b_t}$ is the consumption decision in period *t*, conditional on taking fertility decision b_t. Equation (7) shows that the conditional Euler equation for optimal consumption allocation between period *t* and *t+1* is as such that the marginal utilities of consumption in both periods are equal, conditional on optimal fertility choices. I assume households have a constant relative risk aversion utility function of the following form:

$$U_t(C_t) = \frac{1}{1-\gamma}\left(\frac{C_t}{\exp(\alpha_t)}\right)^{1-\gamma}, \tag{8}$$

where γ is the coefficient of risk aversion and concavity requires γ to be positive. The function $\exp(\alpha_t)$ can be interpreted as a taste shifter and may depend on predetermined variables such as age and the number of children, for instance:

$$\alpha_t = \alpha + \alpha_1(age_t) + \alpha_2(age_t^2) + f(B_t) + u_t. \tag{9}$$

In the empirical section the intercept α is allowed to be household specific and the function $f(B_t)$ is a set of dummy variables for the number of children (one, two, or more than two). By substituting (8) into (7) the conditional Euler equation can be written as:

$$\left(\frac{1+r}{1+\delta}\right)\left(\frac{C_{t+1}}{C_t}\right)^{-\gamma}\left(\frac{\exp(\alpha_{t+1})}{\exp(\alpha_t)}\right)^{\gamma-1} = 1 + e_{t+1}, \tag{10}$$

with $E_t[e_{t+1}] = 0$. Taking logarithms on both sides of equation (10), using a Taylor approximation, and introducing subscript *h* for a household, I obtain the linearized Euler equation (e.g., Browning and Lusardi, 1996, pp. 1804-1805):

$$\Delta c_{ht+1} = \alpha_0 + \Delta\alpha_{ht+1} + u_{ht+1}. \tag{11}$$

with $\Delta c_{ht+1} = \Delta \log(C_{ht+1})$, and Δ is a difference operator. Note that by taking differences the household specific effect drops out of the equation. Given the discussion above, the error term u_{ht+1} may not be assumed uncorrelated with $\Delta\alpha_{ht+1}$ since fertility outcomes are potentially endogenous and are affected by random shocks that are revealed at the beginning of period $t+1$. This is taken into account by using instruments for the number of children in period $t+1$ in the empirical analysis.

As discussed at length in the introduction, consumption is often observed to track income. This study does not aim to provide an answer to why consumption may track income and at this point takes as given that there may be excess sensitivity of consumption with respect to (expected) income changes. To test for excess sensitivity John Campbell and Gregory Mankiw (1990) and Annamaria Lusardi (1996) propose to add the growth of household income to the Euler equation (equation (11)):

$$\Delta c_{ht+1} = \alpha_0 + \Delta\alpha_{ht+1} + \beta\Delta y_{ht+1} + u_{ht+1}. \qquad (12)$$

with $\Delta y_{ht+1} = \Delta \log(Y_{ht+1})$. The parameter β is interpreted as a measure for excess sensitivity of consumption to expected income changes. If the Rational Expectations Permanent Income Hypothesis holds then this parameter is estimated to be insignificantly different from zero. When estimating equation (12) I take the endogeneity of fertility and income changes into account.

3. DATA: THE DUTCH SOCIO-ECONOMIC PANEL

The micro data used in this study are taken from the Socio-Economic Panel (SEP) of the Netherlands. The panel started in 1984 and is conducted by Statistics Netherlands. About 5000 households respond to the survey in each wave and in principle every household member over 15 completes the questionnaire. Each respondent is asked questions about his or her socio-economic and demographic situation. Up to 1990 the survey has been conducted twice a year, a wave in April and a wave in October. Information on earnings has been collected in the October waves and information on household wealth is collected in the April waves. From 1990 onwards the survey is conducted only once a year and all information is collected in May. Available for this study are the waves up to and including 1994. Not all waves are, however, usable for this study since information on households' financial wealth is only available from 1987 onwards and information on labor income is not available for the year 1994. More details on these data can be found in Rob Alessie, Annamaria Lusardi and Trea Aldershof (1997).

As discussed in the introduction, I compare households' situations before and after the birth of their children and this restricts the sample to only those households for which the first birth is observed within the observation period. Also, as is commonly done, only couples, either married or cohabiting, are being considered to avoid issues concerning household formation. This leaves us with around 300 households per year. Observations with missing values on any of the relevant variables (mainly on wealth holdings) and the top and bottom 5% of the consumption distribution are excluded from the sample. This causes a further 30% reduction of our sample. The resulting sample contains information on just over 200 households per year over the years 1987-1993. This is an unbalanced panel. On average a household is observed for 4.3 years and 15.4% of the households are observed over the whole observation period. In total I use 1522 observations.

Employment is defined as being in paid employment and an employed woman on maternity or parental leave is registered in the data as being employed. Household income includes earnings of both the man and woman in the household, child allowances, money transfers made to the household (for instance an inheritance) and interest payments on financial assets. Household income is net of income tax and social security contributions. Household savings is the sum of liquid savings and home savings within one year. Liquid savings includes money put in checking and savings accounts, savings certificates, money lent to other people, changes in the investments in stocks, bonds, and the change in the value of cars owned by the household. From this measure the change in debt and loans is subtracted. Home savings is the change in the value of the house and mortgage. Household consumption is defined as household income minus household savings. All financial statistics are reported in 1994 Euros (1994 Dutch Guilders divided by 2.20371). Educational attainment of both the man and woman in the household is observed in three levels. Level 1 is at most primary education or secondary education, level 2 is intermediate vocational education and level 3 is higher vocational education or a university degree.

Table 8.1. Sample statistics per year

Year	1987	1988	1989	1990	1991	1992	1993
Number of households	213	232	234	235	221	201	186
Variables	*Sample Averages*						
Panel A: Women							
Age	26.6	27.2	28.1	28.8	29.8	30.5	31.5
Educational attainment							
level 1	23.0	27.2	20.5	19.1	24.0	17.9	18.3
level 2	51.6	51.7	54.7	55.7	52.9	56.2	57.0
level 3	25.4	21.1	24.8	25.1	23.1	25.9	24.7
Employment	57.7	53.0	47.9	42.6	36.7	36.8	31.2
Panel B: Men							
Age	29.2	29.9	30.6	31.3	32.3	33.4	34.1
Educational attainment							
level 1	20.2	22.0	15.4	14.9	26.7	15.9	16.1
level 2	45.1	46.1	47.0	46.0	37.1	43.8	42.5
level 3	34.7	31.9	37.6	39.1	36.2	40.3	41.4
Employment	91.1	90.5	93.2	94.5	95.5	94.5	96.8
Panel C: Household characteristics							
Birth rate	17.8	24.6	29.9	17.4	26.7	29.9	25.8
Childless	63.4	52.2	38.9	31.5	24.4	17.9	7.5
One child	33.8	37.5	39.3	37.4	32.1	30.8	31.7
Two children	2.8	9.9	20.9	28.9	39.4	43.8	49.5
Three children	0.0	0.4	0.9	2.1	4.1	7.5	11.3
Married	78.4	81.9	86.8	88.1	90.5	92.5	96.8
Homeowner	51.6	53.9	59.8	66.8	68.3	73.1	74.2

Table 8.2. Average household income, consumption and savings per year (in 1994 Euros)

Year	1987	1988	1989	1990	1991	1992	1993
Income	19266	19340	19999	19956	21416	19896	20964
Consumption	17110	17422	18032	18746	21059	16620	17564
Total savings	2156	1918	1967	1210	357	3276	3400
Liquid savings	163	-391	330	836	-411	-426	-301
For homeowners:							
Home savings	2143	2965	1918	163	888	4417	4511

Tables 8.1 and 8.2 report the relevant sample statistics. Table 8.1 shows that educational attainment of the woman in the household remains relatively stable over time; over half of the women have an intermediate vocational education and around a quarter has a higher vocational education or a university degree. Several sample statistics show that the sample ages over time, this is due to the sample selection criteria. For example, the female employment rate decreases and the number of children increases over time.

As discussed above, the time between the 1989 and 1990 wave of the panel is less than one year because the month of interview changed from October to May. This shortening of the observation period causes fewer births for 1990. Statistics on the age distribution of children show that most households (49.5%) have at the end of the observation period two children. Marital rate increases from 78.4% in 1987 to 96.8% in 1993, which is likely to be an age effect. The homeownership rate increases from 51.6% in 1987 up to 74.2% in 1993. Table 8.2 reports on household income, consumption and savings over time. The low savings in the recession year 1991 is in line with the National Accounts.

To examine the situation of households around births the data are centered on the year of birth of the first child (Tables 3 and 4). I only have 5 observations 7 years before having the first child (YB = –7) and this is considered too few to report reliable statistics. Table 8.3 shows that the average age at which women give birth to their first child is just over 28 years. This is in line with Gijs Beets and Pauline Verloove-Vanhorick (1992) who report an increase in the average age at which Dutch women give birth to their first child from 25 in the early 1960's to 28 in the early 1990's. Several years after the birth of the first child couples have about two children, which is in line with the descriptive statistics reported in Hans Bloemen and Adriaan Kalwij (2001) using different data from the Netherlands. Most couples are married for some time before having children. Couples that divorce are (by construction) removed from the sample from the time of divorce since they essentially start two separate new households. The female employment rate declines from around 80% before having children to around 25% in the first years after giving birth to the first child. This is in line with the empirical evidence from the labor supply literature that the presence of children has a negative effect on female labor supply (Thomas Mroz, 1987, Bloemen and Kalwij, 2001). Male employment rates are over 90% in most periods.

Table 8.4 reports on both the sample mean and median of household income, consumption and savings in the years around the time of births. Median household income drops from around 22,000 Euro before the birth of the first child to around 18,000 Euro after the birth of the first child. Median household consumption decreases when children enter the household. The decrease in income with the birth of a child is on average larger than the decrease in consumption, which results in households saving less in the immediate years following first birth. Liquid savings (last columns) are in the immediate years following first birth on average negative, which implies households draw on their savings accounts when children arrive in the household to partially offset the reduction in income. Although one can argue selection issues may bias this picture, these observations are very much in line with the earlier work of Smith and Ward (1980) for the US who report a reduction in consumption consequent on the arrival of an infant in the household and with Browning and Ejrnaes (2002) for the UK who conclude that households save to deal with financial consequences of having children.

Table 8.3. The situation of households around the time of births. YB is the years from first birth. For example, YB = –3 is three years before and YB = 3 is three years after the birth of the first child

YB	Number of observations	Age of the woman	Birth rate (%)	Number of Children	Married (%)	Female employment rate (%)	Male employment rate (%)
-7	5	-	-	-	-	-	-
-6	21	24.8	0.0	0.0	52.4	81.0	81.0
-5	41	24.8	0.0	0.0	41.5	78.0	90.2
-4	70	26.2	0.0	0.0	58.6	81.4	88.6
-3	87	26.9	0.0	0.0	71.3	88.5	95.4
-2	127	27.0	0.0	0.0	70.9	81.9	93.7
-1	174	27.7	0.0	0.0	85.6	78.2	92.5
0	189	28.4	100.0	1.0	93.1	34.9	92.6
1	200	29.0	12.0	1.1	95.5	27.5	95.0
2	179	29.3	36.3	1.5	96.6	22.3	93.9
3	140	30.3	36.4	1.8	97.1	23.6	92.9
4	118	31.0	19.5	1.9	99.2	18.6	94.1
5	93	31.8	12.9	2.0	96.8	17.2	96.8
6	54	32.5	13.0	2.2	100.0	13.0	98.1
7	24	33.5	8.3	2.3	100.0	16.7	100.0

Table 8.4. The financial situation of households around the time of births. YB is the years from first birth. For example, YB = –3 is three years before and YB = 3 is three years after the birth of the first child

YB	Income		Consumption		Savings		Liquid savings	
	mean	median	mean	median	mean	median	mean	median
-7	-	-	-	-	-	-	-	-
-6	19580	20885	17960	17573	1621	1720	-1785	1453
-5	20482	20769	18109	17613	2372	2452	-389	1246
-4	21164	21846	17173	16976	3991	2902	795	811
-3	23120	23139	19506	18549	3613	3091	405	1592
-2	22195	21902	19217	18673	2978	2538	1614	1778
-1	21202	21622	18405	17702	2797	1633	441	-8
0	19274	19199	17406	16216	1869	1133	-1064	-606
1	18953	18075	17751	16568	1202	751	-44	-249
2	18546	17726	17644	16547	902	279	-127	-102
3	19127	18094	18535	16978	591	1044	-1264	-459
4	18846	17850	18451	17677	395	332	451	219
5	21116	18046	19051	17172	2065	1011	319	-166
6	20536	18047	16170	15635	4366	2511	1935	731
7	21151	19183	16902	17042	4249	3351	-4400	-953

4. AN ANALYSIS OF CONSUMPTION AND INCOME GROWTH AND THE ROLE OF CHILDREN

This section analyzes, based on the economic model outlined in section 2, to what extent household consumption is affected by a change in the number of children and predicted income. Furthermore, I provide insights in the determinants of household income changes around the time of births.

As argued in section 2, outcomes of fertility decisions are potentially endogenous and I therefore instrument the demographic variables using as additional instruments the educational attainments of the woman and man, also interacted with age. From the fertility literature it is known that educational attainment in combination with age is a good predictor of outcomes of fertility decisions (e.g., Bloemen and Kalwij, 2001). Also household employment is treated as potentially endogenous. Therefore all equations in this section are estimated using an

Instrumental Variables (IV) estimator and at the bottom of Table 8.5 all instruments are reported. Since panel data are used, clustering is taking into account when calculating the standard errors. Furthermore, I wish to emphasize that time-constant unobserved household specific preferences are eliminated since all equations are specified in differences between two periods. As a consequence, the sample used for estimation is reduced to 1172 observations. I include, without reporting on them, in all equations year dummy variables to account for aggregate (macro) shocks. I present for all estimated equations an R^2 as a goodness-of-fit measure and an over-identification test statistics for model misspecification.

4.1 Income Growth

Before turning to the estimation of the conditional Euler equation I first analyze the determinants of income growth using a reduced form approach. The estimation results are reported in columns (1) and (2) of Table 8.5. In the first specification, column (1), I include as explanatory variables the age and age squared of the woman in the household and three dummy variables for the number of children in the household. I also include age squared of the man and educational attainment of both the man and the woman but I omit these estimates from Table 8.5 for presentational reasons. The over-identification test statistic is equal to 108 and with a critical value of 18.3 I reject the null-hypothesis of no misspecification. Having said this, the results show a decline in income of over 30% when children arrive in the household. A closer inspection of why this model does not pass the modelspecification test shows that the employment status of the woman needs to be included. For this reason the model in column (2) includes variables for female employment and, for completeness and without affecting the results, male employment. This model passes the modelspecification test. After controlling for employment the estimates of the dummy variables for children in the household turn insignificant. The dominating picture that emerges from columns (1) and (2) is that women leaving employment after having given birth is the principle channel through which children reduce household income. This result is in line with the conclusions of Smith and Ward (1980).

Table 8.5. Estimation results. The parameter estimates and statistics in bold are significant at a five percent level. (Y = household income, C = household consumption)

	(1)		(2)		(3)		(4)	
Dependent variable	Δln(Y)		Δln(Y)		Δln(C)		Δln(C)	
Explanatory variables	p.e.	s.e.	p.e.	s.e.	p.e.	s.e.	p.e.	s.e.
Δ(age)/10	-1.20	1.37	-4.06	2.36	-0.09	1.32	0.80	1.28
Δ(age squared)/100	-0.03	0.22	-6.16	9.99	-0.09	0.25	-0.09	0.23
Δ(number of children = 1)	**-0.30**	**0.05**	0.02	0.07	**-0.26**	**0.10**	-0.09	0.10
Δ(number of children = 2)	**-0.37**	**0.08**	0.09	0.09	**-0.39**	**0.15**	-0.18	0.15
Δ(number of children ≥ 3)	**-0.49**	**0.13**	0.23	0.13	**-0.75**	**0.23**	**-0.48**	**0.24**
Δ(employment status woman)			**0.30**	**0.06**				
Δ(employment status man)			**0.65**	**0.11**				
Δln(Y)							**0.62**	**0.17**
Goodness of fit, R^2	0.07		0.17		0.05		0.06	
Over-identification test statistic	**108**		2.9		22.2		7.3	
(Degrees of freedom, Critical value)	**(10, 18.3)**		(8, 15.5)		(14, 23.7)		(13, 22.4)	
Number of observations	1172		1172		1172		1172	

* p.e = parameter estimate, s.e. = standard error.

** The set of instruments contains dummy variables for the years 1988-1993, Δ(age)/10 and Δ(age squared)/100 of the woman interacted with the level of education, female and male employment status in the previous period, the level of education of the man and woman, dummy variables for the number of children in the previous period, Δ(age of the man)/10 and Δ(age squared of the man)/100 interacted with the level of education of the man.

*** All regressions include time dummy variables and the age squared of the man, the income growth equations also include educational attainment of the man and woman.

4.2 The conditional Euler equation

The estimation results of the conditional Euler equation for consumption, i.e. equation (11), are reported in column (3). The arrival of children in the household yields a significant negative effect. Given the economic model of section 2 this is interpreted as children reducing the marginal utility of consumption. However, one has to interpret this result with caution since the model just passes the modelspecification test (22.2 versus a critical value of 23.7). Column (4) extends this model by allowing for excess sensitivity of consumption to expected income changes, i.e. equation (12). This model passes the modelspecification test. The effects of children on consumption now turn insignificant. When testing for it, the three fertility variables turn out to be jointly insignificant. One way of interpreting this result is that, once controlled for predicted income changes, households deal with the costs of having children by changing demand patterns. Empirical evidence on how demand patterns in the Netherlands change when children arrive in a household is presented in Adriaan Kalwij, Rob Alessie and Peter Fontein (1998).

Browning and Ejrnaes (2002) test for a precautionary motive by looking at the estimate corresponding to the effect of age squared. This estimate is insignificant both in columns (3) and (4). The most striking result in column (4) is the significant excess sensitivity estimate of 0.62. This suggests that a 1% reduction in household income yields a 0.62% reduction in household consumption. This finding is in contrast with the conclusion of Browning and Ejrnaes (2002) that once controlled for children consumption does not track income. Most estimates using US data are in the range of 0.2 to 0.7. Rob Alessie and Annamaria Lusardi (1997), also using the Socio-Economic Panel of the Netherlands, find no significant excess sensitivity of consumption to income changes. A comparison of results, however, has to be interpreted with caution since there is actually no real economic interpretation of this reduced form coefficient. It may depend, for example, on the sample used. The sample used in this study consists of young households who may face tight liquidity constraints, have long planning horizons and strong precautionary motives. Nevertheless, based on the findings here it seems unlikely that consumption no longer tracks income on a household level once controlled for demographics (fertility outcomes). One way of harmonizing the contrasting conclusions here (and in earlier US studies) and of Browning and Ejrnaes (2002) is that their results are based on a quasi-panel data and are not likely to hold when employing household level panel data.

5. SUMMARY

Using a panel of Dutch households over the period 1987-1993, this chapter provides a detailed analysis of households' consumption decisions around the time of births, and the role income, children and employment play in this process. The main empirical findings are summarized as follows:

- Households are observed to save on average more before than after having given birth to their first child. This is line with the predictions of a standard lifecycle model of consumption behavior where households make provisions for future consumption needs (i.e. a consumption smoothing motive).
- Households do not reduce savings enough to offset the reduction in income due to women leaving employment, and consumption is therefore observed to decrease with the arrival of children in the household. This is in line with the earlier findings of Smith and Ward (1980) and Apps and Rees (2001).
- The empirical results show that women leaving employment after having given birth is the principle channel through which children reduce household income.
- I conclude that consumption tracks income around the time of births. The estimated excess sensitivity of consumption to predicted income changes suggests that a 1% reduction in income yields a 0.62% reduction in consumption. This implies a rejection of the Rational Expectations Permanent Income Hypothesis.

ACKNOWLEDGEMENTS

I wish to thank Siv Gustafsson, two anonymous referees, Rob Alessie, Richard Blundell, John Ermish, Arie Kapteyn, Eiko Kenjo, Edwin Leuven and the seminar participants at the Departments of Economics at the Universities of Copenhagen and Oxford, the 1999 meeting of the European Society for Population Economics in Turin, and the Fall 2001 meeting of the European Low-Wage Employment Research Network in Braga, and the Scholar conference on "Education and Postponement of Maternity" at the University of Amsterdam, October 2002, for helpful comments and suggestions. Financial support of the TMR network on Savings, Pensions and Portfolio Choice is gratefully acknowledged (TMR Grant number ERBFMRXCT960016). The data were provided by Statistics Netherlands; the views expressed in this paper are those of the author and do not necessarily reflect the views of Statistics Netherlands. This chapter has been published in the Review of Economics of the Household under the title 'Consumption and Income Around the Time of Births' (Kalwij, 2005, Volume 3, Number 1, pp 75-89) and I thank the publisher for granting permission to reprint it with several minor editorial changes.

REFERENCES

Alessie, Rob, and Annamaria Lusardi. (1997). "Saving and income smoothing: Evidence from panel data", *European Economic Review*, 41, pp. 1251-1279.

Alessie, Rob, Annamaria Lusardi and Trea Aldershof. (1997). "Income and wealth over the life-cycle: evidence from panel data", *Review of Income and Wealth*, 43, pp. 1-32.

Apps, Patricia, and Ray Rees. (2001). "Household Saving and Full Consumption over the Life Cycle", *IZA discussion Paper*, No. 280, IZA, Bonn.

Attanasio, Orazio and Martin Browning (1995). "Consumption over the life cycle and over the business cycle", *American Economic Review*, 85, pp. 1118-1137.

Attanasio, Orazio and Guglielmo Weber (1995). "Is consumption growth consistent with intertemporal optimization? Evidence from the Consumer Expenditure Survey", *Journal of Political Economy*, 103, pp. 1121-1157.

Beets, Gijs, and Pauline Verloove-Vanhorick. (1992) "*Een slimme meid regelt haar zwangerschap op tijd*", Swets & Zeitlinger B.V., Amsterdam/Lisse.

Bloemen, Hans, and Adriaan Kalwij. (2001). "Female Labor Market Transitions and the Timing of Births: A Simultaneous Analysis of the Effects of Schooling", *Labour Economics* (8) 5, pp. 593-620.

Browning, Martin, Angus Deaton and Margaret Irish (1985). "A profitable approach to labor supply and commodity demands over the life-cycle", *Econometrica*, 53, pp. 503-544.

Browning, Martin, and Mette Ejrnaes (2002). "Consumption and Children", *working paper* no.06, Centre for Applied Microeconomics, University of Copenhagen.

Browning, Martin, and Annamaria Lusardi. (1996). "Household Saving: Micro Theories and Micro Facts", *Journal of Economic Literature*, Vol. 34, pp. 1797-1855.

Campbell, John, and Gregory Mankiw. (1990). "Permanent Income, Current Income and Consumption", *Journal of Business & Economic Statistics*, 8, pp. 265-279.

Carroll, Christopher, and Lawrence Summers (1991). "Consumption growth parallels income growth: some new evidence", in B.D. Bernheim and J.B. Shoven (eds) *National Saving and Economic Performance*, Chicago University Press for NBER, Chicago, pp. 305343

Flavin, Marjorie A. (1981). "The Adjustment of Consumption to Changing Expectations about Future Income", *Journal of Political Economy*, Vol. 89, no.51, pp. 974-1009.

Gourinchas, Pierrre-Oliver, and Jonathan Parker (2002). "Consumption over the lifecycle", *Econometrica*, 70(1), 47-90.

Hall, Robert. (1978): "Stochastic implications of the life-cycle permanent income hypothesis: theory and evidence", *Journal of Political Economy*, Vol. 86, pp. 971-988.

Heckman, James J. (1974). "Life cycle consumption and labor supply: an explanation of the relationship between income and consumption over the life cycle", *American Economic Review*, 64, pp. 188-194.

Kalwij, Adriaan S. (2000). "The Effects of Female Employment Status on the Presence and Number of Children", *Journal of Population Economics*, 13, pp. 221-239.

Kalwij, Adriaan S. (2003). "Female Employment and Fertility Decisions: an Analysis of the Effects of Household Financial Wealth", *Applied Economics Quarterly*, Vol. 49, Issue 3, pp. 231-252.

Kalwij, Adriaan S. (2005). "Consumption and Income Around the Time of Births, *Review of Economics of the Household*, Vol. 3, no.1, pp. 75-89.

Kalwij, Adriaan, Rob Alessie and Peter Fontein (1998). "Household commodity demand and demographics in the Netherlands: a microeconometric analysis", *Journal of Population Economics*, Vol. 11, 4, pp. 551-577.

Lusardi, Annamaria. (1996). "Permanent Income, Current Income, and Consumption: Evidence From Two Panel Data Sets", *Journal of Business & Economic Statistics*, Vol. 14, No.1, 81-90.

Mroz, Thomas A. (1987). "The sensitivity of an empirical model of married women's hours of work to economic and statistical assumptions", *Econometrica*, 55, 4, 765-799.

Nagatani, Keizo (1972). "Life cycle saving: theory and fact", *American Economic Review*, 62, pp. 344-353

Pakes, Ariel. (1994). *Estimation of Dynamic Structural Models: Problems and Prospects* Part II: Mixed Continuous-Discrete Models and Market Interactions, in: C. Sims and J.J. Laffont (eds), Proceedings of the 6th World Congress of the Econometric Society, Cambridge U.K.: Cambridge University Press.

Smith, James P, and Michael P. Ward. (1980). "Asset Accumulation and Family Size", *Demography*, 17 (3), pp. 243-260

Thurow, Lester (1969). "The optimum lifetime distribution of consumption expenditures" *American Economic Review*, 59, pp. 324-330.

Zeldes, Stephen P. (1989). "Consumption and liquidity constraints: an empirical investigation", *Journal of Political Economy*, 97, pp. 305-346.

Chapter 9

FAMILY FORMATION IN EAST AND WEST GERMANY BEFORE AND AFTER UNIFICATION

MICHAELA KREYENFELD

1. INTRODUCTION

After unification, East Germany has been undergoing a major reconstruction of its society and economy. Compared to pre-unification times, when women's full-time employment was universal, career tracks highly pre-determined and the compatibility of work and family life supported through an array of family policies, childrearing and employment are no longer as compatible in post-unification East Germany. Furthermore, career options have become more diverse, which involved, on the one hand, better possibilities to turn higher education into higher earnings, on the other hand, high risks of unemployment. Against this background, one would expect that, compared to pre-unification times, the variation in the timing of fertility by women's educational level has increased.

In this chapter, we utilize data from the German Socio-Economic Panel (GSOEP) to investigate the role of role of women's education in the transition to the first child in East and West Germany before and after unification. In the following section, we give a brief account of the institutional changes that have occurred in East Germany after unification (Section 2). We then elaborate our theoretical considerations on the role of women's education in fertility (Section 3). The subsequent part consists of the empirical analysis where we employ piecewise-constant event history models to the analysis of first birth risks (Section 4). The last part summarizes the major results (Section 5).

2. INSTITUTIONAL CONTEXT

2.1 The German Democratic Republic

In the GDR, encompassing family policies relieved the costs of children and supported the compatibility between work and family life. Basic needs (such as

Siv Gustafsson and Adriaan Kalwij (eds.), Education and Postponement of Maternity, 225–236.

housing and food) were heavily subsidized and mainly centrally allocated (Vortmann 1988, Cornelius 1990, Schmähl 1992, Trappe 1995, Frerich and Frey 1993, Trappe and Rosenfeld 2000, Kreyenfeld 2004). The costs of children were reduced by an array of monetary transfers and 'in-kind subsidies'. For example, the allocation of housing space was centrally regulated and in order to get or change an apartment, one had to apply to the local municipalities (Frerich and Frey 1993: 427f.). Young couples did not immediately receive an own apartment, but having a child or getting married was an important reason to get priority access to it. New mothers were given a 'birth grant' of 1,000 Mark, provided they had taken part in medical check-ups during pregnancy (Gysi and Speigner 1983). Upon marriage, couples could apply for a 'marriage loan' of 5,000 Mark which was partially cancelled out when a child was born and it completely cancelled out with the birth of a third child.

Gender equality was a major goal on the political agenda of the GDR and already in the 1950s, public policies were directed towards encouraging women to participate in the labor market (Obertreis 1986: 74ff.). In the 1960s, the East German government particularly focused on reducing the gender gap in educational levels and labor market positions. Firms were requested to set up women's promotion schemes, and women were encouraged to retrain and take up further education (Trappe 1995). In the 1970s, when population policies became of great significance, public policies tried to more rigorously address the problems that arise from combining full-time employment and family life. The most notable policy measure in this context was the increase in the provision of public day care in the following years. By the beginning of the 1970s, about a third of all children ages 0-3 attended public day care. By the middle of the 1980s, the percentage of children ages 0-3 in public day care had increased to more than 70 percent (Statistisches Amt der DDR 1990). In 1976, the 'Babyjahr' was introduced which was basically a one-year period of paid parental leave. Initially, women could only take advantage of it after the birth of a second or higher order birth. Since 1986, women could also use it after the birth of the first child. The 'Babyjahr' was directed to women only, i.e. fathers could not take it. In this context, East German policies have frequently been criticized for never really addressing gender issues. Although the public provision of day care solved some of the major incompatibilities of work and family life, household tasks continued to be the responsibility of women (Pascall and Manning 2000: 254).

Apart from a parental leave period of one year, men and women were both expected to be continuously employed full-time. East German legislation was set up in such a way that, in case of divorce, women were essentially not granted maintenance claims. Neither did single motherhood entitle to social benefits (Berghahn and Fritzsche 1991: 144ff., Frerich and Frey 1993: 396). There was basically no unemployment and the labor market provided highly structured employment careers. The risks of status downward moves were minimized by the principle of 'status adequate job placement' which meant that workers were primarily allocated to jobs by their formal educational qualifications (Huinink et al. 1995, Solga and Konietzka 1999, Zühlke 2000, Szydlik 2002). Wages were basically centrally set, i.e. workers were classified into different wage groups according to the requirements of the job, which in turn strongly related to their vocational and educational qualifications. Apart from the basic wage, which made up about 70 to 80 percent of the total wage, firms offered extra bonuses to their workers for over-time, shift work, out-standing work performance, etc. (Frerich and Frey 1993: 133f., Szydlik 1994). However, in comparison to the West German wage structure, the East German wage structure was fairly compressed (Bird et al. 1994: 391, Frick et al. 1995: 85, Krueger and Pischke 1995: 412).

2.2 Institutional Changes after Unification

The 'Fall of the Berlin Wall' (in November 1989) is usually considered as the landmark of the dissolution of the East German system. Eleven months later, in October 1990, the Unification Treaty ('Einigungsvertrag') was ratified, which basically prescribed that the East German legal and political system was to be replaced by the West German system. This involved, for example, that the 'Babyjahr' was abolished in favor of the 'Erziehungsurlaub'. While the 'Babyjahr' offered a relatively high level of income replacement for the period of one year, the parental leave regulation in the Federal Republic of Germany (FRG) provide a long period of leave (of currently up to three years) combined with a low level of income tested benefits. While during GDR-times, men and women were urged to be employed full-time, the new tax and transfer system is widely believed to encourage married women's labor market withdrawal (Gustafsson 1992, Gornick et al. 1998). The most important measure in this context is the system of 'income splitting', which provides tax relieves for married one-earner couples (Dingeldey 2001).

In light of the rapid institutional transformation, it was widely believed that also the encompassing public day care system of the GDR would soon be cut down to West German levels (Nauck and Joos 1995: 25, Rindfuss and Brewster 1996: 273, Rindfuss et al. 1996, Adler 1997: 44, Lechner 1998: 473, Kopp 2000: 109). However, public day care was one of the institutions presumably least affected by the institutional changes. Although day care centers had been closed down, there is still a fairly broad coverage of public full-time care in the eastern states of Germany. For example, in the year 2002 about 40 percent of all children ages 0-3 attend public day care in the eastern states of Germany, while this is the case for less than 5 percent in the western states (Statitisches Bundesamt 2004). Against this background, one can contend that East German women encounter much better chances of combining working and family life than West Germans even after unification.

Nevertheless, it is clear that the problems that arise from combing childrearing and employment have increased after unification. Opening hours of the day care centers have become less flexible and day care places are more strongly rationed, if compared to pre-unification times (Hank et al. 2001). While public day care was essentially free of charge during GDR-times (apart from a small contribution for the meal at lunchtime), parents now have to pay a childcare fee ('Elternbeitrag') for the use of public day care. Compared to liberal market regimes, the prices for the use of public day care are still low and they are charged according to the household income of the parents (Hank and Kreyenfeld 2003). Hence, it is possible that day care fees discourage some parents from the use of public day care. Furthermore, the GDR-regulations provided an array of policies that supported mother's employment, such as extra days of holiday for women with two or more children and paid leave when a child was sick. In principle, similar regulations exist in the FRG as well. For example, parents can take up to 10 days of paid leave when their child is sick and up to 20 days if they have two or more children. In competitive labor markets, parents might, however, be more cautious to take advantage of such regulations than in a labor market where employment tracks are very much pre-determined.

The change in the economic system was followed by a thorough restructuring of the East German labor market. Compared to GDR-times, East Germans were now subject to a labor market where both up- and downward mobility were more likely. On the one hand, this involved the possibility to turn higher education into higher earnings and better career opportunities (Bird et al. 1994: 391, Brinkmann and Wiedemann 1995, Frick et al. 1995: 85, Krueger and Pischke 1995: 412, Mayer et al. 1999). On the other hand, this involved high unemployment rates and, compared to pre-unification times, less pre-determined and less stable employment tracks. Although the German government introduced large-scale publicly funded training measures, job-creation programs and early retirement schemes, unemployment rates increased rapidly in the aftermath of unification (Brinkmann 1999, Lutz et al. 1999: 269). Women and particularly those without formal qualifications were most severely affected by unemployment and they encountered the greatest difficulties to re-enter the labor market (Bielinski et al. 1995). In 1995, for example, about half of all women without any formal qualifications were unemployed, while on the other hand there was very little unemployment (about 5 percent) among women who had a university degree. Engelbrech and Reinberg (1997: 11) speak in this context of a 'polarization' with highly qualified employed women on the one hand, and non-working women without sufficient formal qualifications on the other.

The new institutional constraints in the FRG did not only involve high risks of unemployment, but they also provided a new flexibility regarding working hours and employment behavior. When the labor market situation of East German women deteriorated, one could have suspected that some women would have taken advantage of the newly available option of part-time work or the 'home-maker model' (Dorbritz 1997: 243, Huinink 1999: 129). Similar to their West German counterparts, they would reduce their working hour or completely withdraw from the labor market after childbirth.

Empirical evidence shows that mother's labor market participation has clearly declined in East Germany after unification. Compared to pre-unification times, East German mothers are more often employed part-time and return to the labor market much later than they did before (Engelbrech und Jungkunst 1998, John and Stutzer 2002). However, mother's employment rates in East Germany are still fairly high if compared to the situation in the West. Table 9.1 shows, for example, that only about 15 percent of West German mothers are employed full-time, while this applies to roughly 40 percent of all East German mothers in the year 2002.

Table 9.1. Employment rates of mothers 1990-2002 (column percent)

	West Germany				*East Germany*			
	1990	*1994*	*1998*	*2002*	*1990*	*1994*	*1998*	*2002*
Employed full-time	17	16	15	14	69	54	51	41
Employed part-time	32	32	33	36	20	14	16	23
Not employed	51	52	52	50	11	32	34	36
Sample size	734	763	754	739	744	702	575	456

Notes: The sample comprises women aged 18 to 45 whose youngest child is 18 or younger.
Source: German Socio-Economic Panel 2002, sample A+C (own calculations).

3. THEORETICAL CONSIDERATIONS

3.1 Education and First Birth

Women's education and employment have presumably been the most important parameters to explain fertility variations in contemporary societies (Rindfuss et al. 1988, Becker 1993, Hirschman 1994). Women with a higher educational attainment are more inclined to pursue an employment career. They earn higher wages, encounter higher opportunity costs of child rearing which reduce their propensity of having children (Becker 1960, 1993). Apart from the negative effect of education on family size, recent studies have highlighted the role of education in the postponement of family formation (Blossfeld and Huinink 1991, Liefbroer and Corijn 1999, Gustafsson 2001). Conceptually, two paths are distinguished by which higher education leads to higher ages at first birth:

It has been argued that childrearing and educational participation is incompatible in most societies (Hoem 1986, Rindfuss et al. 1988, Blossfeld and Huinink 1991). Students are subject to monetary and time constraints and there are "normative expectations in society that young people who attend school are 'not at risk' of entering marriage and parenthood" (Blossfeld and Huinink 1991: 147). More highly educated women will therefore be older at first birth, because they are in education for a relatively long period of their lives during which they postpone parenthood.

The second argument refers to the period after completion of education. If a woman interrupts her employment career to care for her child, she will encounter opportunity costs of forgone earnings and her human capital will depreciate. Furthermore, during this period she does not accumulate any work or firm experience and might miss out on vital opportunities of career building (Taniguchi 1999, Albrecht et al. 1999, Gustafsson et al. 2000, Gustafsson 2001). Since more highly educated women experience a steeper age-earning profile, the period of career building is considered to be particularly crucial for them. "Having a child early in one's career limits the time available for extra courses or the time to work long hours; this is often needed to enter the career track. These kinds of consequences are often much less negative later in a woman's career. Thus the overall opportunity costs of childbearing for highly educated women may be higher early in their career than somehow later in their careers" (Liefbroer and Corijn 1999: 54). Based on these considerations, women's higher education should lead to higher ages at first birth.

3.2 Education and First Birth in the GDR and FRG

The previous argumentation is based on various assumptions. These assumptions, however, do not hold well for communist Eastern Europe. First of all, one assumption is that a competitive labor market punishes career interruptions, particularly during the phase of career building. If a woman withdraws from the labor market during this time, her human capital depreciates, she will miss out on career options, and she will be unable to catch up on them after she returns to the labor market. In a labor market that provides highly structured employment tracks, there should be less need to strategically time childbirth in accordance with the employment career. If it is possible to interrupt the employment career and resume it later on, there is no reason why an earlier interruption should be more harmful than a later one. Second, it is usually assumed that childrearing and employment are incompatible and that a woman is forced to interrupt her employment after childbirth. The shorter the career interruptions, however, the less negative should be the impact of parenthood on employment. Among other aspects, the availability of public day care is often considered to be crucial in this respect (Kravdal 1996, Hank and Kreyenfeld 2003). Finally, one usually assumes traditional gender roles, i.e. that it is the woman who reduces her labor market engagement after childbirth.

The latter assumption fits to East and West Germany for the period before as well as after unification (Böckmann-Schewe et al. 1993: 50ff., Trappe 1995). The first and second assumptions, however, do not hold equally well in the two parts of Germany. Childrearing and employment were fairly compatible in the former East Germany. Furthermore, employment decisions were basically not a matter of choice in the centrally planned labor market of the GDR. Instead, women's full-time employment was universal, and women, irrespective of their educational levels, were expected to swiftly return to full-time employment after the 'Babyjahr'. Employment careers were highly pre-determined by educational qualifications. This involved that employment interruptions should have mattered to a much lesser extent for the subsequent employment career than in a labor market where career advancements depend more strongly on the performance on the job. Against this background, one would expect that there was less variation in the timing of fertility by women's educational level in the GDR.

After unification, childrearing and employment have become less compatible than before unification. The labor market entails greater risks, but also greater chances of experiencing job mobility. Women without formal qualifications encounter high unemployment risks, limited career options and relatively low opportunity costs of childrearing. Women with a high educational attainment have better earning prospects, better career options and should rather postpone parenthood to later and more stable stages in their employment careers. Against this background, one would expect an increase in the variation in the timing of first birth by women's educational levels in the eastern states of Germany, if compared to the GDR.

4. DATA, VARIABLES AND METHOD

In the following, we use data from the German Socio-Economic Panel 2002 (GSOEP) to investigate the role of women's education in the transition to the first child for the time before and after unification. The GSOEP consists of various subsamples, i.e. a 'West German sample', a 'foreigner sample', an 'East German sample' etc. (Haisken-DeNew and Frick 2003). For this analysis, we only use women of the 'West German sample' (sample A) and of the 'East German sample' (sample C). We furthermore restrict the analysis to the birth cohorts 1951-1980. There are 4,811 valid female respondents in sample A and C. We exclude women with incomplete fertility or educational histories which leaves the sample with 4,275 respondents.

The dependent variable in our study is the transition to first birth. A case is censored at age 35 or when the last interview was conducted. The major independent variable is a time-varying covariate for woman's education. We distinguish a university degree, a vocational degree, no degree and periods in education. We also control for calendar period. We distinguish the time prior and after 1990. In principle, the GSOEP provides a rich set of information on wages, household characteristics and attitudes (Haisken-DeNew and Frick 2003). Most variables are, however, only surveyed prospectively. The East German sample has been surveyed first in 1990 and only few variables are therefore available for the time before unification. This explains why we limit the analysis to only two independent variables.

We apply a piecewise constant event history model to investigate the transition to first birth. In the piecewise constant model, the baseline hazard is assumed to be constant for pre-defined time intervals, but it is allowed to vary across these time segments. When $ln\ h(t)$ is the natural log of the intensity of the event, $h_0(t)$ the baseline, x_1 a matrix of time-constant covariates, $x_2(t)$ a matrix of time-varying covariates, β_1 and β_2 parameter estimates, one yields the following general relationship

$$ln\ h(t) = h_0(t) + \beta_1 x_1 + \beta_2 x_2(t) \quad (1)$$

In our study, the baseline hazard is the age of the respondent, measured in years from age 15. We divide the time axis at the ages 20, 25 and 30. In order to estimate the model, we use the event history module in STATA 8.1 and the extension for piecewise constant models provided by Jesper Sorensen (Stata Corporation 2003).

5. FINDINGS AND DISCUSSION OF RESULTS

Table 9.2 displays the results of the event history model. In West Germany, educational participation strongly reduces first birth risks. There is also a strong negative gradient of educational level. Compared to women without a degree, women with a vocational training degree encounter a 30 percent lower first birth risk. For university graduates, first birth risks are cut by almost 50 percent. There is a significant negative effect of calendar period, which corresponds to the continuous postponement of first birth over time. In East Germany, first birth risks decline sharply after unification. There is a negative effect of educational participation, which is, however, less pronounced than in the West. Educational attainment has a negative gradient, but the coefficients are not significant.

From the analysis in Table 9.2, it is impossible to tell whether the role of education in the timing of first parenthood has changed after unification. In order to address this issue, we also employ an interaction of the period indicator and education (Table 9.3):

For West Germany, the results for the time prior and after unification are alike. There is a very strong negative effect of educational participation and a pronounced negative gradient of educational level. In East Germany before unification, the effect of educational participation is significant, but not as strong as in the West. This suggests that educational participation and parenthood were more compatible in the GDR than in the FRG. Furthermore, there is no significant effect of educational level on first birth risks. This corresponds to previous findings that show that educational differences in the timing of fertility in the GDR can be explained fully by differences in the length of educational participation (Kreyenfeld 2004). After unification, the East German pattern becomes similar to the West German one. There is now a negative gradient of educational level and educational participation strongly reduces first birth risks.

Table 9.2. Piecewise constant event history model, relative risks of transition to first birth

	West Germany			*East Germany*		
	exp(b)	*t*		*exp(b)*	*t*	
Age*)						
15-20	0.064			0.151		
21-25	0.107			0.345		
26-30	0.170			0.346		
30-45	0.151			0.121		
Education						
In education	0.16	-12.70	***	0.24	-5.31	***
Low degree	1			1		
Vocational degree	0.71	-2.82	***	0.76	-1.04	
University degree	0.53	-4.26	***	0.78	-0.83	
Period						
Before 1990	1			1		
After 1990	0.85	-2.72	***	0.37	-12.37	***
Log Likelihood (0)	-2890			-1706		
Log Likelihood	-1984			-1170		

Notes:*) absolute risks, Significance: * at 10%; ** at 5%; *** at 1%.
Source: German Socio-Economic Panel 2002.

Table 9.3. Piecewise constant event history model, relative risks of transition to first birth

	West Germany			*East Germany*		
	exp(b)	*t*		*exp(b)*	*t*	
Age*)						
15-20	0.065			0.088		
21-25	0.108			0.200		
26-30	0.171			0.204		
30-35	0.153			0.072		
Education before 1990						
In education	0.15	-11.45	***	0.41	-2.14	**
Low degree	1			1		
Vocational degree	0.71	-2.40	***	1.31	0.66	
University degree	0.53	-3.44	***	1.51	0.94	
Education after 1990						
In education	0.16	-9.51	***	0.16	-4.24	***
Low degree	0.83	-0.69		1.22	0.38	
Vocational degree	0.59	-3.62	***	0.49	-1.73	***
University degree	0.44	-4.25	***	0.41	-1.92	***
Log Likelihood (0)	-2890			-1706		
Log Likelihood	-1983			-1167		

Notes:*) absolute risks, Significance: * at 10%; ** at 5%; *** at 1%.
Source: German Socio-Economic Panel 2002.

6. CONCLUSIONS

In this chapter, we investigated the role of women's education in the transition to the first child in Germany for the time before and after unification. The former GDR government provided extensive family policies which supported the compatibility of childrearing and employment and tight labor market institutions predetermined employment tracks. We supposed that these institutional parameters were conducive to an early family formation and could explain why there existed only small differences in the timing of fertility by women's educational levels. Since East and West German women are subject to fairly similar labor market constraints and family policies after unification, one would expect a convergence in fertility patterns which also involves a greater variation in the timing of fertility by women's educational level.

In the empirical part of this chapter, we employed piecewise-constant event history models to the analysis of first birth risks in East and West Germany. In the former GDR, educational participation and parenthood was more compatible than in the West and there was little variation in the timing of fertility by educational attainment. Compared to the situation before unification, parenthood and educational participation is less compatible in present day East Germany. Furthermore, the variation in the timing of first birth by woman's education attainment has substantially increased after unification in East Germany.

REFERENCES

Albrecht, J.W., P.A. Edin, M. Sundström and S.B. Vroman. 1999. Career interruptions and subsequent earnings: A reexamination using Swedish data. *Journal of Human Resources* 34(2): 295-311.

Adler, M.A. 1997. Social change and decline in marriage and fertility in Eastern Germany. *Journal of Marriage and the Family* 59(1): 37-49.

Becker, G.S. 1993. *A Treatise on the Family*. Enlarged edition. Harvard University Press.

Becker, G.S. 1960. An economic analysis of fertility. *Demographic and Economic Change in Developed Countries*. NBER Conference Series No. 11. Princeton: 209-231.

Berghahn, S., A. Fritzsche. 1991. *Frauenrecht in Ost und Westdeutschland: Bilanz, Ausblick*. Berlin: Basisdruck-Verlag.

Bielinski, H., C. Brinkmann and B. Kohler. 1995. Erwerbsverläufe seit der Wende in Ostdeutschland: Brüche und Kontinuitäten. Ergebnisse des Arbeitsmarkt-Monitors über berufliche Veränderungen 1989 bis 1994. IAB Nürnberg. *IAB Werkstattbericht* Nr. 6.

Bird, E.J., J. Schwarze and G.G. Wagner. 1994. Wage effects of the move toward free markets in East Germany. *Industrial and Labor Relations Review* 47(3): 390-400.

Blossfeld, H.-P. and J. Huinink 1991. Human capital investments or norms of role transition? How women's schooling and career affect the process of family formation. *American Journal of Sociology* 97(1): 143-68.

Böckmann-Schewe, L., A. Röhrig and C. Kulke. 1993. Berufsverlauf und weiblicher Lebenszusammenhang: Kontinuitäten und Brüche im Leben von Frauen in den neuen Bundesländern. *Zeitschrift für Frauenforschung* 11(4): 47-63.

Brinkmann, C. 1999, Instrumente aktiver Arbeitsmarktpolitik in Ostdeutschland. In: Wiedemann, E. (et al.) (eds.): *Die arbeitsmarkt- und beschäftigungspolitische Herausforderung in Ostdeutschland.* Nürnberg: Bundesanstalt für Arbeit: 311-351.

Brinkmann, C. and E. Wiedemann. 1995. Arbeitsmarktrisiken im ostdeutschen Transformationsprozess: Ergebnisse des Arbeitsmarkt-Monitors 1989 bis 1994. *Mitteilungen aus der Arbeitsmarkt- und Berufsforschung* 28(3): 323-338.

Cornelius, I. 1990. Familien- und Bevölkerungspolitik in der DDR. *Arbeit und Sozialpolitik* (8/9): 308-316.

Dingeldey, I. 2001. European tax systems and their impact on family employment patterns. *Journal of Social Policy* 4: 563-672.

Dorbritz, J. 1997. Der demographische Wandel in Ostdeutschland - Verläufe und Erklärungsansätze. *Zeitschrift für Bevölkerungswissenschaft* 22 (2-3): 239-268.

Engelbrech, G. and M. Jungkunst. 1998. Erwerbsbeteiligung von Frauen und Kinderbetreuung in ost- und westdeutschen Familien. *IAB Werkstattbericht 2/98*. Nürnberg: Institut für Arbeitsmarkt und Berufsforschung.

Engelbrech, G. and A. Reinberg. 1997. Frauen und Männer in der Beschäftigungskrise der 90er Jahre. Entwicklung der Erwerbstätigkeit in West und Ost nach Branchen, Berufen und Qualifikationen: eine Untersuchung auf Basis der Mikrozensus-Daten. IAB Nürnberg. *IAB-Werkstattbericht* Nr. 11.

Frerich, J. and M. Frey. 1993. *Handbuch der Geschichte der Sozialpolitik in Deutschland.* Band 2: Sozialpolitik in der Deutschen Demokratischen Republik. München.

Frick, J.R., R. Hauser, K. Müller and G.G. Wagner. 1995. Income distribution in East Germany in the first five years after the fall of the wall. *Economic Policy in Transitional Economies* 5(4): 79-108.

Gornick, J.C., M.K. Meyers and K.E. Ross. 1998. Public policies and the employment of mothers: a cross national study. *Social Science Quarterly* 79(1): 35-54

Gustafsson, S. 1992. Separate taxation and married women's labor supply: A comparison of West Germany and Sweden. *Journal of Population Economics* 5(1): 61-85.

Gustafsson, S. 2001. Optimal age at motherhood. Theoretical and empirical considerations on postponement of maternity in Europe. *Journal of Population Economics* 14: 225-247.

Gustafsson, S., C. Wetzels and E. Kenjoh. 2000. Can postponement of maternity in the 1990s be explained in changes in time spent out of market work? Paper presented at the ESPE 2000 Conference in Bonn (Germany).

Gysi, J. and W. Speigner. 1983. *Changes in the life patterns of families in the German Democratic Republic.* Berlin: Academy of Sciences of the GDR. Institute of Sociology and Social Policy.

Haisken-DeNew, J. and J. Frick. (et al.) 2003. *Desktop Companion to the German Socio-Economic Panel Study (GSOEP).* Berlin: German Institute for Economic Research (DIW).

Hank, K., K. Tillmann and G.G. Wagner. 2001. Außerhäusliche Kinderbetreuung in Ostdeutschland vor und nach der Wiedervereinigung. Ein Vergleich mit Westdeutschland in den Jahren 1990 – 1999. *Zeitschrift für Bevölkerungswissenschaft* 26: 55-65.

Hank, K. and M. Kreyenfeld. 2003. A multilevel analysis of child care and women's fertility decisions in Western Germany. *Journal of Marriage and Family* 65: 584-596.

Hirschman, C. 1994. Why Fertility Changes. *Annual Review of Sociology* 20: 203-233.

Hoem, J. M. 1986. The impact of education on modern family-union initiation. *European Journal of Population* 2:113-133.

Huinink, J. 1999. Die Entscheidung zur Nichtehelichen Lebensgemeinschaft als Lebensform – Ein Vergleich zwischen Ost- und Westdeutschland. In: Klein, T., Lauterbach, W. (eds.): *Nichteheliche Lebensgemeinschaften. Analysen zum Wandel partnerschaftlicher Lebensformen.* Opladen: Leske und Budrich: 113-138.

Huinink, J., K.U. Mayer and H. Trappe. 1995. Staatliche Lenkung und individuelle Karrierechancen: Bildungs- und Berufsverläufe. In: Huinink, J. (et al.) (eds.): *Kollektiv und Eigensinn: Lebensverläufe in der DDR und danach.* Berlin: Akademie-Verlag: 88-143.

John, B. and E. Stutzer. 2002. Erwerbsverhalten von Erziehungsurlauberinnen. *Zeitschrift für Familienforschung* 3: 215-233.

Kopp, J. 2000. Geburtenentwickung in Ost- und Westdeutschland. Trends, regionale Unterschiede, Erklärungen. In: Bertram, H. (et al.) (eds.): *Solidarität, Lebensformen und regionale Entwicklung.* Opladen: Leske und Budrich: 82-135.

Kravdal, Ø. 1996. How the local supply of day-care centers influences fertility in Norway: A parity-specific approach. *Population Research and Policy Review* 15(3): 201-218.

Kreyenfeld, M. 2004. Fertility decisions in the FRG and the GDR- An analysis with data from the German Fertility and Family Survey. *Demographic Research, Special Collection* 3(11): 276-318. available under: http://www.demographic-research.org/

Krueger, A.B. and J.S. Pischke. 1995. A comparative analysis of East and West German labor markets: before and after unification. In: Freeman, R.B./ Katz, L.F. (eds.): *Differences and Changes in Wage Structures.* Chicago: University of Chicago Press: 405-445.

Lechner, M. 1998. Eine empirische Analyse des Geburtenrückgangs in den neuen Bundesländern aus der Sicht der neoklassischen Bevölkerungsökonomie. *Zeitschrift für Wirtschafts- und Sozialwissenschaft* 118(3): 463-488.

Liefbroer, A. and M. Corijn. 1999. Who, What, and When? Specifying the Impact of Educational Attainment and Labour Force Participation on Family Formation. *European Journal of Population* (15): 45-75.

Lutz, B., T. Ketzmerick and B. Wiener. 1999. Ausschlußrisiken und Grenzen herkömmlicher Arbeitsmarktpolitik – Einige Lektionen aus der ostdeutschen Entwicklung seit 1990/91. Der Zerfall der Beschäftigungsstrukturen der DDR 1989-1993. In: Wiedemann, E. (et al.) (eds.): *Die arbeitsmarkt- und beschäftigungspolitische Herausforderung in Ostdeutschland.* Nürnberg: Bundesanstalt für Arbeit: 267-287.

Mayer, K.U., M. Diewald and H. Solga. 1999. Transitions to post-communism in East Germany: Worklife mobility of woman and men between 1989 and 1993. *Acta Sociologica* 42(1): 35-53.

Nauck, B. and M. Joos. 1995. East joins west: child welfare and market reforms in the special case of the former GDR. *Innocenti Occasional Papers. Economic Policy Series* 48. Florence: UNICEF International Child Development Centre.

Obertreis, G. 1986. *Familienpolitik in der DDR 1946-1980.* Opladen.

Pascall, G. and N. Manning. 2000. Gender and social policy: comparing welfare states in Central and Eastern Europe and the former Soviet Union. *Journal of European Social Policy* 10(3): 240-266.

Rindfuss, R., P. Morgan and G. Swicegood. 1988. *First Births in America: Changes in the Timing of Parenthood.* Berkeley: University of California Press.

Rindfuss, R.R., P.S. Morgan and K. Offutt. 1996. Education and the changing age pattern of American fertility: 1963-1989. *Demography* 33(3): 277-290.

Rindfuss, R.R. and K.L. Brewster. 1996. Childrearing and fertility. *Population and Development Review* 22(Supplement): 258-289.

Schmähl, W. 1992. Sozialpolitik und Systemtransformation: zur Bedeutung und zur Veränderung von Sozialpolitik im Prozeß der deutschen Vereinigung. In: Schmähl, W. (ed.): *Sozialpolitik im Prozeß der deutschen Vereinigung.* Frankfurt am Main: Campus-Verlag: 26-58.

Statistisches Bundesamt, 2004. *Sozialleistungen. Tageseinrichtungen für Kinder am 31.12.2002.* available under: http://www.destatis.de/basis/d/solei/tab_juhilf.htm.

Solga, H. and D. Konietzka. 1999. Occupational Matching and Social Stratification. *European Sociological Review* (1): 25-47.

Stata Corporation 2003. *Stata Reference Manual. Release 8.* College Station (Texas). Stata Press.

Statistisches Amt der DDR. 1990. *Statistisches Jahrbuch , '90.* Berlin.

Szydlik, M. 1994. Incomes in a planned and a market economy: the case of the German Democratic Republic and the 'former' Federal Republic of Germany. *European Sociological Review* (10): 199-217.

Szydlik, M. 2002. Vocational education and labour markets in deregulated, flexibly coordinated and planned societies. *European Societies 4(1): 79-105*

Taniguchi, H. 1999. The timimg of childbearing and women's wages. *Journal of Marriage and the Familiy* 61: 1008-1019.

Trappe, H. 1995. *Emanzipation oder Zwang? Frauen in der DDR zwischen Beruf, Familie und Sozialpolitik.* Berlin: Akademie-Verlag.

Trappe, H. and R.A. Rosenfeld. 2000 How do children matter? A comparison of gender earnings inequality for young adults in the former East Germany and the former West Germany. *Journal of Marriage and the Family* 62(2): 489-507.

Vortmann, H. 1988: Soziale Sicherung in der DDR. *Aus Politik und Zeitgeschichte* B 32: 29-38.

Zühlke, S. 2000. *Beschäftigungschancen durch berufliche Mobilität? Arbeitslosigkeit, Weiterbildung und Berufswechsel in Ostdeutschland.* Berlin: Sigma-Verlag.

Chapter 10

EDUCATION AND ENTRY INTO MOTHERHOOD IN THE CZECH REPUBLIC DURING STATE-SOCIALISM AND THE TRANSITION PERIOD 1970-1997

VLADIMÍRA KANTOROVÁ

1. INTRODUCTION

During the 1990s, the economic and social environment in which Czechs lived was subject to dramatic transformations including the transition from a centrally planned to a market economy, the democratization of politics and changes to the welfare state. The total fertility rate in the 1980s was slightly over 1.9 children per woman, yet it dropped throughout the 1990s to fairly low levels, in particular between 1996 to 2001 (1.13 to 1.19 children per woman). The mean age of mothers at first birth rose from 22.5 in 1989 to 24.6 in 1999. This development is not unique in that most countries of Central and Eastern Europe have experienced a substantial decline in fertility since the onset of politic and economic transition in 1989 (Kučera et al. 2000).

The Czech experience of the 1990s provoked a discussion on the nature and underlying factors of recent demographic changes (e.g. Rychtaříková 1995, 2000, Rabušic 1996, Fialová and Kučera 1997). These investigations were based on macro-level associations between reproductive behavior and the economic and social development of the Czech Republic. In this discussion frequent reference was made to the "economic crisis thesis" and the "second demographic transition thesis", which mostly were being considered as mutually incompatible hypotheses. The aim of this contribution is to look at the changes in the timing of entry into motherhood on the individual level and to look at the role of women's education in two specific contextual situations – during state socialism in the 1970s and 80s, with a centrally planned economy, and during the profound societal and economic transition of the 1990s.

The education of women has generally been regarded as a very important determinant of first birth timing. Life course studies on first birth transition offer two explanations for differences in first birth timing among women with different

Siv Gustafsson and Adriaan Kalwij (eds.), Education and Postponement of Maternity, 237–258.

education levels (Hoem 1986, Blossfeld and Huinink 1991). First, being enrolled in education; second, education attainment. The major theoretical assumption in these studies is that the effect of education on first-birth risks needs to be viewed in a dynamic way; from a methodological view this means the inclusion of women's education as a time-varying variable that distinguishes between the periods in and out of education. In this way, the impact of being enrolled in education can be distinguished from the *net* impact of the education level on first-birth risks.

Empirical studies report opposing results as concerns the effect of women's education attainment on the timing of first birth. Some studies report that higher education attainment is associated with deferred childbearing (e.g. Bloemen and Kalwij 2001, Liefbroer and Corijn 1999). The authors argue that women with higher education are more inclined to pursue an employment career and postpone childbearing to a later stage. Others do not find any significant effect of education attainment on birth timing (e.g. Gustafsson et al. 2002, Blossfeld and Huinink 1991). Blossfeld and Huinink (1991) for example claim that delayed first births among better educated women are largely linked to continuing education activity, whereas a higher education level has no net inhibiting effect on first-birth risks.

The chapter is organized as follows: Next, we describe changes in the institutional context such as in the education system, the presence of women in the labor market, economic returns to education and family policies. The theoretical framework is based on the economic approach to the timing of births (e.g. Gustafsson 2001). Within this framework, we discuss childbearing decisions under state socialism and during the transition period, and highlight major differences between these periods that may be a reason for the postponement of first birth in the 1990s. In particular, we look at education differences in the timing of first birth. Our empirical analysis is based on data from the Czech Fertility and Family Survey of 1997. We apply an event-history analysis to the transition to first child. The analysis proceeds in two steps and in both we compare behavior under state socialism with behavior during the transition period. In the first step, we investigate the effect of education attainment on first-birth risks. In the second step, we study first-birth risks since completion of studies in order to provide a deeper insight into the relationship between education duration and the timing of entry into motherhood in the life course of women.

2. CHANGES IN THE INSTITUTIONAL CONTEXT

2.1 Education – Structures and Changes

Many aspects of the state-socialist education system (the number and type of schools, the length of education, the number of students admitted every year to different kinds of schools, the admission requisites) were planned according to the needs of the economy. The purpose was to provide white-collar workers with technical education and especially manual workers with technical apprenticeship for industry. The education system did not experience any major changes or reforms in the 1970s and 1980s. The state-socialist regime strongly promoted an education path leading to apprenticeship and the length of this education was generally two to three years (women were 16 to 17 years old at completing education). Upper-secondary education with school-leaving certificate (maturita) lasted four years (women were around age 18 at completing education). Places in university education were limited and admission was based not only on the academic qualification of students, but also on other requirements (such as Communist party membership of students or their parents).

In the 1990s, the inherited education system had a low level of flexibility and a weak capacity to fully absorb the education aspirations, especially for university education, of young adults. Furthermore, the baby boom cohort born in the mid-1970s entered into upper-secondary and tertiary education. In the 1990s, interest in the lowest structural level (apprentice schools) decreased to the benefit of upper-secondary education with a certificate (maturita). While in the school year 1989/90, 61% of post-elementary school students enrolled in apprentice schools, it was down to 46% in 1997/98 (Čerych et al. 1999). During the 1990s, more possibilities for further study opened up for young adults after completion of upper-secondary education. Students could now study in a non-university sector of tertiary education (of 1 to 3 years duration), which offered more specialized (social work, lower medical professions, languages) or market-oriented (management, marketing) studies. However, young people strongly perceived a limitation still to be the low capacity of universities.

To conclude, differences in the structure of paths and wider opportunities for attending tertiary education extended the period spent in education. The proportion of young women at age nineteen enrolled in education increased from 15% in 1992 to 40% (20% in upper-secondary and 20% in tertiary education) in 1999 of the total female population of this age. Among women aged 20 to 22 in 1999, 20% of them enrolled in education activities; this compares to 12% in 1992 (OECD 2001). Despite this development, however, the Czech education system was behind not only the countries of the European Union, but also Poland and Hungary as far as the expected average years of schooling in 1999 (15 years for men and 15.2 years for women) is concerned (OECD 2001).

2.2 The Presence of Women in the Labor Market

Strict labor market regulations developed in the centrally planned economy. Employment was defined as a state-guaranteed social right and not as an outcome of market forces. On the whole, work contracts were permanent and the degree of mobility between jobs was low. Due to low wage levels and an official ideology that emphasized the role of women's work in gender equality and emancipation, financial and ideological pressure on women to enter paid employment was strong. Thus, nearly all women participated in the labor market after completion of studies. The proportion of women to the total number employed has been very stable and fluctuated around 46-47% since the 1960s. At the end of the 1980s, participation in the labor force reached over 80% of women at the economically active age (70% if women on paid maternity leave were excluded from the active labor force).

Differences in the female labor force participation by level of education were small (Pailhé 1998). The model of 'continuous employment' was typical for Czech women, who combined work and family life during their reproductive years with only short interruptions of work during maternity and parental leave (Čermáková 1997). Moreover, the majority of women worked full-time. Contrary to some expectations, a massive withdrawal of women from paid employment did not occur during the transition period (Pailhé 1998). This was the result of both the continued economic need for two incomes in a family and women's unwillingness to give up paid employment.

The usual participation of both partners in the labor market led to the formation of the dual earner family model. The families in which the man only was employed and the woman stayed at home were very rare – in 1998, housewives formed a mere 4% and women on parental leave represented just 4.2% of the female population aged 15+ (Kuchařová 1999). With increases in female education attainment and labor force participation, one can presume that husbands and wives are less likely than before to define the role of women traditionally; yet much of the research suggests that traditional gender roles in work and family persist. Empirical evidence points out that childrearing responsibilities were shared along traditional gender roles (Čermáková et al. 2000). The division of labor in Czech households was characterized by housework mostly being done by women. In 1996, the quantitative difference in the division of work between men and women living in a two-income family was that men devoted an average of 48.5 hours per week to their jobs and women 42.5 hours, while on average men spent 10 and women 25 hours on housework (Křížková 1999).

2.3 Economic Returns to Education in the Centrally Planned and Transition Economy

During state socialism, earnings were set by certain categories for all employees according to centrally determined wage grids (Munich et al. 1999). The aim was that differences in individual incomes should be as small as possible. The decreasing significance of education in individual income differentials was a long-term trend during the 1970s and 80s and the rewarding system was characterized by the predominance of factors such as age and seniority (Večerník 1996). Education played a role more so in other channels than in wage differentials. These channels offered various perks such as a second job, extra money, access to scarce goods or services, useful contacts or improved working conditions, thus resulting in a higher quality of both the work and private life (Večerník 1996).

The transition from a centrally planned economy to a market economy led to a fundamental transformation of the occupational structure, an expansion of the private sector and a growing demand for qualified workers with specialized education. Firms began to act according to market forces and output, employment and wages were set by firms rather than a planning center (Svejnar 1999). Education, on-job experience and work performance were valued higher in areas where modernization was introduced, and over-employment decreased. However, other areas were influenced by the 'soft conditions' for transformation leading to the sustenance of inefficient firms. All these factors brought wider differences in employment contracts, wages, accessibility of non-wage advantages and employment security.

In the 1990s, the transition to a market economy introduced more economic incentives to obtain higher education; these were lacking in the preceding era. Greater importance was placed on higher education and this opened up new opportunities in the labor market, ensuring access to more stable jobs with relatively higher earnings. Following the collapse of communism, wage regulations were quickly abolished, and a number of studies summarized in Svejnar (1999) provide evidence of a rapid increase in income dispersion during the transition, underlined in part by an increase in returns to education[1]. Therefore, the income level of female university educated employees rose from 133% of the average female income in 1988 to 145% in 1992 and to 160% in 1996 according to Microcensus data (Večerník 1999, Table 1). Despite equal pay legislation and nearly overall employment of women in all sectors of the economy, both the state-socialist and transition economies were characterized by a gender wage gap, which is not different from that in market economies (Jurajda 2001, Pailhé 2000).

Table 10.1. Average wage by education attainment and gender, the Czech Republic (Percent)

Education	Total			Men			Women		
	1988	1992	1996	1988	1992	1996	1988	1992	1996
Elementary	90.5	75.7	69.9	90.5	81.0	73.0	93.1	80.3	74.6
Upper-secondary:									
- without maturita	95.4	92.9	87.6	95.4	90.3	85.9	93.9	85.2	81.8
- with maturita	101.4	103.7	106.9	102.2	104.5	110.3	104.3	112.6	112.7
Tertiary	134.0	144.0	164.7	124.6	140.0	161.3	133.1	145.4	160.7
Average	100.0	100.0	100.0	100.0	100.0	100.0	100.0	100.0	100.0
In % of total	100.0	100.0	100.0	115.3	119.3	116.4	79.6	77.8	81.7

Source: Microcensus 1989, 1992 and 1996 (Večerník 1999).

Moreover, having higher education was kind of an 'insurance' against economic uncertainty. Between 1993-1997, the unemployment rate of university educated women was around 2% and for women with elementary education it was between 8 to 15%, for the others it fluctuated between 4 and 8%. While the general unemployment rate of women was between 4.5-7% between 1993 and 1997, among 15 to 19 years old women this percentage was more than 3 times higher (CSU 2003).

2.4 Population and Family Policies

In the discussions on fertility in the Czech context, the question on population policies and the role of the state in general is of importance (e.g. Heitlinger 1976, Frejka 1980, Wolchik 2000). The relevant measures of pronatalist policies were introduced in the first half of the 1970s. In 1968, paid maternity leave was extended to 26 weeks. Prolonged maternity leave with a job guarantee was granted until a child reached 2 years of age (in the mid-1970s, it was extended to 3 years). Maternity allowance (at the time representing around 40% of the average female salary) was introduced in 1971 starting with the birth of second child and paid until the child reached 2 years of age (Kocourková 2002). However, for many families forgone earnings of women were an important part of the budget and women usually returned to work earlier than the period guaranteed by law (Fialová and Kučera 1997).

A massive development of childcare facilities during state socialism was the result of economic and ideological arguments for a high labor force participation of women. Public day care for children over age 3 was easy accessible and not costly (subsidized by municipalities). In the 1980s, kindergartens offered places to over 85% of children aged 3 to 5 and places in nurseries corresponded to 15% of children aged 0 to 2 years (Kučera 2001).

State support for families included not only direct cash transfers such as child allowances[2], but also subsidies in kind for day-care centers, nursery schools, after-school care, school canteens, transport, summer camp, or indirect subsidies on food and manufactured goods intended primarily for children (Fialová and Kučera 1997). All this had a strong compensatory effect on the overall budget of families with children[3].

State housing policy preferred married couples with children over others in all types of newly constructed housing (Kučera 2001). Loans for young married couples up to age 30 were introduced in 1973 and repayments were partly cancelled at the birth of a child[4]. Therefore, population policy promoted an early start of family formation, gave a great advantage for families with children and preferred married to cohabiting couples.

After 1990, the system of indirect social assistance, which in the past consisted of various price cuts and subsidies from the public budget, was reduced. The state abolished some measures (such as annulling of state guarantee for newly-weds loans in 1991). Since inflation was high in the early transition period, child allowances and other family benefits in cash reduced in value. Eligibility criteria for some family benefits (e.g. child allowances) were changed to means-tested benefits in 1996.

The system of maternity and parental leave (up to four years) became more generous[5] but granted little flexibility to combine childrearing and employment. In addition, parental-leave benefits were far below income replacement levels, being based on a flat rate principle. Throughout the 1990s, the provision of places in kindergartens for the total aggregate of children aged 3 to 5 remained stable at between 85 to 90% (CSU 2001). By contrast, the greatest reduction occurred in the number of public nurseries for children aged 0 to 2 (to 1% of the population of same-aged children in 1997, see UZIS 1998) causing difficulties for women willing to return to work before the child reached age 3. The growth of fees lead to the diminished affordability of kindergartens and nurseries for low-income families because the average monthly charge for pre-school facilities was approximately 10% of the average wage in that period (Čermáková et al. 2000). As a result of these trends, the reconciliation between childrearing and paid employment for mothers with small children became increasingly difficult.

3. THEORETICAL CONSIDERATIONS ON THE ROLE OF EDUCATION IN THE TIMING OF FIRST BIRTH

According to the economic approach, the role of female human capital plays a central part in the timing of birth (e.g. Gustafsson 2001). The relative costs of children are affected significantly by changes in the value of the time that women have at their disposal. This is because the cost of mother's time is a major part of the total cost of producing and rearing children (Becker 1993). The economics of family provides a comprehensive framework for the role of women's education in the context of 'market' economies. Among the components that must be included in the costs of children the 'career planning hypothesis' discusses: (i) the opportunity costs of time spent with children instead of being in the labor market, (ii) the depreciation of the value of education and experience while caring for a child, and (iii) net direct child costs (Cigno and Ermisch 1989, Cigno 1991, Walker 1995; these models are discussed in Gustafsson 2001). The authors considered the economic costs of having a child at different stages of a woman's life. These considerations are not the same for women with different socio-economic characteristics – such as education. Even if the effect of women's education is theoretically disputed (Gustafsson 2001), it is generally considered to be harmful having children during the 'career building' phase, in particular so for women with higher education (e.g. Liefbroer and Corijn 1999, Gustafsson et al. 2002).

However, the contextual framework for which these explanations have been developed is different to the conditions under state socialism and perhaps the transition to a market economy in the Czech Republic. First, the theoretical concept assumes that career interruption is penalized and, moreover, that it is dependent on the stage of career at which the work interruption due to childbirth is taken. Second, the economic returns to education are held to be the result of market mechanisms. However, these assumptions need to be questioned when looking at overall employment, definite work contracts and wage grids in a centrally planned economy. Third, the theory assumes an incompatibility between childrearing and women's employment. Nevertheless, the population policy of the state under socialism aimed at alleviating women's childcare responsibilities by supporting public childcare. In what follows, we discuss the context of childbearing decisions under state socialism and the transition period and highlight the major differences. In particular, we look at education differences in the timing of first birth.

Under Czech state socialism, most women participated in labor market activities and future earnings were highly predictable according to wage grids. When earning levels were largely dependent on age and the timing of work interruption due to childbirth had no major influence on women's future employment and earnings, it was generally considered better for women to have children early in life, that is when earnings were the lowest (as noted also by Fialová and Kučera 1997). Furthermore, the withdrawal from the labor market after childbirth was on the whole temporal and the compatibility of work and childrearing was supported by public childcare provisions. Besides, strong incentives provided by public policies favored low age at first childbirth. Easier access to housing for couples with children and reduced repayment of newly-wed loans at the birth of each child are examples of such policies. There were few education differences in income or the standard of living, because of wage regulations, an important redistribution of incomes and various kinds of subsidies from public sources. Therefore, (i) the opportunity costs of forgone earnings, (ii) the depreciation of the value of education or job experience while caring for a child, and (iii) net direct child costs applied to a similar extent to all women. We consequently assume that there was little differentiation by education attainment in first birth risks (when controlled for different education duration).

In the 1990s one observed the decline in period fertility, along with a rise in the mean age of mothers at first birth. The fact that in the 1990s women spent more time in education than before can explain at least in part the observed postponement of entry into motherhood. Young women involved in longer education paths formed a family later in life. Besides, there was a prolongation of the period between the end of studies and the formation of family during which young women established their position in the labor market and society in general. An intriguing question is whether this development was proportional in all education groups or whether the education differentiation in the timing of first birth was rising. Finding out whether and how women's education had an effect on the transition to first birth might contribute to the understanding of the fertility decline of the 1990s.

In economic terms, it can be argued that the (i) indirect costs of children (opportunity costs of mothers' time spent with children) continued to rise as the market economy widened options for young people, the labor market became more competitive and education and job-related experience gained in importance. Apparently, (ii) the depreciation of female human capital while caring for a child also became a more important factor in considering fertility decisions. However, there existed differences by education attainment. While these considerations were of comparatively low importance to women with lower earnings and/or higher uncertainty on the labor market (with a higher risk of unemployment and difficulties to find a job), they rose for women with relatively high earnings and good career prospects. Thus, it became for women increasingly important to time motherhood with respect to their employment career, in particular so for those with higher education. The hypothesis following from this argument is that the education differentiation of fertility augmented in the 1990s and women with higher education had comparatively lower risks of first birth.

The second hypothesis is based on different arguments than the previous one and discusses the role of 'economic hardship' accompanying the transition to a market economy. Expenditures on children were rising during transition (through inflation or the canceling of subsidized prices) and the subsidies for families from public resources declined substantially. Therefore, in terms of economic theory (iii) net direct costs of children increased. The growing uncertainty resulting from the overall economic insecurity disproportionately affected young people and young families (Večerník 2001, Forster and Toth 2001). The former might have delayed childbirth because financial resources to fulfill the basic needs of the family were lacking. This argument supports the hypothesis emphasizing economic and social difficulties experienced in the 1990s, which created a specific and almost a 'crisis' behavior that was manifested in a decline of fertility (Rychtaříková 2000). On the individual level, the possible behavioral response to the economic hardship could affect the groups of women who were the 'losers' in the economic transition to a considerably higher degree than those who were not. Women with low education had relatively less paid and less stable jobs, and they faced greater difficulties in establishing themselves on the labor market than their counterparts with higher education. They therefore faced stronger financial constraints when it came to family formation. Moreover, the subsidies for families from public resources formed an important part of the family budget. Thus, diminishing state financial support for families had a greater impact on these women. The hypothesis following from this argument is that there was higher education differentiation in fertility in the 1990s and women with a lower education level refrained comparatively more often from first childbirth than those with a higher education level.

To sum up, we formulated two competing hypotheses with different expectations concerning the role of education in the decline of first births in the 1990s. The following empirical analysis will help to assess their validity.

4. DATA AND METHOD

4.1 Sample Selection

The data used in the empirical analysis are from the Fertility and Family Survey of the Czech Republic, conducted in November-December 1997 (Rychtaříková and Kraus 2001). It contains information on 1,735 women and 721 men, the latter who are current partners of women in the sample. In our analysis, we use the female part of the sample only (Note 6). The women surveyed were born 1952-1982, and were 15-45 years old at the time of the interview in November 1997. The data provide us with full retrospective histories of childbearing and education paths.

In our analysis, we partition the data sample, primarily because two different structures of the socioeconomic incentives influenced entry into motherhood. We construct two separate parts of the data set (Note 7) – one for the 1970s and 80s and the second one from January 1990 until the time of the interview. In this way, we obtain distinct effects of the explanatory variables for each period.

4.2 Analytical Procedure

We apply proportional hazard model for the transition to first birth, where the effects of covariates on the hazard of occurrence is multiplicative. The hazard function for $\ln\mu_i$ as a log-hazard of occurrence of the event at time t for i^{th} woman is defined as:

$$\ln \mu_i(t) = y(t) + \sum_j \beta_j x_{ij}(t) \tag{1}$$

where x_{ij} are covariates with β_j as the respective regression parameters, y(t) is the log-hazard function by age of mother with t as the time passed since the 15th birthday. The baseline hazard by age of woman is a piece-wise linear spline in the log-hazards (generalized Gompertz). For the estimation of the hazard models we use the aML software – Version 1.04 (Lillard and Panis 2000). Further useful characteristics (such as several duration splines) are described in the empirical analysis where we apply them.

4.3 Description of Variables

We are interested in the event of first birth (expressed in month and year of birth). The date of first childbirth is backdated by nine months to obtain an approximate date of conception. This is because events that occurred after conception might be influenced by conception itself (e.g. the end of participation in education, caused by pregnancy). The event of first child conception is studied from women's age 15. Because of the very young age pattern of first order fertility we limit our analysis to age 35. After excluding 26 cases[8], we work with 1709 female life histories. The total number of first births is 887 in the 1970s and 80s and 333 in the period 1990-1997. All events are reported in month and year. We attribute the occurrence of the event to the middle of the respective month.

Our time-varying variable on education attainment is constructed as a categorical variable. 'No upper-secondary certificate' applies to education without secondary school leaving certificate (maturita). 'Upper-secondary certificate' corresponds to an upper-secondary education with secondary school leaving certificate (maturita). 'University degree' applies to a part of life after university graduation. Periods 'in education' are assigned only to full-time participation in education[9].

Table 10.2. Sample composition of childless women by education

Total number of individuals, period 1970-1997	100%	1709
Education ever obtained:		
upper-secondary certificate (maturita)	41%	697
university degree	5%	78
Ever been in education (at ages 15 and above):		
any education	94%	1604
after upper-secondary certificate	12%	209

Source: Czech Fertility and Family Survey of 1997 (author's own calculations).

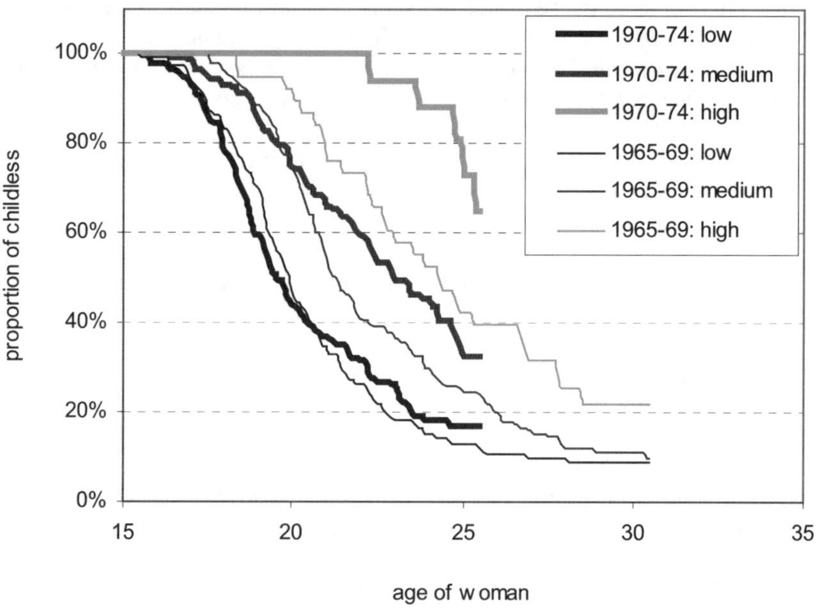

Figure 10.1. Transition to first birth: Proportion of childless women by age and final education level, cohorts 1965-69 and 1970-74.

Notes: (1) Method: Kaplan-Meier survival plots; dependent variable: transition to first child measured since age 15. (2) Final education attainment is measured at the date of interview. Women in education at date of interview are excluded. Levels of education attained: low (no upper-secondary certificate), medium (upper-secondary certificate), high (university degree). (3) Number of cases in the analysis for the 1965-69 cohort: 321 women, and for the 1970-74 cohort: 322 women. (4) Data: Czech Fertility and Family Survey of 1997.

5. FINDINGS AND DISCUSSION OF RESULTS

5.1 How Did Education Attainment Affect the Timing of First Birth?

There are two aspects to the possible influence of education on entry into motherhood. First, being enrolled in education; second, education attainment.

Young women in the state-socialist period did not appear to perceive the incompatibility between childbearing and education to be *very* strong. Becoming pregnant and giving birth to a first child while being a student was not an extremely rare event. According to FFS data, in the 1970s and 80s every sixth first child (17.7%) was conceived when the women surveyed were still in education. Less than half of them (7.8% of all first children) were born when their mothers were still students. This points to the sequence of events in a short period: *conception – end of education – birth of first child* (10% of all first births) or *conception – birth of first child – end of education* (7.8% of all first births) as contrasted to *end of education – conception – birth of first child* (82.2%). Most women completed their education even if they were pregnant or already a mother[10]; moreover many pregnancies took place in the last year of school or university. During 1990-1997, the proportion of first children that were conceived and/or born while the mothers-to-be were still in education dropped to 10% and 5% respectively.

Starting with survival curves of the transition to first birth disaggregated by final level of education, one observes a postponement of first birth from the cohort born in 1965-69 to that born in 1970-74 (Figure 10.1) especially for women with higher final levels of education.

In the analysis, we take the education variable as time-varying with differentiation of the periods in education and out of education. We estimate a proportional hazard model in which we include woman's age and the education characteristics only (Table 10.3). As expected, in both periods being in education lowered the risk of entry into motherhood compared to women who had already finished education. Therefore, since the years spent in education prolonged during the 1990s (Section 2.1), the period in women's life when it is not considered as appropriate to give birth to a child – due to incompatibility between education and childrearing – also extended, leading to a postponement of first births.

As concerns the *net* effect of education attainment, having a university degree as opposed to an upper-secondary certificate increased the transition to the first child in the 1970s and 80s (but not significantly). Whether this may merely be the consequence of a timing effect – resulting from a comparatively high intensity of first birth in a brief period shortly after the end of studies – we will discuss later in the analysis of first birth risks after the completion of education. Women with no upper-secondary certificate had a relative first birth risk that is higher by 18% compared to those with an upper-secondary certificate (maturita).

In the period 1990-97, women with no upper-secondary certificate had a 37% higher risk of first birth compared to women with at least an upper-secondary certificate. Therefore, women with lower education entered transition to first birth more rapidly than their counterparts with higher education. It follows that higher educated females were contributing to the observed decline in first birth risks more so than other women did.

Table 10.3. Transition to first birth: Effects of women's education

Baseline by age of woman:									
			(SE)						
Intercept	-4.51		(0.30)	***					
Slopes:									
Age 15-18	0.90		(0.11)	***					
Age 18-19	0.39		(0.13)	***					
Age 19-22	0.02		(0.04)						
Age 22-25	-0.03		(0.05)						
Age 25-35	-0.11		(0.03)	***					
	Period 1970-1989				**Period 1990-1997**				
	b	exp(b)	(SE)		b	exp(b)	(SE)		
Education obtained:									**1990-1997**
Out of education:									**reference**
no upper-secondary	0.15	1.16	(0.08)	**	-0.21	0.81	(0.10)	**	1.36
upper-secondary certificate		1.00			-0.52	0.59	(0.11)	***	1.00
university degree	0.11	1.12	(0.20)		-0.47	0.63	(0.27)		1.05
In education:									
no upper-secondary	-0.76	0.47	(0.13)	***	-1.31	0.27	(0.30)	**	0.45
upper-secondary certificate	-1.04	0.35	(0.19)	***	-1.88	0.15	(0.33)	***	0.26
Log Likelihood	-5,653								
Observations	1,709								
First births	1,220								

Notes: (1) Event-history model (generalized Gompertz) with age of mother as piecewise linear spline; (2) Reference category = upper-secondary certificate in the period 1970-1989; (3) Significance: * at 10%; ** at 5%; *** at 1%; (4) Data: Czech Fertility and Family Survey of 1997.

5.2 The Timing of Entry into Motherhood after the End of Education

To investigate further the effect of education attainment on entry into motherhood, we distinguish between the effect of the time passed since the end of education and the effect of the woman's age. Thus, we examine the period after participation in education and its relationship with family formation. We introduce along with the age of women another 'time clock' (i.e. the time passed since the end of education). If there are multiple clocks in the model (by age of women and time passed since education completion), they combine additively to form the overall risk of first birth in the log-hazard. Women complete their studies at a certain age and this is when we consider the 'time clock' for the time passed since the end of education to start ticking[11].

The mathematical representation is as follows:

$$\ln \mu_i(t) = y(t) + c(t\text{-}e_i) + \sum_j \beta_j x_{ij}(t) \quad (2)$$

where c(t-ei) is a time dependent linear spline term which enters the model only if the woman in question completed her education and ei is indicating the time of education completion relative to age of woman. In our results, the spline for the effect of studies completion is characterized by an immediate effect (constant) and a later development (with a change in slope of effect at 2 or 4 years from the end of studies). In the present analysis, the effect of education completion interacts with the covariate education level. It has three categories: no upper-secondary certificate, or an upper-secondary certificate or a university degree.

In order to interpret the coefficients, it is easier to visualize them in a graph. The multiplicative effects of the time passed since the end of studies are added to the hazard of first birth by women's age at the ages typical for completing education at the respective level (Figures 10.2 and 10.3).

In the 1970s and 80s, the risk of conception doubled (after completion of studies at an upper-secondary or lower level) or tripled (after completion of a university degree) immediately after a woman subject to our analysis left school. For a few years, the risk was rising or stable and then declining (Figure 10.2). Education completion was strongly perceived as the beginning of the family formation period. In particular, women with university education had a high risk of entry into motherhood shortly after completion of university studies and the risk declined thereafter. This may be the result of societal norms on early entry into motherhood, the 'ideal' age these women already passed by having undergone university studies (for that period, the mean age of mothers at first childbirth was 22,0 to 22,5 years while the usual age of university completion was between 22 and 24 years). Therefore, they tended to have their first child comparatively swiftly after the end of education, and age differences in entry into motherhood relative to women with other education levels were less than different lengths of participation in education.

Differences between education groups in the role that the time passed since education completion played in first birth risks were more important in the 1990s than the previous two decades. Particularly women with a university degree had low risks of first childbirth after completion of studies, with a subsequent rise in risks thereafter (Figure 10.3). This reveals that the period between education and family formation constituted a distinct part of life in which young educated women established their position on the labor market and pursued their education attainment. At the opposite end, women with no upper-secondary certificate still had increased risks of first childbirth shortly after the completion of studies. These women had comparatively limited prospects on the labor market and were less motivated to translate their education qualifications into labor market activities.

To conclude, the change in the timing of entry into motherhood after studies completion is a significant feature of the relation between education and first birth in the 1990s.

Table 10.4. Transition to first birth: Effects of time elapsed since end of education

	Period 1970-1989	(SE)			Period 1990-1997	(SE)	
Baseline by age of woman							
Intercept	-5.58	(0.32)	***	Intercept	-5.78	(0.70)	***
Slopes:				Slopes:			
15-18 years	0.95	(0.13)	***	15-18 years	0.68	(0.29)	**
18-19 years	0.38	(0.15)	**	18-20 years	0.01	(0.14)	
19-22 years	0.04	(0.05)		20-25 years	-0.12	(0.08)	
22-25 years	-0.06	(0.07)		25-28 years	-0.17	(0.12)	
25-35 years	-0.03	(0.06)		28-35 years	-0.24	(0.11)	**
Time elapsed since end of education:							
No upper-secondary certificate:							
Constant	0.93	(0.17)	***		1.97	(0.43)	***
Slope: 0-2 years	0.14	(0.10)			0.02	(0.21)	
Slope: 2+ years	-0.08	(0.04)	**		0.08	(0.06)	
Upper-secondary certificate:							
Constant	0.50	(0.21)	**		1.16	(0.56)	**
Slope: 0-2 years	0.22	(0.13)	*		0.02	(0.30)	
Slope: 2+ years	0.00	(0.05)			0.21	(0.10)	**
University degree:							
Constant	1.22	(0.42)	***		-0.84	(0.92)	
Slope: 0-4 years	-0.17	(0.20)			0.66	(0.52)	
Slope: 4+ years	0.04	(0.23)			0.19	(0.09)	**
Log likelihood	-5,548						

Notes: (1) Event-history model (generalized Gompertz) with age of mother as piecewise linear spline; (2) Significance: * at 10%; ** at 5%; *** at 1%; (3) Data: Czech Fertility and Family Survey of 1997.

Figure 10.2. Transition to first birth: Effects of time elapsed since end of education for different education levels, period 1970-1989.

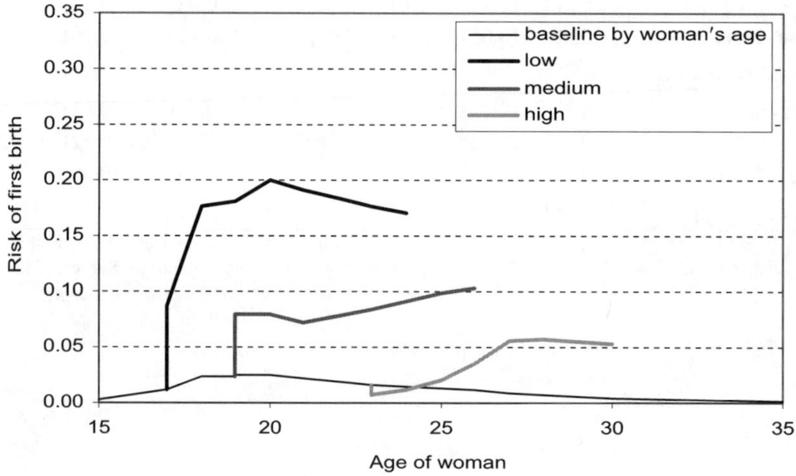

Figure 10.3. Transition to first birth: Effects of time elapsed since end of education for different levels of education, period 1990-1997.

Notes: (1) Levels of education attained: low (no upper-secondary certificate), medium (upper-secondary certificate), high (university degree). (2) The age at the end of education is the following: no upper-secondary certificate: 17 years; upper-secondary certificate: 19 years; university degree: 23 years. (3) Data: Czech Fertility and Family Survey of 1997.

6. CONCLUSIONS

We investigated the role women's education played in the entry into motherhood, looking at two specific contextual situations – the state socialism of the 1970s and 80s, with a centrally planned economy, and in the societal and economic transition of the 1990s. The event-history analysis of the Czech Fertility and Family Survey of 1997 showed several findings:

1. Education differentiation had a small impact on first-birth risks in the 1970s and 80s.
2. Women faced high risks of transition to first birth immediately after the completion of education, and in particular so university graduates.
3. There was an increase in the impact of a woman's education on timing of entry into motherhood after 1990. Women with an upper-secondary certificate or university degree had comparatively lower first-birth risks than their counterparts with a lower education level.
4. In the 1990s, the period between studies completion and entry into motherhood prolonged, and this was especially evident for university graduates.

In the interpretation of our results, we stress the importance of the institutional environment (political setting, institutions of the labor market, the education system and public policies) in fertility behavior. In the Czech society of the 1970s and 80s, the labor market provided little room for up- and downward mobility (obligatory overall employment, no unemployment, rigid rules for career advancement and wage grids based mainly on age). In view of this situation, the timing of work interruptions related to maternity leave did not have any major influence on future women's employment and earnings, since both of them were institutionally regulated. At the same time, population policy facilitated the reconciliation of childrearing with women's employment. Furthermore, these policies motivated young couples to marry and enter parenthood early. This combination of, on the one hand, the lack of incentives and weak constraints on the labor market and, on the other hand, incentives provided by population policies led to universal and early entry into motherhood with little impact of education differentiation.

For the period 1990-1997 we formulated two contrasting hypotheses explaining the decline in first-birth risks in the 1990s and a greater education differentiation in the timing of entry into motherhood compared to the previous period. In the first hypothesis, we made the supposition that the increased evaluation of education and greater education differentiation of labor market opportunities and constraints brought about increasing opportunities for highly educated women. Following from this, highly educated women should have lower first-birth risks. The second hypothesis perceived economic hardship associated with economic transition as the most important factor having an influence on reducing first-birth risks. Accordingly, women with a low education status should have lower risks of entry into motherhood.

The empirical analysis lent no support to the second hypothesis. On the contrary, the study supported theoretical assumptions that changes in opportunity structures and institutional settings induced changes in fertility behavior among young women. The transition to a market economy was characterized by profound and swift changes in the framework conditions of the labor market – such as entry and exit patterns, earnings, and evaluation of education or job experience. Women with higher education made use of the new employment opportunities and career prospects, and their education received greater importance in terms of prestige or income than in the state socialist era. Women seemed to postpone family formation to a time after the consolidation of employment – this means acquiring some job experience, making the most of the education attained and creating improved conditions for prospective maternity leave with the right to a period of job protection[12].

We compared two institutional settings with different economic evaluations of women's education (see Section 2.3) and different career options for highly educated women. We conclude that the way in which women's education is rated on the labor market and the possibilities to reconcile women's employment with childrearing seem to influence the effect women's education has on the timing of first births.

Against the background of our results, the intriguing question arises whether low first-birth risks in the 1990s are related to (i) a postponement of entry into motherhood, or to (ii) an increase of childlessness among Czech women. However, this question stays at present unanswered. One may assess the importance of both effects in the decline of fertility in the 1990s when the cohorts of women born in the 1970s reach the age limit of childbearing. Meanwhile, an interesting finding of our analysis is that women with a higher education seemed to postpone entry into motherhood or to a refrain altogether from childbearing more so than women with a lower education.

As concerns the policy implications of our results, one might question the development of family policies in the 1990s. It then became difficult to reconcile employment and childrearing especially for mothers with children below age 3. Public childcare for children below this age was very limited and the system of parental leave was inflexible (as concerns combining parental leave with part-time work or employment at home). The prevalent type of family with children below age 3 was mainly that the man was the breadwinner (being in full-time employment) and the woman was temporarily a housewife staying at home and being financially dependent on the male partner. Such prospects play an important role in childbearing decisions of young women, especially those with a higher education. Therefore, family policies in the Czech Republic need to take a new direction: they should address the issues of public childcare for children below age 3, the parental leave system and work time flexibility.

ACKNOWLEDGEMENTS

This paper was originally published in *Demographic Research*, 2004, Special Collection 3 *Contemporary Research on European Fertility: Perspectives and Developments*, Article 10, pp. 245-274 with the title "Education and Entry into Motherhood: The Czech Republic during State Socialism and the Transition Period (1970-1997)" (http://www.demographic-research.org/). The author (Vladimíra Kantorová) wishes to thank the Max-Planck-Gesellschaft, which holds the copyright of the original article, for the permission to reprint it in the present book.

NOTES

1 On the basis of micro data from the Social and Stratification Surveys of 1984 and 1993, for one additional year of education, earnings increased in the pre-transition period by 2.4% for males and 4.2% for females and in the early transition period by 5.2% for males and 5.8% for females. Those with university education experienced a particularly large earnings increase. Unlike the earnings return on formal education, the earning return on experience declined (Chase 1998).

2 Child allowances were given to all dependent children, but not to an equal amount per child. It was mostly to the benefit of families with 3 children. In the 1970s and 1980s, child allowances for two children represented 15 to 20% and for three children 35 to 40% of the average monthly wage (Kučera 2001).

3 In the 1980s, average transfers (cash benefits, benefits in kind including the provision of day-care centers, nursery schools, after-school care, transport and school canteens and income tax relief or rent subsidies) per child per month equaled approximately 15% of an average monthly salary and in total represented around 10% of total government expenditures (Kroupová and Huslar 1991).

4 From the loan to newly wed of 30 000 CZK (i.e. around 14 times the average monthly wage in 1973) to be repaid in 10 years, 2000 CZK were cancelled at the birth of the first child and 4000 CZK at the birth of the second and each following child.

5 Maternity leave was guaranteed for 28 weeks (36 weeks for lone mothers) and maternity allowance was equal to the amount of sickness leave allowance (since 1993, it has been 69% of the daily basis of income with a certain maximum amount). After this period, one of the parents had the right to stay on parental leave. In 1990 parental leave was prolonged up to the child's third birthday including job protection and in 1995 it was extended by another year but without further job protection. However, in reality in some cases the 3 years job protection rule failed due to an unstable business environment in which many new companies shut down and many companies rationalize or cancel individual branches or work positions (Čermáková et al. 2000). Mothers (or in rare cases father) on parental leave received a fixed flat rate contribution (in 2001, 25% of the average monthly female wage). In general, mothers stayed at home with their children for a longer period compared to the 1970s and 80s.

6 To use in our analyses information on the women's partners would be in many aspects very helpful with respect to the theoretical assumptions and explanations, since most of them deal with couples as a unit of observation. However, there are methodological obstacles using this information in the case of the Czech Fertility and Family Survey. First, we have only 721 partners to 1735 women. Second, we consider first births and the male partner who answered questions on his life history at the time of the interview in 1997 was not necessarily the partner with whom the woman had her first child or was under the risk of first childbirth.

7 In the first part covering the period of the 1970s and 80s, censoring is attributed at 1 January 1990 or when the women reached age 35. The second part contains parts of women's life histories experienced from 1st January 1990 to April 1997. All women who became 15 years old after 1990 are included. Women who celebrated their 15th birthday before 1990 are considered only if they were childless and not pregnant in January 1990. In practice, the observations on these women start at their respective age on 1 January 1990 and pre-1990 parts of female life histories are not included. Censoring was made at

April 1997 (eight months before the date of the survey) and when the women reached age 35. For the months February and March 1997, we use the start of pregnancies leading to first childbirth, with the child expected to be born in November or December 1997.

8 We excluded 26 female records form the analysis. In 2 cases the women conceived their first child before age 15 and in 23 cases women did not reach age 15 before April 1997, i.e. the date of censoring of observations.

9 'Out of education' periods are distinguished only if longer than 12 months; if they are shorter, this part of the female life history is treated as 'in education'. Part-time education is not included in periods of enrollment in education, but any completion certificate gained is considered in the variable of education attainment.

10 One of the questions in the Fertility and Family Survey questionnaire in the section on education histories is whether the education spell was finished successfully or not. In the 1970s and 80s, among women who were pregnant while being in education, only less then 15% did not complete successfully their education (own calculations from FFS).

11 In the present analysis, the end of full-time education is considered as the date at which the woman finished her education. If there is another education spell that started less than 16 months after the end of the previous education period, then the schooling is considered as not yet finished.

12 Since the motivation for changes in the timing of births have to be supported by the possibility of introducing these changes; the quick spread of contraceptive use in the 1990s was of major importance. Not surprisingly, the use of modern contraceptive methods did not expand in the same pace across different education groups; contraceptive use among Czech women appeared to increase with the education level (Wynnyczuk and Uzel 1999).

REFERENCES

Becker, G.S., 1993. *A Treatise on the Family. Enlarged edition*. Harvard University Press, Cambridge.

Bloemen, H., and Kalwij, S., 2001. "Female labor market transitions and the timing of births: a simultaneous analysis of the effects of schooling." *Labour Economics* 8: 593-620.

Blossfeld, H.-P., and Huinink, J., 1991. "Human capital investments or norms of role transition? How women's schooling and career affect the process of family formation." *American Journal of Sociology* 97: 143-168.

Čermáková, M., 1997. "Postavení žen na trhu práce (Women in the labor market)." *Sociologický časopis* 33: 389-404.

Čermáková, M. et al. 2000. *Relations and Changes of Gender Differences in the Czech Society in the 90s.* Institute of Sociology at the Academy of Sciences of the Czech Republic, Praha.

Čerych, L., Koucký, J., and Matějů, P., 1999. "School system and educational development." In: Večerník, J., and Matějů, P. (eds), *Ten Years of Rebuilding Capitalism: Czech Society after 1989.* Academia, Praha: 44-69.

Chase, R.S., 1998. "Markets for communist human capital: Returns to education and experience in communist Czech Republic and Slovakia." *Industrial and Labor Relations Reviews* 51: 401-423.

Cigno, A., 1991. *Economics of the Family.* Clarendon Press, Oxford.

Cigno, A., and Ermisch, J., 1989. "A micro-economic analysis of the timing of first births." *European Economic Review* 33: 737-760.

CSU, 2001. *Statistická ročenka* 2000 (Statistical Yearbook 2000). Czech Statistical Office, Praha.

CSU, 2003. *Labour Force Surveys* 1993-2002. Czech Statistical Office, Praha.

Fialová, L., and Kučera, M., 1997. "The main features of population development in the Czech Republic during the transformation of society." *Czech Sociological Review* 5: 93-111.

Forster, M.F., and Tóth, I.G., 2001. "Child poverty, and family transfers in the Czech Republic, Hungary and Poland." *Journal of European Social Policy* 11: 324-341.

Frejka, T., 1980. "Fertility trends and policies: Czechoslovakia in the 1970s." *Population and Development Review* 6: 65-93.

Gustafsson, S., 2001. "Optimal age at motherhood. Theoretical and empirical considerations on postponement of maternity in Europe." *Journal of Population Economics* 14: 225-247.

Gustafsson, S., Kenjoh, E., and Wetzels, C., 2002. "The role of education on postponement of maternity in Britain, Germany, the Netherlands and Sweden." In: Ruspini, E., and Dale, A. (eds), *The Gender Dimension of Social Change*

The Contribution of Dynamic Research to the Study of Women's Life Courses. The Policy Press, Bristol: 55-79.

Heitlinger, A., 1976. "Pro-natalist population policies in Czechoslovakia." *Population Studies* 30: 123-165.

Hoem, J.M., 1986. "The impact of education on modern family-union initiation." *European Journal of Population* 2: 113-133.

Jurajda, S., 2001. "Gender wage gap and segregation in late transition." CERGE-EI Working Paper, Praha.

Kocourková, J., 2002. "Leave arrangements and childcare services in Central Europe: policies and practices before and after the transition." *Community, Work & Family* 5: 301-318.

Křížková, A., 1999. "The division of labour in Czech households in the 1990s." *Czech Sociological Review* 7: 205-214.

Kroupová, A., and Huslar, O., 1991. "Children at the turning point: Economic reform and social policy in Czechoslovakia." In: Cornia, G.A., and Sipos, S. (eds), *Children and the Transition to the Market Economy*. Aldershot, Avebury: 149-177.

Kučera, M., 2001. "Rodinná politika a její demografické důsledky v socialistickém Československu (Family policies and their demographic consequences in socialist Czechoslovakia)." In: *Česko-francouzský dialog o dějinách evropské rodiny* (Czech-French dialogue on history of European family). *Cahiers du CEFRES* 22, CEFRES, Praha: 53-68.

Kučera, T., Kučerová, O., Opara, O., and Schaich, E. (eds), 2000. *New Demographic Faces of Europe*. Springer, Berlin.

Kuchařová, V., 1999. "Women and employment". *Czech Sociological Review* 7: 179-194.

Liefbroer, A.C., and Corijn, M., 1999. "Who, what, where, and when? Specifying the impact of educational attainment and labour force participation on family formation." *European Journal of Population* 15: 45-75.

Lillard, L.A., and Panis, C.W.A., 2000. *aML Multilevel Multiprocess Statistical Software, Version 2.0*. EconWare, Los Angeles.

Munich, D., Svejnar, J., and Terrell, K., 1999. "Returns to human capital under the communist wage grid and during the transition to market economy." University of Michigan Business School. Working Paper 272. www.wdi.bus.umich.edu.

OECD, 2001. *Education at a Glance OECD Indicators – 2001 Edition*. www1.oecd.org/els/education/ei/eag.

Pailhé, A., 2000. "Gender discrimination in Central Europe during the systemic transition." *The Economics of Transition* 8: 505-535.

Pailhé, A., 1998. "L'offre de travail des femmes en Europe Centrale dans la période de la transformation systémique." *Révue d'études comparatives Est-Ouest* 29: 11-40.

Rabušic, L., 1996. "O současném vývoji manželského a rodinného chování v České republice (On marriage and family trends in the Czech Republic)." *Demografie* 38: 173-180.

Rychtaříková, J., 1995. "Recent changes in fertility and families in the Czech Republic." *Studia demograficze* 4: 35-46.

Rychtaříková, J., 2000. "Demographic transition or demographic shock in recent population development in the Czech Republic?" *Acta Universitatis Carolinae Geographica* 1: 89-102.

Rychtaříková, J., and Kraus, J., 2001. *Fertility and Family Surveys in Countries of the ECE Region. Country Report: Czech Republic*. Economic Commission for Europe/United Nations Population Fund, New York/Geneva.

Svejnar, J., 1999. "Labor markets in the transitional Central and East European Economics." In: Ashenfelter, O., and Card, D. (eds), *Handbook of Labor Economics*. Elsevier Science, Amsterdam: 2810-2857.

UZIS, 1998. *Zdravotnická ročenka* 1997 (Czech Health Statistics Yearbook 1997). Institute of Health Information and Statistics of the Czech Republic, Praha.

Večerník, J., 1996. "Earning disparities in the Czech Republic: The history of equalization." *Czech Sociological Review* 4: 211-222.

Večerník, J., 1999. "Inequalities in earnings, incomes, and household wealth." In: Večerník, J., and Matějů, P. (eds), *Ten Years of Rebuilding Capitalism: Czech Society after 1989*. Academia, Praha: 115-135.

Večerník, J., 2001. "From needs to market: Changing inequality of household income in the Czech transition." *Working Paper 370,* University of Michigan Business School, www.wdi.bus.umich.edu.

Walker J.R., 1995. "The effect of public policies on recent Swedish fertility behaviour." *Journal of Population Economics* 8: 223-251.

Wolchik, S. L., 2000. "Reproductive policies in the Czech and Slovak Republics." In: Kligman, G., and Gal, S. (eds), *Reproducing Gender: Politics, Publics and Everyday Life after Socialism*. Princeton University Press, Princeton: 58-91.

Wynnyczuk, V., and Uzel., R., 1999. "Czech Republic and Slovak Republic." In: David, H. P. (ed), *From Abortion to Contraception: A Resource to Public Policies and Reproductive Behavior on Central and Eastern Europe from 1917 to the Present.* Greenwood Press, Westport: 91-119.

Chapter 11

ASSORTATIVE MATING BY EDUCATION AND POSTPONEMENT OF COUPLE FORMATION AND FIRST BIRTH IN BRITAIN AND SWEDEN

SIV GUSTAFSSON AND SEBLE WORKU

1. INTRODUCTION

The purpose of this chapter is to analyze whether the effect of longer education on timing of maternity works primarily through the timing of couple formation or through postponement of maternity once the couple is formed. We consider the effects of education of each spouse together and separately on postponement of couple formation and the time elapsed from couple formation to timing of first birth.

In Western Europe, the period spent in education has increased over time, and fertility is very low. A number of studies, including Siv Gustafsson, Cecile Wetzels, Jan Dirk Vlasblom and Shirley Dex (1996) and Eiko Kenjoh (2004), show that relative to mothers in Britain, Germany and the Netherlands, Swedish mothers are much more likely to have entered employment within 24 to 60 months after first birth. This difference may be explained by the Swedish policies of paid parental leaves, subsidized childcare, and separate taxation of earnings, which have been effective in Sweden since the early 1970s. These policies are intrinsically pronatalist. One purpose of this chapter is to analyze whether in Britain, where family policies are much less generous and reforms in this area have been introduced only since the 1990s, duration to first birth is longer relative to Sweden.

Our theoretical conception is that individuals have a preferred age for couple formation and timing of birth that fits their human capital investment plans. They also have a fair idea of desirable traits for the marriage candidate when searching in the marriage market. The timing of union formation depends not only on the successful completion of human capital investment but also on the successful search for the right candidate. In our empirical work, we adopt a two-stage method of estimation. We first determine who marries whom by a multinomial logit model and then use predicted probabilities of the spouse's education level in hazard models to analyze the duration from age 13 to union formation and the duration from union to first birth.

Siv Gustafsson and Adriaan Kalwij (eds.), Education and Postponement of Maternity, 259–283.

This chapter is organized as follows: section 2 discusses the theoretical framework, section 3 gives a descriptive country comparison, section 4 motivates our empirical strategy, section 5 presents our estimates of the mating function, section 6 presents our results on the durations to couple formation and first birth, and section 7 concludes.

2. THEORETICALCONSIDERATIONS AND EARLIER WORK

There are two basic questions addressed in this chapter: "Who marries whom?" and "What causes postponement of couple formation and first birth?" Gary Becker (1973, 1981) suggested that if an attribute complements a similar attribute in a partner, this leads to positive assortative mating: 'likes' marry 'likes'. Spouse's education is most likely complementary, so that a highly educated person profits from marrying someone with a similar education. Evidence of positive assortative mating by education has been found for the United States (Robert Mare, 1991) as well as for many European countries (Hans-Peter Blossfeld and Andreas Timm, 2003). However, education can have the opposite effect: if sex ratios of highly educated people diverge from unity a less educated woman may marry a man with a higher education than her own because he can't find a highly educated available candidate at the optimal time of couple formation, or vice-versa. Search on the marriage market may also take longer.

In Blossfeld and Timm (2003), which has inspired our thinking on the mating function, the focus is on explaining 'upward marriage' as opposed to 'homogamous marriage' and 'downward marriage' with regard to educational attainment levels of men and women. The same structure of analysis is used in Blossfeld and Timm (2003) for all 14 countries included in their analyses.[1] For example, in Germany older cohorts of women married upwards because the educational sex ratios of these cohorts were favorable for upward marriage.

In general, results show that successful search in the marriage market depends on the availability of marriage candidates or sex ratios (see Shoshana Grossbard-Shechtman 1984, 2003; David Lam 1988; Theodore Bergstrom and David Lam 1989; Bergstrom 1997; Hiromi Ono 2002). Furthermore, John Ermisch (2003) presents a theory of search in the marriage market, where the probability of matching with someone of lesser quality, for example lower education, depends on the offer arrival rate, the proportion of others with higher education in the marriage market, the probability of divorce, the personal discount rate, and the expected life-time discounted values of marrying a highly educated person versus staying single or marrying a less educated person.

Theories of search in the marriage market and assortative mating take optimal age at couple formation as exogenous. For example, Bergstrom and Lam (1989) and Bergstrom (1997) assume that men prefer to marry a woman three years younger and they exploit the large year to year variation in Swedish fertility rates for empirical estimation of their model.[2] However, empirical results show that women postpone motherhood until after finishing education, e.g. for Germany, Hans-Peter Blossfeld and Johannes Huinink (1991) show that the probability of marrying or having a birth is very low for women who are students. Similar results are found for Britain, Germany, the Netherlands, and Sweden in a cross-country analysis on the role of education in postponement of maternity (Siv Gustafsson, Eiko Kenjoh and Cecile Wetzels, 2002a).

It seems reasonable to think of optimal age at union formation and optimal age at first birth as the outcome of a plan for investments in human capital and career planning (see Siv Gustafsson, 2001). With this approach it becomes important to study consequences for lifetime earnings of different timing of first birth, as is theorized in Alessandro Cigno (1991, chapter 8) and Siv Gustafsson and Cecile Wetzels (2000). One can think of optimal age at first birth as a financial constraint. Seeing this decision from a man's point of view, career planning and ability to provide financially for a family would not give different results for optimal timing. For a woman, who in most cases has to carry most of the time costs of children, the career planning motive can lead her to postpone first birth beyond the point that would suit a husband who is two years older and more financially secure. For a woman it may be optimal to delay motherhood until her opportunity costs of childcare in terms of her career have decreased, leading her to first complete her education and establish herself on the job market. Formally, timing of first birth depends on the opportunity cost of time, plus the foregone human capital cost. The opportunity cost of time consists of wage multiplied by periods not worked in the labor market due to childcare requirements. The capital cost consists of human capital investments foregone multiplied by the forgone returns to human capital investments due to the child's presence. The optimal timing then maximizes lifetime earnings or equivalently minimizes the opportunity cost plus the capital cost (Cigno, 1991, ch. 8; Gustafsson, 2001).

The time costs of marriage, even if not zero, are likely to be much smaller than the time costs of caring for a small child. Due to the availability of reliable contraception the two decisions can be separated and the explanatory variables can have different effects on timing of couple formation and timing of first birth. We therefore develop the analysis as two separate decisions.

3. DESCRIPTIVE COUNTRY COMPARISIONS

We use several waves from the British Household Panel Survey (BHPS) for the years 1991-1998 for Britain (Marcia Taylor 1999) and the Household Market and Non-Market Activities Survey (HUS) covering the years 1984-1998 (Anders Klevmarken and Paul Olovsson, 1984), which is a similar household panel survey for Sweden.

Our analysis is performed on the select sample of couples who had at least one child by 1998, the woman having been born between 1930 and 1979. Our sample makes use of information on both husband and wife. We treat unmarried cohabitation as equivalent to marriage. The data sets provide information on year of birth and education completed by both husband and wife. The data also provide complete fertility history and information as to when the couples moved in together (collected in waves 2 and 8 for the British data and using the full panel for the HUS). Women or men for whom we could not match the natural father or mother of the first child, or with other missing values, were discarded. Our sample consists of 3,072 couples (1,960 cases for Britain and 1,112 for Sweden).[3]

Education is a key variable. In our data we know the highest education level achieved by the individual. The philosophy behind making educational levels comparable across countries has been to determine the level of education corresponding to the US 'high school' and call that medium education, whereas less education than what corresponds to 'US high school' is called low education and more than 'high school' is called a high level of education. Implementing this rule we defined medium education level as that normally taking 12-14 years of fulltime study. We use the average time it takes to achieve the education level given in the data to determine whether an education is high, medium or low. (The education variable was developed for earlier cross-country comparative work by Gustafsson and co-authors, see Wetzels (2001) and Kenjoh (2004) for further details on this variable).

In Table 11.1 we compare the mean age at the life events of women in couples. Swedish women are on average older at finishing education and union formation than their British counterparts but younger at first birth for a given education level: British couples, where both husband and wife have higher education, while younger at couple formation are almost two years older at the birth of a first child. Looking at the age differences between partners, women in both countries form unions with partners 2 to 3 years older than themselves with the exception of highly educated Swedish women married to less educated men who are 3.6 years older than themselves.

Table 11.1 also demonstrates that there is educational assortative mating in both countries. The proportions are similar: both countries have 59% of couples with the same levels of education, followed by a higher level of husband's education (29% for Britain and 28% for Sweden), and lastly a higher level of wife's education (12% for Britain and 13% for Sweden). Among couples with the same educational levels, couples in which both have low levels take the biggest share in both countries.

Figure 11.1 shows the Kaplan-Meier estimates for the three life events: age at finishing education, at union, and at first birth for each country by gender. In our data, all individuals finish education, form a union and have a child, so the survival function for not yet having these events goes to zero. Parenthood occurs later among men than women and translates in such a way that at age 25 about 60-70 per cent of the men are not yet fathers as compared to close to 30-50 per cent of the women. Also we notice marked cross-national differences in the gap between age at finishing education and union formation, the gap in the incidence being wider among British men. The duration between union and first birth is shorter for Swedish couples, about 2 years on average, whereas it is about 3 years on average for British couples. Some Swedish husbands finish their education after couple formation and having their first child. The curve for finishing education crosses the other two curves for Swedish husbands at about age 30.

Table 11.1. Women's mean age at life events by education

	Mean age at			**Age difference**		
	Finishing education	Couple formation	First Birth	between spouses	Number of observations	Percent
A. Britain						
Education Equal						
HH	21.9	24.5	29.6	1.7	88	4.5
MM	19.1	22.6	26.3	2.6	222	11.3
LL	15.8	21.3	23.9	2.7	846	43.2
Total					1156	59.0
Husband higher						
HL	16.2	23.1	26.9	2.5	73	3.7
HM	20.1	24.2	28.3	1.8	98	5.0
ML	16.2	21.9	25.1	2.2	391	19.9
Total					562	28.7
Wife Higher						
MH	22.0	23.2	27.5	1.9	40	2.0
LH	21.2	24.3	27.7	1.3	15	0.8
LM	18.1	22.1	24.8	2.4	187	9.5
Total					242	12.3
Overall Britain	17.1	22.1	25.2	2.4	1960	
B. Sweden						
Education Equal						
HH	23.5	25.6	27.8	1.9	103	9.3
MM	20.1	22.9	25.5	2.6	56	5.0
LL	16.6	23.2	23.5	3.0	493	44.3
Total					652	58.6
Husband Higher						
HL	17.7	24.6	24.8	2.3	103	9.3
HM	20.6	22.6	24.9	2.6	49	4.4
ML	17.5	23.4	23.8	2.0	160	14.4
Total					312	28.1
Wife Higher						
MH	21.9	25.9	27.2	0.9	36	3.2
LH	21.9	25.0	25.7	3.6	35	3.1
LM	19.9	22.7	23.8	3.0	77	6.9
Total					148	13.3
Overall Sweden	18.4	23.6	24.4	2.6	1112	
Overall both countries	17.6	22.6	24.9	2.5	3072	

H = education level high, M = medium, L = low.
HH = education levels of both husband and wife are high. Other educational sorting defined analogously for husband-wife educational combinations.
Source: Own computations based on the BHPS 1991-1998 and HUS 1984-1998.

Figure 11.1. Britain and Sweden: Men and women in couples, Kaplan-Meier estimates survival functions

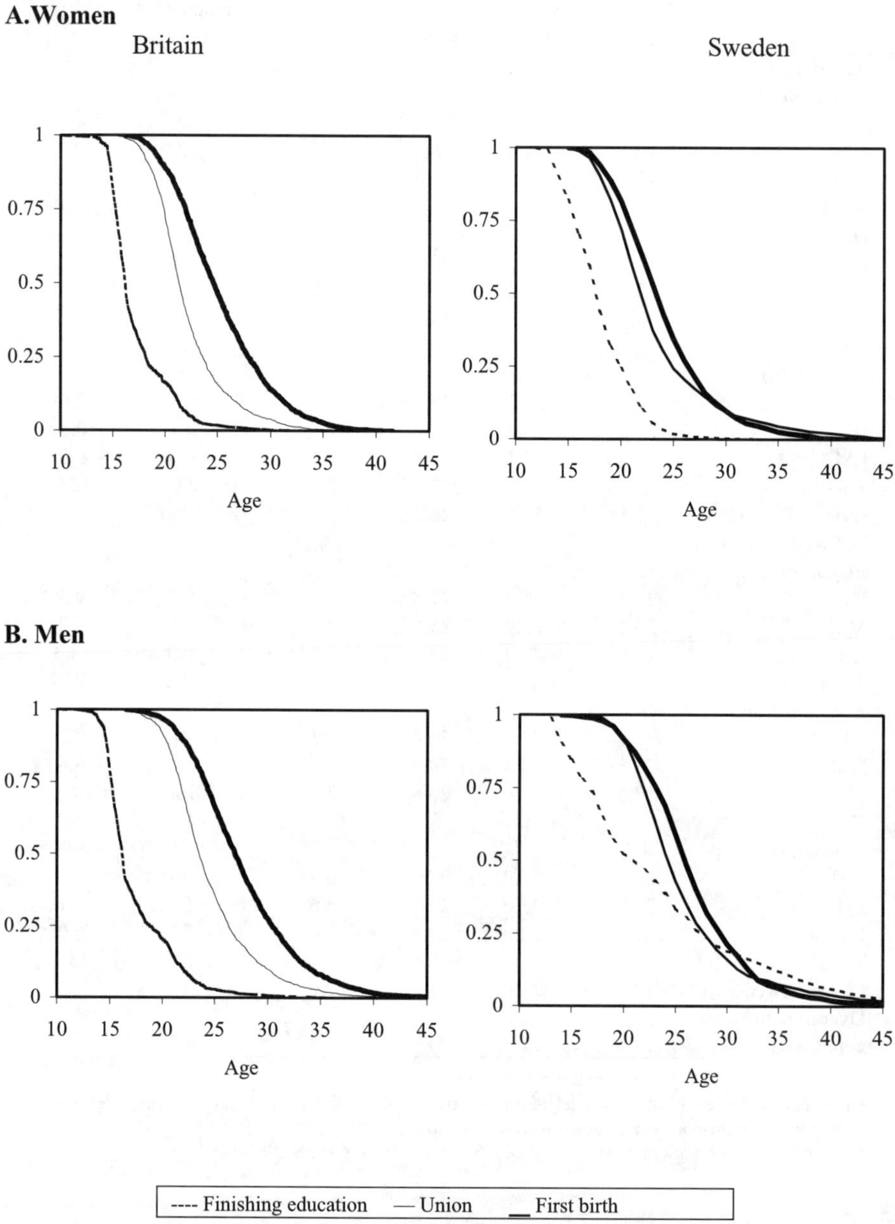

Source: Own computations based on the BHPS 1991-1998 and HUS 1984-1998

Table 11.2. The change in marital sorting by cohort

	A. Britain		Born in				B. Sweden		Born in			
	1930s	1940s	1950s	1960s	1970s	All cohorts	1930s	1940s	1950s	1960s	1970s	All cohorts
Education equal												
HH	1	25	29	33	0	88	8	47	36	12	0	103
MM	21	55	64	77	5	222	3	17	26	10	0	56
LL	148	247	203	221	27	846	107	189	121	69	7	493
Percent	66.1	61.6	53.6	57.8			65.6	60.5	53.8	56.5		
Husband higher												
HL	8	20	24	20	1	73	22	49	24	7	1	103
HM	10	18	33	35	2	98	4	15	20	9	1	49
ML	42	109	133	101	6	391	22	61	53	22	2	160
Percent	23.3	27.7	34.4	27.2			26.7	29.9	25.5	23.6		
Wife higher												
MH	1	10	20	8	1	40	3	14	12	7	0	36
LH	1	3	7	4	0	15	3	8	18	6	0	35
LM	25	44	39	74	5	187	8	18	30	19	2	77
Percent	10.5	10.7	12	15			7.8	9.6	17.6	19.9		
Total observations	257	531	552	573	47	1960	180	418	340	161	13	1112
Mean age difference	1.4	2.2	2.4	3.1	3.2	2.4	1.3	2.5	2.8	3.6	5.5	2.6

The percentage educational column distribution for persons born in the 1970s is not shown because of too few observations.
Source: Own computations based on the BHPS 1991-1998 and HUS 1984-1998.

Table 11.2 presents the distribution by cohorts of couples in the marriage market. The pattern of marital sorting changes over cohorts. Assortative mating is predominant for all cohorts but the proportion of both men and women with medium or higher education increases for younger cohorts. The number of men who marry women with lower education than themselves is at maximum for men born in the 1950s for Britain and for the cohorts born in the 1940s in Sweden. The age difference between spouses is slightly higher among Swedish couples, with men being older than women. The age differential rises from a little more than a year in the oldest cohort to more than 3 years among cohorts born in the 1960s. This increasing age differential between husband and wife is rather counterintuitive because one would think that spouses would become more similar to each other over time as women's life chances increase and men can share their breadwinning obligations with their wives.

4. EMPIRICAL STRATEGY

The decision about whom and when to marry is a simultaneous decision. Different chapters in Blossfeld and Timm (2003) struggle with the simultaneity of these decisions. Nan Dirk De Graaf, Wilma Smeenk, Wout Ultee and Andreas Timm (2003) use a first stage duration analysis and a second stage multinominal logit on who marries whom. We use a two step method inspired by Joris Ghysels (2003) who built his model based on Richard Blundell and Richard Smith (1994).[4]

The first step consists of estimating a mating function for the choice of the spouse, using a multinomial logit model. The purpose is to sort males and females into couples by predicting the level of education of the husband given the level of education of the woman, her individual socio-economic characteristics, and marriage market variables.

The multinomial logit model provides a set of probabilities for the j choices (marrying a high, medium, or low education person) for a decision-maker with characteristic X_i (William Greene 2003, p. 721).

$$Prob(Y_i = j) = \frac{e^{\beta_j' X_i}}{\sum_k^j e^{\beta_k' X_i}}, \quad for\ j = High, Medium, Low \tag{1}$$

This expression can be normalized by setting $\beta_1 = 0$ and rewriting it as:

$$Prob(Y_i = j \mid X_i) = \frac{e^{\beta_j' X_i}}{1+\sum_k^j e^{\beta_k' X_i}}, \quad for\ j = High,\ Medium \tag{2}$$

For positive fitted β values the probability of marrying a man of high or medium education (relative to a man of low education) increases and for negative fitted β values the probability of a certain match decreases. The estimates of the multinominal logit result in three predicted probabilities for each woman: her probabilities of marrying a man with high, medium or low education. Since we need to have one and only one predicted education level for each woman's husband, we use that prediction which has the highest probability.

The second stage of our empirical analysis consists of estimating separately hazard-rate models of the durations from age 13 to union formation and from union formation to first birth. We use parametric duration Weibull models and, together with other variables, we use the predicted educational combinations from step one as explanatory variables [5]. The rate of entry into a union or first birth is defined as:

$$h(t) = \lim_{\Delta \to 0} \frac{\text{Prob}(t \leq T \leq t+\Delta | T \geq t)}{\Delta} = \lim_{\Delta \to 0} \frac{F(t+\Delta) - F(t)}{\Delta S(t)} = \frac{f(t)}{S(t)} \qquad (3)$$

where T is a random variable and t is a realization of T. T has a continuous probability distribution f(t). The cumulative probability distribution is F(t) (Greene 2003, p. 792). The hazard rate h(t) without any covariates can be estimated by the Kaplan-Meier product limit estimator, as shown in Figure 1 above the survival function S(t) for the three life events.

A parametric duration model, different from the nonparametric Cox proportional model, assumes a particular functional form for f(t) and S(t) and therefore for the hazard function h(t). The probability of someone forming a union or having a first birth, given that it has not happened yet, is likely to increase sharply with age since we start at age 13. We therefore adopt a Weibull distribution, which allows for such a shape. The hazard function for the Weibull model takes the form:

$$h(t) = p(\lambda t^{p-1})e^{-(\lambda t^{p})}, \quad \text{where } \lambda = e^{X\beta} \qquad (4)$$

and λ and p– the duration dependence variable–are parameters to be estimated. Since we only use observations of individuals who experienced both events, union formation and first birth, our coefficients are interpreted as durations and are not contaminated by the probability of experiencing the event.

Individual differences in the hazard functions are characterized partly by the observed explanatory variables x_i and in part by the unobserved characteristics of the individual. In addition to the observed heterogeneity captured by our included variables the relationship between decisions regarding timing of union formation and first birth may also be affected by unobserved heterogeneity. James Heckman and James Walker (1990) distinguish between two different types of unobservables: those known to the interviewed person in the survey and unknown to the analyst, and those unknown to both. If unobservable characteristics are correlated with the observables, then not including an estimate of the unobservables will lead to incorrect inference regarding the impact of observables on the timing of events and to problems of identification.

There are a number of ways of extending duration models to account for heterogeneity. A direct approach is to model heterogeneity in the parametric model by defining the survival function conditioned on the individual specific effects, adding to this model a term for the unobserved heterogeneity. This is the same principle as incorporating a disturbance term in a regression model. We use a

Gamma distribution for the unobserved heterogeneity. Thus the model can be rewritten as:

$$h(t) = p(\lambda t^{p-1})[S(t)]^{\theta} \quad (5)$$

where θ is a parameter for unobserved heterogeneity, with $\theta = 0$ being the case of no unobserved heterogeneity.

Although we may have solved some of the econometric mistakes by our choice of a two step model and the use of the parametric Weibull model that controls for unobserved heterogeneity, we have probably at least two sources of possible bias. First, the way that we selected our sample may introduce a selection bias. (We had used a selected sample so that we could get spouse information, see also Marco Francesconi, 2002, and Ghazala Naz, Øivind Anti Nilsen and Steinar Vagstad, 2005). In our case, the larger the differences in age at union formation and age at maternity for cases included in our study, and those not included, the larger is the potential selection bias. In the appendix to this chapter, we show how age at first birth behaves when using all women rather than only women for whom we know the husband's characteristics. Table A1 shows that for women in couples it hardly makes a difference whether we know the husband's education and time at couple formation or not. For all women, including those who are single when giving birth, there is a difference. Age at maternity is lower for women who are single when having their first birth. The difference is very small for Sweden but larger for Britain, where teenage pregnancies are more common.

Another reason for biased estimates is that if we do not account for all variables likely to influence the decisions, there may be an omitted variable bias. Using a sample consisting only of women in couples allows using information about the husband, which if not used in the estimations may have resulted in an omitted variables bias. The result is that one must choose which bias is more acceptable.

5. THE MATING FUNCTION

The results of the multinominal logits for women's choice of the education level of their husbands are given in Table 11.3 for Britain and Table 11.4 for Sweden. The education level of the woman, her social background, and marriage market conditions are used as explanatory variables to predict the education level of her husband. We include the woman's education level-high or medium-with low education as the comparison group.

The number of years spent in fulltime education is entered as an additional variable. The latter variable is correlated with the level of education because it takes more years to achieve a high level of education than a low level, but the correlation is not perfect since there is a variation of the number of years in school within an educational level. Table 11.3 shows that relative to women of low education British women of medium education are 22 times more likely to marry a highly educated man (relative to a man of low education). The relative risk ratios in Tables 11.3 and 11.4 show double comparisons. Also, if given the educational level she spent more years in school, her chances of marrying a high or medium educated man, other things equal, increase, because there are statistically significant and positive relative risk ratios for duration in school in Table 11.3.

Table 11.3. Britain: Multinomial logit models of choice of spouse for women

	High		Medium	
	RRR	z	RRR	z
High education [a)]	14.04	1.21	0.27	-0.60
Medium education	22.70	2.19	2.57	1.05
Duration in school *	1.20	5.22	1.14	4.56
Born in 1930s [b)]	0.76	-0.88	0.82	-1.04
Born in 1940s	0.91	-0.40	1.13	0.84
Born in 1950s	1.29	1.11	1.55	2.84
Born in 1970s	0.74	-0.46	0.76	-0.75
High social class [c)]	2.13	4.20	1.37	2.54
Missing social class	0.66	-0.93	0.84	-0.71
Foreign descent or non white [d)]	0.71	-1.09	1.13	0.68
Missing race	0.95	-0.18	0.80	-1.28
Mother worked at age 14 [e)]	1.37	1.77	1.23	1.84
Mother work information missing	3.89	2.86	1.18	0.49
Marriage opportunities for high educated **	1.32	0.32	1.21	0.21
Marriage opportunities for medium educated* *	1.72	0.48	0.87	-0.11
Marriage opportunities for low educated **	5.90	1.44	8.48	1.60
Medium educ. by marriage oppor. for high educated	0.53	-0.69	0.90	-0.10
Low educ. by marriage oppor. for high educated	1.49	0.44	1.09	0.09
Medium educ. by marriage oppor. for medium educated	1.18	0.14	1.25	0.18
Low educ. by marriage oppor. for medium educated	0.88	-0.11	1.45	0.30
Medium educ. by marriage oppor. for low educated	0.27	-0.98	0.15	-1.35
Low educ. by marriage oppor. for low educated	0.68	-0.29	0.17	-1.33
Number of observations				1960
Log Likelihood				-1646.49
LR Chi square (44)				503.07
Likelihood ratio index				13.25%
Percentage of overall correct predictions				60.1%
Observed frequency		259		653
Predicted frequency		152		378
Average predicted probability		0.13		0.33

1. Outcome being married to a low educated man is the comparison group
2. Reference categories for the explanatory variables: a) Low education; b) Born in 1960s; c) Low social class; d) Originally from the country; e) Mother was home at age 14
3. * Duration in school is duration from age 13 to finishing school
4. ** (Number of high (or medium or low) educated men in period t: (M_t)/ Number of high (or medium or low) educated women in period t+2: (F_t +2))
5. ∇ is a joint significance at 95% of significance level with a likelihood ratio test

Source: Own computations based on the BHPS 1991-1998.

Table 11.4. Sweden: Multinomial logit models of choice of spouse for women

	High		Medium	
	RRR	z	RRR	z
High education [a)]	2.65	1.31	1.86	0.77
Medium education	0.75	-0.43	1.41	0.55
Duration in school *	1.31	6.38	1.16	3.77
Born in 1930s [b)]	2.60	2.17	0.86	-0.40
Born in 1940s	3.00	2.42	1.34	0.76
Born in 1950s	1.58	1.52	1.14	0.52
Born in 1970s	0.89	-0.13	0.42	-1.05
High social class [c)]	2.04	3.25	1.43	1.66
Missing social class	0.47	-0.70	1.06	0.09
Foreign descent [d)]	1.25	0.83	1.38	1.36
Missing decent	4.84	0.88		
Mother worked at age 14 [e)]	1.19	0.96	0.89	-0.69
Mother work information missing	0.88	-0.10	0.00	-23.12
Marriage opportunities for high educated **	1.15	0.79	0.90	-0.5
Marriage opportunities for medium educated* *	0.68	-0.58	1.00	0
Marriage opportunities for low educated **	1.21	0.83	1.13	0.51
Medium educ. by marriage oppor. for high educated	1.09	0.41	1.36	1.29
Low educ. by marriage oppor. for high educated	0.83	-0.98	1.19	0.82
Medium educ. by marriage oppor. for medium educated	1.28	0.29	0.66	-0.45
Low educ. by marriage oppor. for medium educated	1.49	0.54	1.05	0.06
Medium educ. by marriage oppor. for low educated	0.98	-0.08	1.04	0.14
Low educ. by marriage oppor. for low educated	0.83	-0.70	0.95	-0.20
Number of observations				1112
Log Likelihood				977.98
LR Chi square (44)				279.78
Likelihood ratio index				12.51%
Percentage of overall correct predictions				61.5%
Observed frequency		255		252
Predicted frequency		205		28
Average predicted probability		0.23		0.23

Source: Own computations based on the BHPS 1991-1998.

We control for woman's birth cohort because, as shown in Table 11.2 above, the educational level of both men and women has increased over time. To identify the social background of the women we use three variables: a dummy variable for 'mother worked' when the respondent was 14 for Britain and 16 for Sweden, measures of parents' social class, and a dummy for foreign origin. For Britain we also include a dummy variable for native and non-white.[6] To measure social class in Britain, we used the parent's job grading of the Goldthorpe-Hope (GH) Scale obtained directly from waves 1 and 8 of the BHPS. This measure is based on rank values that vary from 1 to 124 and a scale value that goes from 17.52 to 82.05. The value of the scale is based on information about detailed occupation classification together with detailed breakdown of the prestige of an occupation. If the GH scale is available for both parents we take the mean value, but if it is only available for one of the parents we use it as it is. We construct three groups by dividing the scale into parts at the 33rd percentile (low social class), between the 33rd and 66th percentile (medium), and from the 67th percentile and up (high social class).

A dummy variable is created if social class is missing. In the Swedish case, the social class variable is constructed by combining the highest level of schooling of the respondent's father with his occupation when the respondent was aged less than 16. The results in Tables 11.3 and 11.4 show that being from a high social class increases the probability of marrying a highly educated man, other things being equal, in both Britain and Sweden. Foreign descent or race, other things being equal, has no influence on the probability of marrying a man with medium or high education.

We created marriage opportunity indicators as sex ratios per one-year cohort and each education level–high, medium, low–to control for changes in the distribution of educational attainment over time and across cohorts for both sexes. These variables control for the availability of marriage candidates with a given educational level. In constructing this index a man of cohort t is assumed to prefer marriage to a woman of cohort $t + 2$ who has the same level of education as he. The sex ratios have been computed as:

$$\frac{M_t^s}{F_{t+2}^s} \tag{6}$$

where s = high, medium or low and t = cohort and M is the number of males and F the number of females. Thus the marriage opportunity variables are constructed for each level of education and by single years of birth cohort. We also included interactions of women's own education and the marriage market variables. The marriage market variables and those interacted with woman's own education are not significant, except for one: when marriage market opportunities are favorable for low education women in Britain they are more likely to marry a man who has high or medium education.

We used the estimated models in Tables 11.3 and 11.4 to predict the probabilities of being in each of the outcomes of the dependent variable: marrying a spouse of high, medium or low education. For each individual, three predicted probabilities are obtained. Because we need one predicted value for each couple, we chose the highest one of these three probabilities.

The last row of Tables 11.3 and 11.4 respectively compare observed and predicted frequencies of husband's education level. This average predicted probability, which is computed across all women, shows proportions of husbands with high, medium and low education that are very close to what is shown in Table 11.1 above.

Table 11.5 shows the results using the rule that assigns the maximum of the three probabilities of the education of each woman's husband. The results of the predictions are broken down by the nine educational groupings used in the second step of our estimations. It is clear from Table 11.5 that our model overpredicts assortative mating (homogamy) substantially: we predict 88% and 83% of homogamous marriages respectively for Britain and Sweden whereas the observed proportion of homogamous marriages was only 59% in both countries, as seen from Table 11.1 above.

The case where both partners have low education is particularly, overpredicted. In contrast, the number of cases where the husband has higher education than his wife, is severely underpredicted in both countries. According to Table 11.1, in 28 percent of the couples in both countries the husband is more educated than the wife, but according to Table 11.5 only 3 to 4 percent are predicted to be in this situation.

Table 11.5. Predicted versus observed educational levels

	Britain			**Sweden**		
	Actual	Predicted	pred.%	Actual	Predicted	pred.%
Education equal						
HH	88	139	7.1	103	160	14.4
MM	222	327	16.7	56	23	2.1
LL	846	1 260	64.3	493	740	66.6
Total	1 156	1 726	88.1	652	923	83.0
Husband higher						
HL	73	0	0.0	103	12	1.1
HM	98	13	0.7	49	33	3.0
ML	391	47	2.4	160	4	0.7
Total	562	60	3.1	312	49	4.4
Wife higher						
MH	40	4	0.2	36	1	0.1
LH	15	0	0.0	35	13	1.2
LM	187	170	8.7	77	126	11.3
Total	242	174	8.9	148	140	12.6
Total number	1960		100.0	1112		100.0

Source: Own computations based on the BHPS 1991-1998.

6. DURATIONS TO COUPLE FORMATION AND FIRST BIRTH

The second step of our analysis are the two Weibull hazard models with individual unobserved heterogeneity and predicted intra-couple education group, based on the mating function estimated in step 1. The results of the two duration estimations are presented in Table 11.6.

The dependent variables are the durations from age 13 to union formation, and the duration between union formation and first birth. Union formation is measured as the time at which the couple moved in together. For the BHPS, the date of union is collected both in the second wave (1992) and the eighth wave (1998). The data are collected by asking the date of first cohabitation, the end of cohabitation, and date(s) of marriage(s)/divorces. We use the date of moving together of that man with whom the woman lived when her first child was born. Also the family compositions are consistently given in the entire panel. In the BHPS, first birth questions are asked both in the second and eighth waves. The questions were put to all respondents aged 16 and over for both males and females. Furthermore, first-born children are given identification numbers that makes it possible to trace both their parents. Therefore, we can check whether the husband is the biological father of the child. In the HUS, the current marital status and time when the current partners moved in together are given in all the waves. In the HUS, the first birth question comes in the first 2 waves and the last 3 waves in the non-response and supplementary samples.[7] The family composition data allows one to relate biological fathers to their children.

In the duration analysis we work with both fixed and time varying variables. The fixed variables include the nine educational groups of predicted husband's education for a given wife's education, estimated by our first step presented above.[8] Further, we use the same fixed social background variables as in the mating function and birth year splines to control for birth cohort.

We have merged the British and Swedish data in order to be able to compare the duration to couple formation and to first birth between the two countries, *ceteris paribus,* and include a dummy for 'Sweden'. Another fixed variable is the unemployment rate when the woman was 20 years old. Total unemployment rate at age 20 for each one-year birth cohort is obtained from the ILO yearbook of labor statistics and OECD historical statistics for both countries. For example, if a woman was born in 1931, we use the unemployment rate for 1951.[9] Whereas labor market situation, as measured by unemployment rate, may produce longer durations to couple formation and first birth, we did not include this variable in the mating function for we think that it is unlikely to affect the choice of partners. The unemployment rate at age 20 has a strongly significant, but rather small, negative effect on the duration to couple formation of 6 percent, and no significant effect on the duration to first birth. This indicates that people may wait longer before moving in together if labor market conditions are bad, but they do not wait longer before they have their first child.

The rest of the explanatory variables in Table 11.6 are time-varying: they increase for every period that the person is still at risk, i.e. has not yet experienced the event being explained. Note that a period is a year in the duration to couple formation, but months are recomputed to fractions of a year, whereas in the duration from union formation to first birth a period equals one month.

If an estimated coefficient in Table 11.6 is less than one that an event occurs given that it has not yet occurred, a lower probability in comparison to the reference group is the case and a coefficient larger than one means a higher probability. Since everyone in our sample experiences the events of couple formation and first birth the estimated coefficients are also measures of durations. The duration until an event occurs is the inverse of the probability that it occurs. Therefore, a lower probability means a longer duration and a higher probability means a shorter duration.

For the educational groupings the case of both husband and wife having low education (LL) is the reference category. These couples are the ones who move in together earlier than couples of other educational groups, because all the other educational groups have estimated coefficients below 1. Our estimates in Table 11.6 therefore show the expected duration from age 13 to union formation by educational groups. The estimates for the educational groups are not very precise, i.e. the z-values are smaller than 2 for positive effects, or larger than –2 for negative effects.

The time varying variable 'being in school' has a strong negative effect both on couple formation and on having the first birth once the union is formed.

The country comparison is quite interesting. It shows that, other things being equal, relative to their British counterparts Swedish couples are older when they move in together. This shows up in a probability less than one i.e. 0.73 in Table 11.6, which is statistically strongly significant. In contrast, once a Swedish couple has been formed, they have their first birth sooner. The duration from couple formation to first birth is shorter or equivalently the probability of having a first birth is higher, 1.63 and strongly significant.

The objective behind the Swedish family policies is to make it easier for women to combine education, work, and family life. This is supported by extended paid and protected parental leaves and an extensive system of subsidized early childhood education and care. Parental leaves including maternity leave amount to 18 months. The first 12 months of leave is paid at 80% of wages up to a certain maximum, while one month for the father and one month for the mother is compensated by 90% of the salary of the parent who is on leave. Another 3 months are paid at a low flat rate and the last 3 months are unpaid. But the most child-friendly aspect of Swedish parental leave policies is the great degree of flexibility. The national social security board keeps the account on line. Parents can check electronically how many days they have been using and how many days are left. Parents can divide their total parental leave time as they want, ranging from both parents staying at home half the time, to one or the other parent fulltime at home.

They can also choose to be paid only e.g. 75 percent of the entitled payment, in which case they get more days (Gustafsson and Kenjoh 2004). By contrast, British family policies are less generous: every mother is entitled to 18 weeks of maternity leave, and those mothers who worked continuously for at least a year before having the child are entitled to an additional 29 weeks of leave. The first 6 weeks of leave are paid at 90% of wages and another 12 weeks at a low flat rate. After the maternity leave either parent can take a parental leave that is unpaid but job-protected and can last up to 13 weeks.

Table 11.7 shows the predictions made using the models in Table 11.6.[10] Comparisons of the actual to the predicted durations show that the values fairly well replicate the main features of the data for the durations starting from age 13 but slightly overestimate the durations after the end of education to each of the events. The actual durations are not shown in Table 11.6, but are implicit in Table 11.1 and Figure 11.1. Women form their union about 5 years after the end of education in both countries, but postpone motherhood 3 more years in Britain. Figure 11.1 and the results of Table 11.6 show that birth occurs more quickly in Sweden once the couple has been formed. Interestingly, for women marrying a person with lower education than themselves, the duration to union from age 13 is shorter, though motherhood takes much longer to occur. Lesser educated women wait longer after finishing education than more educated women. The educational system can be seen as a marriage market with students searching among other students for a mate, as pointed out, among others, by Blossfeld and Timm (2003). However, the duration from union to birth is somewhat longer for women born in the 1950s and 1960s as compared to women born in the 1930s and 1940s, but the difference is less than a year on average. The results of Tables 11.6 and 11.7 show that education of both spouses matters. The longest duration from age 13 to birth is if both spouses have high education, and the shortest if both spouses have low education.

Table 11.6. Duration analysis with Weibull model with individual unobserved heterogeneity and predicted education group

	Duration from woman's age 13 To union in years		Duration from union to first birth in months	
	Coefficient	Z	Coefficient	Z
Log current age	0.00	-52.8	1.81	2.10
Education equal: HH [(a)]	0.70	-1.72	0.56	-2.66
MM	0.72	-1.89	0.93	- 0.39
Husband higher: HL	0.77	-0.88	0.71	-1.07
HM	0.73	-1.33	0.60	-2.03
ML	0.74	-1.95	0.65	-2.63
Wife higher: MH	0.86	-0.28	0.77	-0.48
LH	0.52	-1.75	0.82	-0.50
LM	0.91	-0.53	0.94	-0.35
Being in school	0.14	-10.43	0.84	-2.39
1-2 years after school [b)]	0.24	-7.93	0.22	-11.88
3-4 years after school	0.80	-3.69	1.26	3.14
5-6 years after school	0.77	-4.39	0.93	-1.11
7-8 years after school	1.01	0.18	1.00	0.03
9-10 years after school	1.44	4.06	0.95	-0.64
11-12 years after school	1.99	5.7	0.86	-1.51
>12 years after school	5.68	13.81	1.21	1.76
High social class [c)]	0.84	-3.72	0.99	-0.22
Missing social class	0.91	-1.05	1.25	2.18
Foreign descent [d)]	0.79	-3.85	1.34	4.37
Missing race	1.10	1.34	1.25	3.03
Mother worked at age 14 [e)]	0.97	-0.73	1.02	0.43
Mother work information missing	0.82	-1.63	0.87	-1.00
Unemp. rate when the woman was 20	0.94	-5.36	1.01	0.95
Sweden [f)]	0.73	-6.48	1.63	8.05
Birth years splines: From 1930 to 1939	1.03	2.42	1.01	0.68
From 1940 to 1949	0.99	-0.71	0.98	-0.86
From 1950 to 1959	1.00	0.24	0.98	-1.34
From 1960 to 1969	1.06	3.35	1.05	2.74
From 1970 to 1979	1.17	3.31	1.10	1.81
Weibull shape parameter	3.45	194.44	0.00	-0.16
Unobserved heterogeneity	-17.66		-2.60	-5.92
Number of observations		3072		3072
Time at risk		29649		102435
Log Likelihood		945.50		-4812.58
Likelihood Ratio Chi square statistics				410.34
with degrees of freedom (39)		5752.75		

Reference categories for the explanatory variables: a) LL; b) Still in school; c) Low social class; d) Originally from the country; e) Mother was home at age 14; f) Britain Also included in the model are marriage market opportunity variables and their interaction with education.

Source: Own computations based on the BHPS 1991-1998 and HUS 1984-1998.

However, a highly educated woman who marries a man of low education has her baby earlier than if she marries a highly educated man. In general, it is the case that the higher the education of one of the spouses, given the other spouse's education, the longer the duration to first birth.

Moreover, in Table 11.7 we notice cohort effects in the distribution of the durations. Unions do occur earlier after finishing education for the youngest cohorts. The last two rows of Table 11.7 show the country differences, other things being equal. Swedish women enter union later but have their first birth earlier. Swedish women stay in school longer (Table 11.1), but once they finish school and form a union, they are quicker to start a family. Generous family policies and good childcare facilities may have caused this outcome: pronatalist policies may have reached their goal. Although the Swedish policies have been motivated by equal opportunities for women and men, they are intrinsically pronatalist.

Table 11.7. Predicted mean durations in years for married women born 1930-1979 in Britain and Sweden

	Predicted mean duration from				
	Women's age 13 to birth (1)	Women's age 13 to union (2)	Union to birth (3)	Woman's end of education to union (4)	Woman's end of education to birth (5)
Equal					
HH	16.1	12.9	3.7	3.3	6.5
MM	14.1	10.5	3.2	3.6	7.2
LL	11.6	9.7	2.5	6.6	8.5
Husband higher					
HL	14.8	13.9	2.2	5.3	6.2
HM	16.1	12.5	3.4	3.1	6.7
ML	14.9	11.0	4.2	4.9	8.8
Wife higher					
MH	15.2	12.3	3.1	4.6	7.5
LH	14.5	13.2	2.8	6.7	8
LM	12.0	9.4	2.8	4.5	7.1
By cohorts					
Born in 1930s	12.9	11.2	2.3	7.8	9.5
Born in 1940s	12.3	11.0	2.4	6.5	7.8
Born in 1950s	13.0	10.1	3.1	4.9	7.8
Born in 1960s	12.2	9.0	3.1	4.2	7.4
Born in 1970s	8.5	6.4	2.1	2.4	4.5
Britain (N = 1960)	12.8	9.5	3.1	5.4	8.7
Sweden (N = 1112)	12.0	11.5	2.2	6.1	6.6
Overall mean (N = 3072)	12.5	10.2	2.8	5.6	7.9

1. (1)-(3) were predicted directly from the three different models, but (4) and (5) were calculated by taking the predictions in (1) and (2) and subtracting the actual duration from age 13 to end of education.

2. Chi square tests are performed between the observed and expected frequencies using intervals of durations. The tests signal a significant difference between the two but of course the test is very sensitive to the choice of the number of intervals and to whether or not including the extremes.

Source: Own computations based on the BHPS 1991-1998 and HUS 1984-1998.

7. CONCLUSIONS

Both in Sweden and in Britain there is positive assortative mating by education and 59% of the women in each country are married to a man with the same educational level. In our mating functions for the British and Swedish marriage markets respectively, the results of assortative mating by education are more pronounced in Britain than in Sweden, as shown by much larger and statistically significant relative risk ratios. Although we correctly predict the education level of the husband for 60 percent of our couples in both countries, our mating functions overpredict the same education level cases and underpredict the unequal education level cases.

The education level of both spouses, the duration of schooling, and a high level of unemployment at age 20 reduce the rates of transition into both union formation and first birth, or equivalently increase the duration. In particular, we notice a larger duration until each of the two events if both spouses have high education. The two events happen sooner if both spouses have low education. Yet, a highly educated woman married to a man of low education gives birth earlier than if she was married to a highly educated man, which indicates that education of each spouse matters. After the end of education, women wait more than 5 years to form their union, and wait 2-4 years more to have a child. In our duration analysis performed on merged data for Sweden and Britain we find that other things being equal Swedish couples form their union later than British couples, but once the union is formed they have their first birth sooner. This is in line with the generous family policies in Sweden that make it more affordable to have a child earlier. Also looking at the predictions made from the model the younger cohorts are more likely to form unions earlier but postpone childbearing, which is what one would expect given that contraceptives have become widely acceptable and more reliable.

Given that Sweden was a forerunner in accepting contraceptives and unmarried cohabitation, we expected that the country comparison might indicate earlier couple formation in Sweden. However, we do not find this. Perhaps this is an indication that the greater freedom was used to intensively search a sequence of more than one potential marriage candidate. Since we only analyze the couple that resulted in the first birth of thc woman, wc havc not rcscarched the possibility that a different and childless couple relation preceded the one we focus on.

ACKNOWLEDGEMENTS

This chapter was originally published in *Review of Economics of the Household*, 2005, vol. 3, no. 1, pp. 91-113. A very early and different paper, co-authored by Eiko Kenjoh, was presented at the Scholar seminar on Education and Postponement of Maternity, University of Amsterdam. We are thankful for comments from Michael Lindahl, Adriaan Kalwij, Andrey Launov and other seminar participants at the University of Groningen, the University of Lund and ESPE 2004. Further, we thank Eiko Kenjoh for giving us the country comparable education variable, which she constructed for earlier work (see Kenjoh, 2004).

NOTES

1 Countries included in the Hans-Peter Blossfeld and Andreas Timm (2003) are: West Germany, Flemish Belgium, France, the Netherlands, Italy, Spain, Great Britain, United States, Denmark, Sweden, Hungary, Slovenia and Israel.

2 Theodore Bergstrom and David Lam (1989) estimate this model on Swedish birth cohorts of men born from 1895 to 1942 and women born from 1898 to 1945. They assume, that the difference $a^*_m - a^*_f$ is 3 years, so that a man always wishes to be 3 years older than his wife. According to this assumption the deviation of the marriage age from the preferred marriage age of a male will depend on the availability of women three years younger. Because of period fluctuations in the total fertility rates the sex ratio M_t/F_{t+3} fluctuated in their study between 0.9 and 1.25.

3 For Britain, we started with 6079 women and 5593 men out of which 4052 women and 3236 men had first birth, 2120 were matched as couples; only for 1960 couples was the date of union known. For Sweden, we started with 3033 women and 2248 men out of which 2068 women and 1303 men had first birth, 1112 were matched as couples. In the econometric literature Robert Moffit (1984), James Heckman and James Walker (1990) and Hans Blomen and Adriaan Kalwij (2001) suggest solutions for the problem of selection bias. We acknowledge that we do not solve the problem of selection bias. We are focusing on durations including only couples who have experienced both events, which gives us a pure duration effect which is not contaminated by the effect of experiencing the event (Joseph Hotz et al., 1997).

4 However both Joris Ghysels (2003) and Richard Blundell and Richard Smith (1994), on whose work Ghysels built, estimate a linear model in their first step. The estimated values of the endogenous variable as well as the corresponding residuals serve as explanatory variables to the second step of the estimation process. Since our first step is multinomial logit estimated by maximum likelihood, we do not have any residuals to introduce in the second step of our estimation.

5 The reason we choose a parametric duration model rather than a nonparametric Cox proportional hazard model is that STATA provides an opportunity to estimate unobserved heterogeneity for parametric duration analysis but not for the Cox method.

6 The ethnicity variable in the BHPS is directly taken from the data set. The question is posed in such a way that the respondent self-classify himself or herself into the different ethnic grouping given (white, Black-Caribbean, Black-African, Black-other, Indian, Pakistani, Bangladeshi and Chinese). We aggregated this variable to distinguish only whether the person is of white race or not. In the Swedish case, the closest question to the ethnicity variable is a question asked about the citizenship of the parents of the respondent. We assigned the respondent to be of Swedish descent if both parents are Swedish citizens, and if either of the parents is a foreign citizen we assigned the respondent to be of foreign origin.

7 The collection of the HUS data started in 1984 with 1500 households. The panel was interviewed again in 1986 and 1988. A new wave of about 1000 households with a supplementary sample to increase sample size was collected in 1993. In this data collection those who had not responded in 1986 and 1988 were approached again. The last wave of the HUS panel was collected in 1998.

8 The coefficients of Table 11.4 do not change much if actual educational groups are used as explanatory variables instead of predicted educational groups.

9 Alicia Adsera (2003) shows that age-specific unemployment rates have a major impact on fertility rates. She used age-specific unemployment rates from late 1960s onwards, gender-specific and activity specific unemployment rates from 1960-1997, but these are not available for earlier cohorts.

10 Chi-square tests are performed to test whether the observed frequencies differ significantly from the expected frequencies. Frequencies were computed on different intervals of durations. The tests suggest very strong evidence against the null hypotheses.

APPENDIX

A. The construction of the education variable for Sweden:

Respondent's education categories as obtained from the HUS data set and assigned years of schooling.

Qualification obtained	Normal years of schooling
1. Did not complete elementary school	7
2. Elementary school, normally 6-8 years	8
3. Vocational training > 1 year beyond elementary school-leaving examination etc	9
4. Intermediate school-leaving examination, comprehensive school etc	9
5. Vocational training > 1 year after intermediate school-leaving examination etc	10
6. Higher school examination (technical/ three year gymnasium)	12
7. Education at least one year beyond higher school examination	14
8. College/university examination	16

Finally the years of study have been grouped as 16 high, 10 to 14 medium and 7 to 9: low.

B. The construction of the education variable for Britain:

Respondent's education categories as obtained from the BHPS data set and assigned years of schooling.

Qualification obtained	Normal years of schooling
1. No qualification	8
2. Apprenticeship	8
3. CSE Grade 2-5,Scot G	8
4. Commercial qualification, No O levels	9
5. GCE O levels or equivalent	11
6. GCE A levels	13
7. Nursing qualification	14
8. Other higher qualification	15
9. Teaching qualification	15
10. First degree	16
11. Higher degree	19

Finally the years of study have been grouped as 16 and 19 years to be high, 12 to 15 medium and below 12 as low.

C. The construction of the social class variable for Sweden:

Father's occupation categories when the respondent was 16 as obtained from the HUS data set:

1. Farmer, fisherman
2. Small businessmen or working in the family business
3. Manager of business
4. Salaried employee/supervisor in the private sector
5. Salaried employee/supervisor in the public sector
6. Industrial worker in the private sector
7. Worker in the private sector
8. Worker in the public sector
9. Other

Categories 3,4,5 are ranked as high occupation category; 2,7,8 and 6 are ranked as medium occupation category and 1 as low category.

Father's education level when the respondent was 16 as obtained from the HUS data set:
1. No schooling
2. Elementary school at least 6 years
3. Vocational school
4. Intermediate school-leaving examination, comprehensive school/adult education
5. Gymnasium (upper secondary school)
6. University college

7. Other school

Categories 5 and 6 are taken as high level category; 3,4 and 7 are taken as medium education category and 1 and 2 as low category.

Finally occupation and education are combined to create the social class variable as shown below.

Occupation	Education	Social class
Low	Low	Low
Low	Medium	Low
Low	High	Medium
Medium	Low	Low
Medium	Medium	Medium
Medium	High	High
High	Low	Medium
High	Medium	High
High	High	High

D. The age at finishing education

The age at finishing education is calculated in the following way. In the BHPS, we have one variable indicating the school leaving age and another one indicating the age at which further education is ended. We use the latter if the person receives further education and the former if not. In the HUS, age at finishing education is not directly available. We compute age at finishing education by using information on years of schooling since elementary school and add seven as primary schooling starts at age seven. In proceeding this way, we implicitly assume that women do not interrupt schooling. Also since respondents are asked to transform their part-time studies to full time into their full-time equivalent, we cannot distinguish if the education they have is full-time or part-time.

Appendix Table A1. Selectivity analysis on mean age of the mother at first birth

I.	*Time period in which the first child was born*					
	1950s	1960s	1970s	1980s	1990s	Total
A. Kenjoh 2004, also includes women born before 1930s						
Britain	24.9	23.9	27.2	24.5	25.4	
Number of obser.	590	738	801	931	357	3417
Sweden	24.8	23.8	24.5	25.7	27.0	
Number of obser.	402	613	620	405	210	2250
B. Our sample in this chapter: women for whom we know a) the education of both husband and wife and b) the date they moved in together						
Britain	22.5	23.5	25.0	25.4	28.2	
Number of obser.	112	412	506	601	329	1960
Sweden	21.3	23.3	24.7	25.7	27.0	
Number of obser.	70	352	367	235	88	1112
C. All women who have a child and for whom we know a) the education of both husband and wife and b) we do not know the date they moved in together						
Britain	22.5	23.4	25.1	25.4	28.5	
Number of obser.	101	351	441	489	238	2120
Sweden	21.6	23.4	24.7	25.7	27.2	
Number of obser.	145	402	407	249	94	1297
D. All women who have at least one child and for whom we know the education level						
Britain	22.1	23.4	24.4	24.4	26.7	
Number of obser.	410	837	1013	1105	687	4052
Sweden	21.5	23.3	24.5	25.6	27.0	
Number of obser.	240	591	621	408	212	2072
II.	*Time period in which the woman is born*					
	1930s	1940s	1950s	1960s	1970s	Total
B. Our sample in this chapter: women for whom we know a) the education of both husband and b) the date they moved in together						
Britain	25.3	24.9	25.7	25.1	21.4	
Number of obser.	257	531	552	573	47	1960
Sweden	25.2	24.5	24.6	23.4	20.8	
Number of obser.	180	418	340	161	13	1112
C. All women who have a child and for whom we know a) the education of both husband and wife and b) we do not know the date they moved in together						
Britain	25.3	24.8	25.6	25.0	21.1	
Number of obser.	269	566	580	627	78	2120
Sweden	24.7	24.5	24.4	23.5	20.8	
Number of obser.	281	460	373	170	13	1297
D. All women who have at least one child and for whom we know the education level						
Britain	24.9	24.4	24.9	24.3	20.9	
Number of obser.	671	1003	1012	1080	286	4052
Sweden	24.4	24.3	24.6	24.0	21.4	
Number of obser.	429	687	592	315	49	2072

Source: Own computations based on the BHPS 1991-1998 and HUS 1984-1998.

REFERENCES

Adsera, Alicia (2004), "The Changing Fertility Rates in Developed Countries. The Impact of Labor Market Institutions." *Journal of Population Economics*, 17, 17-43.

Becker, Gary S. (1973), "A theory of marriage: Part I." *The Journal of Political Economy*, 81, 813-846.

Becker, Gary S. (1981, 1994, 1st, 2nd ed.), *A Treatise on the Family*, Cambridge Massachusetts: Harvard University Press.

Bergstrom, Theodore C. (1997), "A Survey of Theories of the Family." In: Mark R. Rosenzweig and Oded Stark (eds.), *Handbook of Population and Family Economics*, Amsterdam: Elsevier.

Bergstrom, Theodore C. and David A. Lam (1989), "The Effects of Cohort Size on Marriage Markets in Twentieth Century Sweden." In: *The Family, the Market and the State in Industrialized Countries*. Oxford, Oxford University Press.

Bloemen, Hans and Adriaan Kalwij (2001), "Female Labor Market Transitions and the Timing of Births: a Simulteneous Analysis of the Effects of Schooling." *Labor Economics*, 8, 593-620.

Blossfeld, Hans-.Peter (1990), "Changes in the Educational Careers in the Federal Republic of Germany." *Sociology of Education*, 63, 165-177.

Blossfeld, Hans-Peter and Johannes Huinink (1991), "Human Capital Investments or Norms of Role Transition? How Women's Schooling and Career Affect the Process of Family Formation." *The American Journal of Sociology*, 97, 143-168.

Blossfeld, Hans-Peter and Andreas Timm, (ed.) (2003), *Who Marries Whom? Educational Systems as Marriage Markets in Modern Societies*, Dordrecht: Kluwer Academic Publishers.

Blundell, Richard and Richard J. Smith (1994), "Coherency and Estimation in Simultaneous Models with Censored or Qualitiative Dependent Variables.", *Journal of Econometrics*, 64, 355-373.

Cigno, Alessandro (1991), *Economics of the Family*, Oxford: Clarendon Press.

Cigno, Alessandro and John F. Ermisch (1989), "A Micro-Economic Analysis of the Timing of Births." *European Economic Review*, 69, 318-328.

Columbia University, Undated, *Clearing House on International Developments in Child, Youth and Family Policies*, Author: www.childpolicyintl.org.

Ermisch, John F. (2003), *An Economic Analysis of the Family*. Princeton: Princeton University Press.

Francesconi, Marco (2002), "A Joint Dynamic Model of Fertility and Work of Married Women." *Journal of Labor Economics*, 20, 336-380.

Ghysels, Joris (2003), *The Work and Care Game*: *An Empirical Analysis of Household Decision Making in the European Union*, Doctoral dissertation, Universiteit Antwerpen.

Goldthorpe, J.H. and Hope K. (1974), *The Social Grading of Occupations: A New Approach and Scale*, Oxford: Oxford University Press.

Greene, William H. (2003), (5th ed.), *Econometric Analysis*, Upper Saddle River, New Jersey: Prentice Hall. International Inc.

Grossbard-Shechtman, Shoshana A. (1984), "A Theory of Allocation of Time in Markets for Labor and Marriage." *Economic Journal*, 94, 863-83.

Grossbard-Shechtman, Shoshana.A., (ed.) (2003), *Marriage and the Economy: Theory and Evidence from Advanced Industrial Societies*, New York and Cambridge: Cambridge University Press.

Gustafsson, Siv S. (2001), "Optimal Age at Motherhood: Theoretical and Empirical Considerations on Postponement of Maternity in Europe." *Journal of Population Economics*, 14, 225-247.

Gustafsson, Siv, Cecile Wetzels, Jan Dirk Vlasblom and Shirley Dex (1996), "Labor Force Transitions in Connection with Child Birth. A Panel Data Comparison Between Germany, Sweden and Great Britain." *Journal of Population Economics*, 9, 221-246.

Gustafsson, Siv S. and Eiko Kenjoh (2004), "New evidence on work among new mothers. What can trade unions do?" *Transfer., European Review of Labor and Research*, 10, 34-47.

Gustafsson, Siv and Cecile Wetzels (2000), "Optimal Age for First Birth: Germany, Great Britain, the Netherlands and Sweden." In Siv Gustafsson and Danièle Meulders (eds.), *Gender and the Labor Market, Econometric Evidence of Obstacles to Achieving Gender Equality*, London: MacMillan

Gustafsson, Siv, Eiko Kenjoh and Cecile Wetzels (2002a), "The Role of Education in Postponement of Maternity in Britain, Germany, the Netherlands and Sweden." In Elisabetta Ruspini and Angela Dale (eds.), *The Gender dimension of Social Change. Tthe Contribution of Dynamic Research to the Study of Women's Life Courses*. Bristol: The Policy Press.

Gustafsson, Siv, Eiko Kenjoh and Cecile Wetzels (2002b), "The Labor force tranditions of First-time Mothers in Britain, Germany, the Netherlands and Sweden." In Hugh Mosley, Jacqueline O' Reilly and Klaus Schömann (eds.), *Labor Markets, Gender and Institutional Change:Essays in Honour of Günther Schmid*, Chaltenham and Northampton: Edward Elgar.

Heckman, James J. and James R. Walker (1990), "The Third Birth in Sweden." *Journal of Population Economics*, 3, 235-275.

Hoem, Jan (1986), "The Impact of Education on Modern Family-Union Initiation." *European Journal of Population*, 2, 113-133.

Hotz, V. Joseph, Jacob A. Klerman and Robert J. Willis (1997), "The Economics of Fertility in Developed Countries." In: Mark R. Rozenzweig and Oded Stark (eds.), *Handbook of Population and Family Economics*, 1A. Amsterdam: Elsevier.

ILO, 1950-1960, *The Year Book of Labor Statistics*, International Labor Office, Vol. 12 –Vol. 20, Geneva.

Klevmarken, Anders N. and Paul Olovson (1993), *Household Market and Nonmarket Activities: Procedures and Codes 1984-1991*. Stockholm: Almqvist & Wiksell International.

Kenjoh, Eiko (2004*), Balancing Work and Family Life in Japan and Four European Countries: Econometrics Analysis on Mothers' Employment and Timing of Maternity*, Amsterdam: Thela Thesis, No. 337.

Lam, David (1988), "Marriage Markets and Assortative Mating with Household Public Goods." *Journal of Human Resources*, 23, 462-487.

Mare, Robert D. (1991), "Five Decades of Educational Assortative Mating." *American Sociological Review*, 56, 15-32.

Naz, Ghazala, Øivind Anti Nilsen and Steinar Vagstad (2004), "Education and Completed Fertility in Norway, Chapter 12 of this book.

OECD (1969), "Labor Force Statistics 1956-1967." *OECD Economic Outlook*, Paris.

OECD (1999, 2001), "Historical Statistics 1960-1988, 1970-1999." *OECD Statistics*, Paris.

Ono, Hiromo (2002), "Women's Economic Standing, Marriage Timing and Cross-National Contexts of Gender: The Case of Japan, US and Sweden." *Working Paper*. Ann Arbor: University of Michigan.

Taylor, Marcia (ed.) (1992), *British Household Panel Survey User Manual*, Volumes A and B, Essex University ESRC Research Centre on Micro-Social Change.

Wetzels, Cecile (2001), *Squeezing Birth into Working Life: Household Panel Data Analyzes Comparing Germany, Great Britain, Sweden and The Netherlands*. Aldershot: Ashgate Publishing Ltd.

Chapter 12

EDUCATION AND COMPLETED FERTILITY IN NORWAY

GHAZALA NAZ, ØIVIND ANTI NILSEN, AND STEINAR VAGSTAD

1. INTRODUCTION

Increased education levels and decreased overall fertility seems to be an empirical regularity in most OECD countries (Council of Europe, 2001; OECD, 2001a). Micro-based studies in various other countries as well also report a negative relationship between women's education and fertility (see for instance, Gardner, 1973; Rindfuss et al., 1980; Schultz, 1993; and Weinberger et al., 1989). One explanation for the negative correlation between education and fertility is the time-use and opportunity costs. Economic theory acknowledges the importance of parental time, especially the mother's time in the upbringing of children (see for instance, Becker, 1965; Schultz, 1973, Gronau, 1973). The trade-off between fertility and labour market work is an important and widely accepted economic explanation of the observed negative association between women's education and total fertility. An increase in the education increases the wages and employment opportunities of a woman, inducing substitution out of time intensive activities such as children (see Moffitt, 1984; Birdsall, 1988; Becker, 1991; Schultz, 1993; Bloemen and Kalwij, 2001). Economists have estimated strong negative effects of women's wages on fertility (see for instance, Heckman and Walker, 1990b; Merrigan and St.-Pierre, 1998).

The Scandinavian countries have not experienced the same dramatic drop in total fertility over the last decades as compared to most other OECD countries. At the same time, female labour force participation and average education levels are high in Scandinavia. Some recent empirical studies using Scandinavian data suggest a positive association between education and third birth of married women, given that they already have got two children (see Hoem and Hoem, 1989; Kravdal, 1992; Rønsen, 1998; Naz, 2000). However, the positive association between education and third birth does not imply that females' education increases completed fertility as there is evidence that the percentages of childless women and women with only a

Siv Gustafsson and Adriaan Kalwij (eds.), Education and Postponement of Maternity, 285–306.

single child are higher for those who have the longest schooling (see for instance, Lappegård, 1999). A higher proportion of childless women and women with only a single child may offset the positive association between education and third birth observed in previous studies. Therefore, to evaluate the relationship between females' education and total fertility, it is important to look at childlessness together with the total number of children given that one gets children at all.

The first objective of this chapter is to investigate the association between completed fertility and education of married women in Norway. Empirical evidence suggests that women with high education tend to marry men with even higher education (see, for instance, Winch, 1958; Vandenberg, 1972). This is referred to as positive assortative mating in the marriage market (see Becker, 1991). Assortative mating implies that the education of the husbands ought to be taken into account when measuring the association between women's education and fertility. Due to assortative mating two kinds of indirect effects of females' education can take place. First, marrying a man with higher education and correspondingly higher income works as an income effect (similar to the effect of a labour-free income), which may affect fertility positively. Empirical studies verify the positive association between husbands' income and fertility (see for instance; Heckman and Walker, 1990a, 1990b; Merrigan and St.-Pierre, 1998). Second, assortative mating may also affect fertility through specialisation. The literature on household economics suggests that a large part of the gains from marriage stem from specialisation between husband and wife: the husband specialises in the labour market while the wife is specialising in household production.[1] There is ample evidence for specialisation within the household. Married men work longer hours in the market and have substantially higher wages than unmarried men. Moreover, married women have lower wages and work more at home than unmarried women (see Gronau, 1986; Daniel, 1992; Korenman and Neumark, 1992). We may also expect that increased husband's education implies more specialisation within the family, leading to a reduction of the opportunity cost of bearing children for women. We first estimate the gross effect of females' education on fertility. Thereafter, we decompose this effect into a "husband effect" and a "net effect".

In Western countries child bearing is not confined to marriage, but rates of fertility within marriage is higher than those outside the marriage. The opportunity cost of children may be different for married and unmarried women. Thus, the second objective of this chapter is to analyse and discuss the difference in completed fertility for married and unmarried women.[2] The fact that married women get more children than unmarried ones needs no further explanation. We find that education is positively correlated with fertility for married women but negatively for unmarried ones, and this is perhaps more of a puzzle. We argue that in Scandinavia both married and unmarried women are to a large extent insured against what can be called direct costs of giving birth (e.g. costs of medical care, day-care subsidies, public schooling), while they are not insured against more indirect losses, for instance against foregone career opportunities, or the less tangible emotional costs. Single women can be expected to suffer a larger career loss from childbirths as compared with married or cohabitating women, for several reasons. First, married women may have supportive husbands, implying that for married women career and family is compatible. Recent time use surveys show that Norwegian men, especially when wives are working full time, share the responsibility of child-care (see Rønsen, 2001). Consequently, for married women the career disadvantage associated with childbirths should be smaller as compared with unmarried (single) women.[3] Moreover, the career loss may differ across parity levels: it is reasonable to believe that loss of career is largest for the first child, for instance due to fixed time-costs of having children. Since, empirically, the marginal fertility decision of the average unmarried woman is whether or not to have the first child, while the marginal decision of the average married woman is whether to have a third child, this is another explanation of the difference between married and unmarried women's fertility response to education.

The Norwegian data set used, based on census data from public registers, is unique along several dimensions. First, since the data are based on the census, we do not have only a small number of observations as in surveys. Our final sample includes more than 8,000 individuals. By using the Norwegian data we are able to meet some of the critique of existing literature; limited samples, the lack of information about spouse characteristics and the incidence of childlessness. These shortcomings may have plagued former studies, giving imprecise or erroneous results.

The rest of the chapter is organised as follows. In the next section we give a brief description of some institutional features of Norwegian women's fertility, educational level and labour force participation together with a description of the fertility patterns in Norway over the last decades. Section 3 presents the data and some summary statistics. In Section 4 we discuss the theoretical differences in fertility between married and unmarried women. The empirical specification is discussed in Section 5. In Section 6 we present and discuss our empirical results. Section 7 concludes our findings.

2. INSTITUTIONAL BACKGROUND[4]

The relative high fertility accompanied with a high educational level in the Scandinavian countries may be due to institutional settings in these countries. First, Norway and Sweden have labour markets characterised by strongly compressed wage distributions, especially for women (see for instance OECD, 1993; Kahn, 1998). This means that female wages and thereby the direct costs of bearing children are not much affected by education, and that any measured effect of education therefore might have a less direct cause. Second, the Scandinavian countries have quite generous arrangements for maternal leaves – arrangements that to a large extent insure a woman from an income loss due to childbirths (see OECD, 2001b).[5] Also the level of governmental transfers to parents has increased over time. However, this insurance against short-term income losses from childbirths does not eliminate the importance of more indirect costs attached to loss of career. We will return to this point below.

Figure 12.1 (Source: Statistics Norway) illustrates the total fertility for Norway. The figure indicates that the fertility from 1983 has somewhat increased. Note however, that this pattern covers the fact that women seem to postpone their childbirths. As Figure 12.2 (Source: Statistics Norway) illustrates, women today get their children later in their lifecycles as compared with earlier generations. In addition, we find that completed fertility of younger generations seems to be small relative to older generations.

The educational level in Norway is increasing, similar to most other countries. This pattern is especially evident for females. For instance, in 1952 only 15 percent of the students in graduate schools and universities were females, while this share was 55 percent in 1994. Only at the PhD level the female share of students is still lower than for males. When we look at the median age at first birth by educational length for various cohorts (shown in Figure 12.3), we see that the age of first birth is higher for the more educated groups and that the age of first birth has increased for all educational groups over time.

The labour force participation rates of females are relatively high in Norway as compared with other countries, especially among younger cohorts. However, many women choose to work only part-time. For instance, the proportion of working women who chose to work part-time was 46% in 1994.

Figure 12.1. Total fertility

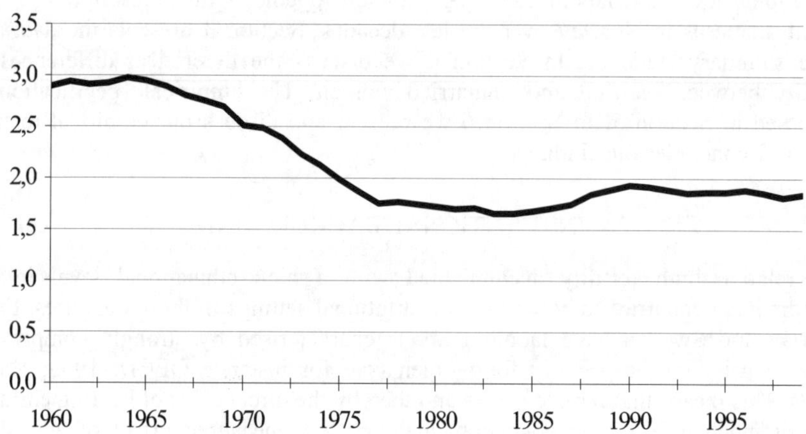

*Figure 12.2. Cohort fertility; accumulated birth rates*1000*

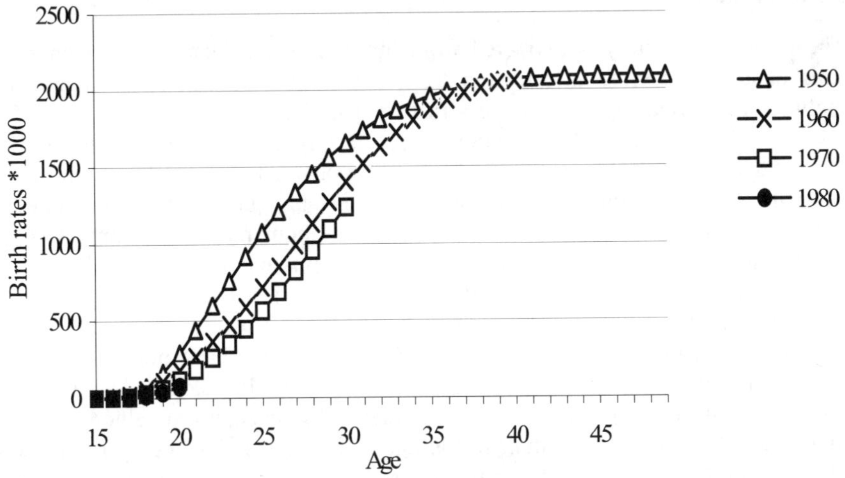

Figure 12.3. Median age at first birth, by educational groups

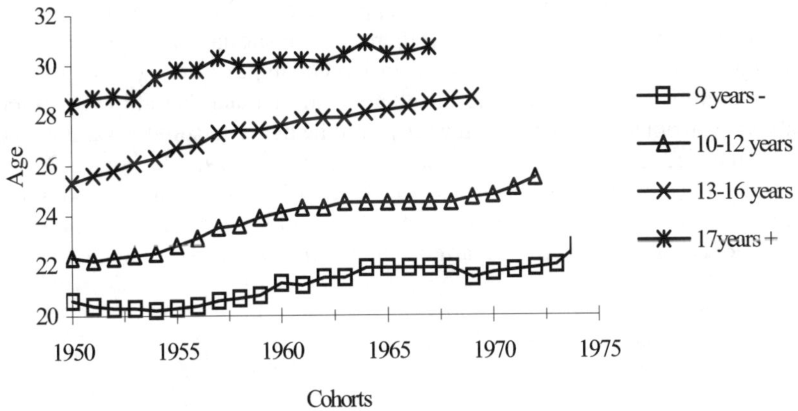

3. DATA

3.1 Data sources

The data in this study is extracted from the Norwegian Database of Generations. This database provides information from public and administrative registers and includes all individuals born in every fifth year in the period from 1950 to 1995. For all the cohorts there is information about family characteristics, education and variables describing the labour market attachment of the individuals. The time of sampling of the different variables varies. For instance, family status, the length and type of education, and variables describing the labour market attachment is given every tenth year, while childbearing is recorded annually.

Primarily due to missing birth data we have restricted attention to women born in 1955 (Data for the 1950 cohort is hampered by severe under-registration of births for the years 1968-71, while cohorts from 1960 onwards have not completed their fertile period at the end of registration period (1995)). The sample has information until 1995. By concentrating on the 1955 cohort of women, we are able to follow the individuals through most of their fertile age. Missing variables cut our data to 86% of the entire Norwegian 1955 female cohort. There are 4,341 unmarried and 20,201 married women in the remaining data. The data used in our study include information about changes in marital status, recorded in the database as monthly events. Using this monthly information, we construct our final sample such that the unmarried ones never have been married, while the married ones have been married to the same husband all the time. That means that divorced, widowed or remarried women are excluded from our sample. This exclusion is done to get as homogeneous sample as possible. However, note that there will be substantial heterogeneity in our sub-sample of unmarried women, as this group encompasses cohabitating women as well as single women. There is no information in the data that allow us to identify cohabitating women.[6] If so, we believe it would be better to split the sample between *de facto* married women (including cohabitating ones) and single women. Modelling and analysing the relationship between family-formation and -dissolution and fertility is beyond the scope of this chapter. Thus all the presented results should be interpreted as conditional on the marital status in the various sub-samples.

In order to get information about husbands' characteristics we include only those married women in our sample whose husbands are found in the data (3,873 observations). As the Database of Generations provides information for only the individuals who are born in every fifth year in the period from 1950 to 1995, we include only women with husbands born in one of the years 1950, 1955, 1960 or 1965. One might worry that this sub sample may not be representative of all the married women as it selects only the women whose husbands are of the same age, 5 years younger, or 5 or 10 years older. Note however, that we will test whether the sub sample of women with husbands included in the database are similar as those women with husbands not found in the database.

3.2 Variables

The dependent variable is number of children ever born to the women when they are 40 years old. Our educational variable is the level of education for the respondent.[7]

As already discussed, education may affect fertility in several ways. In particular, education affects one's earnings potential (through employment opportunities as well as wages) and therefore education is a proxy for the economic resources available for the prospective parents (i.e., "income") as well as a proxy for time costs of raising children. An alternative proxy for the income potential could have been some measure of actual income (for instance income in a single year or an average over several years). However, since fertility has a strong effect on women's labour supply, actual income is clearly not exogenous, and we have therefore chosen to exclude income variables in our study, knowing that this might introduce problems due to omitted relevant variables. We report mean income of married and unmarried women in Table 12.1.

As discussed in the introduction, assortative mating may give rise to indirect effects of education on fertility. Therefore, to get a more complete picture of the effect of women's education on their completed fertility, it is important to control for spouse characteristics. In this study we include spouse education, measured as number of years of schooling. Spouse income is excluded. This exclusion is based on the same arguments as for the exclusion of women's own income.

We have also included the age difference between husband and wife, defined as husband's age minus woman's age.[8] Another variable included is the age at marriage. Women who get married early have a longer period where the likelihood of an additional child is greater. An additional reason for including age at marriage is that this variable might partly control for a woman's "social status," since

Table 12.1. Descriptive statistics

	Married (husband in sample)	Married (husband not in sample)	Unmarried
Number of children			
Mean	2.27	2.23	0.77
Variance	1.03	1.09	0.94
Distribution (%)			
0	5.3	6.6	52.5
1	10.7	11.1	25.2
2	46.3	46.0	16.7
3 +	37.7	36.3	5.6
Age at first birth			
(conditional on having at least onechild)	24.5	24.3	27.1
Age at marriage	23.7	23.6	
Years of schooling			
Mean	11.7	11.6	12.0
Distribution (%)			
- 11	52.9	55.5	47.3
12 - 15	33.6	32.4	34.7
16 +	13.4	12.1	18.0
Age difference (husband - wife)			
Distribution (%)			
-10 years	0.4		
-5 years	3.9		
0 years	56.7		
5 years	39.0		
Mean income (1989, 1992, and 1995)			
(1995 prices, 1000 NOK)	123.3	122.6	143.0
Regions (counties)			
Distribution (%)			
Oslo (*Oslo, Akershus*)	12.8	16.6	16.7
East (north) (*Hedmark, Oppland*)	7.2	8.8	9.0
East (south) (*Østfold, Vestfold, Buskerud*)	28.6	17.7	18.0
South (*Telemark, Vest-Agder, Aust-Agder*)	6.5	10.5	9.8
West (*Rogaland, Hordaland, Sogn- og Fjord.*)	15.6	22.2	21.7
Mid (*Møre- og Romsd., S.-Trøndelag, N.-Trønd.*)	13.6	14.6	15.0
North (*Nordland, Troms, Finnmark*)	15.8	9.7	9.9
Number of observations	3873	16328	4341

individuals with high income and high education are likely to get married late. Other fertility studies, such as Kiernan (1989) and Santos Silva and Covas (2000) find a negative effect of a late marriage on the probability of having children.

Since the average educational level varies across regions, it is important to control for place of residence. We have included seven regional dummies, using Oslo as the base case. If we had ignored the geographical aspect, the educational variable might just have picked up regional differences. The regional dummies might also control for regional differences in the costs of raising children, together with regional differences in the income potential for both women and men.

3.3 Descriptive statistics

Some descriptive statistics are given in Table 12.1. There is a marked difference between unmarried and married women: close to 80% of the unmarried women get no or one child, while more than 80% of those who marry get two or more children. The numbers reported in Table 12.1 reveal that the mean of the level of education is higher for unmarried as compared with married. Furthermore, highly educated women are over-represented among those who never marry. This is probably also one explanation for the higher income among unmarried compared to the married ones. In Table 12.1 we also present summary statistics for married women who have been married to the same husband all the time but whose husband are not found in the database. The broad picture reveals only minor differences between the two groups. We therefore base our regressions on married women for whom we have information about husbands' characteristics.

Table 12.2. Years of schooling of wives and husbands. Number of couples

	Husbands						
Wives	-9	10-11	12-13	14-15	16-17	18+	Total
-9	163	176	183	26	18	5	571
10-11	288	388	541	155	67	41	1480
12-13	69	131	265	114	57	57	693
14-15	27	48	157	137	100	139	608
16-17	17	29	88	78	109	79	400
18+	1	2	5	11	14	88	121
Total	565	774	1293	521	365	409	3873

Table 12.2 shows the years of schooling for women and husbands. The educational attainment is positively correlated, clearly illustrating the positive assortative mating discussed above: the frequencies are highest close to the diagonal.

Table 12.3 illustrates the correlation between couples' education and number of children. We see that the number of children is positively correlated with the husbands' education, while the correlation with the wives' education is not clear.

Table 12.3. Years of schooling of wives and husbands. Number of children

	Husbands						
Wives	-9	10-11	12-13	14-15	16-17	18+	Mean
-9	2.31	2.24	2.19	2.50	2.44	2.20	2.26
10-11	2.27	2.30	2.30	2.36	2.24	2.37	2.30
12-13	2.07	2.20	2.18	2.26	2.47	2.56	2.24
14-15	2.11	2.10	2.42	2.31	2.45	2.50	2.38
16-17	1.82	2.10	2.28	2.19	2.10	2.24	2.18
18+	1.00	1.50	1.60	1.91	1.43	2.22	2.05
Mean	2.23	2.25	2.27	2.30	2.27	2.38	2.27

4. FERTILITY AND MARITAL STATUS

The opportunity cost of children may differ for married and unmarried women. Furthermore, the cost of having an additional child may vary with the parity levels. To refine our discussion of career losses and costs associated with costs of children, we look at the difference dependent on the marital status.

We start by noting that the expected number of children, denoted y, can be written as:

$$E(y) = P(y > 0) \times E(y | y > 0) \tag{1}$$

Differentiation with respect to female education, denoted *edu*, yields the following expression for the marginal effect of education on fertility:[9]

$$\frac{\partial E(y)}{\partial edu} = \left[\frac{\partial P(y > 0)}{\partial edu} \times E(y|y > 0)\right] + \left[P(y > 0) \times \frac{\partial E(y|y > 0)}{\partial edu}\right] \tag{2}$$

Equation (2) shows that the effect of education on fertility can be decomposed into the effect on the probability of getting at least one child (the first term on the right hand side) and the effect on the expected number of children, given that a woman already has got at least one child (the second term on the right hand side).[10]

Additional education opens new career opportunities, and therefore increases the potential opportunity costs of having children. Norwegian women are to some extent insured against income losses stemming directly from childcare, while "losses of career" remain. As discussed in the introduction, unmarried women may suffer a larger career loss from childbirths compared to married women. Since unmarried women often do not have a partner in the household to share the time-consuming activity of caring for and raising children, they may suffer a larger career loss from childbirths as compared with married women. If it is true that single women experience a tougher career drop than do married women, we may expect to find that $\partial P^{married}(y>0)/\partial edu > \partial P^{unmarried}(y>0)/\partial edu$. For similar reasons, we may expect that $\partial E^{married}(y|y>0)/\partial edu > \partial E^{unmarried}(y|y>0)/\partial edu$.

5. EMPIRICAL SPECIFICATION

To see the effect of a set of background variables and characteristics on women's completed fertility, we use a count data model.[11] A first choice could be a Poisson model. The Poisson model assumes the equality between mean and variance for the dependent variable. However, when the assumption of equidispersion is violated the estimated parameters from a Poisson model are consistent but not efficient. We see in Table 12.1 that there is over-dispersion (when variance is greater than mean) as well as under-dispersion (when variance is smaller than mean) in the number of children, depending on what (sub-) sample we are looking at. For the case where we have over-dispersion we could use a negative binomial model. The negative binomial model, however, does not account for under-dispersion. Instead, we adopt a strategy where we use a restricted generalised Poisson regression model (RGPR). This model has the convenient feature that it allows for both over- and under-dispersion.[12] The RGPR model has previously been used by Wang and Famoye (1997) to analyse completed fertility.[13]

In the RGPR model the probability function for the response variable Y_i (here; the number of children) is given by:

$$f_i(y_i \mid \mu_i, \alpha) = \left(\frac{\mu_i}{1+\alpha\mu_i}\right)^{y_i} \frac{(1+\alpha y_i)^{y_i-1}}{y_i!} \exp\left(-\frac{\mu_i(1+\alpha y_i)}{(1+\alpha\mu_i)}\right) \tag{3}$$

where $y_i = 0, 1, 2,..,$ and $\mu_i = \exp(\mathbf{x}_i\beta)$. The $\mathbf{x}_i$-vector includes the covariates and an intercept, while β is a vector of regression parameters. The inclusion of the α-parameter is an extension of the standard Poisson model, such that when $\alpha = 0$, the probability function in eq. (3) reduces to the Poisson model.

The log-likelihood function for the RGPR model is given by:

$$LogL(\alpha,\beta) = \sum_{i=1}^{N} \left\{ y_i \log\left(\frac{\mu_i}{1+\alpha\mu_i}\right) + (y_i - 1)\log(1+\alpha y_i) - \frac{\mu_i(1+\alpha y_i)}{(1+\alpha\mu_i)} - \log(y_i!) \right\} \tag{4}$$

where $\alpha > min(-\frac{1}{\max(\mu_i)}, -\frac{1}{\max(y_i)})$. We report the marginal effects and the corresponding z-values.[14] The marginal effect of covariate *j* is calculated as:

$$\frac{\partial E(y \mid \mathbf{x})}{\partial x_j} = \frac{1}{N}\sum_{i=1}^{N} \beta_j \hat{\mu}_i \tag{5}$$

where $\hat{\mu}_i = \exp(\mathbf{x}_i\hat{\beta})$. Let $c(\hat{\beta})$ denote the vector of all the marginal effects. Using the delta method we may estimate the covariance matrix of the marginal effects as:

$$V(c(\hat{\beta})) = \left(\frac{\partial E(c(\hat{\beta}))}{\partial \hat{\beta}}\right)' Var(\hat{\beta}) \left(\frac{\partial E(c(\hat{\beta}))}{\partial \hat{\beta}}\right) \tag{6}$$

The reported *z*-values of the marginal effects are based on this latter expression.

We also report consistent Akaika information criterion for the estimated models, CAIC defined as[15]

$$CAIC = -2LogL + k \cdot (\ln(Number\ of\ obs) + 1) \tag{7}$$

where *LogL* is the log likelihood. The minimum *CAIC* indicates the "best" model. We have also calculated the proportion of correct predictions. Finally we have calculated the following χ^2-value;

$$\chi^2 = \sum_{m=0}^{M} \frac{(n_m - \hat{n}_m)^2}{\hat{n}_m} \tag{8}$$

where n_m denotes the observed number of individuals with m children, and $\hat{n}_m$ is the estimated number with the same count. We let m go from 0, while we have merged the last cells such that $M \in \{7,8,9,10\}$ since $\hat{n}_m$ for $m \geq 7$ becomes very small, leading to unproportionally small denominator (and large ratios) in expression (8).

6. RESULTS AND DISCUSSION

To study the effect of females' education on completed fertility we split our sample into married and unmarried women[16] and run regressions using the RGPR model. The results are given in Table 12.4.

The results presented in Column 1 are the results for married women without controlling for any husband characteristics. We find that females' education is positively associated with completed fertility at age 40. One year of additional education is associated with 0.027 more children. The positive association between females' education and fertility is in contrast to empirical findings in various other countries. The findings give no support to the theories focusing on the costs of time, saying that higher education leads to higher wages and thereby higher opportunity costs of having children.

However, the positive and significant effect of education might be due to the combination of assortative mating and omitted husband's characteristics. If we do not control for husbands' education, the covariate *women's education* would not only pick up the effect of women's own education, but also the effect of their husbands' education. We decompose the "gross effect" of married women's own education on fertility into a "husband effect" and a "net effect". To find the "net effect" of women's own education, we include also their husbands' educational level together with the age difference between husband and wife. These results are given in Column 2 of Table 12.4. We see that when we control for husbands' characteristics the positive effect of females' education becomes smaller and insignificant. The findings of small and insignificant effects of education on completed fertility are in line with the results found by Moffitt (1984) using US data, and by Kalwij (2000, table 4) and Bloemen and Kalwij (2001) using Dutch data. The effect of husband's education is positive and significant. One year of additional education of a husband is associated with 0.033 more children. This positive and significant effect is in contrast with international findings. For instance, Santos Silva and Covas (2000) using Portuguese data, Kalwij (2000) and Bloemen and Kalwij (2001) using Dutch data, all find negative but insignificant effects of husband's education on fertility. One interpretation of the positive and significant effect of husband's education is as follows: Norwegian females' education does not affect fertility directly, but only through assortative mating. Women with high education tend to marry men with even higher education and this assortative mating provides an income effect that affects fertility positively. The results suggest that it is the income potential for husbands and not women's own income potential (reservation wage) that is important for women's complete fertility.[17]

Table 12.4. Restricted Generalised Poisson Regression Results

	Married		Married		Unmarried	
	Marg.eff.	z-value	Marg.eff.	z-value	Marg.eff.	z-value
Woman's education	0.027	3.000	0.008	0.871	-0.033	-9.988
East (north)	0.056	0.674	0.076	0.907	0.105	1.153
East (south)	0.009	0.127	0.003	0.041	-0.257	-5.324
South	0.205	2.561	0.203	2.558	-0.167	-2.363
West	0.353	4.927	0.355	5.042	-0.095	-1.787
Mid	0.259	3.457	0.258	3.469	0.120	1.991
North	0.299	3.597	0.310	3.756	0.342	4.787
Age at marriage	-0.056	-12.803	-0.060	-13.606		
Age difference			-0.020	-2.974		
Husband's education			0.033	4.333		
α(coefficient)	-0.097	-96.370	-0.097	-98.157	0.097	5.618
Log likelihood	-5568.8		-5555.8		-5061.0	
Number of obs.	3873		3873		4341	
Number of children						
μ (predicted)						
mean	2.27		2.27		0.77	
max	2.96		3.06		1.34	
y (actual)						
mean	2.27		2.27		0.77	
max	10		10		6	
CAIC	11230.2		11222.7		10206.5	
Correctly predicted	0.64		0.64		0.86	
χ^2	620.9		627.4		131.7	

Notes: The reference category is women living in the Oslo region.An α=0 indicates that the RGPR reduces to Poisson model. The marginal effects of the regional dummies are measuring the change of dummy variable from 0 to 1. χ^2 is defined in the main text.

Concerning the age difference, we see that women married to older men tend to get fewer children.[18] However, with the relative large age differences in our sample (5, 0, –5, and –10 years) care should be taken when interpreting this result. Still, based on the reported marginal effect in Column 2, an increase of one year in the *age difference* between the husband and the wife will lead to 0.020 less children.

The marginal effect of *Age at marriage* is negative but small. This tells us that women who get married earlier are likely to get more children. An obvious reason is that an early marriage also leads to a longer period of marriage, and thus, a longer period where the likelihood of an additional child is greater. Another potential explanation is that the age at marriage is a proxy for the somewhat imprecise definition "social status". Women with lower social status tend to get married earlier, and also get more children. Based on the reported marginal effect, decreasing age at marriage with one year leads to 0.06 more children. Given that women with lower social status take less education, the total difference between women with various social backgrounds may be significant. Finally, we see that the fertility pattern varies by regions, and that most of the regional dummies are statistically significant.

As already pointed out, our sample of married women includes only women whose husbands are born in 1950, 1955, 1960 or 1965. We have tested whether there are any substantial differences between the sub-sample of married women for which the husbands are in the sample and the sub-sample for which the husbands are not in the sample. We merge the two sub-samples, and run a RGPR model where we include a sample dummy (1 if husband in sample, 0 otherwise) separately, in addition to interaction terms between the explanatory variables (as used in Column 1, Table 12.4) and the sample dummy. None of the interaction variables are individually significant, except for age at marriage. The marginal effect is small, but still it is an open question to us why this coefficient is statistically significant (*t*-value = 2.00). The summary statistics do not reveal any differences between the two sub-samples. Furthermore, a chi-square test of joint-significance of all the interaction variables in the RGPR model strongly rejects the hypothesis that there are any differences between the two sub-samples ($\chi^2_{df=8} = 9.11$).

The last columns of Table 12.4 illustrate the association between education and fertility of unmarried women at age 40. We see that education of unmarried women is negatively related to fertility. One year of additional education is associated with 0.033 less children. This is significantly different from what we found for married women.[19] As already mentioned, our sample of unmarried women is rather heterogeneous including cohabitating (*de facto* married ones), as well as single women. Furthermore, we should keep in mind that that our sample split of married women and single women is not exogenous, since marital status is affected by the presence and the number of children. Still, when we find the effect of education to be significantly negative for unmarried women, we expect the true negative effect of education on single women's fertility to be even stronger.[20] From the summary statistics we also know that married women tend to have more children than unmarried women. The discussion in Section 4 encompassed the ideas about fertility and marital status. The numerical values of all the expressions in equation (2) are given in Table 12.5.

Table 12.5. Fertility and Education by Martial Status

	$\frac{\partial P(y>0)}{\partial edu}$	$E(y \mid y>0)$	$P(y>0)$	$\frac{\partial E(y)}{\partial edu}$	$\frac{\partial E(y \mid y>0)}{\partial edu}$
Married	0.000	2.40	0.934	0.008	0.008
Unmarried	-0.022	1.62	0.475	-0.033	0.006

Table 12.6. Regression results, Probit model

	Married		Married		Unmarried	
	Marg. eff.	z-value	Marg. eff.	z-value	Marg. eff.	z-value
Woman's education	0.001	0.882	0.000	0.338	-0.022	-7.321
East (north)	0.000	0.006	0.000	0.009	0.039	1.109
East (south)	-0.013	-1.127	-0.014	-1.159	-0.128	-5.099
South	-0.011	-0.719	-0.011	-0.741	-0.103	-2.909
West	-0.006	-0.526	-0.006	-0.571	-0.073	-2.563
Mid	0.001	0.060	0.001	0.073	0.048	1.597
North	0.007	0.619	0.008	0.661	0.192	6.885
Age at marriage	-0.006	-10.541	-0.006	-10.699		
Age difference			-0.002	-1.298		
Husband's education			0.001	0.812		
Log likelihood	-751.6		-750.1		2862.1	
Pseudo-R^2	0.063		0.065			
Number of obs.	3873		3873		4341	

Notes: The reference category is women living in the Oslo region. The dependent variable is equal to one if a woman has one or several children, and zero otherwise. The marginal effects of the regional dummies are measuring the discrete change of a dummy variable from 0 to 1.

Numerical values for $\partial E(y)/\partial edu$ are taken from the results reported in Table 12.4. To calculate numerical values for $\partial P(y>0)/\partial edu$ we run probit regressions, reported in Table 12.6.[21] Finally, the numerical values for $E(y \mid y>0)$ and $P(y>0)$ and are calculated from the reported numbers in Table 12.1. Given these numbers, we get an expression for $\partial E(y \mid y>0)/\partial edu$ by rearranging equation (2).[22]

Looking at the results in Table 12.5, the first thing we note is that the differences in the characteristics for the two groups are as expected. For instance we find that one additional year of education is associated with 2.2% decrease in the probability of having at least one child of unmarried women, while increased educational level does not affect the probability of childlessness for married women. We also see that there is a substantial difference between married and unmarried women in the expected number of children given that the woman has at least one child, $E(y \mid y>0)$. Note however, that this difference is not driven by education since $\partial E(y \mid y>0)/\partial edu$ is small and more or less the same for married and unmarried women (0.008 and 0.006, married and unmarried women respectively). Thus, the significant difference in the importance of education for the completed fertility may be caused by the effect of education on childlessness. This is consistent with the hypothesis that that unmarried women experience a tougher career drop as a consequence of having children than married women do.

In contrast to married women, we find the regional dummies of South and West to be negative for unmarried women. This is as expected since these two regions comprise the "Bible-belt" in Norway.

In Table 12.4 we also report the estimated α-s. For none of the (sub-) samples, α is equal to zero. These estimates confirm what we already saw in the descriptive statistics; for the sub-samples of married there is under-dispersion, while there is over-dispersion for the sub-sample of unmarried. With the assumption of equidispersion violated, a standard Poisson model would give inefficient estimates.

To see the prediction properties of the RGPR model, we show relative frequencies for the number of children in Figure 12.4 and 12.5. The actual frequencies (denoted *sample*) and the predicted frequencies (denoted *Generalised Poisson*) are given. The predictions are based on the estimates given in Table 12.4, Column 2 and Column 3 (*Married*, and *Unmarried*, respectively). The fit for *Unmarried* is rather good. However, for the *Married* sample there is an underprediction of the mode and overprediction of the tails of the distribution. Similar findings are also reported by Santos Silva and Covas (2000). Looking at the CAIC criterion, we see that CAIC is somewhat smaller for *Unmarried*, indicating somewhat "better" model fit for this sub-sample relative to the sub-sample of married women. We also see that the proportion of correctly predicted values is higher for the *Unmarried*.

Figure 12.4. Single women

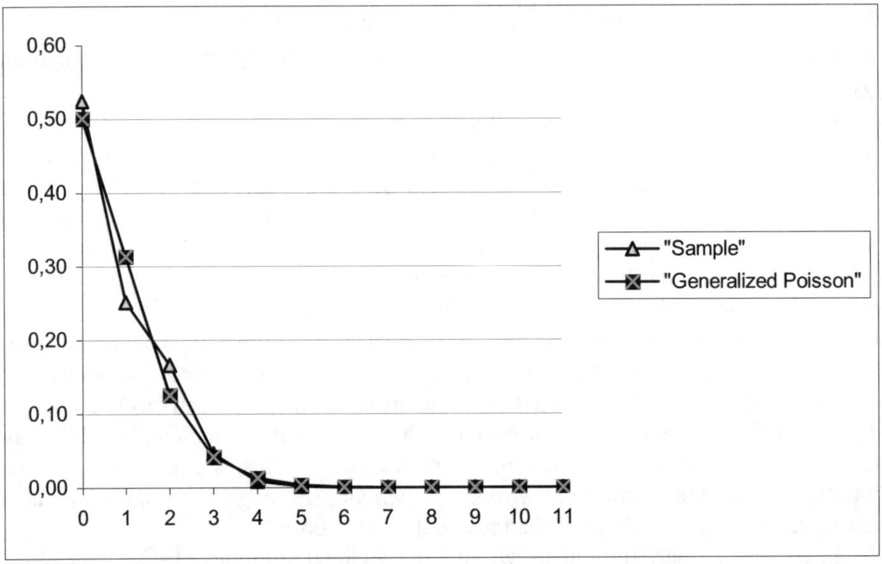

Figure 12.5. Married women (husband on sample)

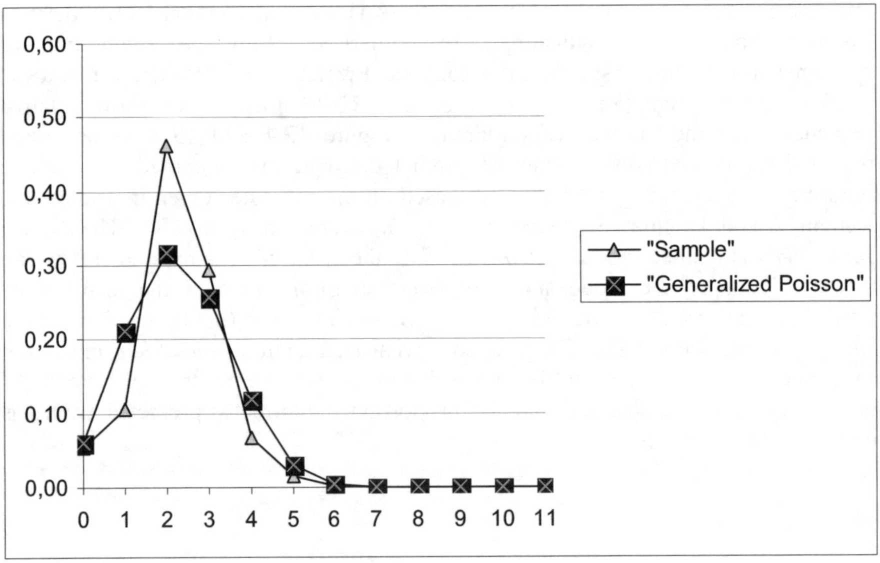

7. CONCLUDING REMARKS

The main objective of this chapter has been to investigate the relationship between completed fertility and education for women in Norway. There are of course many decisions (and coincidences) leading to the total number of children. A fully satisfactory dynamic model is hard to construct and we have chosen a simplified model approach. Thus, our results should be interpreted with great care.

We find that the effect of married women's education on fertility is positive. The effect of education becomes much smaller and insignificant when we control for husbands' education. At the same time we find that husbands' education affects women's fertility positively. These findings suggest that married women's education does not directly affect fertility but goes through assortative mating in the marriage market. Given this pattern, one may ask why is it so important to distinguish the effects working via the husband from other effects? Consider two different thought experiments. In the first we "give" a random woman one extra year of education. This will affect her fertility directly, and also make her marry a man with somewhat higher education, which also affects fertility. Next consider giving one extra year of education to *all* women. For each of them we can compute the direct effect, but when every woman acquires more education, the average woman cannot possibly expect to marry some man with higher education, leaving them with only the direct effect.

In contrast to our findings for married women we find that there is a negative relationship between education and the completed fertility of unmarried women. The career losses attached to childbirths may explain this difference between married and unmarried women. We find that the association of women's education with the expected number of children, given that they have at least one child, is almost the same for married and unmarried women. However, education increases the probability of remaining childless for unmarried women but has no effect for married women. In Norway, as in the rest of Scandinavia, there has been consensus of that it should be possible to combine motherhood and career. If our findings really are caused by women' concern about career losses attached to having children, this indicates that the Scandinavian welfare state has not fully succeeded. Nevertheless, the effect of education on completed fertility is small, which might be an indication that the policy of encouraging high fertility and high labour force participation among women has been successful.

From aggregate statistics we know that an increased level of education leads to a higher incidence of living single. When we see a pattern in most OECD countries with more and more individuals taking higher education while the overall fertility decreases, this might be due to the decision of marriage or cohabitation, and not an effect of education on the fertility *per se*. Most women do not want to have children unless they have a husband so if men want to postpone marriage and children it is also going to affect women's decisions. Thus, to get a better understanding of the overall effect of increased education on the total fertility one needs to analyse family formation and fertility decisions jointly. This will be at the core of our future research.

ACKNOWLEDGEMENTS

We wish to thank Espen Bratberg, Siv Gustafsson, Adriaan Kalwij, Alf Erling Risa as well as seminar audiences at the University of Bergen, the ESPE'01 conference and the workshop "Education and Postponement of Maternity" (Amsterdam, October 2002) for valuable comments and suggestions to earlier versions of this chapter. We also wish to thank the Norwegian Research Council for financial support.

NOTES

[1] Some degree of specialisation according to comparative advantages is predicted by practically any kind of model of intra-family decision-making, (see for instance Becker 1973, 1985; Weiss 1997).

[2] Married and unmarried women are not exclusive groups but our sample comprises of unmarried women who never got married by the age 40. It is quite uncommon for women to get married and give birth to a child after 40 given that they never got married earlier. Therefore, it is interesting to compare fertility choices of unmarried women of age 40 with the married ones.

[3] It should be noted that this reasoning distinguishes between married or cohabitating women on the one hand and single women on the other, while our data does not distinguish between cohabitating and single women, only between married and unmarried women (that may be either single or cohabitating). While this feature of our data certainly calls for caution when interpreting the estimates for the unmarried women, it should not affect the qualitative predictions regarding differences between married and unmarried women.

[4] Most of the information in this section stems from NOU (1996:13).

[5] For instance, the current Norwegian maternity leave system gives the women the choice between a maternity leave compensation of 100% of work income for 42 weeks, or 80% for 52 weeks. This compensation requires a minimum of 6 months' paid work previous to giving birth for eligibility, and comes in addition to the universal child benefit. Consequently, for the "normal" family the cost of children does not vary much across income and educational groups.

[6] According to aggregate statistics, almost 37 percent of unmarried Norwegian women of age 40-44 were living as cohabitants in year 1995 (Source: Statistics Norway).

[7] The level of education is measured by the total time which the completed education *normally* takes. This may of course deviate from the time actually spent in education.

[8] Since the age difference is a discrete variable which in our data set can only take values –10, –5, 0 and 5, it could have been treated as a categorical variable. However, for most of our observations (about 95,6%, see Table 12.1) the age difference is either 0 or 5, and then it should not make much difference whether a continuous or categorical approach is chosen.

[9] Note that while y is a discrete variable, $E(y)$ and $E(y|y>0)$ should be thought of as continuous functions. Similarly, *edu* should be thought of as a continuous variable, despite the fact that it takes only discrete values in our data.

[10] For a variety of reasons, married women get more children than their unmarried sisters: $P^{married}(y>0) > P^{unmarried}(y>0)$ and $E^{married}(y|y>0) > E^{unmarried}(y|y>0)$.

[11] See Cameron and Trivedi (1998) for a comprehensive review of count data models.

[12] For more details, see for instance Famoye (1993).

[13] Recent literature on fertility has pointed out advantages of using hurdle models since this will allow for separation between the presence and the number of children (see Winckelmann 2000). See also the special issue of Journal of Population Economics 13 (2), 2000. A more complete model would include the dynamic processes of selection into educations, the timing of births, labour supply, and family-formations and -dissolutions. But such a dynamic multi-process model is hard to construct and beyond the scope of this analysis. Still, we believe our simplified modelling strategy can shed some light over the total effect of increased education on completed fertility in Norway.

[14] The corresponding coefficients are available from the authors on request.

[15] See for instance Gurmu and Trivedi (1996).

[16] Note that this sample split is endogenous and is inline with many other studies in the literature.

[17] To test the robustness of our results we also ran regressions by including the square of women's educational level. Even though the size of the marginal effects varied somewhat but we found the overall picture to be similar as reported in Table 12.4. Including husbands' level of education reduces the importance of married women's own education. Finally, the goodness-of-fit criteria do not change significantly when we include the additional regressor. In total, these additional results confirm the results reported in Table 12.4.

[18] Note that the age difference can not be separately identified from the age of the husband.

[19] This test is done by merging the two sub-samples using interaction variables, and then testing the significance of the interaction coefficients.

[20] Underlying this latter expectation is an assumption that cohabitating women behave as married women, and thus, the effect of education on fertility for cohabitating women would be positive.

[21] Note that only 5.3 percent of married women are childless. This skewness, in favour of women with at least one child, may give unreliable results in a standard binary choice model. Thus, the probit results for married women should be interpreted with great care.

[22] Note that since Table 12.5 is assembled using different sources, there are no easy way to calculate standard errors. Standard errors are therefore not reported.

REFERENCES

Becker, G. S. "A theory of the allocation of time." *Economic Journal*, 75.299 (September 1965): 493- 517.

Becker, G. S. "A theory of marriage." *Journal of Political Economy*, 81.2 (March-April 1973): 813-846.

Becker, G. S. "Human capital, effort, and the sexual division of labor." *Journal of Labor Economics*, 3.1 (January 1985): 33-58.

Becker, G. S. *A treatise on the family*. Harvard University Press, 1991.

Bloemen, H., and A. S. Kalwij . "Female Labor Market Transitions and the Timing of Births: A Simultaneous Analysis of the Effects of Schooling." *Labour Economics*, 8.5 (2001): 593-620.

Birdsall, N. "Economic approaches to population growth." in Chenery H. and T.N. Srinivasan (ed) *Handbook of Development Economics*. North Holland, 1988.

Cameron, C. A., and P. K. Trivedi. *Regression analysis of count data.* Cambridge University Press, 1998.

Council of Europe. *Recent demographic development in Europe*. Council of Europe Press, 2001.

Daniel, K. "Does Marriage make men more productive?" Working Paper No. 92-2 (1992): Economic Research Center, NORC.

Famoye, F. "Restricted Generalized Poisson Regression Model." *Communications in Statistics – Theory and Methods* 22 (1993): 1335-1354.

Gardner, B. "Economics of the size of North Carolina rural families." *Journal of Political Economy*, 81.2 (March-April 1973): 99-122.

Gurmu, S., and P. K. Trivedi. "Excess Zeros in Count Models for Recreational Trips." *Journal of Business and Economic Statistics*, 14.4 (1996): 469-477.

Gronau, R. "The effect of children on housewife's value of time." *Journal of Political Economy*, 81.2 (March-April 1973): 168-199.

Gronau, R. "Home-production - a survey." in: O. Ashenfelter and R. Layards (ed) *Handbook of labor economics*. North-Holland, 1986.

Heckman, J. J., and J. R. Walker. "The third birth in Sweden." *Journal of Population Economics*, 3 (1990a): 235-275.

Heckman, J. J., and J. R. Walker. "The relationship between wages and income and the timing and spacing of births: evidence from Swedish longitudinal data." *Econometrica* 58 (1990b): 1411-1441.

Hoem, B., and J.M. Hoem. "The impact of women's employment on second and third births in modern Sweden." *Population Studies*, 43 (1989): 46-67.

Kahn, L. M. "Against the Wind: Bargaining Recentralisation and Wage Inequality in Norway 1987-91." *Economic Journal*, 108.448 (May 1998): 603-645.

Kalwij, A. S. "The Effects of Female Employment Status on the Presence and Number of Children." *Journal of Population Economics*, 13.2 (2000): 221-239.

Kiernan, K. E. "Who remains childless?" *Journal of Biosocial Science* 21 (1989): 397-398.

Korenman, S., and D. Neumark. "Marriage, motherhood, and wages." *Journal of Human Resources*, 27.2 (Spring 1992): 233-255

Kravdal, Ø. "The emergence of a positive relation between education and third birth rates in Norway with supportive evidence from the Unites States," *Population Studies*, 46 (1992): 459-475.

Lappegård, T. "Akademikerne får også barn, bare senere (Academics also get children, only later)." Statistics Norway. *Samfunnsspeilet*, 5 (1999): 7-14.

Merrigan, P., and Y. St.-Pierre. "An econometric and neo-classical analysis of the timing and spacing of births in Canada form 1950 to 1990." *Journal of Population Economics*, 11 (1998): 29-51.

Moffitt, R. "Profiles of Fertility, Labour Supply and Wages of Married Women: A Complete Life-Cycle Model." *Review of Economic Studies*, 51.2 (April 1984): 263-278.

Naz, G. "Determinants of fertility in Norway," Working Paper 1400 (2000): Department of Economics, University of Bergen, Norway.

NOU. *Offentlige overføringer til barnefamilier*, 13 (1996): Statens Trykning, Oslo.

OECD. *Employment Outlook*, Paris: OECD, 1993.

OECD. *Education at a glance*, Paris: OECD, 2001a.

OECD. *Employment Outlook*, Paris: OECD, 2001b.

Rindfuss R. R., L. Bumpass, and C. R. John. "Education and fertility: implications for the roles women occupy." *American Sociological Review*, 45 (1980): 431-447.

Rønsen, M. "Fertility and public policies - evidence from Norway and Finland" mimeo, Statistics Norway, 1998.

Rønsen M. "Market Work, Child Care and the Division of Household Labour." Report 3/2001. Statistics Norway, 2001.

Santos Silva J. M. C, and F. Covas. "A modified hurdle model for completed fertility." *Journal of Population Economics*, 13 (2000): 173-188.

Schultz, T. W. "The Value of Children: An Economic Perspective," *Journal of Political Economy*, 81.2 (March-April 1973): 2-13.

Schultz, T. P. "Returns to women's education." in E. M. King and M. A. Hill (ed) *Women's education in developing countries: barriers, benefits, and policies*. Baltimore: Johns Hopkins University Press, 1993.

Vandberg, S. G. "Assortative mating, or who marries whom?" *Behavior Genetics*, 2.2 (1972):127-157.

Wang, W. and F. Famoye. "Modeling household fertility decisions with Generalized Poisson regression." *Journal of Population Economics*, 10.3 (1997): 273-283.

Weinberger, M. B., C. Lloyd, and A. K. Blanc. "Women's education and fertility: A decade of change in four Latin American Countries," *International Family Planning Perspectives*, 15.1 (1989): 4-28.

Weiss, Y. "The formation and dissolution of families: Why marry? Who marries whom? And what happens upon divorce?" in: Rosenzweig, M.R. and O. Stark (ed): *Handbook of population and family economics*. North-Holland, 1997.

Winch, R. F. *Mate selection*. New York: Harper, 1958.

Winckelmann, R. *Econometric Analysis of Count Data*, 3d. ed. Berlin, Springer Verlag, 2000.

AUTHOR INDEX

SUBJECT INDEX

F

N

O

P

European Studies of Population

1. J.-P. Gonnot, N. Keilman and C. Prinz: *Social Security, Household, and Family Dynamics in Ageing Societies.* 1995 ISBN 0-7923-3395-0
2. H. van den Brekel and F. Deven (eds.): *Population and Family in the Low Countries 1994.* Selected Current Issues. 1995 ISBN 0-7923-3396-9
3. R. Cliquet and C. Thienpont: *Population and Development.* A Message from the Cairo Conference. 1995 ISBN 0-7923-3763-8
4. H. van den Brekel and F. Deven (eds.): *Population and Family in the Low Countries 1995.* Selected Current Issues. 1996 ISBN 0-7923-3945-2
5. H.A. de Gans: *Population Forecasting 1895–1945.* The Transition to Modernity. 1999 ISBN 0-7923-5537-7
6. D. van de Kaa, H. Leridon, G. Gesano and M. Okólski (eds.): *European Populations: Unity in Diversity.* 1999 ISBN 0-7923-5838-4 (HB)
7. J. de Beer and L. van Wissen (eds.): *Europe: One Continent, Different Worlds.* Population Scenarios for the 21st Century. 1999 ISBN 0-7923-5840-6 (HB)
8. J. de Beer and F. Deven (eds.): *Diversity in Family Formation.* The 2nd Demographic Transition in Belgium and The Netherlands. 2000 ISBN 0-7923-6461-9
9. E. Tabeau, A. van den Berg Jeths and C. Heathcote (eds.): *Forecasting Mortality in Developed Countries: Insight from a Statistical, Demographic and Epidemiological Perspective.* 2001 ISBN 0-7923-6833-9
10. M. Corijn and E. Klijzing (eds.): *Transitions to Adulthood in Europe.* 2001 ISBN 0-7923-6965-3
11. G. Wunsch, M. Mouchart and J. Duchêne (eds.): *The Life Table.* Modelling Survival and Death. 2002 ISBN 1-4020-0638-1
12. H.-P. Blossfeld and A. Timm (eds.): *Who Marries Whom?* Educational Systems as Marriage Markets in Modern Societies. 2003 ISBN 1-4020-1682-4
13. T. Frejka and J.-P. Sardon: *Childbearing Trends and Prospects in Low-Fertility Countries.* A Cohort Analysis. 2004 ISBN 1-4020-2457-6
14. G. Dalla Zuanna and G.A. Micheli (eds.): *Strong Family and Low Fertility: A Paradox?* New Perspectives in Interpreting Contemporary Family and Reproductive Behaviour. 2004 ISBN 1-4020-2836-9
15. S. Gustafsson and A. Kalwij (eds.): *Education and Postponement of Maternity.* 2006 ISBN 1-4020-4715-0

European Studies of Population